I0091127

Violence, Peace & Everyday Modes of Justice and Healing in Post-Colonial Africa

Edited by

Ngonidzashe Marongwe, Fidelis Peter Thomas Duri & Munyaradzi Mawere

Langaa Research & Publishing CIG
Mankon, Bamenda

Publisher:
Langaa RPCIG
Langaa Research & Publishing Common Initiative Group
P.O. Box 902 Mankon
Bamenda
North West Region
Cameroon
Langaagrp@gmail.com
www.langaa-rpcig.net

Distributed in and outside N. America by African Books Collective
orders@africanbookscollective.com
www.africanbookscollective.com

ISBN-10: 9956-550-42-6

ISBN-13: 978-9956-550-42-5

© Ngonidzashe Marongwe, Fidelis Peter Thomas Duri
& Munyaradzi Mawere 2019

All rights reserved.
No part of this book may be reproduced or transmitted in any form or by any
means, mechanical or electronic, including photocopying and recording, or be
stored in any information storage or retrieval system, without written permission
from the publisher

List of Contributors

Ngonidzashe Marongwe is a Lecturer in the History and Development Studies Department, Simon Muzenda School of Arts, Culture and Heritage Studies, Great Zimbabwe University located in Masvingo City, Zimbabwe. He holds a PhD in African History from the University of the Western Cape (UWC), South Africa. He is a past Andrew Mellon Foundation Doctoral Fellow at the Centre for Humanities Research, UWC (2009–2010 & 2012); and a SEPHIS fellow at the Centre for the Study of Culture and Society, Bangalore, India (2011). His research interests include African governance, political violence, gender, military history and terrorism. Ngonidzashe has edited several books such as *Myths of Peace and Democracy: Towards Building Pillars of Hope, Unity and Transformation in Africa* (2016); *Violence, Politics and Conflict Management in Africa: Envisioning Transformation, Peace and Unity in the Twenty-First Century* (2016); and *Contested Spaces, Restrictive Mechanisms and Corridors of Opportunity: A Social History of Zimbabwean Borderlands and Beyond since the Colonial Period* (2018).

Fidelis Peter Thomas Duri is a Senior Lecturer in the Department of History and Development Studies at Great Zimbabwe University in Zimbabwe. He is a holder of a PhD in History from the University of the Witwatersrand in Johannesburg, South Africa. He has particular interest in the field of social history. He has published a number of books and articles which focus on environmental history, socio-cultural dynamics, subaltern struggles, African border studies and politics in Zimbabwe during the colonial and post-colonial periods. He has also reviewed and edited a number of scholarly books and articles and is also a member of the editorial boards of international journals such as the *Zimbabwe Journal of Historical Studies* and the *International Journal of Developing Societies*.

Munyaradzi Mawere is a Professor in the Simon Muzenda School of Arts, Culture and Heritage Studies at Great Zimbabwe University in Zimbabwe. He holds a Ph. D in Social Anthropology, Master's

Degree in Social Anthropology, Master's Degree in Development Studies, Master's Degree in Philosophy and, a B. A (Hons) Degree in Philosophy. Before joining this university, Professor Mawere was a lecturer at the University of Zimbabwe and at Universidade Pedagogica, Mozambique, where he has worked in different capacities as a senior lecturer, assistant research director, postgraduate co-ordinator, and professor. He is an author of more than 70 books and over 250 academic publications with a focus on Africa straddling the following areas: poverty and development, African philosophy, society and culture, democracy, politics of food production, humanitarianism and civil society organisations, urban anthropology, existential anthropology, cultural philosophy, area studies, experimental philosophy, environmental anthropology, society and politics, decoloniality and African studies. Some of his bestselling books are: *Humans, Other Beings and the Environment: Harurwa (Edible stinkbugs) and Environmental Conservation in South-eastern Zimbabwe* (2015); *Theory, Knowledge, Development and Politics: What Role for the Academy in the Sustainability of Africa?* (2016); *Democracy, Good Governance and Development in Africa: A Search for Sustainable Democracy and Development,* (2015); *Culture, Indigenous Knowledge and Development in Africa: Reviving Interconnections for Sustainable Development* (2014); *Myths of Peace and Democracy? Towards Building Pillars of Hope, Unity and Transformation in Africa* (2016); *Harnessing Cultural Capital for Sustainability: A Pan Africanist Perspective* (2015); *Divining the Future of Africa: Healing the Wounds, Restoring Dignity and Fostering Development,* (2014); *African Cultures, Memory and Space: Living the Past Presence in Zimbabwean Heritage* (2014); *Violence, Politics and Conflict Management in Africa: Envisioning Transformation, Peace and Unity in the Twenty-First Century* (2016); *African Philosophy and Thought Systems: A Search for a Culture and Philosophy of Belonging* (2016); *Africa at the Crossroads: Theorising Fundamentalisms in the 21st Century* (2017); *Colonial Heritage, Memory and Sustainability in Africa: Challenges, Opportunities and Prospects* (2016); *Underdevelopment, Development and the Future of Africa* (2017), and *Theorising Development in Africa: Towards Building an African Framework of Development* (2017); *African Studies in the Academy: The Cornucopia of Theory, Praxis and Transformation in Africa?* (2017); *GMOs, Consumerism and the Global Politics of Biotechnology: Rethinking Food, Bodies and Identities in Africa's 21ˢᵗ Century* (2017); *Human Trafficking and Trauma in the Digital*

Era: The Ongoing Tragedy of the Trade in Refugees from Eritrea (2017); *The Political Economy of Poverty, Vulnerability & Disaster Risk Management: Building Bridges of Resilience, Entrepreneurship and Development in Africa's 21ˢᵗ Century* (2018); and *Jostling Between "Mere Talk" and Blame Game? Beyond Africa's Poverty and Underdevelopment Game Talk* (2018).

James Hlongwana is a Senior Lecturer of History in the Department of History and Development Studies at Great Zimbabwe University. He holds a Master's Degree in History from the Midlands State University in Zimbabwe. He is currently a PhD candidate in the Department of History at the University of North West in South Africa. Hlongwana has written several articles in international journals. His research interests concern conflict and borderland issues.

Nancy Mazuru is a Lecturer in the Department of History, Archaeology and Development Studies at Great Zimbabwe University. She holds a Master of Science degree in Development Studies from the Women's University in Africa. Currently, she is a PhD candidate for Development Studies at the University of the Witwatersrand, Johannesburg.

Conrad Chibango is a Senior Lecturer of Religious Studies in the Department of Philosophy and Religious Studies at Great Zimbabwe University. He is interested in analysing religious and social policies and practices in contemporary developing societies. His work is mainly shaped by his particular interest in the interaction between religion and development as well as between religion and law. He is a PhD holder in Canon Law with the Pontifical Urban University, Rome, and a Master of Development Studies with the University of KwaZulu-Natal. He attained a BA Honours in Religious Studies at the University of Zimbabwe. Outside his academic activities, Conrad Chibango is a member of the Catholic Commission for Justice and Peace (CCJP) where he is actively involved in promoting social justice in grassroots communities.

Tobias Marevesa is a New Testament Lecturer in the Department of Philosophy and Religious Studies, under the Simon Muzenda School of Arts and Humanities at the Great Zimbabwe University where he teaches New Testament Studies and New Testament Greek. He is pursuing doctoral studies at the University of Pretoria in South Africa. His areas of interest are New Testament studies and politics, Pentecostal expressions in Zimbabwean Christianity, culture, human rights, and gender-based violence. He has also published in the area of New Testament studies and conflict-resolution in the Zimbabwean political landscape. He has attended and presented a number of papers in both regional and international conferences and has published articles in reputable international journals. He is a member of the New Testament Society of Southern Africa (NTSSA), Reading Association of Nigeria (RAN), Association for the Study of Religion in Southern Africa (ASRSA), African Consortium for Law and Religion Studies (ACLARS), and the International Consortium for Law and Religion Studies (ICLARS). He is serving as an External Examiner in a number of Teachers' Colleges in Zimbabwe.

Prosper Hellen Tlou is a Lecturer in the African Languages Department at the Great Zimbabwe University. She received her Master of Arts and Bachelor of Arts Honours degrees from the University of Venda (UNIVEN), Bachelor of Arts Degree at Great Zimbabwe University and is teaching Tshivenda language at Great Zimbabwe University. She currently serves as a Tshivenda coordinator in the Department of African Languages and Literature. Her research interests include Linguistics, Onomastics and Sociolinguistics.

David Tobias is a Lecturer in the History and Development Studies Department at Great Zimbabwe University, Masvingo, Zimbabwe. He is a holder of a Bachelor of Arts degree obtained with the University of Zimbabwe. He further graduated with a Master's degree in African History from the Midlands State University. Currently he is working on his PhD proposal on the Zimbabwean land reform and agrarian issues. Tobias is a prolific writer and publisher. He has written several articles and book chapters on Zimbabwean political violence, effects of economic sanctions in

Zimbabwe, xenophobic attacks in South Africa, globalisation and inequalities.

Jacob Tagarirofa is a Lecturer and Coordinator for Peace, Conflict and Governance in the Department of Sociology at Great Zimbabwe University, Masvingo, Zimbabwe. His current research interests concentrate on gender and conflict in the post-colony. Over the years, he has contributed several chapters in books and has published numerous articles in, amongst others, *International Journal of Politics and Governance*. He holds a BSC in Sociology from Great Zimbabwe University and an MA in Development Studies from the University of the Western Cape, South Africa. He is currently studying for his PhD in African Studies (Gender, Peace and Conflict) with the University of the Free State, South Africa

Erasmus Masitera is a Lecturer in the Department of Philosophy and Religious Studies at the Great Zimbabwe University, Masvingo. He holds a DPhil in Philosophy from the University of Pretoria, South Africa. Erasmus is interested in researches that deal with traditional African social and political issues and connected philosophies. He has also published widely in the stated areas.

Tinashe Mawere holds a PhD in Women's and Gender Studies from the University of the Western Cape (UWC), an MA in African and Diasporan Literature in English and a BA Honours in English and Communication from the Midlands State University (MSU), Zimbabwe. He is a past Andrew Mellon Doctoral Fellow in the Programme on the Study of the Humanities in Africa (PSHA) at the Centre for Humanities Research (CHR) at the UWC. He joined the UWC Writing Centre in 2011 as a Writing Consultant and has been working there to date. He does part-time lecturing on Academic Literacies, Language and Communication at the UWC and the Cape Peninsula University of Technology (CPUT). He is also a part-time Researcher and Editor at the South African History Online (SAHO). He has also taught Communication Skills and English as a Foreign Language at MSU. Currently, he is a post-doctoral fellow at the University of Pretoria.

Steyn Khesani Madlome is a Full-time Lecturer at Great Zimbabwe University in the Simon Muzenda School of Arts, Culture and Heritages Studies, African Languages and Literature Department. He holds a PhD degree in Xitsonga, Masters of Arts in Xitsonga from the University of Venda, Bachelor of Arts degree from Great Zimbabwe University and a Diploma in Education from Mutare Teachers college. His areas of research are applied linguistics, culture, indigenous knowledge systems and Afrocentricity.

Osborn Risimati Chauke holds a PhD in Xitsonga from the University of the North. He was born in Xifaxani village under chief Xikundu in 1964. He attended the following schools: Shikundu Secondary (J C), Ripambeta High, Lemana High and Giyani High in 1985 (Matriculation). He obtained BA Paed in 1989, then BA Hons (1990). He taught at Shikundu High School before being employed as a lecturer at Lemana College of Education in 1993. Chauke obtained his MA at RAU in 1998. He was the first student to graduate with a PhD in the Department of Xitsonga in 2004 at University of the North. Chauke became a grade 12 examiner for a long time. He wrote the following books: Gama ra nsele (novel), Swa Chavisa (drama), Vutomi, Tihove and Torha emananga (poetry antologies), Vutomi i Rimpfani (poetry), Mahlo ya nkwahle (drama), Magandlati (novel), Tshwana hi rihanti (novel) Migiringiriko ya Xitsonga (Language), A hi tinyungubyiseni Giredi ya 9-12 and a Vatsonga Documentary (co-authored) shown on SABC TV 2. Chauke OR is also well known for being one of the writers of a soapie called MINA HI MINA which won an MTN top award.

Table of Contents

Chapter 1
Violence, peace and everyday modes
of justice and healing: Whither post-colonial
Africa? An Introduction...1
*Ngonidzashe Marongwe; Fidelis Peter Thomas
Duri &Munyaradzi Mawere*

**Part I: The Scourge of
Violence in Post-Colonial Africa**.......................................29

Chapter 2
The Zimbabwean democratization paradox:
Popular protests, violence, and
state responses, 2013-2016 31
David Tobias and Jacob Tagarirofa

Chapter 3
Violent house demolitions in
Harare, Zimbabwe, 2014-2016:
A violation of people's rights..49
Nancy Mazuru

Chapter 4
Female rapists and sperm harvesting:
Narratives of violence and occultism
in post-colonial Zimbabwe 73
*Ngonidzashe Marongwe, David Tobias
& Tinashe Mawere*

Chapter 5

Unearthing the gender and religious
conflict conundrum: The curse of Africa 95

Jacob Tagarirofa

Chapter 6

Ritual murder during the new millennium:
An analysis of the triggers and impacts of
ritual killings in Zimbabwe 107

Nancy Mazuru

Chapter 7

Victims of **FRELIMO** and **RENAMO** brutality:
The Ndau people of Mossurize District of
Mozambique, 1978-2017 127

James Hlongwana

Chapter 8

Social media, infidelity and domestic
violence in 21st century Zimbabwe 145

Nancy Mazuru

**Part II: In Pursuit of Peace Through
Everyday Modes of Justice and Healing** 165

Chapter 9

Political violence and "common sense" justice:
Kuripa ngozi as a transitional justice mechanism
among the Shona people in Zimbabwe's rural areas 167

Ngonidzashe Marongwe

Chapter 10
Appeasing the dead and cleansing the living:
The pursuit of peace in the aftermath of political
violence in 21st century Zimbabwe 191
Fidelis Peter Thomas Duri

Chapter 11
Healing Zimbabwe: Impact of the Catholic
Church's response to political violence on
people at grassroots level 219
Conrad Chibango

Chapter 12
Vanishing traditions? Girl children as
sacrificial lambs in the context of Shona
indigenous transitional justice mechanisms
in 21st century Zimbabwe 249
Fidelis Peter Thomas Duri

Chapter 13
Cultural interpersonal communication
and naming: The case of peri-urban
Beitbridge in Zimbabwe 275
Prosper Hellen Tlou

Chapter 14
The moral significance of the *Dare* system
in seeking justice and peace among the
Shona people of Zimbabwe.. 291
Erasmus Masitera

Chapter 15
Indigenous and Christian forms of
national healing: A case for the Global
Political Agreement in Zimbabwe 313
  Tobias Marevesa

Chapter 16
Conflict, justice and peace from an
African indigenous cultural perspective:
The case of the Vatsonga people of Mozambique,
South Africa, Swaziland and Zimbabwe 327
  Steyn Khesani Madlome & Osborne Risimati Chauke

Chapter 17
The prospects of peace, healing and
justice in 21ˢᵗ century Africa:
Concluding Remarks 345
  *Fidelis Peter Thomas Duri, Ngonidzashe Marongwe
  & Munyaradzi Mawere*

Chapter 1

Violence, Peace and Everyday Modes of Justice and Healing in Post-colonial Africa

*Ngonidzashe Marongwe; Fidelis Peter Thomas Duri &
Munyaradzi Mawere*

Introduction

Undeniably, violence, in various proportions, genres and manifestations, has had an enduring historical legacy in Africa, as in many other parts of the world, helping to generate complex results, emotions and legacies. As Ndlovu-Gatsheni (2009) has rightly argued, Africa has undergone cycles of violence across the pre-colonial, colonial and post-colonial epochs. In recent history, as Marongwe and Mawere (2016) opine, overt violence became banalised on the African continent from the 1960s due to the entrenchment of the decolonisation process and since then almost all nations on the continent have suffered violent episodes of various proportions and modes. As Marongwe and Mawere argue, outside of the liberation wars, the violent struggles have included, *inter alia*, armed disputes in the Horn of Africa, service delivery protests and xenophobic attacks in South Africa, "confrontations over the distribution and access to resources like land and minerals, border conflicts, ethnic and religious tensions and over access to- or denial of- state apparatus" (*Ibid*: 1). Among others, the above-mentioned struggles have contributed to "the militarisation of many African states leading to *coup de tats* and counter *coup de tats* in countries like Nigeria, the Democratic Republic of the Congo (DRC) and Libya; the emergence and sustenance of regimes that have employed coercive tactics to remain in power at differing moments in many countries like Zimbabwe, Equatorial Guinea and Kenya" as well as "the rise of religious fundamentalisms in places like Nigeria dominated by the Boko Haram, the growth of the al-Qaeda cells in the Sudan, Egypt, Mali, Tanzania and South Africa, and the Al-

1

Shabaab in Somalia and Kenya" (*Ibid*). The latter part of religious-based or religious-linked fundamentalist violence has found expression as terrorism and/or as War against Terror.

In Zimbabwe and many other countries of Africa, other underreported genres of violence have emerged, including sexual assaults, gender-based, epistemic, political and economic violence. On the whole, the violence has generated differing results, including state destruction and formation; deaths and population decreases; economic losses and gains; social formations and stratifications; subjects and subjectification; rulers and the ruled; as well as colonialism and coloniality.

It is for this major reason that in this volume, we have committed some chapters (2 to 8) on the subject of violence, to largely focus on the hidden dimensions of violence encapsulated in house demolitions as in Nancy Mazuru's chapter, the violence of entrapment of the borderland Ndau people in James Hlongwana's chapter and the often under- reported forms of violence caused by social media, and ritual murders, again by Nancy Mazuru, among others. In Duri's chapter on avenging spirits (*ngozi*) and violence, which is largely about the deployment of a Shona jurisprudential and restorative justice process of method of solving disputes, the hidden dimensions of violence of appeasing spirits (or *kuripa ngozi* in Shona), including the violation of girl children's rights are laid bare. Hence, the chapter shows the paradox of this method where there are some violations that are perpetrated allegedly for communal good.

At the same time, it seems apparent that attempts at forging lasting peace out of the ashes of the above mentioned episodes and modes of violence using international actors and state institutions have brought dwindling returns for the continent. At best, what has happened is that "armed peace" or what Johan Galtung (1964) calls negative peace, in which, and at best, only the physical manifestations of violence have been tackled without necessarily bothering to set the parameters that could serve to reduce the impacts of the long term and sometimes structural underpinnings of violence, has been achieved. There is, in this regard, need for an examination of some possible ways that could aid in the establishment of comprehensive peace. In the Galtung (1964) formulation, this is positive peace. To

Galtung (1964: 2), positive peace involves the elimination of structural violence and the institution of moves towards the "integration of [a] society". This means that in the end, as Grewal (2003: n.p.) opines, peace should entail a cocktail of negative peace that is the "absence of violence, pessimistic, curative, peace not always by peaceful means" but sometimes by coercion or violent means and positive peace that is "structural integration, optimistic, preventive, peace by peaceful means".

From the foregoing, a comprehensive articulation of peace must be read as "the absence of violence in all its forms- physical, social, psychological, and structural" (Reardon, 1988: 16). As Grewal (2003) argues, a clear understanding of the contours of violence, therefore, inadvertently leads to a greater comprehension of what justice and peace ought to be. Largely, this could be a useful basis for the erection of some pillars of justice that the African continent so desires desperately. In pursuit of the ideals of positive peace, most chapters in this volume speak to how the deployment of everyday lived experiences and common sense modes of conflict resolution and management, such as avenging spirits or *ngozi* or *uzimu* in the Zimbabwean Shona and Ndebele communities, respectively could help concretise positive peace and justice.

The germane theme of justice remains a huge conundrum for Africa, as it is for the rest of the world. It is at the centre of many chapters in the volume. But, what is justice? This is an amorphous subject that has several meanings to different people, which inadvertently continues to generate huge and sometimes acrimonious debates. Amongst the huge debates on what justice is, a resort to one of the founding theorists on the subject, Aristotle, provides important insights. Ancient Greek philosopher, Aristotle, who has bequeathed to the world a profound understanding of justice, as cited in Winthrop (1978:1202), says justice speaks to practising "complete virtue" towards others, which may mean that one sacrifices self-virtues for the others. To this, Masaka (2017:61) adds that justice is "the disposition that resides in a being to treat others as one generally expects to be treated." In the words of Winthrop (1978:1202), this entails "a habit of some sort which issues in actions that we could call just and which assures that these actions are undertaken with the

3

intention of their being just." On the whole, Aristotle equates justice to legal/legality and equal/equality with legality determined by abiding by laws set in a political community and equality bringing fairness to that community (Winthrop, 1978). Aristotle further discusses two realms of justice that help to attain fairness in a community, that is, distributive justice and corrective justice. The former speaks to the fair parcelling out of goods and other entitlements. The latter, relates more to justice that is pronounced by courts in which the goal is to rectify losses and illegal gains (*Ibid*). In addition to these forms of justice is retributive and restorative justice. Retributive justice is generally a system of justice based on the punishment rather than on rehabilitation of offenders as is the case of *ngozi* in Shona culture. In other words, retributive justice entails that those who commit wrongful acts morally deserve to suffer proportionate punishment. On the contrary, restorative justice is a system of justice which generally focuses on the rehabilitation of offenders through reconciliation with victims and the society at large.

All these conceptualisations of justice speak to what is right based on a people's comprehension of their worldview. Different people have different outlooks on justice based on, among others, their history, religion, existing laws/codes of conduct and ethics/morality. Many chapters in the second part of this volume, titled: *In Pursuit of peace through everyday modes of justice and healing*, relate to this theme of justice by discussing variegated ways that can be used to enhance justice outside of the statist and so-called formal channels, broadly in the common sense realm, including some Christian organisations such as the Catholics Bishops' pastoral letters espoused in Conrad Chibango's chapter. However, many chapters contained herein try to discuss the search for justice through retributive and restorative means. It would seem that the discussions around *ngozi/uzimu* intend to transcend the limits of corrective justice as it relates to the re-actifying of the loss by those who will have been murdered, where the broad question is: how does punishing the murderer ameliorate the loss of the murdered? The same question was posed by Aristotle (paraphrased in Winthrop, 1978:1204) who averred that corrective justice "must rectify the murder's gain and the victim's loss; but the dead victim's loss is rectified by the murder's loss is not obvious."

What emerges from the Chapters by Marongwe, Duri, and Marevesa for example, is that *ngozi/uzimu* based justice re-actifies at different levels, including the physical, metaphysical, the individual and community level, as well as the production and reproduction levels.

Whilst various researches have been conducted on the subjects of violence, peace and justice, the enduring and perturbing questions, which have almost become rhetorical, have remained including: What are the underpinnings of violence? How has violence been manifested? What have been the effects of violence? What is the connection between violence and the apparent absence of peace and justice on the continent? What can be done to end the cycles of the violence? Is it possible, as Marongwe and Mawere (2016) question, for Africa and Africans in Africa to enjoy peace and justice? What, also, is the link between violence and state formation, mobilisation for power, the preservation of sovereignty, state administration and state collapse in Africa? What may be the possible connections between the attainment of peace and the efforts towards justice?

These questions remain instructive. The aim of this book is to wade into this huge debate and trouble some of the disputations that have undergirded the subjects of violence, justice, healing, reconciliation and peace. However, we ask them alongside the germane question: What can be done beyond the state and formal levels to undercut violence? This volume responds to the questions raised with pioneering chapters that are rooted in specific case studies and ethnographic studies on either the occurrence of violence, establishment of peace, peculiar modes of justice/transitional justice or the contribution of everyday modes of healing that can or have been used to undercut the continuation of violence at different strata of society. This, broadly, moves the debate from the more formalised state-led/state-driven, 'modern' and often prosecutorial articulations of peace, justice and healing to the more informal and sometimes "common-sensical" notions, in the Antonio Gramsci (1999: 419) formulation, of the same, which involves emphasising everyday societal philosophies. Notwithstanding the fact that this "philosophy by the man in the street" may be "fragmentary, incoherent and inconsequential, in conformity with the social and cultural position of those masses whose philosophy it is" (Gramsci, 1998: 419), which makes it "an ambiguous, contradictory and multiform concept" (*Ibid*: 423) its value lies in that it is "embedded [in] and [is composed of] spontaneous beliefs and assumptions characterising the conformist thinking of the mass of people in a given social order" (*Ibid*). This includes, among others, modes that may be considered traditional, religious, those based on restitution or those that are rooted in specific contexts but lying outside the purview of the state or formal institutions that can be utilised at the individual, family and more localised levels for the betterment of the society. It is for this reason that some chapters in this volume have deliberately focussed on the more hidden and subtle forms of violence that the people of the continent of Africa and elsewhere have suffered, their effects and how they can be gotten rid of.

On the whole, the chapters in this volume tackle, largely through peculiar and in-depth case-studies, expressions and theorisations of violence, manifestations of peace and the manifestations of the different methodologies of everyday modes of pursuing justice among the Zimbabwean communities. What remains instructive and outstanding about the chapters is that they have been pitched at the interdisciplinary level. As such, most of the chapters have been rooted in combinations of humanities and social sciences related disciplines such as, History, Sociology, Anthropology, Ethnography, Literature, Ethnomusicology, religion and culture. The book is divided into two large sections. The first section titled "The scourge of violence in post-colonial Africa" is made up of chapters that deal with complex occurrence of violence at the national, political and personal levels. The second section of the book deals with peace, justice and healing through non-state actors. As such, it is aptly titled "In pursuit of peace through everyday modes of justice and healing".

The book project derives inspiration from the two widely publicised 'common sensical' conflict resolution and transitional justice strategies experienced in Rwanda and Mozambique following harrowing episodes of violence. These violent episodes were the 1994 genocide and the 16 year Mozambican post-independence civil war, respectively. To end the cycles of violence following the genocide, Rwanda instituted the *gacaca* courts while in the Gorongosa region of Mozambique, the state acceded to the deployment of the *magamba* spirits to help in the resolution of some of the conflicts. These transitional justice mechanisms are assumed to be a part of restorative justice mechanisms that sought to "repair, restore and establish responsibility" (Clapham, 2012: n.p). Broadly as restorative transitional justice mechanisms, they strove for "victim-oriented structure [that] reflects the shift in emphasis from crime as a violation of laws answerable to the state, to an understanding of crime as harm done to individuals and communities" (*Ibid*).

The section further argues that although the above mentioned traditional transitional justice mechanisms have their own challenges, and in some cases failed to achieve set aims, they showcase the possibility of adopting or at least improving traditional or cultural-based transitional justice for local communities, which helped the respective communities to advance varying levels of healing, justice, reconciliation and peace. In this regard, the book considers them as useful *dispositifs*. To this end, as Louis Althusser (cited in Adam David Morton, YR : 42) advances, a *dispositif* is "a series of general theses on history which are literally contradictory, yet organised in such a way as to generate concepts not deducible from them, for the purposes of theorising an 'object' which in fact is a determinative object." As such, a troubling of some of the cultural methods of conflict management from across Africa helps this book to perceive of the potential hidden in them and the value that local communities have for them, largely as a part of their 'common sense' (see Marongwe in this volume on the common sense framework). Their analysis also serves to recognise their growing profile and an affirmation of their potential in Africa. Broadly, as Marongwe (2013) argues, while these methods were to a large extent expedient, they helped, among other things to expedite peace processes among locals, reduce the work load of the Western-style courts, and above all, to prove that indeed traditional African methods can be integrated with the Western justice to bring lasting reconciliation and peace to previously conflict-ridden communities.

What should also not escape attention is the fact that many sub-Saharan African people notwithstanding the several hundreds of years of interactions with European-based civilisation, are still largely guided in their everyday living, by traditional/cultural or common sense beliefs. As such, their worldviews on justice, peace and healing are also heavily influenced by this cultural rootedness. This understanding is also affirmed by the Zimbabwe government's Organ for National Healing, Reconciliation and Integration's (ONHRI, 2009: 23) "Concept Paper", which was the organ's Green Paper, which averred that "long-lasting healing may not take root without national and local ceremonies by the people and their leaders, consistent with cultural timetables, practices and community participation." Perhaps based on this, it is, thus, little of a surprise that there is a growing list of African countries whose community members have made use of cultural based transitional justice methods in combination with Western prosecutorial transitional justice mechanisms. This burgeoning list includes Rwanda, which adopted the *gacaca* following the harrowing genocide of 1994, Mozambique which adopted *magamba* spirits in the aftermath of the 1975 to 1992 civil war and the continuing efforts to use *mato oput* by the Acholli of northern Uganda in the wake of the Lord's Resistance Army's continued terror-inclined war tactics (Sriram and Pillay, (2009). The other advantage of the traditional methods is that serious crimes, especially those involving senior army officers and senior party/militia and government officials, are dealt with at the prosecutorial levels and the many, usually, petty crimes, are then quickly resolved at the levels of the traditional transitional justice schemes. As well, even the more serious ones will also need to be resolved at the village courts to help make the resolving at the community and metaphysical level possible. The combinations have also proved very effective in quickening the processes of attaining transitional justice, especially in situations where the scale and pace of trials in post-conflict situations in Africa has been worryingly slow. To exemplify, Sriram (2009: 17) has established that by 2009, the International Criminal Court (ICC) trials for Rwanda and Sierra Leone had yielded only 40 and 10 convictions for perpetrators, respectively.

Another critical factor to consider is how these various traditional and cultural practices help to engender the transition from negative peace to positive peace in the respective communities. As Johan Galtung (1964:2) says "the difference between negative and positive peace is that negative peace articulates the absence of the more apparent and physical forms of violence, including wars while positive peace describes the absence of structural violence and where there are moves towards the 'integration of [a] society." In this regard, positive peace tackles the root causes of conflict and ensures long term peace in societies.

At another level, the traditional transitional justice mechanisms also help to integrate local communities through encouraging the participation of the common villagers and the involvement of spirits, which in the Mbiti (1969) formulation represent the living dead. The involvement at both the physical and metaphysical levels borrows from the thinking that crimes committed, even when they are perpetrated at the individual level, are generally taken as crimes committed against the larger community (Eppel, 2001) involving both the living and the living dead. The involvement of the 'living dead' usually involves the appeasing of spirits, which is crucial in linking the living with their fore bearers. In this African metaphysics or "ontology of invisible beings", (Ramose cited in Nabudere, 2008: 3), the living-dead are venerated for their influence on the lives of the living. As such, the adoption of culturally rooted or traditional transitional justice mechanisms, therefore not only renders restorative justice at the physical level to the victims possible, but it also helps to appease the spirits of the departed, which connects the present with their historically bequeathed tradition.

In the sections below, we briefly discuss how the *gacaca* and *magamba* spirits were used as vital parts of the mechanisms for restorative transitional justice in Rwanda and Mozambique respectively, as well as the lessons that the larger African continent can draw.

Gacaca

Gacaca is a Customary Dispute Resolution system (or an African harmony model) widely used in Rwanda since pre-colonial times to resolve disputes between the aggrieved party and the wrongdoer. As Sherif (2017: 100) notes "gacaca court system is an epitome of Rwandans' traditional practice reincarnated to speed up trials in post-genocide Rwandan society to heal issues of genocidal trauma and dispense transitional justice through truth-telling and confession." During this process "apology, compensation and reintegration remain as essential elements" (Fiseha, 2017: 37) of the *gacaca* dispute resolution system. *Gacaca* in Kinyarwanda is "lawn justice" or literally justice on the grass, which is based on pre-colonial, community-based courts where respectable male elders known as *Inyangamuguyo,* that is men of honourable or exemplary conduct (Scanlon and Motlafi, 2009: 301) or "those who detest disgrace" acted as judges. In the traditional sense of the *gacaca* courts, feuding parties would gather together with their relatives before a village assembly that is led by older and supposedly wiser men for the resolution of the dispute (Human Right Watch, 2011). The emphasis here is to achieve a restorative outcome – a social equilibrium – that is for the good of the community, not only the aggrieved party or family. In other words, the process is mediatory but not in the context of the Western system of conflict resolution in which a neutral mediator facilitates the negotiations between the disputants. Gacaca, as other African dispute resolution models, is normally mediated by the elders and the process is participatory as it is not only confined to the disputes alone but to all other actors in the community.

However, the re-established *gacaca* courts, while utilising the format of the past, now differ markedly from the traditional pre-genocide *gacaca* courts in that the re-established *gacacas* operate as a direct arm of the country's justice ministry's National Service of *Gacaca* Jurisdictions (SNJG), which sought retributive justice rather than reconciliation and in which the *inyangamuguyos* were drawn from relatively young villagers than in the past (Human Rights Watch, 2011). These *gacaca* courts were re-established in 2002 but they began trials in 2005 with a new mandate of trying genocide cases (Human Rights Watch, 2011). At their launch, the *gacaca* courts were conceived by the then Vice-President Paul Kagame as "An African solution to Africa's problems" (BBC News, YR: n.p) and as marking "revert[ing] to our traditional methods of conflict resolution" (Human Rights Watch, 2011: np). The *gacaca* courts were tasked with the following five objectives: "Vice-President Kagame officially launched *gacaca* courts to try genocide-related cases and announced five core objectives: Reveal the truth about what happened;

10

Accelerate genocide trials; Eradicate the culture of impunity; Reconcile Rwandans and reinforce their unity; and Prove that Rwanda has the capacity to resolve its own problems" (*Ibid*). A very clear mandate was spelt out to these courts: they had to find justice for the genocide through stressing confession, forgiveness and reparations for the victims (Scanlon and Motlafi, 2009: 302). The background to their re-establishment was that the national prosecuting courts were overwhelmed by the up to one million deaths cases, 250 000 rape cases from the 1994 genocide (United Nations, n.d.: n.p) and the fact that up to 10 000 accused had also died in prisons awaiting trial (*BBC News*, 18 June 2012).

What was also novel was that all the communities were supposed to choose their own judges to hear the trials of the genocide suspects and up to 12 000 courts were established, which managed to successfully try up to 1, 2 million cases nationally by the time of their closure in 2012 (United Nations, n.d.). Over and above this, the *gacaca* courts were also set up against the background of the modern Rwandan court system under duress as most of the judges had been killed during the genocide and most of the conventional courts infrastructures had also been destroyed (Human Rights Watch, 2011). Under the mandate of promoting reconciliation, the *gacaca* courts often allowed those that confessed roles in the genocide to be re-integrated without much or no punishment at all (United Nations, n.d.). On the whole, what emerges is the setting up of the *gacaca* courts amid serious adversities for Rwanda as a nation and for the Rwandese justice system process"

More generally, the "*gacaca* trials… served to promote reconciliation [and reintegration] by providing a means for victims to learn the truth about the death of their family members and relatives. They also gave perpetrators the opportunity to confess their crimes, show remorse and ask for forgiveness in front of their community" (United Nations, n.d.). In this regard, as the Human Rights Watch (2011:n.p) points out, "with trials taking place in the very location where the crimes had occurred and with neighbours, families, and friends looking on, local communities would play an important role in the proceedings and would see justice being done; this in turn would give them greater ownership of the process."

These courts were vital in speeding up the justice process for the victims in a country whose courts had been destroyed during the conflict. In this regard, by 2007, some two years after their re-establishment, there were some 12 000 such *gacaca* courts, which had resolved about 71 405 cases (*Ibid*). The initiative to re-establish *gacaca* courts proved very crucial and effective in conflict resolution because it would have taken the Rwandan judiciary above 150 years to solve these cases, most of which were committed during the 1994 genocide and in a country where about 95 percent of the judiciary personnel had been either killed or exiled and that the judiciary system had perennially been harmstrung by shortages of resources and had also been traditionally driven by the executive (*Ibid*).

We should also not lose sight of the fact that the *gacaca* courts operated alongside the International Criminal Tribunal for Rwanda (ICTR) and the Rwandan national Court System, in a three tier system. The ICTR was mandated to deal with "persons bearing the greatest responsibility for the genocide and other serious violations of international humanitarian law committed between 1 January and 31 December 1994 (United Nations, n.d.). On the other hand, the national court system of Rwanda was supposed to prosecute all "those accused of planning the genocide or for committing serious atrocities, including rape" (*Ibid*). On the whole, the *gacaca* courts were successful in that they "shed light on what happened in their local communities during the 100 days of genocide in 1994, even if not all of the truth was revealed. They say it helped some families find murdered relatives' bodies which they could finally bury with some dignity. It has also ensured that tens of thousands of perpetrators were brought to justice. Some Rwandans say that it has helped set in motion reconciliation within their communities" Human Rights Watch, 2011: n.p).

Notwithstanding these successes, it has been noted, sadly, however, that the *gacaca* promoted "controversial justice" and/or provided justice that fell below international standards (BBC News, 18 June 2012). Among others, this was based on the fact that the *gacaca* courts had an average of 65% conviction rate, giving the *gacaca* courts a mandate that was new with little training offered to the judges, judges lacking adequate training, the failure of the courts to guarantee the security of the accused and the victim families, for being partisan as many Rwanda Patriotic Front (RPF) members were reported to have never been tried by the *gacaca* courts, and their failure to achieve restorative justice through material compensation to the victims (*BBC News*, 18 June 2012). In furtherance to the above, Seay (2017) advances that the *gacaca* courts were instrumentalised by the RPF to underscore its legitimacy and to create a patronage economy, as well as for many participants the courts became a tool for meting out retributive justice. Added to the above were sentiments by some of the victims that not all perpetrators had been brought forward for trial, bitterness at outcomes from both the victims and perpetrators (Human Rights Watch, 2011). The Human Rights Watch (2011: n.p) best sums the shortcomings as:

> basic violations of the right to a fair trial and limitations on accused persons' ability to effectively defend themselves; flawed decision-making (often caused by judges' ties to the parties in a case or pre-conceived views of what happened during the genocide) leading to allegations of miscarriages of justice; cases based on what appeared to be trumped-up charges, linked, in some cases, to the government's wish to silence critics (journalists, human rights activists, and public officials) or to disputes between neighbours and even relatives; judges' or officials' intimidation of defense witnesses; corruption of judges to obtain the desired verdict; and other serious procedural irregularities.

However, as Clapham (2012) advanced, the shortcomings were largely externally driven and also because of the weight of the numerous trials that had to be covered by the *gacaca* courts and not the inherent weaknesses of the *gacaca* courts.

Magamba spirits in Mozambique

The Mozambique civil war was officially ended by the signing of the Rome Accord between the warring parties, FRELIMO and RENAMO in 1992. In many accounts (Igreja and Dias-Lambranca, 2008; Igreja, 2009), this has been viewed as "negative peace". As has already been defined in earlier sections, negative peace deals largely with the eradication of the physical manifestations of violence and conflict and does little if anything to eliminate the deeper causes of violence such as structural causes. In this regard, Igreja (2009) emphasises that the General Peace Agreement of 1992 simply drew the line in the sand for the atrocities of the civil war, by offering a blanket amnesty for the crimes committed during the 16 year old civil war. This modality of amnesty adopted as the transitional justice emphasised a break between the past and the new post-conflict Mozambique, which left many victims unreconciled. While this could have been adopted because of the equilibrium in military power both sides had at the time, it is also widely regarded as having reconciled the top leaderships without necessarily solving the local problems the communities had emanating from the conflict (*Ibid*). Due to the challenges in the Rome Accord, *magamba* spirits were used by the local people of the Gorongosa District to achieve healing following harrowing years of Mozambique civil war.

Magamba spirits were spirits of victims which possessed especially female survivors of the war, who were themselves or their families responsible for killing them or using their body parts for protection from the war (*Ibid*). As Igreja (2009) further notes, besides killing their victims the perpetrators also mixed body parts of the victims in herbs so that they could themselves not fall victim to the war. At other times it was said that the *magamba* spirits also affected [re]production by causing infertility among the perpetrators's female relatives, which caused the females to consult traditional healers over their predicament (*Ibid*). To resolve the misfortunes, traditional healers would go into trance, invoke the *magamba* spirits to come out and speak on who they were, what happened and what they wanted as compensation (*Ibid*). In this way, not only was the truth exposed, but the perpetrators and victims' families came together and compensated each other thereby restoring social harmony as well as economic and social restoration. In addition to this, child soldiers were also reintegrated into their communities after some traditional rituals supervised by traditional healers and traditional authorities.

Of particular importance is the fact that this method was adopted at a local scale, performed in front of all villagers, in the Gorongosa region to complement the General Peace Agreement (AGP), signed in Rome, which had ordered a general amnesty (*Ibid*). Although the effectiveness of this method has not yet been properly evaluated, it no doubt helped to heal the district. However, and notwithstanding the latter aspect, it has to be noted that *magamba* spirits advocated restorative justice through applying "legal concepts such as *ku tongwa* (to judge), *ku vundzissana* (to interrogate one another), *ku bueca* (to confess), *ku lipa* (to pay), *ku lekerera* (to forgive) and *ku verana* (understanding)" (Igreja and Dias-Lambranca, 2008: 79).

However, one of the enduring weaknesses of the *magamba* spirits is their gender bias, apparently against women. In the *magamba* spirits, only dead men and not women can come back as *magamba* spirits in the pursuit of restorative justice (Igreja and Dias-Lambranca, 2008). This reduces the agency of women in the *magamba* spirits healing (*Ibid*).

Chapter summaries

In Chapter 2, Jacob Tagarirofa and David Tobias tackle the violence in the popular protests that occurred in Zimbabwe between 2013 and 2016. As they argue, these popular uprisings were not only "spontaneous and not aligned to any institutionalised political party", but they were also undergirded by violence. The setting of the protests was rooted in the collapse of the Government of National Unity (GNU) comprising ZANU-PF, the MDC-T and MDC-Mutambara that was subsequently followed by worsening livelihoods. The gains of the GNU were swiftly reversed under the ZANU-PF government in the aftermath of its collapse. The areas of concern for the demonstrators, *inter alia*, were unfavourable trade policies especially Statutory Instrument 64 that banned a host of imports that were the cornerstone of many vendors; delays in the payment of wages for government workers; cash shortages; corruption; unmitigated retrenchments following the High Court ruling of July 2015 which stated that employers could legally terminate the employment of workers by giving them three months' notice without paying them off all their dues; a spike in the prices of consumer goods; and more generally, worsening living conditions.

Under this milieu, the demonstrators began to call for a more responsive governance dispensation in the country, which spoke to the need for greater democratisation, an end to harsh economic policies and the need for President Mugabe to step down. Some of the major participants were vendors, civil servants, other workers, pro-democracy activists and some clergymen. These calls were largely unwelcome by the ZANU-PF government that increasingly drew on its coercive apparatus of the security forces to brow beat the demonstrators and/or to cause the disappearance of some of the leading protestors, such as Itai Dzamara. This led to violence and counter violence from the two sections. What is also profound about this chapter is that it unravels the intricacies of the popular protests that gripped the country in the period under review and promised to herald a refreshing political-economic dispensation for the country.

In yet another illuminating chapter, which forms Chapter 3 of this book, Nancy Mazuru illustrates the hidden forms violence of the state in the post-colonial Zimbabwean dispensation as manifested in house demolitions. By focussing on house demolitions in the so-called undesignated areas in and around environs, such as Budiriro, Chitungwiza, Glen Norah, Epworth, and along the Harare International Airport Road, Mazuru meticulously teases out how such destructions, which are constitutive of involuntary or forced displacement feed into the violation schemes of human rights. To Mazuru, the demolitions of these houses in Harare should be considered as part of the long line of strong arm and military-style pogroms that have led to displacements and violation of people's fundamental rights, including Operation *Gukurahundi* from 1982 to 1987 meant to deal with the dissident menace, the Churu Farm evictions of 1992 ahead of the Commonwealth Heads of Government Meeting (CHOGM), the 2000 Fast Track Land Reform Programme that simultaneously settled blacks on previously white-owned farms as it displaced the white farmers and violated the rights of those in the opposition, the 2005 Operation *Murambatsvina*/Remove the Filth, the 2002, 2005 and 2008 political violence and the 2014 Tokwe-Mukosi Dam evictions. As such, the violent displacement of people had become endemic and routinized in post-colonial Zimbabwe, hence she calls for its halting. As she laments:

A striking feature among house demolitions or forced displacement in Zimbabwe lies in the brutal manner in which the operations have been carried out as well as the non-availability or inadequate and unclear plans by the government to compensate the victims, thereby violating a plethora of human rights and causing serious living hardships.

Regarding the 2014 to 2016 demolitions and subsequent displacements, what emerges from this illuminating chapter in terms of the violation of human rights and statutes is that some of the houses were pulled down at night and/ or in rainy weather.

Another tangent that emerges clearly from Mazuru's chapter is the undertone of politically motivated reasoning for the demolition of urban homes. Among others, Operation *Murambatsvina*/Operation Remove Filth and the 2014-2016 house destructions seemed to target the urbanites following successive electoral defeats of the ruling ZANU-PF party in urban constituencies. To this extent, it has become a truism in Zimbabwe that urban parliamentary constituencies in Zimbabwe have since 2000 been MDC/MDC-T strongholds. Broadly, they have been perceived to have rejected the ruling ZANU-PF party, hence the urbanites have routinely been condemned by senior ZANU-PF and state officials as having sold out to imperialist agencies. In the end, Mazuru ably demonstrates that the house destructions violated a lot of rights, including the right to adequate housing, freedom from arbitrary interference with one's home, the rights to privacy and family, and the right to political choice.

In the fourth chapter, Ngonidzashe Marongwe, David Tobias and Tinashe Mawere, consider the discursive narratives that have emerged following the rise in cases of female rapists in post- colonial Zimbabwe. They do this by problematizing the nexus of the violence of female sexual assaults and rape and occultism in an economy under duress. Guided by the germane question: what narratives have emerged from these reported cases of female sexual rape?, the triumvirate argues that whilst there was a wide array of discourses that have emerged to account for the proliferation of female rapists who were accused of harvesting their male victims' sperms, at the centre of these was the collection of the sperms for reasons related to witchcraft and sorcery meant to enrich the collectors. This was part of efforts to escape the biting and worsening economic challenges the country was facing. As they argue: "these cases illustrate how the deepening economic crisis in the country led to desperate survival strategies. In this case, the desperate means to eke survival in a desperate economy invoked a resort to occultism, which in itself also demonstrates very deep levels of desperation." As well, the chapter ably contends that the reported cases help to debunk the oft cited legal, and everyday discourses on sexual rape, which is thought to be only performed by males (who have penetrative ability with their penises) on females. As they aptly put it:

> What these cases further showcase is the disruption of the commonly-held notions of the distribution of gender stereotypical victimization, agency and power between males and females. Largely, the narratives that emerge portray discourses of women as natural and perpetual victims of violence and rape by projecting, too, that men can be unwilling victims of sexual violence in the society.

The fifth chapter by Jacob Tagarirofa examines, through the deployment of a multiple case study methodology, the nexus between religion, gender and conflict. Tagarirofa rightly observes that religion, together, with ethnicity, is a major cause of conflict in the world. Set, more generally under the hidden question concerning the position of women in religious conflicts, Tagarirofa contends that it is rather erroneous to regard women solely as victims in conflicts. As he contends, "Although women do suffer in most religious conflicts, their capacity should not be seen with rigid identity lens since they can alter their spaces and practices according to the dictates of the conflict situation." This argument builds on revisionist feminist scholarship that has called for a more troubled reading concerning gender and victimhood or agency. Through this narrative, the chapter, thus, calls for a consideration of the agentic roles that some women have performed instead of concentrating only on their victimhood in war situations and other situations of conflict. Among others, Tagarirofa presents compelling evidence from situations in which some women helped "to end bloody conflicts, to brokering peace accords in Sierra Leone and Liberia. In Nigeria's bloody Boko Haram terrorist attacks, women have been seen taking care of the victims of conflicts way before the formal medical teams arrive."

In Chapter 6, Nancy Mazuru troubles the causes and the impacts of the seemingly "antiquated and illegal" practice of ritual killings in post-colonial Zimbabwe. To Mazuru, while ritual killings have a long historical genealogy and have been on the decline in the modern era, in some parts of Africa, the killings have endured to the present day. For Zimbabwe, Mazuru argues that the pervasiveness of the practice in the new millennium is rooted in the "crisis" that entrenched massive unemployment and poverty which overall worsened existential conditions of the majority of Zimbabwe. And, as the existential needs were worsened, many people resorted to superstitious belief systems and spiritual solutions to mitigate the suffering, including ritual killings, which were premised to bring in better economic fortunes to private citizens and to declining businesses.

In Chapter 7, James Hlongwana discusses the placement of the borderland Ndau people found along the Zimbabwe-Mozambican border, literally between a hard rock and a difficult place, in which they suffer violence from the feuding FRELIMO and RENAMO protagonists. Based on an ethnographic study in the Mossurize District of Mozambique, which is a RENAMO stronghold, the chapter problematises the intricate dimensions of the overt and sometimes hidden dimensions of violence that have befallen the civilians of the district, sometimes spilling into the neighbouring Manicaland Province of Zimbabwe. While the physical violence of the contestation over control of the district is apparent, the violence is largely hidden and is seldom in the news given that it is tucked away in a rural setting, seemingly away from the media lenses. As well, the physical manifestations of the FRELIMO-RENAMO conflict have led to the violent displacement of many Mossurize District residents. In his words, Hlongwana amply captures the predicament of the civilians of Mossurize pointing out that:

While RENAMO employs terror to force the civilian population into submissive posture, FRELIMO implements counter-insurgency tactics against the same population. Both parties have resorted to murder, looting, destruction of homes and animals. To avoid capture and subsequently loss of life people have taken refuge either in forests, mountains and steep-sided river valleys or in neighbouring Zimbabwe, leaving their property and animals at the mercy of FRELIMO and RENAMO soldiers. By 2017, the Mossurize District countryside resembled a virtually deserted region with sporadic gunfire as part of the order of the day.

In Chapter 8, Nancy Mazuru meticulously consider how the widespread use of the social media platforms such as WhatsApp, Twitter, Skype and Facebook have impacted on infidelity in sexual liaisons and worsened the cases of domestic violence in Zimbabwe among intimate partners. She does this, notwithstanding and without minimising the positive impacts of social media in easing communication and networking challenges across the world, including availing spaces for advertisements, re/connections, business associations, and for the dissemination of social news relating to birthdays, deaths and/ or weddings. To Mazuru, however, "there is a strong interrelationship between social media, infidelity and domestic violence in Zimbabwe" because:

> Social media has become one of the most used methods of finding out former and new love partners as well as sending love messages and sexting. These platforms are used by both married and unmarried people. Many social networks also provide an online environment for people to communicate and exchange personal information for dating purposes. Of paramount importance to note is the fact that social media has rapidly heightened the rates of infidelity among couples, thereby increasing marital disputes, divorce and domestic violence in the country.

Ngonidzashe Marongwe, in Chapter 9, discusses how the practice of appeasing avenging spirits (*kuripa ngozi*) among the Shona people of Zimbabwe can add the country's search for the seemingly illusive transitional justice in the post-colonial era. Marongwe's chapter gives a pithy theorisation of *ngozi* and *kuripa ngozi* as largely rooted in the need for restorative peace and justice. The purpose of the chapter, as Marongwe puts it, is to help the discussion for "victim-based" transitional justice mechanisms that can help to stamp out the culture of violence and impunity. Building on earlier studies, including those by Sriram and Pillay (2009), the chapter presents a compelling argument for the adoption of everyday healing processes rooted in community traditions alongside government-led and/ or internationally known transitional justice practices. As Marongwe puts it, *kuripa ngozi's* value in Zimbabwe lies in that:

> Besides transcending the binary between peace and justice, *kuripa ngozi* would be suitable for rural areas because it is a well-known practice, cost-effective, quick, is supportive of socio-economic rights, and is less encumbered technically. Its potential usage also undercuts the thread of passiveness of communities in transitional justice that has been marked by blanket amnesties. *Kuripa ngozi* is also informed by pragmatic concerns under Zimbabwe's conditions of severe political polarity.

In Chapter 10, Fidelis Duri discusses the significance of appeasing avenging spirits as a ritual mechanism for the resolution of the history of politically-motivated violence in post-colonial Zimbabwe. For Duri, the chapter is based on the apparent failure by the "Zimbabwe's criminal justice system in handling murder cases in general and those related to politically-motivated violence in particular in a manner that brings about reconciliation and lasting peace to the generality of the population." The failure undergirded by a compromised criminal justice system in Zimbabwe in which there was partisan appointment of magistrates and judges that overall resulted in the partial trial of politically-related crimes. As Duri ably presents, this stemmed from the close links between the judges and magistrates with the ruling ZANU-PF party and/or the security services that had a history of closeness to ZANU-PF. As a result of this partiality in the trial of the cases, Duri, thus, calls for a consideration of avenging spirits, known as *ngozi* and *uzimu* among the Shona and the Ndebele, respectively, as "African indigenous justice mechanisms … in an effort to achieve peace and reconciliation in conflict and post-conflict communities that were decimated by political violence during the new millennium." The main difference between Duri's Chapter 10 and Marongwe's Chapter 9 is that Marongwe's chapter focusses on the broader application of avenging spirits whilst Duri's specifically troubles the use of the fear of avenging spirits in resolving politically-related cases of murder and violence. On the whole, the two chapters complement each other and they add critical insights into the efficacy of age-old mechanisms based on the power of avenging spirits in resolving violent disputes and the establishment of long term peace and justice.

Conrad Chibango, in Chapter 11, discusses the efficacy of the Catholic Church's pastoral letters in healing grassroots communities of Zimbabwe that have been ravaged by seemingly unending cycles of politically-motivated violence and conflict. With a history that can be traced back to the 19th century letters by Popes Pius IX and Leo XIII, pastoral letters are documents that have been written by priests, bishops and Popes of the Roman Catholic Church articulating, condemning and/or seeking a redress to critical issues of their times that contributed towards the suffering of the citizens. Broadly, the chapter, which builds on an acknowledgement of the negative effects of the long genealogy of violence in Zimbabwe, laments the ambivalent impact of the pastoral letters in rebuilding ruptured communities. On the one hand, the letters have provided a platform for the knowledge empowerment of the community members, yet on the other hand, the author laments the limited effects of the letters due to the entrenched fear that prevents the members from openly implementing the ethos of these, which leads to his call for a newer *modus operandi*. On the whole, as he surmises, "although the Catholic Church's pastoral documents have empowered people with knowledge and skills to assess the moral position on the use of political violence, their impact on grassroots communities has remained compromised, largely due to fear. The chapter also acknowledges that an emerging approach, which engages various stakeholders from the community in discussing peace building and dealing with conflict cases, may be one of the effective steps towards healing Zimbabwe." The chapter illustrates the repeated attempts by the Catholic Church in seeking to provide avenues for the mending of broken communities that were afflicted by past conflicts that have the potential to recur.

In Chapter 12, Fidelis Duri discusses the hidden forms of violence in the Shona jurisprudential system of appeasing avenging spirits (*kuripa ngozi*) when it involves marrying off young girls. For Duri, this is against the set ethos of *kuripa ngozi* as a restorative justice concept. As part of the restorative justice, the age-old practice of *kuripa ngozi* has almost always involved marrying off young girls as part of the compensation package to appease an avenging spirit in addition to the payment of cattle and money. Based on a wide range of cases drawn from across Zimbabwe, Duri ably argues that the practice is a "betrayal of justice" because the girl who is pledged, literally, becomes "a slave and wife to a member of the deceased's family." This is because of reasons such as that the girl usually got married off to an adult man and seldom to a boy of her age; the violation of the young girl's rights and liberties based on the coercing of girls to marry older men without any alternative; as well as the practice being gender insensitive. As a result, there have been many cases in post-colonial Zimbabwe where the young girls who would have been married off ran away. In addition, there have been a lot of arrests by the Zimbabwe Republic Police as the marrying off of young girls violate the country's constitutional provisions. Over and above this, there have been a lot of demonstrations against the continuation of the practice by girl-child and women rights advocacy groups. In his words, Duri contends that:

> The cultural practice of marrying off a young girl in order to appease the avenging spirit of a murdered person is both ambivalent and self-defeating in that it sacrifices the rights and liberties of girl children, and at times boy children, under the guise of seeking peace and justice. As a jurisprudential institution, it causes societal discord by appeasing the dead and their bereaved families at the expense of innocent young people whose childhood and adulthood are both compromised.

In Chapter 13, Prosper Hellen Tlou discusses how the Vhavenḓa people have deployed names for the dual role of identification of perceived conflict areas and as a tool to send different coded messages that advocate for peace in their communities. In the latter case, many of the names used convey messages of wrong doing in an ironic way. In this regard, names of shops, taxis and domestic animals, among other things, are used not only to "identify them but also to communicate different messages to perceived enemies, jealous friends/relatives or people in general. The names vary from protests to advice with the sole aim of maintaining peace. They are also used as a way of reprimanding those whose behaviour is considered socially and morally unacceptable without physically confronting them. The Vhavenḓa see this as a better option to dealing with conflicts as it minimises open friction and animosity." Overall, the chapter depicts the dynamism of conflict resolution strategies by African communities, which if restituted could go a long way in promoting peace and harmony in post-colonial Zimbabwe.

Erasmas Masitera's Chapter 14 pithily interrogates the role of the Shona people's *Dare* (communal meetings) as a moral tool in the formulation and implementation of acceptable behaviour and conduct. As Masitera posits, because the *Dare* system was/is built around the Ubuntu lived philosophy, it thus contains "virtue and deontological ethical" philosophies that promote peace and harmony in society. This means that, the *Dare* system is fashioned in such a way that enables the attainment of social justice and common good of the citizens. In his own words:

> The *Dare* is the best way through which social justice and common good are advanced. In that regard, the *Dare* system is a channel that is utilized to influence behaviour among the Shona people. Besides influencing behaviour, the system also helps in establishing peace, justice and the principle of equality among the Shona people. Thus, this traditional system is a way through which psychologically the Shona people are influenced into a particular way of thinking and behaving. Noteworthy, though, is that the influence is mostly positive, for the good of the community at large, a common good approach.

What is profound from Masitera's chapter is that far away from the *Dare* stifling individual rights, it actually promotes them. However, this is done in a way that does not disturb communal good, but rather promote peace and harmony in society.

In Chapter 15, Tobias Marevesa calls for a combined use of Christian and African traditional religious practices in efforts to end the cycles of violence and impunity recurrent in post-colonial Zimbabwe and in bringing about the much needed reconciliation and healing for the wounded Zimbabwean political community. For Marevesa, the adoption of this multi-pronged approach could have gone a long way in strengthening the efforts the Global Political Agreement (GPA), that brought feuding parties, namely the Zimbabwe African National Union-Patriotic Front led by Robert Mugabe and the two Movement for Democratic Change (MDC) formations, that is MDC-Tsvangirai and MDC-Mutambara that were led by Morgan Tsvangirai and Arthur Mutambara, respectively. As Marevesa contends, the GPA through the constituted arm on healing and reconciliation, the Organ for National Healing Reconciliation and Integration (ONHRI), failed in its mandate to heal Zimbabwe. For him, greater success in entrenching reconciliation, healing and peace could have come from among others if the ONHRI had "incorporated people and institutions with the capacity for conflict resolution drawn from the traditional and religious domains … [including] traditional leaders, traditional healers (*n'angas*), church leaders, spirit mediums, cultural values [and] local communities." The significance of this chapter is that besides adding voice to the use of retributive and restorative justice in Zimbabwe's conflict resolution conundrum, it also draws attention to the potential of Christian-based solutions while raising the often neglected/minimised roles that local leaders such as *n'angas* and chiefs have over their communities, especially as interlocutors between their communities and the living dead in the Nabudere formulation.

The 16th chapter by Steyn Khesani Madlome and Osborne Risimati Chauke discusses some of the common conflicts that afflict the Vatsonga-speaking people who are found in many southern African countries, including Zimbabwe, South Africa, Swaziland and Mozambique. These include interpersonal, intra-group, inter-group and conflicts that occur between the traditional ruling elites and the common subjects. The duo go further to trouble the efficacy of the communities' traditional strategies aimed at resolving these conflicts. On the whole, and drawing from their ethnographic study of the Vatsonga communities, Madhlome and Chauke contend that "some of the major disputes within communities can be settled amicably from an Afrocentric vantage point to the satisfaction of the people involved in the same way or even far much better than other points of view elsewhere." This largely derives from the fact that many African communities are undergirded by Ubuntu values, which consider individual needs and the ultimate good of the community in solving disputes. As well, the chapter shows how in the Vatsonga conflict resolution system, both the wrongdoer and aggrieved part[ies] benefit from the methods employed in resolving their conflict. The chapter ends by recommending the incorporation of African indigenous cultural ways of achieving justice and peace in the process of resolving the numerous conflicts that afflict the African continent in the 21st century.

The last chapter by Marongwe, Duri and Mawere is a conclusion to the book. It provides a meticulous final analysis of all the issues raised and discussed in this volume.

References

BBC News, (18 June 2012), "Rwanda 'gacaca' genocide courts finish work", Available at: http://www.bbc.com/news/world-africa-18490348, Accessed 15 May 2018.

Clapham, C. (2012) "Gacaca: A Successful Experiment in Restorative Justice?", An essay Available at: https://www.e-ir.info/2012/07/30/gacaca-a-successful-experiment-in-restorative-justice-2/, Accessed 15 June 2018.

Fiseha, A. (2017) 'Fundamental features of indigenous dispute resolution mechanisms in Ethiopia', In Abraha, K. et al, (Eds) *Proceedings of the International Conference on the African way of resolving conflicts: The harmony model*, Institute of Population Studies Centre for Dispute Resolution, Mekelle University: Ethiopia.

Galtung, J. (1964) 'An Editorial,' in: *Journal of Peace Research*, Volume 1, Number1, pp 1-4.

Galtung, J. (1969) 'Violence, peace and peace research', Available at: academic.regis.edu/bplumley/Galtung1969JPRViolencePeaceP eaceResearch.pdf, Accessed 21 June 2016.

Grewal, B. S. (2003) 'John Galtung: Positive and negative peace', Available at: www.activeforpeace.org/no/fred/Positive_Negative_Peace.pdf, Accessed 21 June 2016.

Human Rights Watch, (2011), "Justice Compromised: The legacy of Rwanda's community based *gacaca* courts", Available at: https://www.hrw.org/report/2011/05/31/justice-compromised/legacy-rwandas-community-based-gacaca-courts, Accessed 17 May 2018.

Igreja, V and B. Dias-Lambranca, (2008) "Restorative justice and the role of magamba spirits in post-civil war Gorongosa, central Mozambique", in *Traditional Justice and Reconciliation after Violent Conflict: Learning from African Experiences,* International Institute for Democracy and Electoral Assistance (IDEA).

Igreja, V. (2009), "The politics of peace, justice and healing in post-war Mozambique", in C. L. Sriram and S. Pillay, eds, *Peace vs Justice: The dilemma of transitional justice in Africa*, UKZN Press: South Africa.

Marongwe, N. (2013) "Rural women as the invisible victims of militarised political violence: the case of Shurugwi district, Zimbabwe, 2000-2008", *PhD Thesis*, University of the Western Cape, Cape Town: South Africa.

Marongwe, N and M. Mawere, (2016) 'Democracy, violence and peace in one house: The dilemma of post-colonial Africa', in: M. Mawere and N. Marongwe (eds.) *Myths of peace and democracy? Towards building pillars of hope, unity and transformation in Africa*, Bamenda: Langaa RPCIG, pp 1-20.

Masaka, D. (2017) 'Global justice and the suppressed epistemologies of the indigenous peoples of Africa", in: *Philosophical Papers*, Volume 46, Number 1, pp59-84.

Mbiti, J.S. (1969) *African religion and philosophy*, Heinemann: London.

Scanlon, H and N. Motlafi, (2009) "Indigenous justice or political instrument?: The modern gacaca courts of Rwanda", In: C. L. Sriram and S. Pillay, eds, *Peace vs Justice: The dilemma of transitional justice in Africa*, UKZN Press: South Africa.

Seay, L. (2017) "Rwanda's *gacaca* courts are hailed as a post-genocide success. The reality is more complicated", in *The Washington Post*, 2 June, Available at:
https://www.washingtonpost.com/news/monkey-cage/wp/2017/06/02/59162/?utm_term=.6a6c27510a90, Accessed 17 May 2018.

Sherif, A. A. (2017). 'Healing conflicts in Africa through its indigenous institutions : The revitalisation of the Mato Oput Practice and Gacaca System in post-conflict state of Rwanda and Uganda', In: Abraha, K. et al, (Eds) *Proceedings of the International Conference on the African way of resolving conflicts: The harmony model*, Institute of Population Studies Centre for Dispute Resolution, Mekelle University: Ethiopia.

Sriram, C. L. (2009) "Introduction: Transitional Justice and peace building", In: C. L. Sriram and S. Pillay, eds, *Peace vs Justice: The dilemma of transitional justice in Africa*, UKZN Press: South Africa.

Winthrop, D. (1978) 'Aristotle and theories of justice', In: *The American Political Science Review*, Volume 72, Number 4, pp1206-1216.

Part I:
The Scourge of Violence in Post-Colonial Africa

Chapter 2

The Zimbabwean Democratisation Paradox: Popular Protests, Violence and State Responses, 2013-2016

Jacob Tagarirofa & David Tobias

Introduction

The chapter focuses on the popular protests in Zimbabwe in the post-2013 harmonised elections that were won by the Zimbabwe African National Union Patriotic Front (ZANU-PF). The post-2013 elections period also coincided with the collapse of the Government of National Unity (GNU) that had been formed in 2009 and comprised ZANU-PF and the two Movement for Democratic Change (MDC) formations which were the MDC-T and the MDC-M led by Morgan Tsvangirai and Arthur Mutambara, respectively. The post-2013 election period was not only characterized by discontent among many citizens, but also epitomized the reconfiguration of Zimbabwe's democratization milieu since the protests were not only violent, but, spontaneous and not aligned to any institutionalized political party. From 2009 until 2013 when new elections were held the parties had been working as awkward bed fellows who nonetheless laboured towards the country's economic recovery by putting in place dynamic strategies, which, among others, helped to reinvigorate the dying economy, including the dollarisation policy, economic stabilization strategies and economic growth strategies. Regrettably, most of the efforts and work accomplished by the GNU to put the economy on an optimistic trajectory were, arguably, reversed in the post-2013 era as evidenced by delays in civil servants salary dates and the inescapable liquidity crunch. As a result of the reversals, the country witnessed waves of protest movements by the public against the ZANU PF–led government. In this regard, there emerged massive demonstrations and strikes staged by vendors, workers, pro-democracy activists and some clergymen.

The period 2013-2016 characteristically exhibited a trail of violence between the state and its citizens as the demonstrations became confrontations, which turned bloody as demonstrators decried economic degeneration, dysfunctional industries, and corruption in the corridors of power, massive unemployment, cash shortages and forced retrenchments, among others. The demonstrators also called for more democratization of the state, which among others called for the removal of the then long-serving President, Robert Mugabe. The government countered through violent police and other security services crackdown on the defenceless protestors as it continued to blame the international community and western sanctions in stirring violence in the country. Among some of the results of the violence was the diminishing of democratic space and the destruction of economic infrastructure needed for social cohesion.

Methodologically, the research was purely qualitative where data was gathered through oral interviews, analysis of relevant documents, newspapers and desktop research. This chapter therefore argues that, continuous repression and oppression from of the people by state apparatus culminates in spontaneous uprisings and confrontations which degenerate into new legacies of violence and modified political dispensations.

Civil protests against the ZANU PF government since 2013

The lifespan of the GNU came to an end in 2013 when ZANU-PF controversially won the scheduled harmonized elections against the MDC-T. To some people the victory actually sent shock waves since the campaigning period had been relatively peaceful and each party had been given enough time and space to gunner for support. Against such odds, the ZANU-PF party eventually formed the government and sought to consider and implement policies as a way of fulfilling its campaign promises. Since 2013 the generality of the population had their optimistic hopes shattered as the government started to grapple with deepening political, social and economic turmoil which ravaged the country. Among others, there was a consistent downturn especially in the revenue being collected by the

Zimbabwe Revenue Authority (ZIMRA) (*Daily News*, 1 January 2017). Civil society groupings protested against the election outcome and incidences of violence were witnessed. This was not a surprise so if cross-examined against existing contemporary political realities then where, for instance, the state secret security agents were alleged to have been instrumental in fomenting insidious coercion of the citizens into supporting the ZANU-PF party. Again, the fact that all opposition political parties had to seek clearance from the police before they held any rally is a demonstration of how the state repressive apparatus was at play in Zimbabwean politics since most of the opposition rallies were never sanctioned and this again emerged as another bone of contention raised by the protesters. This does not only demonstrate how relevant Althussers' (1971) ideas on state apparatus are in accounting for the incidence of violence and state response in Zimbabwean politics, but, as well qualifies the Marxian view that in every epoch the ruling ideas are the ideas of the ruling class (Giddens, 2000). Against this background, there emerged a myriad of anti-government demonstrations which were in the form of general strikes as outraged citizens turned against the government.

Different groups of people and some individuals with different backgrounds emerged but all displayed a new spirit of resistance and outpoured their anger against the government. The groups included the following: the National Vendors Union of Zimbabwe (NAVUZ) led by Stendrick Zvorwaza, Tajamuka/Sesjikile, a social movement led by Promise Mkwananzi, whose ranks included university students and unemployed graduates, workers specially civil servants who were disappointed by the government's failure to provide fixed dates for their salaries and bonuses, some clergy like Pastor Evan Mawarire who was the leader of the shadowy movement known as 'This Flag Campaign', pro-democracy activists, cross-border traders and members of the opposition political parties (*Daily News*, 3 June 2016). Although some groups and individuals had genuine grievances pertaining to their specific interests and occupations, they shared certain common issues which universally united them as demonstrators. These developments signify the metamorphosis of the democratisation efforts by numerous civic organizations in Zimbabwe since they seemingly sprang spontaneously without any traceable inclination towards opposition political outfits. This is so because, traditionally democratic forces were thought to be known political parties and civic organisations which ran contrary to this nascent development where people just assembled themselves due to the levels of their disgruntlement and mobilised protests against the government. Whilst Itai Dzamara, a so-called pro-democracy activist's disappearance seems to have marked the beginning of the citizen uprisings and popular protests, the subsequent consolidation of those efforts by *Tajamuka/Sesjikile* and This Flag led by Mkwananzi and Mawarire respectively acted as a springboard for the solidification of the mass protests to the extent of calling for state response.

One-man demonstration: bedrock for the popular mass protests

Itai Dzamara was well-known for his one-man demonstrations against the government, a feat which perhaps heightened the spirits of the subsequent citizen movements that followed. Dzamara was a journalist and political activist known in Zimbabwe mostly for his Occupy Africa Unity Square campaign against the government of the then President, Robert Mugabe (*Newsday*, 12 March 2015). He became famous through his hand-delivered petition to the then President of Zimbabwe and the Occupy Africa Unity Square intonation. Dzamara advocated for the occupation of the Africa Unity Square in Harare. This place is located on the heart of the Harare city centre adjacent the Parliament Building. According to Dzamara, the occupation of the square was a way of communicating dissatisfaction in the country's leadership particularly the then President, Robert Mugabe, and his ZANU-PF government (*Bulawayo 24News*, 10 November 2014). This marked the beginning of popular protests as up to 50 people joined him in November 2014 in 'occupying the square', between 0900 hours and 1700 hours. In response, the Zimbabwe Republic Police deployed almost 70 members in heavy riot gear to intimidate the protestors. The Africa Unity Square in Harare is a few blocks away from the offices of the

President and this made the occupation a potential security threat (*Ibid*).

After the demonstrations, Dzamara wrote; "…We occupied Africa Unity Square today, yet again forced the state to respond, and, yet again, demonstrated our goodwill by agreeing to negotiate. We are the people! We are the numbers" (*Ibid*: 5). Those that gathered with Dzamara at the square said they wanted a response from the then President, Mugabe, to the demands for him to admit failure, step down and pave way for a process towards finding a new national plan for governance and leadership (*Ibid*). After going back to the President's office, Dzamara and his two colleagues were taken to a holding area where armed police officers watched them carefully. Dzamara wrote that the intelligence officers from the President's office regarded them as high profile suspects and they deserved high level security. They were transported to the Harare Central Police Station where they were immediately taken to the underground holding bays (*Daily News*, 19 October 2014). Senior police officers came one by one quizzing Dzamara about his agenda of occupying the Africa Unity Square. They warned him of the devastating consequences of the move but he remained adamant. This constituted one of the immediate responses by the government (*My Zimbabwe*, 6 November 2014).

The final episode of the "Occupy Africa Unity Square" demonstration ended sadly for Dzamara as he was severely beaten by the Zimbabwe Republic Police Support Unit force which was deployed in full force. Dzamara was beaten together with his fellow activists and his lawyer. He was taken to a local hospital where he was given treatment. A few hours after he was admitted into hospital, the social media was awash with photos of Dzamara lying unconscious after the beating at the hands of the police (*MyZimbabwe*, 6 November 2014). He shocked the people when he started posting articles on his Facebook page called The News Leader encouraging the people to continue with the peaceful demonstration against the Mugabe government (*Ibid*).

On the morning of 9 March 2015, Dzamara was abducted by five unidentified men while at a barber shop in Harare's Glenview suburb (*Newsday*, 10 April 2015). This background speaks to the validity of the view that 'a match stick burnt bushes'. The resultant effect of Dzamara's individual pursuits and experiences became a cornerstone for the subsequent mass protests that rocked the country through various social groups that were involved in mass protests against the allegedly autocratic government.

Tajamuka/Sesjikile: The springboard for citizen uprisings

Just like the Tunisian uprisings which were ignited by one vendor who burnt himself and instilled rage unto the masses (*MyZimbabwe*, 6 November 2014), the Zimbabwean uprisings seemingly followed the same path as Mkwananzi, the *Tajamuka* frontman, rose to fame after he publicly denounced the government for a myriad of socio-political and economic failures. Tajamuka was an organic idea which began naturally because of the vacuum which was there in terms of cohesive youth mobilisation (*Zimbabwe Independent*, 23 September 2016). There were discussions among various youth formations about the need to create a common platform, obviously to pull together towards democratisation and putting government to task in terms of economic policies and welfare provision to its citizens (Munaki, 2016). It started off as a campaign which would raise the discontent of the young people to government through action and unity, a deliberation which signalled the impending mass citizen protests by disgruntled youths. The fundamentals were that young people from various progressive youth formations must come together for action. Mkwananzi (2016:5) confirms this by affirming that, "*Tajamuka* was never designed to be in the boardroom or in the hotel to discuss anything; it was designed to be in the streets in action with young people, particularly those 40 years and below. Young people from all walks of life, be it opposition parties or civil society, so that it how it started". He further notes that, it later developed into a citizens' movement which paved way for the subsequent and recurrent mass demonstrations and protests by various social groups which were either mistreated or whose livelihoods had been disrupted by government such as vendors, unemployed graduands, and cross-border traders. The *Tajamuka* citizen movement was, however, not taken lightly by the state since its leader was apprehended, and remanded in custody for several days without due regard to the proper legal course (*Ibid*). These pacification attempts were in vain as more mass protests ensued.

This Flag: Resistance through weapons of the weak

Another force that concurrently complemented the *Tajamuka's* protestations was This Flag, a seemingly political, but religious movement led by the clergyman Evans Mawarire. Cherure (2016) wrote that, religious institutions in Zimbabwe were known for glorifying the state due to the prevalent patronage system which came with numerous rewards to the religious leaders. However, the case of This Flag was a bit divergent from the above observation in that, it was the pastor himself who chose to stage a one-man demonstration against the government's shortcomings. He moved around the Harare city centre putting on a flag as a symbolic representation of the queries he had about the government, a move which can be equated to Scott's (1985) notion of the weapons of the poor or weak in their everyday forms of resistance. Scott notes that, the weak in every social or economic setting would resort to informal and unorganised forms of resistance against an oppressive and exploitative system. In the Zimbabwean context, Mawarire put on a flag which is a respected national emblem as his weapon since he seemingly humiliated the state for its alleged failures. His efforts were complemented by many young suffering people and fellow church members who also wore the flag at mass gatherings in the city centre. The disparagement of the national emblem annoyed the government and this resulted in his apprehension and successive temporal incarcerations although he had not used any harmful physical weapon to threaten national security and public order (*Newsday*, 13 December 2016).

Mawarire's call for national prayers at the city centre gatherings which were attended by many people with each holding a burning candle at night, perhaps symbolised the need by the general masses for a brighter future amidst the dark environment of scarce economic opportunities in the country. Employing Scott's idea of hidden forms of power, one is convinced to justify that there is a clear connection between resistance and the ideas of hidden and invisible power. Just as hidden forms of power can be used by powerful actors such as the state to keep certain issues and voices under control, similarly relatively powerless groups such as churches and informal citizens' movements such as This Flag and the likes of *Tajamuka*, can employ strategies of resistance which 'hide' their actions from the powerful, or which use codes such as prayers or mass wearing of a national emblem to make them invisible. Scott (1992) submits that, another example may be found in the rich history of African-American spirituals, which were sometimes used in the times of slavery as codes for communication, disguising hidden messages from the workers under the guise of singing a hymn or folklore. As such, these mass protests in Zimbabwe redefined the nature and pattern of dealing with states which cherish violence as a weapon since protestors devised other strategies which evaded the inescapable hegemonic laws and state brutality.

Unemployed graduands decrying poverty

Major issues raised by the demonstrators especially among the vendors included wide-spread joblessness, poverty, hunger and starvation (Munaki, 2016). A wide range of activists including unemployed graduands protested against the government arguing that Zimbabwe was historically regarded as one of Africa's most promising economies but the government had, through mismanagement, slipped the economy into irreversible decline (Mukaka, 2015). They further cited dysfunctional industries and forced retrenchments as major catalysts for the prevalent abject poverty and the appalling living conditions of the working poor. Others cited the government's economic policies which had throttled investment and the prospects of industrial expansion for enhanced employment opportunities. The protesters also lambasted the policy of indigenisation which was constantly seen as ill-fated and disastrous to the nation. The Indigenisation Act of 2008 which ordered foreign industrialists and other entrepreneurs to cede 51% shares to the locals was perceived disastrous as it discouraged prospective investors (*Daily News*, 23 November 2016).

These protestations illustrate that many sections of the Zimbabwean population were very policy conscious and they could resist any government moves which they felt would jeopardise their livelihoods. This is evidenced by the nature and pattern of protests by many unemployed graduands who gathered in the main streets of Zimbabwe's capital Harare, chanting and singing denigratory slogans and songs against the then President and his government during the period October to November 2016 (*Daily News*, 20 November 2016). These protests incidentally exposed the government's lack of human rights conscience since it retaliated by deploying the police and the army to brutally disperse the protestors (Ibid). The analogy also qualifies Giddens's (1983) Theory of Structuration which avows that individual actors' actions are constrained by socio-political and economic structures in social contexts, yet in turn these individuals have agency, which is the ability to manoeuvre and navigate these social constraints for their survival. As a result, the political structure which traditionally coerces the protestors has proven to be fragile since the protests which constitute the 'actions' by agents have resulted in the reorganisation of the political system since it has been discredited or rendered illegitimate.

Yet still, more other people, especially from the opposition parties, highlighted concern over corruption, nepotism and inefficiency in the corridors of power. They argued that the then President, Robert Mugabe, had been historically surrounded by some officials who were bent on looting, robbing, pilfering and literally raping the national economy instead of finding practical solutions to the deepening economic crisis (*Newsday*, 31 December 2016). The issue of corruption was said to have risen to crisis levels among some government ministers and senior public officials. The CCJP (2000) notes that what actually troubled the public was the fact that corrupt officials that were arrested usually got away with their fraudulent acts. This implied that there was impunity and lawlessness in the country. At times the government accused those who raised concern of lawlessness as hypocrites and puppets who were bent on igniting civil protests and regime change in Zimbabwe (*Ibid*). The impact of corruption scandals only served to compromise the legitimacy of both the ZANU PF party and government. Thus, the demonstrators joined hands and demanded for a better Zimbabwe with a stable and vibrant democracy as the government continued to grapple with challenges of a deepening economic and political crisis. Natural causes also played a hand in tormenting the already violence-ridden society. Devastating drought spells became a permanent feature during the period under study. Although droughts affected the whole nation, the country's southern region was the hardest hit since it has historically been a dry prone area. The available evidence indicates that the occurrence of droughts left more than 4 million citizens requiring food aid by 2017 (*Daily News*, 1 January 2017). The food shortages as much served to deepen the high poverty levels in the country as they worsened food shortages. This scenario happened against the backdrop of the government's failing attempts to import maize to feed the nation, which had serious negative implications on the already overburdened national budget where 97% of government spending was perennially channelled towards the payment of civil servants (*The Worker*, November 2016).

Street vendors and state violence

This section turns to a discussion of the repressive state response to the popular protests by street vendors. The first case illustrates the clashes between the state and vendors that started in July 2015. The clashes were instigated when the then Minister of Local government, Public Works and National Housing gave a seven-day ultimatum to vendors to remove their stalls from the city canters. This was after the realisation that more than 20 000 unlicensed vendors were now operating in the Central Business District (CBD) and city streets in major towns like Harare, Bulawayo, Mutare, Chivhu, Chinhoyi, Masvingo, among others causing congestion as approximately 1.5 million people were now employed in this informal sector across the country's urban cities (Munyuki, 2015). The majority sold fruits and vegetables, cell phones, phone recharge cards, second-hand clothes, belts and foot wear among others. As well, there were fears that the continuation of these illegal trading activities in the city centres were affecting the operations of the licensed business persons and that some of the people involved in the trade were using it as a façade to cover up criminal activities. At another level, the state blamed the vendors for causing disease outbreaks, including typhoid, cholera and other water borne disease (*Newsday*, 15 January 2017).

However, what also should not be forgotten is that usually when people's lives are threatened, people tend to adopt various survival strategies in order to minimize constraints triggered by the crises (Chiumbu and Musemwa, 2012). The survival strategy of resorting to the informal economy did not only demonstrate the government's failure to formulate and effectively implement sound economic policies, but, was also a form of latent protest against the failure of the formal economy. The shift from formal employment by the majority resulted in the exponential increase in the number of vendors throughout the country. This has been so much to an extent that Zimbabwe has been sarcastically dubbed a 'Vending Nation' (Munaki, 2016). The government seemed oblivious to this blatant fact that had a profound bearing on the people's material well-being. Apart from criticizing the vendors for operating without licenses, the other reason cited by both the government and urban authorities was that it was no longer possible to do normal business in the CBD because the vendors had brought congestion.

As a result of this, there were accusations and counter-accusations between vendors and the government. The situation became worse and violence escalated because the vendors were fighting back through a plethora of strategies which included throwing of stones and bricks on both the Zimbabwe Republic Police (ZRP) and municipal police. They took to the streets led by their associations and occasionally delivered several petitions to the parliament, and vehemently resisted eviction orders. There emerged a violent police crackdown on vendors throughout the country. Initially, it was the regular municipal police assisted by the ZRP which unleashed violence on the vendors when the eviction campaign began. Due to the fact that the number of vendors was increasing daily due to the continuously deteriorating economic situation, they were occasionally joined by some disgruntled members of the public (Munyuki, 2015). The government immediately responded by massively increasing the deployment of security agents (*Ibid*). The government's response took a new twist when the Zimbabwe

National Army came in with trucks and tankers against anti-government demonstrators (*Newsday*, 6 November 2016). They used water cannons, seized and burned goods which belonged to vendors and the majority were indiscriminately arrested, beaten and at times released after bail.

On their part, the vendors also formed another formidable force towards the everyday clamour for democracy, human rights and better living conditions, a deliberation which qualified them to categorically be an informal social force. This perhaps augments Fanon's (1963) sentiments on violence and its meaning for the oppressed. He argued that violence is the only effective method which the oppressed poor people can employ to emancipate themselves. The Zimbabwean mass protests epitomize the colonial epoch's characteristic entanglement between the Africans and the colonial masters. The Zimbabwe government's responses by using repression and violence can be likened to what Fanon regarded as a tactic of colonial rule which was maintained through legitimation of violence and repression (Fanon, 1963).

The vendors' argument seemed justifiable. They were frustrated and this made them to continue to resort to the use of force to counter state-sponsored repression. Most of them argued that there was no space in the designated areas for all of them. The interviews conducted revealed that the majority of the vendors had realised that the CBD had become a key market with potential customers while the designated sites were remotely located. The designated areas could not be easily accessed by both vendors and customers and this rendered the vending business virtually unviable. The situation was worsened by the fact that the majority of the vendors were widows, the disabled, uneducated women, unemployed youths and educated graduands who in most cases operated their business while at the same time taking care of their children. In other words, they saw themselves as innocent people whose discontent was justified and erroneously viewed as rebellion and met with utmost brutality. The majority argued that they were just trying to make ends meet as they were profoundly affected by extreme poverty in a terribly harsh economic environment. The situation did not change much as the vendors continued to stage more demonstrations and demanded back their confiscated goods and wares. They accused the government of mismanaging the economy through wrong policies, corruption and greed (*Newsday*, 14 December 2016.

Many vendors were further baffled when they realised that the ZANU-PF party distributed the confiscated goods throughout the country as a way of soliciting for political support. They further argued that, the looming plan to demolish their stalls by the Harare City Council and the confiscation of their wares was unconstitutional since section 74 of the national constitution stipulated that no one can be evicted from his or her property without a court order (*Daily News*, 25 January 2017). It should be underlined that the resistance demonstrated by the vendors was justified since the government's seizure of their wares and their subsequent disposal for political currency violated the constitution. The government's clampdown on vendors was also insensitive given the severe socio-economic hardships that gripped the country.

The cash crisis and subaltern everyday responses

Another source of protests and confrontation during the period was the cash crisis which became critical from March 2016. In October 2016, in an effort to mitigate the cash crisis, the government of Zimbabwe, through the Reserve Bank of Zimbabwe, announced its intention to issue out bond notes as a legal tender. The introduction was done ostensibly under a $200 million export incentive facility allegedly guaranteed by Africa Export-Import Bank to boost exports. There was a flurry of criticism from all circles with many, including the Zimbabwe Congress of Trade Union, MDC, vendors, civic organizations and cross–border traders, with some labelling the move as marking the return of the despised Zimbabwean currency. Throughout 2016, cash queues reminiscent of the 2008 crisis were evident at almost all banking institutions like Commercial Bank of Zimbabwe (CBZ), Central African Building Society (CABS), Banc ABC and Zimbabwe Bank (ZB), among others. Virtually all banking institutions struggled to meet the demand for cash by the generality of depositors (*Newsday*, 30 December 2016). The situation actually spilled into the festive season of 2016 as the demand for cash exponentially increased. Against this backdrop, bond notes were introduced in November 2016 (*Ibid*). Despite the efforts, the ordinary people reacted through spontaneous riots at the banks, hording of the United States dollar and escalation of black market activities in which the much sort for foreign currency was exchanged with bond notes at a profit.

Cross-border traders and the Statutory Instrument 64 of 2016

Another incident of violent protestation was witnessed in the encounter between cross-border traders and the police and army after the introduction of the allegedly suppressive Statutory Instrument 64 (SI64/2016). The government invoked legislation which banned the importation of some foreign consumer goods claiming that it was strategically meant to protect local industries (Makunike, 2017). This angered cross-border traders as evidenced by the responses from the interviewees who argued that the government was actually hiding its finger since they were no industries in the country. According to the traders, there was need for establishment of industries before the ban could be instituted. Most of them saw themselves being further affected since in one way or another, they depended on the importation of foreign goods for resale. At the border with South Africa, he cross-border traders decided to set the Beit Bridge Customs warehouse on fire because that was where the Zimbabwe Revenue Authority (ZIMRA) stored confiscated goods. The government was actually shocked especially given the fact that some South Africans who were bound to lose business by the introduction of the above-mentioned statutory instrument joined in the demonstrations (*Daily News*, 31 December 2016).

One could be forgiven to query the credibility of this enactment of legislation on the mere basis that it was evidently clear that the cumulative deindustrialization of the country was highly attributable to internal factors such as corruption, maladministration, embezzlement of funds by corporate leaders and poor international relations. This is supported by Makunike (2017) who posited that the economic meltdown in Zimbabwe was a function of the collapse of internal organisation due to lack of a political commitment by the ruling elite. On that basis, it can be further argued that, it would therefore be absurd to envisage that the government's introduction of SI64 was sincere and therefore warranted massive reaction from the affected since it directly stifled livelihoods of many cross-border traders whose lives depended much on importation of basic commodities from other countries for resale in Zimbabwe.

The situation became worse when some members of opposition parties openly joined in and demanded that the then President of Zimbabwe, Robert Gabriel Mugabe, should resign (*The Worker*, November 2016). They were perceived by the government as puppets sponsored by the West to effect a regime change in Zimbabwe as the Minister of State Security was to claim (Ibid). Historically, the MDC formations had been regarded as a front for neo-colonialism which was geared to reverse the gains of independence (CCJP, 2000). The government actually became intolerant and suspicious of such demonstrations. In the same vein, Ndlovu-Gatsheni (2003) avers that whenever ZANU-PF's hegemony was threatened, it usually took a nationalistic stance and tried to maintain and retain power and legitimacy through forced mobilization, patronage, cronyism and violence. If this is something to go by, it becomes clear that such approaches breed violent protests which eventually culminate into mass political contestations between the state on one hand and social movements and the general populace on the other.

As a consequence of the eruption of such massive protests, the government of Zimbabwe responded in a number of ways. Apart from massively increased deployment of security agents around the country, the suppression of a myriad of demonstrations was achieved through the use of the constitution of Zimbabwe especially Part 4 , Subsection 113, which deals with public emergency (Constitution of Zimbabwe: 49). Through presidential decrees, all mass demonstrations were outlawed (*Daily News*, 23 November 2016). The President also warned judges who were ruling in favour of demonstrations and opposition party applications (*Daily News*, 25 November 2016). Furthermore, some sections of the Public Order and Security Act (POSA) were invoked to ban such protests by organisations. There was also the effective use of state-controlled newspapers, ZBC and ZTV by the government. These, among others, strongly and constantly warned protestors to desist from further demonstrations. It can be noted that during the period 2013-2016, the government of Zimbabwe was confronted with economic, social and political turmoil which degenerated into visible and violent protestations by disgruntled citizens.

Conclusion

It is evident from the foregoing discussion that there were massive anti-government demonstrations by the citizens of Zimbabwe during the period of 2013-2016. Broadly, the government was blamed for the economic meltdown which saw the impoverishment of the majority. Corruption, sky-rocketing levels of unemployment, deindustrialisation and the growth of the less profitable informal economy, cash shortages, the introduction of SI64 which banned the importation of basic consumer goods, were regarded by many as the instrumental ingredients for the rampant civil disobedience. As a result, the period under study actually speaks to the futility of consolidating democracy and constitutionalism in Zimbabwe since the various responses by the government towards the mass protests seem to have legitimized brutality and deliberate human rights violations through the sanctioned use of police and military forces against the civilians.

It should be noted that, the operational architecture of the Zimbabwean government in the context of these massive protests was not only hegemonic, but, symptomatic of Althusser's analogy of autocratic systems' reliance on repressive and ideological state apparatus. However, such an inclination should not be affirmed as inevitably dogmatic since the resistance by the civilians may in turn have hardened them to be less frightened by future brutal state endeavours and therefore become a time bomb thus qualifying Fanon and Marx's supplication that tyrannical political systems can only be dislodged through a violent, confrontational and bloody revolution waged by the oppressed. The fact that mass demonstrations are often linked to individual protest call for the need to redefine revolutions as processes not only initiated and undertaken

46

by the masses, but also as outcomes of the activities of brave and determined individuals.

References

Alexander, J. (2003) 'Squatters', veterans and the state in Zimbabwe,' in: Amanda Hammar, Brian Raftopoulos and Stig Jensen (eds.) *Zimbabwe's unfinished business. Rethinking land and nation in the context of crisis*, Harare: Weaver Press, pp83-118.

Catholic Commission for Peace and Justice, (2009) *Graveyard governance: A report on political violence in Zimbabwe following the March 2008 harmonised elections*, Harare: Africa Synod House.

Catholic Commission for Peace and Justice, (2000) *Crisis of governance: A report on political violence in Zimbabwe*, volume 1, publisher: city?.

Chigome, J. (2005) *Report on the state of African democracy*, Harare: University of Zimbabwe.

Chiumbu, S. and Musemwa, M. (2012) 'Introduction: Perspectives of the Zimbabwean crises,' In: Sarah Chiumbu and Muchaparara Musemwa (eds) *Crisis! What Crisis? The multiple dimensions of the Zimbabwean Crisis,* Cape Town: Human Sciences Research Council.

Fanon, F. (1963) *The wretched of the earth*, New York: Grove Press.

Giddens, A. (1983) *The constitution of society,* London: Polity Press.

Hlatyayo, L. Mukono, A. and Mukashi, M. (2015) 'Managing Governments of National Unity: Reflections of the Zimbabwe Joint Monitoring and Implementation Committee (JOMIC)' in: *The International Journal of Humanities and Social Studies*, 3 (4): 274-278.

Kuneni, G. (2008) The fate of troubled democracies, Pretoria: Juta.

Machakanja, P. (2009) 'Democracy and multi-party politics in Africa', in: *Journal of Modern African History,* 3 (23): 24-40.

Maposa, R.S. Hlongwana, J. and Muguti, T. (2013) 'Marching forward to the past: Challenges and prospects for the new theology of land in Zimbabwe,' in: *European Journal of Sustainable Development*, 2 (1): 133-148.

Mlambo, A. S. (1997) *The Economic Structural Adjustment Programmes: The Zimbabwean case 1990-1995*, Harare: University of Zimbabwe Publications.

Mukaka, M. (2015) *The politics of African politics*, Plummer Press: Delhi.

Munaki, B. (2008) 'What is politics?' *Mail and Guardian Politics Seminar*, Johannesburg.

Ndlovu-Gatsheni, S. (2003), 'Dynamics of the Zimbabwean crisis in the 21st century', In: *African Journal on Conflict Resolutions*, Volume 3 (1): 99-134.

Scott, J. C. (1985) *Weapons of the weak: Everyday forms of resistance*, Yale University Press: New Haven and London.

Scott, J. C. (1992) *Domination and the arts of resistance: Hidden transcripts*, Yale University Press: New Haven and London.

Utete, C. (2000) *Presidential Report on Land Reform Programme*, Government Printers: Harare.

Zaba F. (2011) Is JOMIC still relevant? Thinking beyond, *Journal of Alternatives for a Democratic Zimbabwe*, 1(16): 9-10.

Daily News, 19 October 2014.

My Zimbabwe News, 24 November 2014.

Bulawayo 24 News, 10 November 2014.

Daily News, 24 August 2016.

Zimbabwe News, 24 August 2016.

Worker, November 2016.

Newsday, 30 December 2016.

Newsday, 31 December 2016.

Daily News, 1 January 2017.

Newsday, 15 January 2017.

Daily News, 25 January 2017.

Zimbabwe Independent, 27 January 2017.

Chapter 3

Violent House Demolitions in Zimbabwe's Harare and Chitungwiza, 2014-2016: A Violation of People's Rights?

Nancy Mazuru

Introduction

The right to housing and shelter is one of the fundamental human rights and it falls under socio-economic rights. However, despite the importance of this right, it has been violated in several ways by many governments across the globe and Zimbabwe is not an exception. The purpose of this chapter is to examine the consequences of house demolitions in Zimbabwe, paying particular attention to the 2014-2016 government-imposed destruction of illegal residential structures in many of Harare and Chitungwiza's residential areas. The major focus is placed on the knocking down of houses that took place along the Harare International Airport Road, Budiriro, Glen Norah, Epworth, and in Chitungwiza. Destruction of urban residential structures is a form of violence that is grounded in forced or involuntary displacement.

The chapter commences with an overview of forced evictions in general, followed by a brief exploration of the trajectory of forced evictions in post-colonial Zimbabwe, examining operations that have been undertaken by the government of Zimbabwe that resulted in the destruction of houses and/or the involuntary displacement of populations. These include the 1983 Operation *Gukurahundi* 'dissident eradication', the 1993 Churu Farm evictions, the 2000 Fast Track Land Reform Programme, the 2005 Operation *Murambatsvina* 'Clear the Filth,' the 2002, 2005 and 2008 political violence and the 2014 Tokwe-Mukorsi flood evictions, among others.

Though the major thrust of the chapter is centred on house demolitions, all these events are important because they help to situate the issue of forced displacements in Zimbabwe in a proper historical context. A striking feature about house demolitions or forced displacement in Zimbabwe lies in the brutal manner in which the operations were carried out as well as the non-availability or inadequate and unclear plans by the government to compensate the victims, thereby violating a plethora of human rights and causing serious living hardships.

Overview of forced evictions in general and house demolitions in particular

Forced evictions usually occur on a large scale in virtually all countries worldwide and this is regardless of the many positive developments in recent years that have significantly strengthened the legal protection against forced evictions under international human rights law (Centre on Housing Rights and Evictions (COHRE), 2002). The practice of forced evictions involves the involuntary removal of persons from their homes or land directly or indirectly attributable to the state (Ibid). The number of people falling victim to forced evictions each year runs into several millions and the human costs associated with such evictions are staggering (UN-HABITAT, 2007). Governments and local authorities in most countries use their powers to evict people who neither have the money nor the power to defend themselves (United Nations Centre for Human Settlements (UNCHS), 2000).

Forced evictions usually occur as a result of development projects, discrimination, urban redevelopment schemes, gentrification, urban beautification, land alienation in both rural and urban areas and in situations of armed conflict and ethnic cleansing (COHRE, 2002). The practice of forced evictions is widespread and it affects persons in both developed and developing countries (Saul et al, 2014). What is astounding is the fact that at least 2 million people in the world are forcibly evicted every year (UN-HABITAT, 2012). In China about 1.7 million people were directly affected by demolitions and relocations related to the Beijing Olympic Games between 2001 and 2008 while in New York City alone, 25,000 evictions, on average were carried out each year during the same period (Ibid). In Nigeria, an estimated 2 million people were forcibly evicted from their homes between 2000 and 2007, and in Zimbabwe, 750 000 people were evicted in 2005 alone (Ibid). Nevertheless, regardless of the causes, under international law forced evictions are considered a *prima-facie* violation of the right to adequate housing and a gross violation of human rights (COHRE, 2002). As such, acts of forced eviction, whether carried out to construct a large dam or a new road, in the context of ethnic cleansing or simply to gentrify a trendy neighbourhood are almost invariably accompanied by attempts by those affected to resist the eviction and to stay in their homes (UN-HABITAT, 2012).

Although there are many factors that cause forced evictions, in the context of urban expulsion, the issue of informal settlements due to housing shortages has emerged as a major factor that cannot be ignored and this is largely due to rapid urbanisation across many parts of the globe. Urbanisation is inevitably increasing throughout the globe but most significantly in the developing world. Over the past centuries and decades, global urban population has rapidly increased from 3% in 1800, 14% in 1900, 30% in 1950 and 47% in 2000 (Bolay, 2006). It is projected that in 2030, the world's urban population will represent 60.2% of the global population, that is, almost 5 billion people of which 4 billion will be from developing countries, out of a total world population of 8.27 billion (Ibid). The megacities of developing countries have populations equivalent to or larger than some of those in developed countries but in much more highly concentrated urban areas at much higher densities (Jones, 2000). In contrast to the developed countries of Europe and North America where urbanisation has been a consequence of industrialisation and has been associated with economic development, in the developing countries of Africa, Latin America and Asia, urbanisation has occurred as a result of high natural urban population increase and massive rural-to-urban migration (McMichael, 2000). However, despite its benefit of generating economic gains, the rapid rate of urbanisation has resulted in several negative consequences particularly in developing countries (Melesse, 2005). Of paramount importance to note is the increase in the demand for affordable housing and urban infrastructure and services, which cities struggle to cope with (UN-HABITAT, 2012). Given a projected urban population increase, the number of people in the most urgent need of housing up to 2030 is estimated to be at least 2.25 billion (*Ibid*). Assuming an average household size of five people, 450 million housing units have to be built worldwide to accommodate this population, that is, 22.5 million units annually or more than 60 000 units each day (*Ibid*).

Due to the rapid growth of cities in developing countries, significant numbers of people are moving to unplanned settlements in the urban peripheries at the expense of agricultural lands and areas of natural beauty (Ibid). Thus, urban growth in Africa, Asia and Latin America is associated with slums, informal settlements, shelter built with little to no basic infrastructure and sanitary provision and with negligible regard of formal planning and building regulations (UN-HABITAT, 2012).

While slums have been taken as a means to solve urban housing shortages by low income earners in most developing countries, Zimbabwe presents a different scenario as there are few slum dwellers in the country. However, informal settlements are rampant just like in other developing countries. While in most developing countries the informal settlements have been witnessed through shanty towns, in Zimbabwe many modern and expensive urban residential properties have been constructed on undesignated land through the operations of land barons, commonly known as 'housing cooperatives.'

Though some of these cooperatives were registered and hence, recognised, this was not the case with a vast majority of them. Taking advantage of the prevailing housing shortages and economic crises, an enormous number of unregistered land barons emerged, offering land prices and payment conditions that seemed to be favourable to a massive number of urban dwellers, compared to the terms dictated by city councils. In addition, in Zimbabwe's most cities, the city councils had not been doing enough with regards to servicing of residential stands for sale (United Nations Human Settlements Programme, 2006). This led to a crisis of housing shortages and faced with such a scenario, many people opted to buy residential stands from land barons. Therefore, forced evictions in general are a common phenomenon in the developing world, triggered by different factors. However, the problem of urban expulsion, which is the major thrust of this chapter is largely embedded in the rapid urbanisation taking place in Zimbabwe and other developing countries coupled with failure by city councils to provide housing to urban dwellers.

The trajectory of forced evictions in post-colonial Zimbabwe

As highlighted earlier, many countries in the world have histories of forcible evictions of people from their residences. In post-colonial Zimbabwe, there have been different factors that directly or indirectly triggered forced evictions of populations and these evictions were of different magnitudes. Since the early years of Zimbabwe's independence, the entire nation has undergone a series of forced evictions imposed by the Zimbabwe African National Union Patriotic Front (ZANU-PF) regime. Operation *Gukurahundi* is one of the earliest episodes that caused mass evictions and massacre of civilians in Zimbabwe. In the early 1980s, the *Gukurahundi* operation ostensibly run as 'a dissident eradication' campaign was unleashed by the national government in the rural districts of Matabeleland and Midlands provinces following a fall-out between the Matabeleland-based Zimbabwe African People's Union (ZAPU) party and the ruling ZANU-PF party (Msipa, 2015). The ruling ZANU-PF party forced many villagers to flee to the City of Bulawayo as refugees (Mpofu, 2012). Due to the grotesquely violent attacks by the government's Fifth Brigade between January 1983 and late 1984 in Tsholotsho, Lupane, Nkayi, Gwanda and Kezi rural areas of Matabeleland, many people fled to Bulawayo, thus fuelling the emergence and growth of illegal settlements (*Ibid*). Operation *Gukurahundi* in Matabeleland province should be regarded as the first wave of political violence in post-colonial Zimbabwe that forcibly displaced citizens from their homes.

The 1993 Churu farm evictions were another episode of forced displacements which rendered several families homeless and landless. In 1993, the ZANU-PF government evicted about 4 000 people from Churu farm, located on the outskirts of Harare (*Zimbabwe Independent*, 4 February 2010. The Churu farm was Ndabaningi Sithole's private estate and he had settled these people on it after they had been evicted from illegal settlements in Harare and left homeless (*Ibid*). Sithole was one of the founding members of the ZANU-PF party in conjunction with Herbert Chitepo, Robert Mugabe and Edgar Tekere in 1963, but he later on formed his ZANU-Ndonga party (Ndlovu-Gatsheni, 2009). Due to political tension between Sithole and Mugabe's regime, the move of resettling the landless people on his private farm did not go well with the ZANU-PF government as it exposed the party's incompetency and lack of respect for human rights (Zimbabwe Independent, 4 February 2010). As such, the government first accused Sithole of not owning the farm albeit the fact that he had legally bought it prior to the settlement of the people (*Ibid*). Through the then Health minister Timothy Stamps, the government declared Churu farm a health hazard that would pollute Lake Chivero (*Ibid*). Despite obtaining a High Court injunction that clearly stated that the Land Acquisition Act was being used as a punitive measure and political weapon, the ZANU-PF government went ahead and forcibly removed the landless residents from Sithole's Churu farm and there were no provisions for their alternative resettlement (*The Zimbabwe Situation*, 3 February 2010). The Churu farm evictions reveal the violent mechanisms used by the ZANU-PF government to suppress opponents or gain political mileage. Since independence, ZANU-PF has blatantly employed the tactic of land seizures and unlawful private property requisition from black political opponents and fellow nationalists to settle old scores and to disenfranchise powerful opposition figures (*Ibid*). Thus, forced evictions in Zimbabwe can be seen as a historical trend.

The emergence of the Movement for Democratic Change (MDC) party in the late 1990s provoked further waves of ZANU PF-induced political violence in the entire country. Kasambala (2005) avows that between 1999 and 2004 large numbers of people were forced to move from their places of residence due to an escalation in political violence and state-sponsored human rights violations throughout the country. McGregor (2010) also states that the political violence that followed the emergence of the MDC in the late 1999 signalled the onset of a new era marked by intense repression, extraordinary rapid economic contraction and displacement on an unprecedented scale. Large numbers of political activists were displaced during election periods as ruling party supporters, especially in the rural areas, targeted and assaulted opposition activists and their immediate families (Kasambala, 2005). The 2002, 2005 and 2008 Zimbabwean elections are widely known as the worst elections where human rights were violated through beatings, assaults, killings and several forms of abuse and this saw some of the victims of political violence abandoning their homes. For instance, after MDC's narrow, but nonetheless historic, victory in the March 2008 parliamentary and presidential elections, state violence to punish its supporters and voters reached high levels through Operation *Makavhoterapapi* (Operation where did you put your vote?) (McGregor, 2010). Between April and June 2008, at least 30 000 persons were displaced in the wake of government-sponsored political violence, particularly in rural areas (U.S Country Reports on Human Rights Practices, 2009). The government did not provide assistance to the Internally Displaced Persons (IDPs), prohibited humanitarian agencies from assisting IDPs or conducting surveys to assess the scope of the problem and refused to acknowledge that its policies had caused internal displacement (Ibid). During the year, when violence levels in rural areas declined in the wake of political talks, many IDPs returned to the rural areas to rebuild their homes and livelihoods that had been damaged and many of them were extorted food, livestock or money by local ZANU PF militias as a condition for their readmission into their communities (*Ibid*). Yet many more who did not choose to return to their original communities integrated into new communities within the country or in the diaspora (*Ibid*).

In addition to the above, in 2000, the government of Zimbabwe embarked on the controversial land reform programme in which it forcibly displaced the whites from their farms and gave them to the blacks (Tofa, 2012). The idea of redistributing the land in itself was indisputable especially considering the damnable inequalities that had sustained structural violence which had for long existed between the minority whites and the majority blacks since the inception of colonialism in Zimbabwe in 1890 (*Ibid*). However, the redistribution itself that followed and coded as the Fast Track Land Reform

Programme (FTLRP) or *jambanja* in the Shona language was not mainly intended to address colonial injustices but to vitiate the opposition support (*Ibid*). This explains why it was characterised by violence, chaos, and multiple ownerships of land by high ranking political figures (*Ibid*). Apart from the brutal way in which it was conducted, including kidnapping and sometimes killing of white farmers, the FTLRP also engendered the widespread displacement of hundreds of thousands of farm workers (*Ibid*). The violent and chaotic nature of the FTLRP disregarded commercial farmers' property rights and violated the right to equal protection of the law and non-discrimination and it created fear and insecurity on white-owned commercial farms (Mapuva, 2016). For the greater part of the new millennium, white farmers continued to lose their farms to ZANU-PF bigwigs.

In 2005, the Zimbabwean government again embarked on a programme of forced evictions and demolitions known as Operation *Murambatsvina* (clear the filth) (Human Rights Watch, 2005). Popularly referred to as "Operation *Tsunami*" because of its speed and ferocity, it resulted in the destruction of homes, business premises and vending sites and an estimated 700 000 people in cities across the country lost their homes, their sources of livelihood or both (Tibaijuka, 2005). The then President, Mugabe, initiated this campaign to rid Zimbabwe of what he told Parliament was "a chaotic state of affairs" in the nation's cities and towns (Ibid). Operation *Murambatsvina* led to widespread internal displacement with hundreds of thousands of people sleeping in the open on disused fields or porches, in the bush, in overcrowded conditions and inadequate shelters, with little or no access to food, water and medical assistance (Ibid). Tens of thousands of homes and hundreds of informal business properties were destroyed without regard for the rights or welfare of those affected (Ibid). The operation was undertaken at the height of the winter season and there was total disregard of the human rights of the people affected (Chitando and Manyonganise, 2011). The evictions and displacements took place in the context of high political polarisation in Zimbabwe following the formation of the MDC as an opposition political party in 1999 (Security Council Report on Zimbabwe, 2005). It had been noted that the urban poor tended to support the MDC rather than the then President Robert Mugabe and his ruling ZANU-PF party (Ibid). The MDC won all urban seats in Harare and Bulawayo in the 2000 parliamentary elections, and again won most of the urban seats in the controversial March 2005 poll (Ibid). Given such a scenario, it is quite probable that Operation *Murambatsvina* was a ploy by the government to disperse MDC supporters from urban areas. In the same line of argument, Sachikonye asserts that having gained 26 out of 30 parliamentary seats in major cities and towns, and continuing to control local government in urban areas, the MDC was viewed as a persistent threat to ZANU PF, hence, the Mugabe regime thus sought to weaken the MDC, punish its urban supporters and "lance the boil of dissatisfaction in heavily populated urban areas before it could reach explosive levels" (Sachikonye, 2011: 27).

Viewed from this perspective, Operation *Murambatsvina* was both retribution against opposition supporters and a pre-emptive strike against urban discontent because the then Minister of State Security, Didymus Mutasa, had previously warned of the possibility of spontaneous uprisings in urban areas as a result of food shortages and economic crises (*Ibid*). The different forms of violence embedded in diverse operations undertaken by the Zimbabwean government validates Chipika and Malaba's (2017) assertion that states in crisis usually invoke security sector operations, under the guise of maintaining peace, security and stability. Operation *Murambatsvina* entailed large scale human rights violations as it arbitrarily forced hundreds of thousands of people to destroy or cede their property without due notice, process or compensation (Kasambala, 2005). The operation also restricted evicted people's freedom of movement by confining them to holding camps and forcibly ejected many of them to the rural areas where they had little or no access to basic services and means of economic support (*Ibid*).

Another remarkable episode of forced evictions that took place in Zimbabwe was the 2014 Tokwe-Mukorsi Dam flood displacements. While authorities from the ruling ZANU-PF party affirmed that the floods were a natural disaster resulting from climate change which caused high rainfall, the victims and the general public in Zimbabwe believed that the occurrence of floods was a convenient excuse used by the government of Zimbabwe to evict people without compensation (Human Rights Watch, 2015). According to the Human Right Watch (2015), many flood victims together with dam project workers asserted that the floods could have been easily prevented by letting out water downstream of the dam wall through water regulating tunnels (*Ibid*). Again, the rights of thousands of people were violated as many of them were not compensated financially and in terms of adequate land. A large majority of them were resettled on one-hectare plots, which were inadequate for producing enough food for their families. In addition to that, most of the flood victims lost their property and livestock in the whole process of evacuation (*Ibid*).

Broadly, this section sought to underscore the need not to disaggregate the house demolitions as a unique case but one that follows a long line of strong arm evictions in post-colonial Zimbabwe. This section has illuminated the long genealogy of military-style evictions that have characterised different sections of the Zimbabwean society at differing moments in the post-colonial period. This, then, ably sets the tone for the section below that deals with house demolitions during the period 2014-2016 in Harare.

The 2014-2016 house demolitions in Harare and Chitungwiza

After the 2005 Operation *Murambatsvina,* house demolitions in Zimbabwe resumed in 2014, and this saw city councils together with the government being blamed by residents and human rights activists for violating people's rights. Between 2014 and 2016, Harare City Council razed to the ground some houses in Budiriro 4, Glen Norah, and Arlington Farm near Harare International Airport while Chitungwiza City Council also knocked down several houses, leaving thousands of residents homeless and exposed to the vagaries of weather in the rainy season (Mutingwende, 2016).

During the time when the houses were destroyed, there were about 70 illegal housing cooperatives operating in Harare (Matenga, 2015). However a large number of the houses that were demolished belonged to three popular housing cooperatives namely: Five Greater Heights, Chronicle Housing Cooperative and Tembwe Housing

Cooperative. These housing cooperatives had developed stands for residential settlement in Glen Norah, High Glen and Budiriro 4 respectively (Charumbira, 2016).

The houses were destroyed on the grounds that they were built on illegal land. For instance, houses along Airport Road were declared illegal as the land was considered reserved for the expansion of the Harare International Airport. However, according to *Newsday* (22 January 2016), these houses were destroyed after the then Zimbabwean President, Robert Mugabe, expressed his disquiet over the settlement, referring to it as an eyesore (Matenga, 2016).

About 200 houses along High Glen and Kambuzuma roads were destroyed because they were considered built on state land that was reserved for a hospital and other amenities (Mavudzi, 2015). Some of the houses that were demolished in High Glen were considered to be built on wet lands, hence Harare City Council wanted to preserve such areas as prescribed by the city's town plan (*Ibid*). However, while the preservation of wetlands seems to be a noble reason, its genuineness becomes controversial especially when other structures built on wetlands in the same city were spared from the demolitions. A vivid example is the Long Chen Plaza Chinese Shopping Mall which was constructed on wetlands in the outskirts of Harare (Mathuthu, 2013). This shopping mall was constructed and opened despite warnings from the Environmental Management Agency (EMA) and several environmentalists (Ibid). Basing on this case, one may be tempted to argue that house demolitions are a problem of the poor and vulnerable segments of societies because those who have financial and political muscles often find their way out.

In Budiriro 4, close to 100 houses built on the land developed by Tembwe Housing Cooperative were destroyed on grounds that they were constructed on land that was reserved for a school (Charumbira, 2016). Hence, these houses were built on illegal land, a common trend related to houses that were demolished in other suburbs. However, some of these housing cooperatives were allegedly linked to ZANU-PF officials (Ncube, 2016). In this regard, just like the Operation *Murambatsvina*, house demolitions in the period under discussion may also be perceived as a strategy by ZANU-PF to target MDC supporters.

House demolitions and human rights concerns

Although the rationale behind the demolition of houses in Harare seemed to be somehow valid, circumstances surrounding the demolition process triggered human rights distress among the general public and human rights advocate groups. As illustrated in Figure 1, some of the houses that were razed down were fully constructed.

Figure 1: *Fully constructed houses being demolished*

Many people raised concern as to why the government waited until houses were fully constructed to destroy them. The general question that was asked by many people is: Where was the city council when all these houses were being constructed?

Some of the houses that were destroyed had electricity connections as shown in the Figure 2, hence the question that arises is why the state-owned Zimbabwe Electricity Supply Authority (ZESA) connected electricity to these houses if they were illegal.

Figure 2: *House demolitions in suburbs with electricity connection*
(Adapted from Newsday, 22 January 2016).

Some of the houses for example in Chitungwiza were demolished during the night (Makunde, 2014). Many respondents expressed concern as to why the Chitungwiza City Council carried out the demolitions during the night. Furthermore, some of the houses in Budiriro, Glen Norah and Arlington Farm were demolished during rainy season thereby exposing the residents and their property to the menace of rain (Matenga, 2016).

Such acts are a violation of the right to housing and shelter as well as international law on forced evictions. Article 11 of the International Covenant on Economic, Social and Cultural Rights (ICESCR) 1966) asserts that states parties should recognise the right of everyone to an adequate standard of living for himself and his family, including adequate food, clothing and housing, and to the continuous improvement of living conditions. It also avers that the state parties should take appropriate steps to ensure the realisation of this right, recognising to this effect the essential importance of international cooperation based on free consent (*Ibid*). The ICESCR (1966) listed eight pre-requisites which should be observed when forced evictions are carried out as a last resort and one of them is that displacements should not take place in particularly bad weather or at night without the consent of the affected persons (*Ibid*). Hence, the demolition of houses during rainy season and during the night that was done by Harare and Chitungwiza City Councils violated the house demolition rules set by ICESCR (1966). However, it should be noted that in general, ICESCR is against the practice of imposed relocations. General Comment Number 7 of ICESCR declares that states must refrain from forced evictions and ensure that the law is enforced against its agents or third parties who carry out involuntary displacements and urges countries to ensure that legislative and other measures are adequate to prevent and if appropriate, punish enforced dislodging carried out without appropriate safeguards by private persons or bodies (*Ibid*).

In addition to the ICESCR, there are several international human rights instruments that protect the right to adequate housing and freedom from arbitrary demolitions. These include Article 12 and Article 25 (1) of the 1948 Universal Declaration of Human Rights (UDHR), Article 17 of the International Covenant on Civil and Political Rights (ICCPR), Article 27 of the United Nations Convention on the Rights of the Child (UNCRC) and Article 14 of the Convention on the Elimination of all forms of Discrimination Against Women (CEDAW) (UN-HABITAT, 2007; Kuveya, 2016). In addition to these international instruments, Section 74 of the Zimbabwean Constitution states that no persons may be evicted from their home, or have their home demolished without order of court made after considering all the relevant circumstances (Constitution of Zimbabwe, 2013). Thus, the manner in which the demolitions were conducted was not only a violation of international human rights instruments but also the Constitution of Zimbabwe.

In addition, Article 12 of the UDHR (1948) and Article 17 of ICCPR (1966) assert that no one shall be subjected to arbitrary interference with his privacy, family, home or correspondence, nor to attacks upon his honour and reputation. Everyone has the right to the protection of the law against such interference or attacks (Ibid). Article 25 (1) of the UDHR (1948) states that everyone has the right to a standard of living adequate for the health and well-being of himself and of his family, including food, clothing, housing and medical care and necessary social services, and the right to security in the event of unemployment, sickness, disability, widowhood, old age or other lack of livelihood in circumstances beyond his control. Similarly Article 27 (1) of the UN CRC (1989) affirms that state parties recognise the right of every child to a standard of living adequate for the child's physical, mental, spiritual, moral and social development while Article 27(3) of the same convention avers that state parties, in accordance with national conditions and within their means, shall take appropriate measures to assist parents and others responsible for the child to implement this right and shall in case of need provide material assistance and support programmes, particularly with regard to nutrition, clothing and housing. Article 14 (h) of CEDAW (1979) avows that women should enjoy adequate living conditions, particularly in relation to housing, sanitation, electricity and water supply, transport and communications.

The demolition of houses in Zimbabwe, therefore, is a violation of human rights in general as well as violation of women and children's rights in particular. Instead of demolishing houses built with hard-earned cash, the government should find ways to legalise these settlements where possible. Zimbabwe ratified many international human rights treaties such as the ICESCR, ICCPR, CEDAW and UNCRC (Thiis and Feltoe 1997). In addition, the country is also bound by the 1948 UDHR (Shizha and Kariwo, 2011). As such, the government has an obligation of making sure that all people enjoy the right to sufficient housing and other rights stated in these instruments rather than violating them. This goes in line with the contention made by UN-HABITAT (2012) that the right to adequate housing is relevant to all states, as they have all ratified at least one international treaty referring to tolerable accommodation and committed themselves to protecting the right to decent shelter through international declarations, plans of action or conference outcome documents.

The nexus between violation of the right to adequate housing and violation of other human rights

The right to adequate housing entails freedoms which include protection against forced evictions and the arbitrary destruction and demolition of one's home, the right to be free from arbitrary interference with one's home, privacy and family; the right to choose one's residence, to determine where to live; and to freedom of movement (UN HABITAT, 2012). The demolition of houses that took place in Harare and Chitungwiza violated all these freedoms, especially considering the brutal manner in which they were conducted. Such forced evictions exhibit the states' lack of respect, protection, and fulfilment of human rights and freedoms.

Human rights are interdependent, indivisible and interrelated (*Ibid*). Owing to the interrelation and interdependency which exist among all human beings, forced evictions often result in other severe human rights violations particularly when they are accompanied by enforced relocation or homelessness (*Ibid*). During interviews, many victims of the house demolitions asserted that the demolitions took place during rainy or winter seasons, thereby exposing the victims to the perils of the weather. Other informants also indicated that soon after the demolition of their houses, they had no other option expect to stay in overcrowded temporary squatter settlements where unavailability of water, toilets, bathrooms, electricity and other amenities was a serious challenge and it was even worse for women in general and those who had infants (Interview with Ngirazi and Machena, 21 December 2016, Harare). Such living conditions violate the socio-economic right to health, right to water and sanitation, right to adequate standard of living and right to clean, unpolluted environment and may also infringe on the right to survival and development, which falls under civil and political rights. This may in turn pose a serious health challenge to people and diarrhoeal and respiratory infections are usually associated with such state of affairs.

Poor housing conditions, as noted by Thomas *et al* (2016), increase the risk of severe ill health or disability by up to 25% during childhood and early adulthood. It also leads to increased risk of meningitis, asthma, and slow growth, which is linked to coronary heart disease (Dickins, 2014). A certain informant, a mother of three infants, sadly narrated how she struggled to survive in those harsh conditions with her three children including a three year old toddler and twin sons aged 6 months (Interview with Muzungu, 21 December 2016, Harare). The same informant stated that her twins were admitted in a hospital because of pneumonia which she largely attributed to the cold weather conditions they were exposed to (*Ibid*).

More so, the psychological effects that house demolitions have on the victims should not be underestimated. In an interview, one woman sadly narrated that:

> I am failing to come to terms with the reality and I cannot express the pain we have as a family. After my husband borrowed a loan from the bank and bought the stand, we thought that life was going to be better since we were going to stay in our own house. This did not go as we expected because we were forced to be tenants again during a time when my husband was supposed to pay back the loan and we have not yet cleared the debt (Interview with Makwavava, 19 December 2016, Harare).

The unpredictability brought about by house demolitions is considered to have the most traumatic effects on human beings (Sarraj and Qouta, 2005). This is worsened by the fact that a home is not only a shelter but also the heart of the family life because there are memories of joy as well as attachment to familiar objects (*Ibid*). UN-HABITAT states that forced evictions have a profound detrimental psychological impact on evictees, in particular children who have been found to suffer both short and long term effects (*Ibid*).

Other informants stated that they lost their food items during the demolition and evacuation process while others averred that some of their perishable food items went into bad state due to unfavourable weather conditions they were exposed to, coupled with unavailability of electricity which made it impossible for them to use refrigerators (Interviews with Muzungu, 19 December 2016; Chakanyuka, 19 December 2016; Magazeni, 20 December 2016, Harare). This violated the socio-economic right to food and nutrition. Thus, the house demolitions worsened food deficiencies among already poverty-stricken communities, thereby aggravating their destitution.

Furthermore, the right to education was not spared. Many of the house demotion victims who were interviewed indicated that they had to transfer their children to other schools in the same city despite the fact that it was during the middle of the school term (Interviews with Madzingeni, 20 December 2016; Chapungu, 20 December 2016; Machingura, 21 December 2016; Chineni, 21 December 2016, Harare). Some pointed out that due to the fact that it was very difficult to secure a place for school children in urban areas, they were forced to transfer their children to rural areas (Interviews with Chakanyuka, 19 December 2016; Magazeni, 20 December 2016, Harare). This scenario posed a negative impact on the academic performance of children. According to Rafferty (2002), the transition from one school to another is a stressful experience for children and is often associated with school failure and a higher rate of school drop outs. The same author also avers that children who enter classroom in mid semester/ term are more likely held to lower expectations by their teachers (*Ibid*). In addition to that, displaced children need to get used to the new school, new teacher and new school work that is discontinuous with the work they were previously doing (*Ibid*). All these consequences were not given due regard when the government embarked on the house demolitions.

Some parents also asserted that their temporary stay in squatter settlements had a negative bearing on the education of their children, especially on issues related to doing homework as well as attending school every day (Interviews with Muchinei, 20 December 2016; and Makuyana, 19 December 2016, Harare). Goux and Maurin (2005) argue that bad housing affects children's ability to learn at school and study at home. In the same line of argument, Louise *et al* (2012) posit that homeless children are two to three times more likely to be absent from school than other children due to the disruption caused by moving into and between temporary accommodation.

One of the house demolition victims stated that she did not transfer her two children from their schools after the demolitions due to the fact that she failed to secure other academies in the city and at the same time she was not willing to transfer them to rural areas (Interview with Makaya, 19 December 2016, Harare). However, her worry was on the distance between their new residential areas and the schools arguing that she barely afforded to raise transport fare on daily basis thereby implying that on many occasions the children had to walk. Jangan (2008) posits that children who walk long distances

66

to school have many challenges on their academic work and this is particularly serious among female pupils and infants. These challenges include tiredness which leads to lack of concentration in class, limited time to do their homework as well as the risk of being robbed, kidnapped or sexually abused on their way to and from school. Thus, in addition to violating the right to education, house demolitions can also lead to the violation of children's right to protection from violence, abuse, maltreatment, neglect and exploitation.

The practice of forced evictions may also result in violations of civil and political rights such as the right to life, the right to security of the person, the right to non-interference with privacy, family and home and the right to peaceful enjoyment of property (UN-HABITAT, 2012). They can also result in people being pushed into extreme poverty thereby posing a risk to the right to life itself (*Ibid*). Therefore, forced evictions constitute gross violations of a range of internationally recognised human rights including the human rights to adequate housing, food, water, health, education, work, security of the person, freedom from cruel, inhuman and degrading treatment, and freedom of movement (United Nations Human Rights council, 2007).

Conclusion

This chapter has examined the impact of house demolitions on the well-being of the affected people. It focused on the demolitions that took place in Harare suburbs such as Budiriro 4, Glen Norah and Arlington Farm near Harare International Airport as well as in Chitungwiza Town between 2014 and 2016. The chapter commenced with an overview of forced evictions and proceeded to give a foretaste of the trajectory of forced displacements in post-colonial Zimbabwe. The chapter has revealed that forced evictions, particularly in form of house demolitions is a violation of the right to adequate housing and several human rights stated in international treaties such as the UDHR of 1948, ICESCR, ICCPR, CEDAW and UNCRC. Through the house demolitions, the government of Zimbabwe violated these rights regardless of the fact that Zimbabwe is a signatory to these international treaties and that it also ratified these treaties. The chapter has also revealed that besides violating the right to housing and shelter, house demolitions also infringe on other human rights such as the right to education, the right to health and nutrition, the right to clean and unpolluted environment, right to food and nutrition, right to adequate standard of living , right to water and sanitation, right to life, survival and development, right to life and confidentiality, right to dignity, right not to be subjected to cruel, inhuman or degrading treatment or punishment, right to freedom from violence.

References

Bolay, J. (2006) 'Slums and urban development: Questions on society and Globalisation' in *The European Journal of Development Research*, Volume 18, Number 2, pp.284-298.

Centre on Housing Rights and Evictions, (2002) Forced Evictions: Violation of Human Rights: Global Survey on Forced Evictions, No. 8, Geneva.

Chakanyuka, K. (Interview, Harare) 20 December 2016.

Chapungu, L. (Interview, Harare) 21 December 2016.

Charumbira, S. (20 January 2016) 'Women, girls bear the brunt of demolitions,' Available at: https://www.newsday.co.zw, Accessed 10 August 2017.

Chineni, M. (Interview, Harare) 21 December 2016.

Chipika, J. T. and Malaba, J. A. (2017) 'Towards a transformative democratic development state in Zimbabwe- the complex journey,' in: Kanyeze, G. *et al* (eds) *Towards democratic developmental states in Africa*, Weaver Press: Harare.

Chitando, E. and Manyonganise, M. (2011) 'Voices from Faith-Based Organisations' in: Murith, T. and Mawadza, A. (Eds.) *Zimbabwe in transition: A view from within*, Auckland Park: Fanele Media.

Dickins, M. (2014) *A-Z of inclusion in early childhood*, Berkshire: McGraw Hill Education.

Goux, D. and Maurin, E. (2005) 'The effect of overcrowding housing on children's performance at school,' in: *Journal of Public Economics*, Volume 89, Number 5-6, pp. 797-819.

Jangan, K. (2008) 'Defying the odds: A study of Grade 11 female students in Eriteria,' in: J. Zajda *et al*, (Eds.) *Education and social inequality in the global culture*, New York: Springer.

Jones, T. L. (2000) 'Compact city policies for megacities: Core areas and metropolitan regions,' in: Jenks, M. and Burgess, R. (eds.) *Compact cities: Sustainable urban forms for developing countries*, New York: Routledge.

Kasambala, T. (2005) *Zimbabwe: Evicted and forsaken: Internally-displaced persons in the aftermath of Operation Murambatsvina*, Human Rights Watch.

Louise, C. *et al*, (2012) *Children and the environment*, Oxford University Press: Oxford.

Machena, W. (Interview, Harare) 21 December 2016.

Machingura, R. (Interview, Harare) 21 December 2016.

Madzingeni, M. (Interview, Harare) 21 December 2016.

Magazeni, T. (Interview, Harare) 21 December 2016.

Makaya, M. (Interview, Harare) 21 December 2016.

Makunde, G. (29 September 2014) 'Chitungwiza municipality demolishes houses at night,' Available at: http://thezimbabwean.co, Accessed 3 August 2017.

Makuyana, P. (Interview, Harare) 19 December 2016.

Makwavava, T. (Interview, Harare) 19 December 2016.

Mapuva, L. (2016) *The dilemma of children's rights to education in the era of the fast-track land reform programme in Zimbabwe revisited*, New Castle: Cambridge Scholars Publishing.

Matenga, M. (2 November 2015) 'More housing demolitions loom,' Available at: https://www.newsday.co.zw, Accessed 3 May 2017.

Matenga, M. (28 January 2016) 'Demolition victims, furniture soak in rain,' Available at https://www.newsday.co.zw, Accessed 22 March 2018.

Mathuthu, M. (18 December 2013) 'Chinese mall opens despite warnings from environmentalists,' Available at: http://nehandaradio.com, Accessed 4 July 2017.

McGregor, J. (2010) 'The making of Zimbabwe's new diaspora,' in: J. McGregor and R. Primorac (Eds.) *Zimbabwe's new diaspora: Displacement and the cultural politics of survival,* New York: Berghahn Books.

McMichael, A. J. (2000) 'The urban environment and health in a world of increasing globalisation: Issues for developing countries,' in: *Bulletin of the World Health Organisation,* Volume 78, Number 9, pp.1117-1126.

Melesse, M. (2005) 'City expansion, squatter settlements and policy implications in Addis Ababa: The case of Kolfe Keranio city suburb,' *Working papers on population and land use change in central Ethiopia,* Trondheim.

Mpofu, B. (2012) 'Perpetual 'outcasts'? Squatters in peri-urban Bulawayo, Zimbabwe,' in: *Afrika Focus,* 25 (2): 45-63.

Msipa, C. G. (2015) *In pursuit of freedom and justice: A memoir,* Harare: Weaver Press.

Muchinei, S. (Interview, Harare) 19 December 2016.

Mutingwende, B. 12 February 2016. 'Corruption induced housing demolitions: An affront to human rights,' Available at: http://www.zimsentinel.com/?p=2186, Accessed 12 June 2017.

Muzungu, C. (Interview, Harare) 20 December 2016.

Ncube, X. (3 June 2016) 'Harare audits land belonging to housing co-ops,' Available at: http://www.zimbabwesituation.com/news, Accessed 20 May 2017.

Ndlovu-Gatsheni, S. J. (2009) *Do 'Zimbabweans' Exist? Trajectories of Nationalism, National Identity Formation and Crisis in a Postcolonial State,* Oxford: Peter Lang.

Ngirazi, R. (Interview, Harare) 21 December 2016.

Ntini, B. (26 January 2015) 'The MDC Renewal Team has watched in disdain the land grabs currently taking place in Harare's suburbs of Budiriro, Southlea Park and Kuwadzana 4,' Available at: http://thezimbabwean.co/2015/01/mdc-renewal-teams-statement-on/, Accessed 4 July 2017.

Rafferty, Y. (2002) 'Educating homeless children in the United States: An overview of legal entitlements and Federal Protections in Mickelson,' in: Mickleson, R.A. (ed.) *Children on the streets of the*

Americas: Globalisation, homelessness and education in the United States, Brazil and Cuba, Routledge: New York.

Saul, B. *et al,* (2014) *The International covenant on economic, social and cultural Rights,* Oxford: Oxford University Press.

Shizha, E. and Kariwo, M. T. (2011) *Education and development in Zimbabwe: A social, political and economic analysis,* Rotterdam: Sense Publishers.

Thiis, Q. and Feltoe, G. (1998) 'Zimbabwe, in: Stokke, H. *et al* (Eds.) *Inter-nation human rights in developing countries: Yearbook 1997,* London: Kluwer Law International.

Thomas, S. *et al,* (2016) 'Promoting mental health and preventing mental illness in general practice,' in: *London Journal of Primary Care,* 8 (1): 1-9.

Tofa, E. (2012) 'The Bible and the quest for democracy and democratisation in Africa: The Zimbabwe experience,' In Masiiwa, R. G. and Joachim, K. (Eds.) *The Bible and politics in Africa,* University of Bamberg Press: Bamberg.

UN-HABITAT, (2012) *Enhancing urban safety and security: Global report on human settlements,* Routledge.

United Nations Human Rights Office of the High Commissioner, (1976). International Covenant on Economic, Social and Cultural Rights, Available at: http://www.ohchr.org/EN/ProfessionalInterest/Pages/CESC R.aspx, Accessed 23 March 2018.

United Nations Human Settlements Programme, (2006) *Enabling shelter strategies: Review of experience from two decades of implementation,* Nairobi: UN-HABITAT.

U.S. Department of state, (2010) *Country Reports on Human Rights Practices for 2008,* Volume 1, Washington D C.

Zimbabwe Independent, (4 February 2010) 'Land: ZANU-PF tool in suppressing dissent,' in: https://www.theindependent.co.zw, Accessed 6 July 2017.

Zimbabwe Situation, (3 February 2010) 'Mugabe's Vengeful Eviction of Black Nationalist Farmers,' Available at: http://www.zimbabwesituation.com, Accessed 12 May 2017.

Chapter 4

Female Rapists and Sperm Harvesting: Narratives, Violence and Occultism in Post-colonial Zimbabwe

Ngonidzashe Marongwe, David Tobias
& Tinashe Mawere

Introduction

This chapter makes a discursive analysis of the intersections of the hidden forms of violence involved in Zimbabwe's female sexual rapists' narrations and acts in post-colonial Zimbabwe. The sexual rape cases allegedly resulted in sperm harvesting and occult beliefs and practices. Beginning with the incident of three Gweru-based sisters from 2011, cases of men who reportedly were 'raped' for their semen rose to become commonplace. As a result, between 2011 and 2017, it had become rather ordinary for newspapers to have weird-like story lines of women 'rapists'. Among these headlines were: "Man forced to service four women" (*Nehanda Radio*, 22 May 2013); "Female 'rapists' back on the prowl" (*The Herald*, 06 June 2017); "3 female 'rapists' take turns to rape soldier" (*Harare24 News*, 27 December 2012) and "Female rapists leave teacher for dead" (*The Standard*, 9 July 2017). Generally, the women in most of the instances reported in the national press allegedly targeted travelling individual men whom they offered a lift before drugging them, giving them dosages of aphrodisiacs, forcing them to have sex with two or three women continuously for days on end before dumping them in bushes, sometimes naked.

By mid-2017, the cases of female rapists had become a serious cause for concern for the public and the law enforcement agents as reported by *The Herald* (06 June 2017) in an article aptly titled: "Female 'rapists' back on the prowl." Chief Superintendent Paul Nyathi of the Zimbabwe Republic Police (ZRP), in warning members of the Zimbabwean public, stated that: "We would like to urge members of the public to be on the lookout for a group of men and women who are giving unsuspecting victims transport and end up abusing them."

The question that has remained unanswered is: what do the 'female rapists' use the sperms collected for? In other words, what narratives have emerged from these reported cases of female sexual rape? A mixed range of reasons have been advanced for the raping of men and collecting their semen. Among others, blogger.3-Mob.com (n.d.) advanced five reasons for sperm harvesting, namely that sperms were used as an expensive delicacy for the rich just like fish eggs or caviar; a key ingredient in skin smoothening and clearing blemishes on the face lotions; for a sperm bank where the semen is sold to couples who cannot have babies; sperm harvesting was a crazy fetish where the women ran some kind of competition to see who collected more; and that the sperms were used in wealth-generating magic (*juju*).

Whilst we admit to the purchase in the slew of explanations proffered above, in this chapter we would like to pursue the occult explanation. The central argument for this chapter is that, first, these cases whether they were true or not, signify both the subversion and re/production of everyday and common sense discourses of sexual assault/rape and gender based violence in the country where women have largely been on the receiving end of the violence. This is, also, in addition to the fact that such cases also defy legal discourses on sexual rape. Second, and critically, these cases illustrate how the deepening economic crisis in the country led to desperate survival strategies. In this case, the desperate means to eke survival in a desperate economy invoked a resort to occultism, which in itself also demonstrates very deep levels of desperation.

The chapter is divided into three sections. The first discusses the various cases that were reported in the national media. The second tackles the nexus between the sperm harvesting escapades and violence, and how the violence of the rape subverts the everyday understanding of sexual and gender-based violence. The third, drawing from the reasons for collecting the sperms, examines the nexus between the deepening economic crisis in Zimbabwe and a resort to occultism, which in itself is illustrative of worsening poverty in the country. This is also in addition to the fact that the deepening of the economic crunch also subverted and/ or reproduced gendered and sexualized discourses around rape.

The larger significance of this chapter is that, as observed by the World Health Organisation (WHO) (n.d.: 154), sexual assault and/or rape on boys and men "has largely been neglected in research." As such, this chapter attempts to unravel that omission by utilizing reported cases of men who have been subjected to sexual assault by women in Zimbabwe. The chapter argues that the omission of male victims of female sexual abusers from the matrixes of rape is founded on the 'common sense' discourses around gender and sexuality. The cases of alleged male rape in Zimbabwe differ from the contexts that the WHO (n.d.) has established for male rape and other types of sexual violations, including in homes, workplaces, schools, by the military under war conditions in prisons and police custody. Generally, the settings that the WHO (n.d.) gives cover situations in which males violate other males either for the gratification of the abusers, as punishment for violating prescribed gender roles, or as a show of power by soldiers and police officers (WHO, n.d.). For this chapter, however, the cases discussed here are about women who allegedly have raped males. In the end, what these cases further showcase is the disruption of the commonly-held notions of the distribution of gender stereotypical victimization, agency and power between males and females. Largely, the narratives that emerge portray discourses of women as natural and perpetual victims of violence and rape by projecting, too, that men can be unwilling victims of sexual violence in the society.

Sexual rape in context

This section defines rape and seeks to highlight the limits of the commonly accepted gendered definition of sexual rape. In doing this, it seeks to redefine the parameters of what constitutes rape and to debunk the oft used but narrow gendered analysis of rape. Thus, it also calls for a reevaluation of the term, especially in the light of some of the cases to be discussed in the next section.

In Zimbabwe, as in many states across the globe, rape is largely considered as gendered. As the WHO (2002:18) established, "Most acts of sexual violence are experienced predominantly by women and girls and perpetrated by men and boys." Even at law, sexual rape is considered to be only performed by males against women. Its definition is based on the deep penetration that can be performed by male penises that violate vaginas or male penises in oral sex and also by male penises that perform anal sex with either males or females. As such, at law only men can rape women and men can only be raped if there is penetration through their anuses by male penises and/ or other objects. According to the World Health Organisation (n.d.: 149) rape, which is a variant of sexual violence, is "defined as physically forced or otherwise coerced penetration – even if slight – of the vulva or anus, using a penis, other body parts or an object." This view on the gendered dimension is succinctly captured in the analysis of one Zimbabwean lawyer cited in Saunyama (2017: n.p) who posited: "There is nothing like a female rapist according to the law. It may only be aggrieved indecent assault. Rape involves penetration, men are not penetrated unless a man is penetrated through the anus. In fact that will not suffice." What, however, emerges is that such definitions, as above, tally with common sense ideas that associate the penis with power and the vagina with passivity. The penis is shown to be the only 'active' object and the vagina as passive and receiving, and weak – devoid of erection and eroticism. So rape is defined as an act of male power and the penis is 'naturalized' as active and powerful and aggressive.

Perhaps drawing from the everyday pressures and narrations and the limited understanding of sexual violence and rape, in Zimbabwe, the law as regards crimes of sexual rape and gender-based violence has tended to protect women and girls more than men and boys. To this extent, government agencies, Faith-Based Organisation (FBOs) and other civil rights movements have gone a long way to institute human rights instruments that seek to protect the rights of girl children. In the process, men have been perceived as the aggressors in sexual (and gender-based) violence as well as the perpetrators of rape. As a result, many men have continued to suffer in silence from the abuse inflicted by their partners (Adebayo, 2014).

Going forward, the impact of this gender-based definition of sexual rape is that it also impacts the understanding, practice and the discoursing of human rights in Zimbabwe in particular, and Africa, more generally. As such, many men have suffered from underreported rape cases, coercive marriages, cohabitation and dating within families. This is because, generally, men are seen as physically stronger than women. As such, any male sexual victimisation by women has been treated with suspicion. In fact, most cases that reflect female brutality against men have seldom been given worthy attention. Socio-culturally, too, males who have fallen victim to female violence have also been considered as weak and feminine. This has resulted in many of them suffering 'silently'. This common sense understanding of sexual assault and violence could also have impacted on the trials of the so-called female rapists as none were convicted of the charges levelled against them. This includes the case of the three Gweru-based female rapists who were eventually acquitted, apparently for lack of incriminating evidence (*Zimeye*, 2012). However, what should not escape mention is that this could have also emerged from the fact that, as already outlined, at law it is difficult to categorise women as rapists.

However, the rise in the incidents of males who were coerced into sexual acts with women between 2011and 2017, calls for a rethink of the notions of rape and gender-based violence. If, as the definitions above demonstrate, women cannot be able to perform rape on men, why was there a spike in the cases of so-called men who had been raped by women? To this extent, if there were some women who forced themselves on unwilling men, as in our case to collect their sperm, should this not be categorised as rape? This latter question then calls for a review of the definition and legal cum and socio-political narratives on rape. The following section deals with some of the reported cases that simultaneously indicate the extent to which men have suffered from both female rapists and also debunks the ethos of male-female rape.

Breaking the 'normal': Female rapists' narrations in Zimbabwe

This section discusses, pithily, some of the documented cases of female rapists. This recitation of the cases is, however, done against the background possibility that some of the cases reported could have been contrived. This possibility should be considered against the background of the import from 'citizen' journalism on news reliability, rooted, largely in the social media platforms such as WhatsApp and Facebook where many unverified, if not false, stories have found space and widely circulated. As Saunyama (2017: page?) posits, some of these stories could have been "made up by men seeking excuses for their own wayward ways". It cannot also be discounted how some men who liked 'fame' could also have utilized the 'being raped' as an opportunity to get 'publicity'. However, whether some of the stories were contrived is not a major issue since we are not so much into the statistics and their reliability. The point is that they remain profound narrations and we argue that narrations are founded on certain prevailing or re/imagined ideas. At the same time, it also stands to reason that some rape cases may have gone unreported. This may be because, as the World Health Organisation (n.p: 154) argues, some of the male victims could have felt "shame, guilt and fear of not being believed or of being denounced for what has occurred. Myths and strong prejudices surrounding male sexuality also prevent men from coming forward." This speaks to the contours of the regimes of the Ranciere (2006:4) "distribution of the sensible", in which there are 'acceptable" and particular ways of "seeing, feeling, acting, speaking [and] being in the world with one another" (Porter, 2007: 17).

It is also instructive to highlight that male sexual assault and/ or rape is neither peculiar to Zimbabwe nor is it something that has a recent history. As WHO (n.d.) contends, males have been sexually violated over millennia and for a variety of reasons, as already highlighted. To this extent, and admittedly, while more females have fallen victim to sexual assault and sexual rape, across the world, the rate of male sexual assault and/ or rape ranges between "3.6% in Namibia and 13.4% in Tanzania to 20% in Peru" (WHO, n.d:154). In Zimbabwe, the rate of sexual assault for males was growing with some provinces such as Mashonaland central recording 1 per cent (Zimvac, 2017: 189). On average, the average for the country was about 0,5 per cent (*Ibid*).

Nonetheless, these narrations of the rape of males by females presented below are intended to set the background and to showcase some of the common *modus operandi* and the countrywide dispersal of the incidents. The first case that caught the attention of the Zimbabwean public took place in 2011 and involved three female 'rapists' from Gweru City in the Midlands Province. According to *New Zimbabwe* (7 November 2011), three women, Rosemary Chakwizira, Sophie Nhokwara and Netsai Nhokwara, were jointly charged and taken to court with a male accomplice, Thulani Ngwenya, on allegations of committing 17 cases of male sexual attacks/indecent assault of male hitch-hikers after being found in possession of 33 used condoms at an accident scene- four of them half full- in the boot of their car. Further, according to *Zimeye* (10 August 2012), the 'rapists' were also found with some herbal concoctions at their Gweru house. Allegations were that the women who were not in the car when it was involved in the accident rushed to the scene of the crush where they pleaded with the police to let them collect the condoms with the sperms upon which they were arrested and dragged to court on suspicion that they were part of a racket of female rapists (*Bulawayo24 News*, 11 October 2011).

In another incident during 2012, a 33-year-old male soldier with the Zimbabwe National Army (ZNA) allegedly became a victim of a sexual rape by three women who had given him a lift in their car to Harare. Allegations are that the male soldier boarded the BMW car with four occupants, three females and a male driver, at AMTEC Motors in Gweru and after driving for a few kilometres, one of the female passengers sprayed some substance in the face of the victim who fell dizzy and was immediately forced to drink some substance that caused him to fall unconscious. Upon regaining consciousness, he noticed that he had been dumped some 100 metres from the Gweru-Harare highway, that his trousers and undergarments had been lowered, that he had been sexually assaulted by the women, and that all his belongings had been dumped close to his unconscious body (*Harare24 News*, 27 December 2012).

Yet another incident happened in the City of Kadoma. According to *Nehanda Radio* (22 May 2013), an unsuspecting 23-year-old man was called to assist with 'directions' by four women who were driving in an upmarket Toyota Hilux double-cab vehicle who seemed stranded along the Kadoma-Patchway highway. Upon reaching the women, the man was allegedly forced into the car at gun point and was driven to Kadoma, where upon reaching the women's residence he was given a plate of *sadza* (corn meal) with chicken allegedly spiced with an aphrodisiac. After feeding, one of the four women demanded that he be intimate with her and her three compatriots. He was allegedly exposed to this kind of sexual assault for two days before he was 'freed' and was given some US$30, a Samsung cell phone and two old pairs of jeans, probably as a thank you, before he was dumped just outside Kadoma. The man was reportedly very weak when he went to report his ordeal to the police and also complained of stomach pains and general body weakness.

Another reported incident happened in Karoi Town (*Nehanda Radio*, 29 March 2012). In the said assault, a Karoi-based Pastor travelling from the town of Kariba, where he had gone to sell tomatoes, hitch-hiked in a Toyota Ipsum car which had three occupants: two men and one woman. Upon approaching Karoi Town, the driver of the vehicle pulled off the road and the two men instructed the Pastor to have sexual intercourse once with the female passenger who was wearing a female condom. After this, the gang demanded that the Pastor surrender the cash he had on him to them.

In 2017, *The Herald* (6 June 2017), citing Superintendant Paul Nyati of the Zimbabwe Republic Police (ZRP), reported two cases of male sexual attacks by females. In the first reported case, a male complainant boarded a blue Nissan Bluebird car with three occupants, one male who was the driver and two females, at Coca Cola Bus Stop intending to go to Chitungwiza Town. Along the way, the driver detoured into a bushy area where one of the females produced a pistol and forced the complainant to have sexual intercourse with her. On finishing, the victim was forced to drink some substance that left him unconscious. In the second case *The Herald* (6 June 2017) reported that a male hitch-hiker from Beatrice Service Centre boarded a white Toyota Noah vehicle with five passengers aboard and was offered a drink, which left him unconscious. Upon regaining consciousness, he found out that he had been sexually abused.

Another case involved a 39-year-old Chitungwiza-based male teacher who was allegedly raped by two women who had offered him a lift to Marondera Town from Chitungwiza (*The Standard*, 9 July 2017). It is reported that the victim got a hiking from a dark blue BMW car with South African number plates, which had four occupants, a male driver and three female passengers, two of whom were sitting in the back. Once in the vehicle, the victim was offered a beer but he turned it down and was instead given a soft drink which was laced with some drug. Upon finishing the drink, the victim felt dizzy and only woke up in some house where the two female passengers demanded that he be intimate with them, in quick succession and continuously for two days. During the ordeal, he was threatened with a gun to do the sex sessions, had a "severely bruised" manhood, lost cash amounting to US$120, and was sometimes forced to perform unprotected sex with one of the women (*Ibid*).

What emerges from the narratives above are some common characteristics that include the fact that the target group were individual male hitch-hikers, which seemed to offer the abusers some kind of power over the victims. This included the fact that the victims would have been taken away from their familiar environs where they could easily escape and were either locked up and drugged inside the abusers' cars or houses and were also threatened with guns and/ or death.

Broadly, too, by operating in teams that sometimes included some male accomplices, the female rapists had an advantage over their individual targets whom they easily overpowered by ganging up against them, sometimes being aided by the fact that they would have sedated them with. Also, from the foregoing, the male accomplices seemed to offer some kind of further protection and their presence added another dimension of male criminality to the female one, which served to create compound violence.

At another level, the fact that the women were usually in the company of a man, probably established them as pawns in the male business. This also confirmed the historical scripts that underpin Zimbabwean women as those with patriarchal servitude and loyalty. Added to the above, operating in groups meant that the victims often were forced to 'continuously' engage in sexual intercourse with the many of their abusers, which necessitated the giving of aphrodisiacs to the male victims to enhance their virility to enable more sperms to be harvested.

At yet another level, there have emerged numerous roles of cars in the sexual assault cases. In this regard, cars were used for kidnapping the victims, for assaulting the victims and for escaping as get away vehicles. Lastly, what has also emerges is that after the assault the male victims would report to the police, which was where the newspapers got their stories.

Occultism and the deepening socio-economic crisis

This section troubles the debate on the reference to occultism that was prevalent in the discourses around the proliferation of the cases of female rapists and sperm harvesting in Zimbabwe between 2011 and 2017. As already indicated in the introduction of this chapter, this is notwithstanding the slew of reasons that have been advanced for the raping of men and collecting their semen. In the final analysis, by focusing on the *juju* and wealth-generating reasoning, the section posits that it is important to analyse how a Zimbabwean citizenry reacted to, and generated, these narratives on witchcraft and sorcery at a moment in which the society sought socio-economic escapism. This is, first, because these stories shocked and surprised many Zimbabweans in interesting and sometimes contradictory ways. Simultaneously, these occult-inclined narrations move away from the tradition of simple and domesticated women to that of complex ones where the women are aggressive sperm hunter-gatherers as well as to narrations that take away the agency of the women by emphasizing occultism, where the women were simple tools of supernatural forces.

As indicated above, the section builds from the last explanation given in blogger.3-Mob.com (n.d.)earlier, and by the online newspaper, *New Zimbabwe* (7 November 2011) that contended that: "Some people in Zimbabwe believe that sperms can make someone's luck improve as it is associated with new life and regeneration." This perception was corroborated in many other interviews that we had for this chapter. The discussion is also intended to provide a variant response to the question, what did the female rapists want from their victims? We seek, also, to make connections between the occult reasoning articulated in the *New Zimbabwe* to the deepening socio-economic hardships in the country during this period.

The guiding framework for this section comes from Adam Ashforth's (2005) study of witchcraft in post-apartheid South Africa's Soweto Township. To Ashforth, increased reference to occult practices was rooted in "spiritual insecurity" that was closely linked to other insecurities, including poverty, violence, political oppression and the scourge of HIV and AIDS. For this chapter, the argument is that as the crisis worsened, there was a resort to some survival strategies that were in the spiritual realm. In addition, Ranger (1987) and Andersson (2002) have also established that increased reference to witchcraft in post-colonial Zimbabwe was a result of the increase of other insecurities among the locals. Related to this, as Marongwe and Maposa (2015) observed, existential challenges also increase spiritual insecurity. On the whole, as Clifford Geertz (1975: 11) shows, the rise in incidences of occult cases in crises is:

> A kind of dummy variable in the system of common sense thought. Rather than transcending that thought, it reinforces it by adding to it an all-purpose idea which acts to reassure the (locals) that their fund of commonplaces is, momentary appearances to the contrary notwithstanding, dependable and adequate.

Taken in the context of deepening poverty and worsening existentialism, including HIV and AIDS, and political repression in Zimbabwe from the onset of the new millennium, the issue of occult practices as a factor mediating survivalism becomes a crucial factor in the people's socio-economic relations.

Below, we highlight two of these interviews that further buttress thinking around witchcraft and the collection of male victims' sperms by the female rapists. Tonderai from Masvingo City argued that:

> There is no other reason for collecting sperms other than for witchcraft purposes. Sperms are mixed with herbs that result in a lot of wealth. Remember, sperms give life to humans and as such when they are mixed with the herbs the process represents killing a life/human

which then results in the body parts used in medicines for generating wealth. The practice of killing humans and mixing their body parts has a long history in Zimbabwe, so the collection of sperms for similar purposes should not surprise us much.

Related to the above, Chiedza, a vendor from Mutare's sprawling Dangamvura Market, averred that she knew of female friends who had made it by collecting male sperms and exporting them to some *sangomas*(witchdoctors) in South Africa. However, she was not sure what the sperms were used for. She said:

> My three friends who have tried this (male raping and sperm harvesting) have had their lives transformed significantly. We worked together here as vendors. However, they are no longer here with me as they have managed to start each their own lucrative businesses, with one having started a hair saloon business in Harare and two others having teamed up to set up a commuter omnibus business in Bulawayo.

Interestingly, the narrations portray women as actors and not passive recipients of phallic pride, phallic lust, phallic pleasure and phallic violence. This is a shift in a number of woman victimhood discourses and sexual discourses that see women as passive objects of male power and male pleasure. Nevertheless, the narrations do not associate the 'action' of women with their agency. Both the narrations and the responses to them refuse to associate the 'rapes' and female rapists' sexual acts with female pleasure. Instead, the incidences are quickly dismissed as occult-related. This makes sense in societies in which discourses around sex are 'unspeakable' in the public and ideas of female sexual pleasure are almost taboo. The suppression of the erotic as a crucial source of power and agency for women is instrumental to the reproduction of patriarchal systems (Lorde, 1982). The close ties between sexuality and power make sexual pleasure and eroticism fields of political significance.

In the context of the female rapists' narratives, the turn to occult practices satisfies grand and male-centred narratives that disassociate women with power. The occult 'sense' demonstrates a systematic suppression of women's sexual and erotic inclinations [and seeks] the conflation of sexuality within the normative cultural and social terrain of the male-centred hetero-sexual order. Related to this, Mawere (2016: page) reflects how Junior Lizzy Zinhu, also known as Beverly Sibanda/Bev's shows have "attracted the policing-authoritative criticism because of breaking national 'morality'" as her "erotic and raunchy dance routines and strip teasing have made her defy the official Zimbabwean imperative to privatize women's sexuality" and domestication.

Sexual assaults and violence

In this section, the attention is on how the sexual assaults by the female rapists interfaced with different forms of violence, especially in its physical and psychological forms. We draw insights from the WHO (2002) definition of violence to make these analyses. According to the WHO (2002: 4), violence "is the intentional use of physical force or power, threatened or actual, against oneself, another person, or against a group or community that either results in or has a high likelihood of resulting in injury, death, psychological harm, maldevelopment or deprivation". From the definition, what emerges is that violence is caused from the outside, can be verbal or actualised, is injurious either psychologically or physically and it leads to, or is intended to produce, an involuntary action. As shall also be explored, the forms of violence the male victims suffered was in some ways associated with Stanage's (cited in Dagenaar (1990:74) terminology including: "abuse, break, cease, damage, defeat, desecrate, dishonour, disagree, disobey, embarrass, erupt, excite, fear, force, harm, humiliate, impair, impede, injure, insult, interrupt, kill, maltreat, mar, murder, obstruct, perturb, prevent, punish, resent, spoil, stop, torture, thwart and wound." However, what also emerges clearly is that the forms of abuse the men suffered were gender-based but they nonetheless debunk the everyday notions of gender-based violence, which is normally about men perpetrating these acts against women.

Physical violence

The first form of violence suffered was a physical one where the victims were abducted and kept locked up for days providing forced sex to their captors. We deploy the United States Department of Health and Human Sciences' Centre for Disease Control and Prevention (2007:n.p) definition of physical violence as:

> The intentional use of physical force with the potential for causing death, disability, injury, or harm. Physical violence includes, but is not limited to, scratching; pushing; shoving; throwing; grabbing; biting; choking; shaking; slapping; punching; burning; use of a weapon; and use of restraints or one's body, size, or strength against another person.

As Saunyama (2017) puts it for one of the male victims, a 48-year-old teacher from Chitungwiza: "He was sexually abused for days by two women who had given him a lift …" At times, the abductions and forced concubinage for days caused other forms of physical violence to the victims, including causing bodily harm. As in the case of the male teacher who besides physical exhaustion from the seemingly unending sex sessions, he also suffered a bruised manhood and developed chest pains (Saunyama, 2017). The other form of physical violence was that at times the victims' hands would be tied or were tied to beds to minimize resistance. Additionally, by being kept locked for days also physically confined the victims in the spaces against their will, which could also have denied them access to medication, access to preferred food and generally to other common freedoms. Literally, the locking up was akin to confinement usually associated with prisons where there is the arbitrary withdrawal of one's liberties. As also highlighted above, the confinement was at times in dingy and dark places that also worsened the fear factor levels of the victims. The placing of the rape victims in solitary confinement also speaks to psychological violence that we turn to in the next paragraph. Broadly, as the case of Robert Sobukwe's six year solitary confinement at Robben Island Prison, illustrates, his body, voice box and spirit were destroyed by the confinement (Mandela, 1995).

It also stands to reason that the chemical substances that were used to weaken and 'capture' victims as well as the aphrodisiacs used to trigger erections probably caused physical damage to the body organs of the victims. This is especially so if the chemicals used were rudimentarily manufactured to make them cheaper or were derived from questionable sources. It is also probable that the rape survivors can suffer in the long run due to the effects of these chemical substances. What could be worse, also, is that potentially large doses could have been administered to achieve, instantly, the desired effects both during the moments of capture and during the moments of sperm harvesting.

Psychological violence

At another level, and closely related to the physical attacks, the rape victims also suffered psychological violence as they were traumatized by the experiences. By definition, psychological violence is:

> The use of verbal and non-verbal communication with the intent to harm another person mentally or emotionally, and/or to exert control over another person. Psychological aggression can include expressive aggression (e.g., name-calling, humiliating); coercive control (e.g., limiting access to transportation, money, friends, and family; excessive monitoring of whereabouts); threats of physical or sexual violence; control of reproductive or sexual health (e.g., refusal to use birth control; coerced pregnancy termination); exploitation of victim's vulnerability (e.g., immigration status, disability); exploitation of perpetrator's vulnerability; and presenting false information to the victim with the intent of making them doubt their own memory or perception (e.g., mind games)" (US Department of Health and Human Services's Centre for Disease Control and Prevention, 2007: n.p).

What makes psychological violence worse is that it has longer term effects (WHO, 2002: 18). What should also not escape attention is the fact that the two forms of violence cannot be cleanly separated as the victims could have felt them simultaneously. This helped to create complex webs of violence with physical and psychological violence, and possibly other forms of violence happening concurrently. As Dagenaar (1990) explains, psychological violence, as separated from physical violence is not easily decipherable. To him, it includes verbal abuse, maltreatment, personal abuse, detentions, solitary confinements, brainwashing and misuse of education (Ibid). As one victim recounted, he felt "confused, traumatized and … dejected," and that he continued to relive the ordeal explaining that "no man would ever want such an experience and as for me, I would give anything to avoid a repeat, even in a dream" (Saunyama, 2017). What can be considered as the cause of the trauma includes threats of death that the victims receive upon abduction. Often, as described above, the captors often had guns that they used to threaten harm and/ or death to the male victims. For a country like Zimbabwe, guns are not very common and gun ownership is seldom. Thus, for someone to have a gun pointed in their face for the first time, was very unnerving. Following this was the blind folding of the victims, which served to add to the anxiety and confusion about where they were to be taken or location they were at. The trauma was also worsened by the fact that mostly the victims were forced to drink unknown aphrodisiacs probably to enhance sperm production. What probably was worse was that the side effects of the aphrodisiacs were not known.

The victims were also traumatized because they were sometimes forced to have unprotected sex against women they knew very little about. This exposed the victims to greater risks of contracting Sexually-Transmitted Diseases like HIV/AIDS and herpes. The trauma that the victims suffered could also be associated with the reversal of sexual roles, where the affected men felt feminized. This feminization could have been particularly so if one considers that Zimbabwe is a very patriarchal society where being a man is associated with control over women and not the other way round. And, for the men to be so powerless against the women rapists could have triggered this as this was a form of humiliation against the male victims. In the end, the fear of being feminized resulted in many of the victims refusing to reveal their identities as they were scared that some society members would ridicule them for being 'women'. What should not escape attention is that the collection of sperms, which are basically a symbol of manhood and power acts out the association of power and dominance with men. It also struck at the heart of the foundation of patriarchy. Patriarchy emanates as the natural hub of all power. For one to be powerful, the initiation portions need to take some form of maleness, which in this case, the sperms provide.

Critically, also, what one is reminded of is that in some sense, the capture and forced sexual intercourse experiences invert the traditional patriarchal marriage practice among the Shona people of Zimbabwe known as *musenga bere*. The *musenga bere* marriage system was used in some traditional Shona societies by men who forced women to marry them by sometimes literally carrying them on their back or on their shoulders to the homes where they kept them for days before they allowed them to go out by which time it would have been very late for them to return to their homes. In the end, the women would remain with their abductors and became their wives (Mawere and Mbindi-Mawere, 2010).

In addition to the above, the trauma was also due to the uncertainty of the date/day of their release from the assaults. In the end, as the WHO (n.d.: 154) asserts:

> Male [rape] victims are likely to suffer from a range of psychological consequences, both in the immediate period after the assault and over the longer term. These include guilt, anger, anxiety, depression, post-traumatic stress disorder, sexual dysfunction, somatic complaints, sleep disturbances, withdrawal from relationships and attempted suicide. In addition to these reactions, studies of adolescent males have also found an association between suffering rape and substance abuse, violent behaviour, stealing and absenteeism from school.

In the end, the different forms of mental torture, as explained above, have the tendency to debase male confidence and honour, especially if the psychological forms of violence are linked to the common sense discourses of masculinity/manhood. The experiences potentially can create permanent psychological wounds that affect future relationships and the male victims' identity negotiation.

Moving forward, probably one of the reasons why the suspected Gweru women won the case might be related to the unwillingness of victims to publicly expose themselves as victims of female rapists. Doing so would degrade their phallic pride and social status, hence the choice for silent suffering.

Secondary violence was also experienced. As Marongwe (2013) explains, secondary violence is one that is felt through the others. In our case, this was when the male rape victims experienced violence through their relations, like spouses, siblings or children. Secondary violence also involved trauma and spirals of violence. To this extent, the relatives of the rape victims also felt as abused and often took the shame together with the actual victims.

Economic violence as a trigger to female rapists

After examining the varying forms of violence that the male victims of female rape could have faced, there is need to consider economic violence that may have undergirded the commission of the raping by the women. This is closely related to how the worsening economic conditions in Zimbabwe could have triggered desperate survival tactics by the citizens. It builds on the ethos of the discussions in Duri (2015) of how famished Zimbabweans fashioned out survival strategies to escape the entrapments of a biting socio-economic crisis that also had negative political consequences.

Conclusion

From the foregoing discussion, it can be concluded that there was a lot of violence inscribed in the sperm-harvesting escapades by female 'rapists'. These range from physical violence to various types of psychological violence. The chapter has also discussed how the collection of the sperms was linked with witchcraft and sorcery. Critically, the chapter has attempted to make connections between the occult-related reasoning with the deepening economic insecurities, which fed into, and fed from a grid of other socio-existential insecurities. At another level, the chapter has also demonstrated how the cases of female rapists that dominated the recent history of Zimbabwe helped to trouble the definitions and practice of rape and sexual assault, which then calls for a relook at everyday simplified connections between gender and victimhood. This is especially so in situations where males are seldom considered as victims of female violence, worse still in cases of sexual assaults.

References

3-Mob.com, (n.d.) 'Female rapists: what happens to all that sperm?' Available at: http://www.3-mob.com/idiotic/sperm/#.WWdyN2dLfIU, Accessed 13 July 2017.

Andersson, J. A. (2002) 'Sorcery in the era of "Henry IV": Kinship, mobility and mortality in Buhera District, Zimbabwe', in: *Journal of the Royal Anthropological Institute*, Volume 8, Number 3, Available at: http://www.jstor.org/stable/3134534, Accessed 14 March 2011.

Ashforth, A. (2005) *Witchcraft, violence and democracy in South Africa*, Chicago: Chicago University Press.

Bulawayo24 News, 11 October 2011. '3 female rapists, caught with 33 condoms full of sperms, named', Available at: http://bulawayo24.com/index-id-news-sc-regional-byo-8209.html, Accessed 13 July 2017.

Dagenaar, J. (1990) 'The concept of violence' In: C. Mangami and A. du Toit (Eds.) *Political violence and the struggle in South Africa*, Macmillan: London.

Duri, F. P. T. (Ed.) (2015), *Resilience amid adversity: Informal coping mechanisms to the Zimbabwean crisis during the new millennium*, Booklove Publishers: Gweru.

Geertz, C. (1975) 'Common sense as a cultural system', in: *The Antioch Review*, Volume 33, Number 1, Available at: http://www.jstor.org/stable/4637616, Accessed 6 March 2012.

Harare24 News, 27 December 2012, '3 female rapists take turns to rape a soldier', Available at: http://harare24.com/index-id-front+page-zk-14725.html, Accessed 13 July 2017.

Lorde, A. (1982) 'Zami: A new spelling of my name', Freedom, CA: The Crossing Press

Marongwe, N. and Maposa, R. S. (2015) 'PHDs, gospreneurship and the Pentecostal new wave in Zimbabwe', in: *Afro-Asian Journal of Social Sciences*, Volume VI, Number 1, pp1-22.

Marongwe, N. (2013) 'Rural women as invisible victims of the militarisation of violence: The case of Shurugwi District, 2000-2009', PhD thesis, University of the Western Cape, Cape Town.

Mandela, N. (1995) *Long walk to freedom: The autobiography of Nelson Mandela*, Boston, New York and London: Little, Brown and Company.

Mawere, M. and A Mbindi-Mawere, (2010) 'The changing philosophy of African marriage: The relevance of the Shona customary marriage practice of Kukumbira', Journal of African Studies and Development Vol. 2(9): 224-233, Available at: www.academicjournals.org/article/article1380012233_Mawere%20and%20Mawere.pdf, Accessed 15 January 2016.

Nehanda Radio, 22 May 2013. 'Man forced to service four women', Available at: http://nehandaradio.com/2013/05/22/man-forced-to-service-four-women/, Accessed 15 July 2017.

Nehanda Radio, 29 March 2013. 'Female rapist pounces on Karoi pastor', Available at: http://nehandaradio.com/2012/03/29/female-rapist-pounces-on-karoi-pastor/, Accessed 19 July 2017.

New Zimbabwe, 7 November 2011. 'Gweru female 'rapists' attacked in street', Available at: http://www.newzimbabwe.com/news-6460, Accessed 13 July 2017.

Ranciere, J. (2006) *The politics of aesthetics*, Translated by Gabriel Rockhill, London: Continuum.

Ranger, T. (1987) 'Review: Healers and hierarchies', in: *Journal of Southern African Studies,* Vol 13, No2, Special Issue on the political and Economy of health in Southern Africa, January 1987, in http://www.jstor.org/stable/2636862, Accessed 15 March 2011.

Saunyama, J. 16-22 July 2017. 'How I was raped by two women', in: *The Standard*, Harare: Zimbabwe.

Standard, 9 July 2017. 'Female rapists leave teacher for dead', Harare: Zimbabwe.

United States Department of Health and Human Sciences' Centre for Disease Control and Prevention, 2007. 'Intimate partner violence: Definitions', Available At: https://www.cdc.gov/violenceprevention/intimatepartnerviolence/definitions.html, Accessed 9 August 2017.

World Health Organisation, (n.d.) 'Chapter Six: Sexual violence', Available at: www.who.int/violence_injury_prevention/violence/global_campaign/.../chap6.pdf, Accessed 31 July 2017.

World Health Organisation, (2002) 'World report on violence and health: Summary', Available at: www.who.int/violence_injury_prevention/violence/world.../en/summary_en.pdf, *Accessed 9 August 2017.*

Zimeye, 10 August 2012. 'Gweru accused female 'rapists' acquitted', Available at: https://www.zimeye.net/gweru-female-rapists-acquited%E2%80%8F/, Accessed 13 July 2017.

Zimbabwe Vulnerability Assessment Committee (Zimvac), 2017. '2017 Rural livelihoods assessment Report', Available at: https://reliefweb.int/report/zimbabwe/zimbabwe-vulnerability-assessment-committee-zimvac-2017-rural-livelihoods-assessment, Accessed 21 January 2017.

Chapter 5

Unearthing the Gender and Religious Conflict Conundrum: The Curse of Africa

Jacob Tagarirofa

Introduction

The chapter seeks to unearth the correlation between gender and religious conflicts. This is because most religious conflicts in Africa epitomize a gendered skewedness when demographically categorizing victims. It departs from the conviction that religious conflicts, whether armed or violent, characteristically embody more masculine than feminine traits yet women remain a more vulnerable demographic sector since they are naturally perceived to be physically weak to defend themselves. This has culminated in the appreciation of the patriarchal nature of religion as an institution to the extent that both in peace and conflict moments, religion epitomizes a domain where the constriction of women's identity, practices and space seem to be legitimized. Most religious conflicts across the continent and even abroad are symptomatic of this gendered structure where, by virtue of social representation, men seem to be the perpetrators and women the victims. Theoretically, the chapter is guided by the radical and post-colonial feminism strands which stress the need for deconstruction of structures and systems that legitimize and perpetuate the dichotomous victimization and vulnerabilities of women in conflicts.

Methodologically, the chapter is mainly qualitative and based on a multi-case study approach. The chapter mainly argues that in most religious conflicts, women suffer more than men since religion symbolically follows the gender skewedness exhibited in the patriarchal system of most African societies. Based on the discussion, the chapter recommends the need for intensive and extensive education and training of societal leaders in conflict-torn contexts to appreciate the equality in humanity between men and women, as a basis for arresting systems and structures which proliferate gendered victimization and susceptibilities in most religious conflicts.

Religion has been defined in multifarious ways by numerous scholars. However, this chapter deploys Tillich's (1963:12) definition which sees religion as "the state of being grasped by an ultimate concern, a concern which qualifies all other concerns as preliminary, and a concern that in itself provides the answer to the question of the meaning of our existence". The writer submits that this definition squarely befits the chapter's analogy insofar as it unequivocally stipulates the significant notion of being grasped by an ultimate concern of one's existence which is more inclined towards one's sense of belonging or identity. As such, in religion, it is the battle for recognition of one's identity and religious values whose existence should not be in vain but very invaluable.

Feminist legal scholars suggests that the construction of social sex and gender roles, combined with generally subordinate social and economic position of women, mean that women suffer in particular ways during and after conflict (Hudson, 2015). It should be noted that the impact of conflict differs to a great extent upon factors like ethnicity, class, age and location. Religion is one of the factors that causes conflict in the modern-day society as it creates a zeal of wanting to be recognized and usually wanting to dominate over the other, thus a case of identity-based conflicts through religion. There is growing awareness of the gender differences and inequalities during conflict and in post-conflict reconstruction. Yet it is misleading to set up a dichotomy that locates women and men in totally different spheres. Weigel (2011) suggests that, religion has often been castigated as the opium of the people in general and the oppressed in particular.

Religion is often described as a specific fundamental set of beliefs and practices that are generally agreed upon by a number of persons or sects. Conflict, also according to Braham (2005), is a confrontation between individuals, or identity groups over scarce resources. According to Braham (2005), a religious conflict is one that is primarily caused or justified by differences in religious ideology and the incidental use of religion as a criteria for distribution of socio-political opportunities and economic resources whereupon others are unfairly disenfranchised. He further argues that, a religious conflict involves believers of two different faiths for the purpose of dominating the other faith in order to expand their faith at the expense of others.

Contemporary religious conflicts increasingly target the civilian population, whereby women often suffer from systematic rape and other forms of sexual violence. Women and men share experiences and are intimately connected to each other through their families and communities. It is therefore the principal concern of this chapter to evaluate the link between religion, gender and conflict using a multi-case study approach.

Religion, conflict and identity

There is abundant evidence to support the view that religious conflicts are more dominant in the world. This is based on the fact that ethnicity and religion are the most important sources of identity for most individuals and attract strong loyalties to the groups. Since women are usually regarded as symbolic bearers of caste, ethnic or national identity, the sexual violence against women is a deliberate strategy in religious conflicts so as to humiliate the entire community (Oakley, 2015). Women are a heterogeneous group of social actors, who on the one hand are determined to take on certain positions and roles in conflicts, but on the other hand deliberately choose to fulfil certain roles based on their strategies and goals (Appleby, 2000). Women must thus not only be seen as passive victims of religious conflicts, but also as capable actors.

Although women do suffer in most religious conflicts, their capacity should not be seen with rigid identity lens since they can alter their spaces and practices according to the dictates of the conflict situation. A case in point is Hutchson's (2014) observation and recognition of the positive role played by Religious Women for Peace (RW4P), a women's organization which builds and provides technical support to organic, nationally-based Inter-Religious Councils (IRCs). The women have managed to establish their own infrastructure and to share with others the tools they need for advocacy, conflict transformation, community mobilization and leadership. As a consequence, every IRC is different, but they share the common goal of breaking down the hatred and fear that lead to and are often the result of religious wars or conflicts. They have achieved amazing successes in numerous areas, from helping to end bloody conflicts, to brokering peace accords in Sierra Leone and Liberia. In Nigeria's bloody Boko Haram terrorist attacks, women have been seen taking care of the victims of conflicts way before the formal medical teams arrived (Mutunja, 2015). This therefore demonstrates how disproportionately women have been wrongly perceived as weak and therefore victims in conflicts due to their identity. However, it should be noted that in so far as women might be significantly active during and in post-conflict contexts, their vulnerability should not be overlooked.

Women's vulnerability in religious conflicts

The view that women are equally subjected to victimhood in most religious conflicts is to a significant extent true as they endure the same trauma, as the rest of the population from bombings, famines, epidemics, mass executions, torture, arbitrary imprisonment, forced migration, ethnic cleansing, threats and intimidation. Valerie (2014) notes that they are also targets of specific forms of violence and abuse, including sexual violence and exploitation. As noted in paragraph 135 of the Beijing Platform for Action, "While entire communities suffer the consequences of armed conflict and terrorism, women and girls are particularly affected because of their status in society and their sex". This is evidenced in the religious conflict that happened in Mali between the Islamic groups led by the National Movement for the Liberation of Azawad (MNLA) against the Malian government during the 2012-2013 crisis, as women did not enjoy equal status with men in any society. There were cultures of violence and discrimination against women and girls which existed prior to conflict, and these were then exacerbated during the religious conflict. Women were the main victims in this conflict as they never had the chance to participate in the decision-making structures of a society, and they were unlikely to become involved in decisions about the conflict or the peace process that followed (Gardam *et al*, 2000).

Another classical example can be drawn from the religious conflict that happened in Sudan which then led to the division of the state into the North that currently belongs to the Islamic people and the South where Christians and traditional believers now belong. Turlock (2008) submits that, the major reason for the 1972 Addis Ababa Agreement which led to a cessation of the north-south civil war and a degree of self-rule was the nature and visible brutality exerted on women by the conflicting religious groups. Christian women were raped and those who were pregnant would have their foetus extracted from their wombs alive and burnt. Such ruthless acts on Christian women were also a weapon to humiliate men especially by exposing that they were powerless to provide security to their wives. This is a candid exhibition of the invincible view that women are the main victims of religious conflicts especially through sexual violence.

Sexual violence as weapon of contemporary warfare

Lewy (2008) posited that, the changes in armed religious conflict over the past years have severely affected women and girls. Women and girls are often viewed as bearers of cultural-religious identity and thus become prime targets. Gender-based and sexual violence have increasingly become weapons of warfare and are one of the defining characteristics of contemporary religious armed conflict. Rape, forced impregnation, forced abortion, trafficking, sexual slavery and the intentional spread of Sexually-Transmitted Infections (STIs), including the Human Immunodeficiency Virus (HIV/AIDS), are elements of contemporary religious conflict. As noted by the Crans Montana Forum of 17-22 March 2016, Shi'a and Sunni, the two main branches of Islam in Morocco, have reached the highest number of forced abortions during religious conflicts and sexual slavery. Their intention was to spread a message to each other thus victimising women across the line to achieve those goals.

A similar case was also observed in the Central Africa Republic (CAR), as the Selaka rebels who are believed to be of the Christian religion raped 100 Muslim women in an effort to spread STIs and to embarrass the Muslims, as it is taboo in the Islamic religion for women to engage in sexual intercourse with persons outside their belief. This, therefore, clearly shows that women are the main victims in most religious conflicts and theirs indeed is a double tragedy since their identity is despised to inferiority in most mainstream religions and at the same time they are reduced to objects of the war since they are often victims of sexual violence in most religious conflicts as noted above.

Socialisation and the conception of gendered identity

Furthermore, social attitudes also affect the vulnerability of women and girls. For example, families have often wrongly assumed that an elderly woman or a woman with children will be safe from harm and have left them to safeguard property while the rest of the family flees. Women and men often do different types of work, frequently as a result of socially prescribed gender roles, and may be exposed to different threats through this work. Women tend to be responsible for the care and nurture of the family and thus shouldering heavy burdens. This has been summed by Conradie (2009:9) as the 'triple gender roles' of women, which are notably observed as reproduction, production and community care. As such, the writer opines that, this collection of roles does not only often go unacknowledged, but in most instances, aid in the vilification of women's identity and consequently cements their disenfranchisement in conflict and broadly militarism. Collection of firewood or water often puts young girls and women at risk of dangers, which include kidnapping, sexual abuse and exposure to landmines. Ritzer (2008) argues that, women are the very active parent in any child's life. They are greatly responsible for the primary socialization of children thus conflicting religious groups are of the view that the role women play is an advantage to their victimisation, as they are forced train and socialize their children into a religious stereotype that is useful and necessary for conflicts to continue. This therefore justifies the reason why the Boko Haram Islamic militia in Northern Nigeria had to kidnap and impregnate about 500 girls and women that resided in the state of Bono since the year 2009 (Human Rights Watch Report, 2014). This vividly illustrates gendered nature of religious conflicts as augmented by various media proclamations of this Boko Haram incident as incited by the very militia to affirm the society the Islamic belief of women's inferior position in Islamic social organisation. The militia purported the western education that the girls were receiving eroded the Islamic cultural values and beliefs, therefore the kidnapping and rape was tantamount to reinstallation and reaffirmation of women's position in Islamic cultural milieu.

Women have always been victims in most religious conflicts throughout history. Girls, even at the adolescent stage, have been subjected to rape, including mass rape. The raping of women is a means for the aggressor to symbolically and physically humiliate the defeated men. Rape or the threat of rape is also used to drive communities off lands or to heighten terror during attacks for instance in the Israeli-Palestinian conflict. In the Buddhist uprising in South Vietnam, women and adolescent girls suffered beatings, food deprivation, and physical and sexual torture if they resisted rape by armed groups (Human Rights Watch, 2014). In the Democratic Republic of Congo (DRC), women and adolescent girls captured by the rebels "were routinely raped by numbers of rebels and any reluctance or attempt to resist usually meant summary execution" (Women Rights Organisation, 2010: 23). The report went on to highlight how throughout the genocide in Rwanda, the rape and mutilation of women and girls by opposing religious groups was carried out, not only as an attack against these females, but as a means to exercise power over and demoralise the men in the women's family, clan and ethnic-religious group (Ibid). With these scenarios, it becomes tenably true that socialization and societal perceptions pose a significant impact of the disparagement of women much to the detriment of rendering them susceptible to sexual violence and abuse in most religious conflicts.

This chapter submits that, besides the above observation, women are the main victims in most religious conflicts as they are viewed as inferior within their communities and are also discriminated against during the times of conflict. Women are generally classified as dependent upon men and they need to be protected during the times of wars. The lack of protection is the one that therefore leads to displacement. Kagwanja (2000:11) alludes to how in Kenya, within the wider politicisation of religion, "refugees from other Somali clans were lumped together with Kenya's religious Somalis", who were already subject to multiple forms of discrimination. Non-Governmental Organisation (NGO) health workers recorded that rape and beatings of refugee women were daily and nightly experiences (Kenya Non-Governmental Organisations Association, 2000). In a different case, this time involving Sudanese refugees in Kenya, Sudanese cross-border militias and male refugees, as well as members of the Kenyan security forces sexually assaulted, gang-raped, and kidnapped women and girls as young as 11 years. Most of the victims were from the Dinka and Mombasa community (Kabaka, 2011). The Kenyan authorities dismissed these reports, and few of the victims brought charges because of fear of reprisals from male refugees (Ibid). This therefore shows that, women are the main victims in most religious conflicts.

Inverted view of women as active agents in conflicts

Women and girls are not only victims of religious conflict; they are also active agents and participants. They may actively choose to participate in the conflict and carry out acts of violence because they are committed to the religious goals of the parties to the conflict. Women and girls may also be manipulated into taking up military or violent roles such as girl soldiers and female suicide bombers through propaganda, abduction, intimidation and forced recruitment. Women and girls may also provide non -military support for war. According to Simon (2015), women can directly support combatants through cooking and cleaning for soldiers, acting as porters and messengers and through performing other tasks required by militaries all in the name of wanting to keep and safeguard their own belief that will be at stake. They can also indirectly support war efforts by developing and disseminating propaganda, encouraging their children to go to war, voting for governments that launch military campaigns under religious bases and fomenting distrust (Ibid). This is evidenced in the religious conflict that occurred between Palestine and India, as some women performed violent roles. Green (2014) notes that, women may infiltrate opposition groups for the purposes of passing information, hide or smuggle weapons, support or care for fighters. For example, in Syria, women supporting the rebel forces smuggled weapons through checkpoints in baskets of fish, under their clothing and via their children (*Ibid*). With this, one can say that women are not always the victims in most religious conflicts but rather voluntarily or involuntarily they are sometimes active agents and participants in the conflict.

Religious conflicts and the reversal of normative gender perceptions

In addition to this, while religious conflicts and instability more often than not entail profound loss, stress and burden, women and girls can gain temporarily from the changed gender relations that may result from armed religious conflict (Higherd, 2014). They can acquire new status, skills and power through taking on new responsibilities. These changes can challenge existing norms about their roles in society. In some religious conflicts such as the Abyssinia-Somalia conflicts, the loss of men through exile, fighting or death has allowed women and girls to assume functions that were normally the prerogative of men. The writer observes that, in these instances, norms about roles and participation of women and girls in decision-making in the household, civil society, the formal economy, and in women, peace and security studies may be altered, to their benefit. This is confirmed by Green (2014) who puts that, conflict usually allows space for impermanent reconfiguration of social and gender relations, and this does not occur essentially. In the above example, women also infiltrated governmental and peacekeeping forces using social contacts (*Ibid*).

As such, it is notably correct to affirm that individual women combined various identities and roles at once, such as displaced person, community activist, small business owner, soldier and homeless person. It is pathetic to note that, the gains that would have been amassed before, are in most cases reversed after the end of the conflict, thus women have less to gain and stand to be major victims in most of the religious conflicts as they suffer social and physical hazards of the conflict, and have their spaces and practices inhibited by incidences of religious conflict.

Conclusion

In conclusion, women and girls face more and different risks and dangers in religious conflict compared to those faced by men and boys. The chapter has noted that there is an impermeable relationship between religions, conflict and gender insofar as these variables seem to proliferate the suffocation of the other. For instance, religion perpetuates conflicts, and the religious conflicts in turn emerge to be gendered since women bear more the brand of victims than men. As such, the essay has reaffirmed the vulnerability of women in most religious conflicts. This has been noted through any analogy of sexual violence as a weapon of contemporary warfare as epitomized by numerous religious conflicts characterizing the continent. This has also been seen to be strengthened by socialization which influences the conception of gender identity and conflicts or armed struggles. Categorically, the social typification of women as inferior beings has misappropriated societal conceptions of their roles and identities in conflict and military discourse much to their marginalisation and vulnerability. Consequently, the call by post-colonial feminists, to review the condition of women's situation in conflict heterogeneously, should be applauded since the circumstances surrounding women are incongruent. Thus the feminist lamentation for the deconstruction of societal structures and systems that perpetuate the continued suffering and victimisation of women should be upheld if the pragmatic emancipation of women from the consequences of religious conflicts is to be attainable. Otherwise, Africa would remain a cursed continent if these religious conflicts proceed unchecked.

References

Appleby, R. S. (2000) *The ambivalence of the sacred: Religion, violence and reconciliation*, Rowman and Littlefield Publishers: New York.

Braham, E. (2005) *Religion and conflict*, Touchstone Books: London.

Gardam, J. (2000) 'Protection of women in armed conflicts' in: *Human Rights Quarterly*, 22 (1): 45-71

Green, H. (2014) *Women, Conflict and Development*, Polity Press: London.

Human Rights Watch, (2014) *Leave non to tell the story: A case of Boko Haram in Nigeria*, Human Rights Watch: New York.

Hudson, V. (2014) 'Missing women and bare branches: Gender balance and conflict,' *Environmental Change and Security Program Report*, Number 11, pp. 20-24

Lewy, G. (1974) *Religion and revolution*, Oxford, New York.

Paul, H. (2004) *Gender and peace-keeping*, Polity Press, Cambridge: UK.

Simona, S. (1995) *Gender and the Israeli-Palestinian conflict of the politics of women's resistance*, New York: Syracuse University Press.

Tillich, P. (1963) *Theology of culture*, Columbia University Press: Columbia

United Nations, (2001) *From Beijing to Beijing +5: Review and appraisal of the implementation of the Beijing Platform for Action*, United Nations: New York.

Women's Commission for Refugee Women and Children. (1997) *Rwanda's women and children: The long road to reconciliation*, Women's Commission for Refugee Women and Children, New York.

Chapter 6

Ritual Murder during the New Millennium: Dissecting the Triggers and Impacts of Ritual Killings in Zimbabwe

Nancy Mazuru

Introduction

Despite being an antiquated and illegal practice, ritual murder is still pervasive in many African countries and Zimbabwe is not an exception. Since the turn of the new millennium, numerous incidents of ritual-related murders have been witnessed in several provinces of Zimbabwe. It is against this backdrop that the present chapter explores the causes of ritual killings in contemporary Zimbabwe as well as the socio-economic and psychological effects of this practice. The chapter commences by situating the phenomenon of ritual murder in a historical context, tracing it from ancient societies across the globe.

The major theme of this chapter is anchored on examining the reasons why ritual murder is still existent in Zimbabwe in particular and Africa in general when several other societies across the world abandoned it years back.

The chapter argues that unemployment and poverty occupy the heart of the problem while strong superstitious beliefs and greed for fast wealth play complementary roles.

Conceptualising ritual murder

Ritual murder in this chapter is taken to be synonymous with human sacrifice because there is no clear-cut distinction between the two concepts. Human sacrifice is the killing of human beings and the use of their body parts for ritual intentions that include some perceived communication with the spiritual world (Carrosco and Sessions, 2011). Similar to human sacrifice, ritual murder is the sacrifice of a human being to a supernatural being or divinity (Steel, 1995). It is an act committed by two or more individuals who rationally plan the crime and whose primary motivation is to fulfil a prescribed satanic ritual (Jenkins, 1994). It can also be defined as the killing of a human being in such a way that the form of killing is at least partly determined by ideas allegedly or actually important in the religion of the killer or the victims (Wasyliw, 2008). It involves people who commit criminal activities characterised by a series of repeated physical, sexual and/or psychological assaults combined with a systematic use of symbols, ceremonies and/or machinations (Perlmutter, 2003).

Human sacrifice in ancient societies across the globe

The practice of murdering people for ritual purposes is not a unique phenomenon in Zimbabwe as it was also common in many other societies, in Africa and beyond. Blood sacrifice has been an integral part of many world societies for about as long as historical records can tell us (Kastenbaum, 2016). It has been a culturally respectable and "normal" phenomenon within prescribed institutional roles in societies from India to Africa to Polynesia to East Asia to Europe and to the New World (Iadicola and Shupe, 2013). Outside Africa, human sacrifice was a common practice among ancient European hunter-gatherer societies (Kastenbaum, 2016). For instance, human remains, many of which showed signs of violence and ritualised murder, were excavated by archaeologists from the peat sphagnum bogs of Ireland, Britain, the Netherlands, Denmark and northern Germany, where acid conditions prevent decay of soft material (Woolf, 2015).

Similarly, in ancient America, human sacrifice was also practiced among the Aztecs, Incas and the Mayas (Selin, 1997; Carrasco, 2012). The Aztecs, who are often referred to as the biggest sacrificers, believed that the Sun God, their Supreme God, required human blood without which the sun would go out, the corn would die and the Aztec society would be destroyed (Ladicola and Shupe, 2003; Mason, 2005; Moczar, 2013).

The Asian continent was also not an exception. Diverse societies in India, Indonesia, Melanesia, Filipinas, China, Japan and many others practiced human sacrifice (Tort, 2017). In ancient China, for example, during the time of the Shang dynasty, human sacrifice was practiced on a large scale in which sacrificial human victims were often war prisoners captured in the incessant border wars that the Shang kings pursued with their unruly neighbours (Mayor and Cook, 2016). Retainer sacrifice was also practiced in ancient China, whereby kings were buried with members of their royal families (including cooks, grooms, butlers) to serve their ruler in the afterlife (Quigley, 2013). In Japan, in the Bushido cult of the Japanese samurai of the 17th to 19th centuries, warriors were required to give complete loyalty to the lords, including self-sacrifice or *Seppuku* (ritual suicide) if it was demanded (Carrosco and Sessions, 1998). In ancient India, human sacrifice was widely practised in the Hindu culture by the Brahmin caste and others (Jacob, 2013). An example is an ancient tribe in India where victims were offered to an earth goddess by shedding blood and planting flesh in the fields purportedly to ensure good crops of turmeric (Quigley, 2013). In India again, children of humble parents were killed so that the wife of an exalted person would therefore conceive (*Ibid*). Hence, human sacrifice was a global trend during the ancient times.

In the ancient Near East, human sacrifice was also practiced among various cultures. Some of the earliest evidence of the practice dates from the 6 000 BCE, among the Mesopotamian peoples (Nemet-Nejat, 1998; Arp, 2013). The Mesopotamians were among the first cultures to develop a practice of retainer sacrifice in which the slaves and servants of the nobility were killed at the time of their masters' death (Arp, 2013). At the sanctuary called Tophet, children were sacrificed to the goddess Tanit and her consort Baal Hammon (Bromiley, 1988).

Human sacrifice was also part of the Jewish tradition (Strenski, 2008). In the Bible, some Israelites sacrificed their sons and/or daughters to the Ammonite deity Molech, to demons and possibly even to Yahweh (Bromiley, 1988). In the Old Testament, Abraham nearly sacrificed his son Isaac to Yahweh (Genesis 22:1-12). The fact that Abraham quickly heeded to the voice of God when he was instructed to offer his only son as a sacrifice clearly demonstrates that this practice was common during that era. In a similar line of argument, Strenski (2008) states that ancient Hebrew human sacrifice and the death of Jesus were part of a surviving Jewish cultural trait of bloody sacrificial victimisation.

In pre-colonial Africa, human sacrifice was also practiced by different ethnic groups and societies for various reasons. According to Larr (2013), there have always been reports in history reaching from Ancient Egypt down to the Bantu regions, of kings who died and were never buried alone. Servants, warriors and royal attendants were buried with their dead masters and in some cases they were buried alive (Lewis, 2001). In Egypt, the ritual killing of human beings was done either on a regular basis or on special occasions in the Nile Valley during the 1st Dynasty and possibly also in pre-dynasty Egypt (Larr, 2013). The Egyptians had a deep-rooted conviction about life after death and they believed that the dead survived and one day they might come back to life (Kansal, 2012). For this reason, slaves, maids and other royal attendants were killed and buried with their kings so that they would serve the corpses in the tombs (Kansal, 2012). For instance, in pre-dynastic and early Egypt, the servants and wives of the deceased Pharaoh were buried with him (Te Velde, 2007; Nwachindu and Ihediwa, 2017). Just like in Ancient Egypt, human sacrifice was also practised in West Africa in kingdoms such as Asante, Benin, Dahomey, Calabar and Ibo and human beings were sacrificed as offerings to gods and to the dead (particularly to dead kings and other elite forbears) (Meyer, 2005; La Fontaine, 2011). In Southern Africa, when Shaka the Zulu king's mother died in 1827, it is alleged that he buried ten girls together (Gaines, 2000).

In Africa, it was the gradual influence of Christian missionaries that brought about a sense of resentment and the campaign to drive home the awareness of the barbaric implication of this senseless act of killing fellow humans for an unknown life beyond perception (Larr, 2013). Nevertheless, even when the act was successfully challenged and tabooed beyond open practice, there continued to be an underground and secret practice of the act even deep into the 19th century (*Ibid*). This, therefore, shows that like many other societies in the whole world, the practice of human sacrifice was rampant in

Africa during the pre-colonial period. However, the only difference is that this practice is now virtually history in many regions of the world, except in Africa (*Ibid*).

Ritual killings in independent Zimbabwe

In order to provide a holistic picture of ritual killings in present-day Zimbabwe, it is important to avoid taking the country in isolation from other African countries. This is largely because many African societies share similar beliefs, traditions and practices which sometimes trigger ritual murder. In addition, the porous borders of these countries allow the trafficking of human body parts to other countries where they are used for different ritual purposes. In Zimbabwe, for example, there is a belief that some of the human body parts are sold to South Africa (*Newsday*, 15 July 2011).

Recently, the practice of ritual killings has been on the rise in many African countries such as Chad, Nigeria, Liberia, Malawi, Tanzania and Burundi, among others. (Shelly, 2010). In the same line of argument, Stapelberg (2014) avers that every year, hundreds of Africans lose their lives in ritual murders by tribal members who go in search of human body parts at the behest of witchdoctors or traditional healers.

In Zimbabwe, incidents and stories of ritual killings have been in existence since time immemorial. However, these cases appear to have increased in the new millennium. In 2004, a woman from Village Eight in the Nyajezi Resettlement Scheme in Nyanga District was reportedly killed by two men for ritual purposes (Dube, 2017). The two men allegedly murdered the woman, became intimate with the corpse before cutting her body parts (including tongue, fingers, breasts, womb and brains) and sucked her blood as part of the ritual process (Ibid). The body parts were reportedly sold to a local businessman who wanted to enhance his supermarket and grinding mill businesses (Ibid).

In February 2007, a man from Murimbika Village, under Chief Dandawa in Karoi District, allegedly killed his nine–year- old son and sold his body parts for ritual purposes (Sachiti, 2015). The man fatally struck his son with an iron bar and sold one of his ears and blood for

Z\$40 million to strangers who needed the parts for ritual purposes (Ibid). Adding to the above incidents, between November and December 2010, three women and a seven-month-old baby were killed in the Stanmore area, near Gwanda Town and their breasts and private parts were cut off in a suspected ritual murder (Nkala, 2014).

Apart from the above, in July 2011, the *Newsday* reported that Masvingo City had been rocked by a spate of suspected ritual murders which led the Masvingo United Residents and Ratepayers Association to hold a meeting with the police in which they demanded the law-enforcement agents to investigate and stop the practice. Prior to this meeting, several incidents in Masvingo had been reported where children or adults were found dead with missing body parts and the general belief among the residents was that the body parts were being sold in South Africa (Maponga, 2012).

In 2010, a married couple from Masvingo's Mucheke Suburb was arrested after they allegedly gave away their seven-year-old son to suspected ritual murderers (*Newsday*, 15 July 2011). In June 2011, a nine-year-old deaf and dumb child, was abducted in Masvingo and went missing for about a week before his corpse was found floating in the Mucheke River (Maponga, 2012). In 2011 again, a 26 year old man from Masvingo's Rujeko Suburb went missing for three days and his body was also found floating in Mucheke River with his lips, ears and nose missing (Maponga, 2012; *Newsday*, 15 July 2011). In another suspected ritual murder, in January 2012, a 19-month-old toddler was abducted while playing outside as her mother was asleep in a house in Masvingo and the dead body was found four days later (*The Standard*, 14 January 2012).

Furthermore, in September 2012, seven people were murdered for rituals in Chinamhora Communal Area near Domboshawa north of Harare in a period of two weeks. Five of them were killed during the same night and their genitals and other body parts were sliced off (*Daily News*, 19 September 2012). In October 2013, two men from Matabeleland South Province were arrested together with their female neighbour for poisoning their six-year-old niece for ritual purposes (Dube, 2013). The two men allegedly hired their female neighbour to kill their brother's daughter in return for a beast, indicating that they wanted to use the body for ritual purposes (*Ibid*).

112

After being promised a beast, woman tricked the girl into drinking a 500-millilitre bottle of a cattle-dipping chemical under the pretext that it was milk and she died a few hours the same day (*Ibid*).

In another ritual murder in February 2014, a 16-year-old pupil from Murowa Village under Chief Nyamweda in the Mhondoro Communal Lands was fatally axed and her body parts were mutilated, allegedly for ritual purposes (Kuvirimirwa, 2014). The incident took place soon after a nine-year-old pupil from the same community had escaped murder with deep wounds on her throat after a man allegedly pounced on her in December 2013. The assailant fled upon noticing that people had seen him (*Ibid*).

Similarly, on 8 April 2014, a two-year-old girl went missing in the town of Marondera and was found dead on 20 April, with her private parts and right leg missing (Dembedza, 2014). Again, in October 2014, a man from Binga District in northern Zimbabwe killed his wife in an act of suspected ritual murder (Ncube, 2014). The man who was a fisherman had allegedly visited a traditional healer in Zambia to look for *juju* to increase his catch of fish and he was instructed to kill his wife and bring her head for ritual purposes (Ncube, 2014). He reportedly beheaded his wife and put her head in a cardboard box (*Ibid*). After committing the crime, he took his two minor children to his parents' home where he intended to leave them before he could proceed to Zambia but when he returned home he found neighbours gathered at his homestead because they had heard some screams. He was subsequently arrested (*Ibid*).

In July 2015, a four-year-old Grade Zero pupil from Insiza District was found dead with her lips, liver and other body parts missing in a suspected case of ritual murder (Tshili, 2015). In a similar event, on 4 December 2015, a businessman from Mt Darwin District was brutally murdered by three men from the Dotito Communal Lands. The men allegedly removed his scalp, left eye and ear in a suspected case of ritual killings (Laiton, 2016).

In July 2016, a four-year-old boy from the city of Gweru was found dead in a gum plantation near Mkoba Suburb with some missing body parts (Ngwenya, 2016). The body, which had missing limps and a damaged skull, was burnt beyond recognition, raising suspicion that the child could have been murdered for ritual purposes (*Ibid*).

Similarly, on 3 February 2017, a 26-year-old man from Glengarry Suburb in Bulawayo was arrested and remanded in custody charged with two accounts of murder, one of which was linked to ritual purposes (Masara, 2017). The man allegedly killed his 30-year-old friend and severed his body parts which he handed over to a South African-based *Sangoma* (traditional healer) in return for US$20 000 and a Toyota Quantum vehicle (*Ibid*). Later, the killer allegedly opened up to a close friend about the murder. When he noticed that his friend could not stomach the disturbing news, he also killed him in an effort to conceal the crime (*Ibid*).

During the same month, a 22–year- old man from Chivi District allegedly killed his 12-year-old brother and dumped his body in a public toilet in what was believed to be a ritual to get rich and find a beautiful woman to marry (Mswazie, 2017). When interrogated by the police, the murderer claimed that he had been instructed by his ancestors in a vision to kill his younger brother in order to get instant riches and a beautiful wife (*Ibid*).

Furthermore, in April 2017, a 41-year-old man and his 42-year-old girlfriend appeared in court for kidnapping and murdering a six-year-old boy from the town of Norton (*NewZimbabwe*, 21 April 2017). The body of the boy was found on 13 April dumped in a small river in a farm in the Msengezi area near Chegutu Town, without eyes and intestines and other body parts (*Ibid*).

Again, in April 2017, a 12-year-old girl from Hwange went missing for 12 days and was later found dead with her private parts and tongue missing (Masara, 2017). In a similar event, in June 2017, a 22-year-old Gwanda man was arrested for killing a mentally-ill and homeless man and severing his head and private parts for ritual purposes after being promised US$25 000 (Muponde, 2017). After he committed the murder, he sent a message from his phone out to a South African number which read "*Isitshebo sesi ready* (the relish is ready)" (*Ibid*).

Similarly, in July 2017, a Karoi man appeared in court for allegedly killing his dump and deaf sister after he had been promised US$4 000 by a local businessman (Mangirazi, 2017). The victim's severed head was recovered a few metres away from the businessman's shop who reportedly needed it to conduct rituals to boost his businesses (Ibid). All these cases are a clear demonstration that ritual killings are still pervasive in present-day Zimbabwe. Thus, given all the above cases, it is clear that ritual killings are still pervasive in Zimbabwe.

Triggers of human sacrifice in Zimbabwe

Since ritual murder is no longer existent in many societies across the globe, it is important to examine some of the major reasons why this practice is still prevalent in Africa in general and Zimbabwe in particular. There are major factors that trigger the increase in ritual killings in Zimbabwe and many other African societies despite its severe condemnation by the law. Perlmutter (2003) asserts that the need to perform such acts can be cultural, sexual, economic, psychological and/or spiritual. In Zimbabwe, although the causes appear to be multifaceted and diverse, poverty and unemployment seem to be the major driving forces behind this scenario. The majority of the aforementioned incidents of ritual killings reveal that the murderers (in most cases the youth) who harvested body parts were promised money and other material things.

Ezeh (2011) posits that poverty and unemployment are the hydra-headed monsters that have led many young people into ritual killing, membership of secret cults, armed robbery, kidnapping, drug trafficking, financial crimes and prostitution, among others. Xiong (2015) argues that unemployment causes poverty and poverty causes crime. Thus, ritual killings in Zimbabwe can be seen as an effort by some people to deal with the problems of poverty and unemployment. According to the Kenya National Assembly Official Record (2009), the opening up of opportunities for the youth is the only way to ensure that they are not tempted to become members of criminal gangs. Thus, the lower the unemployment levels, the lower the poverty levels, and the lower the rate of ritual killings.

However, though unemployment and high poverty levels can be cited as the major triggers of ritual killings in Zimbabwe, there are also other contributing factors which need to be taken into account.

Greed for instant wealth and business enhancement are also contributing factors as evidenced by some of the ritual murders discussed earlier in this chapter. Through instructions from traditional healers, business people hire murderers to harvests body parts to boost their businesses. According to Behrend (2009), ritual killings just like Satanism, witchcraft and cannibalism, can be seen as contradictory effects of global capitalism and the culture of neoliberalism.

Adding to the above, strong superstitious beliefs also play a contributory role to ritual murder cases in many societies. Mbogoni (2013) states that in Africa, the supernatural conforms itself to the faith people have, like people elsewhere, about the way their lives can be negatively or positively influenced by extra human forces. African traditional religion, which is strongly embedded in norms and beliefs, has a strong influence in the practice of ritual killings. From this perspective, it becomes clear that Africa is not only backward in the economic arena but also in terms of beliefs, norms and values.

According to Pearson (2011), human sacrifice is widespread at a fairly primitive level of society, but as societies advance, it generally dies out or becomes sublimated into some form of symbolic sacrifice. This validates modernisation theorists' common notion that developing countries need to abandon their traditional and primitive norms and values and beliefs and replace them with modern ones (Todaro and Smith, 2011). Thus, there is a correlation between a country's level of development and the beliefs, norms and traditions of its people.

Susceptibility to ritual murder

Although anyone can be a victim of ritual murder, there are categories of people who are more vulnerable to this practice. The susceptibility to ritual murder is mainly caused by two factors. Firstly, the victim may be considered to possess the characteristics/ features desired by the murderers or those who want to perform the ritual (Ngubane, 1986). For this reason, victims are carefully chosen (Vincent, 2008). For instance, children's body parts such as the head are mainly prescribed for a failing business to resuscitate (Vincent,

2008). This superstitious belief stems from idea that children have long life to come, hence using their body parts will enable the business to thrive for a long time (*Ibid*).

Secondly, people who are physically weak usually fall prey to the killers. This group of people include children, women, the elderly, people with disabilities, people with mental challenges and the sick (African Commission on Human and People's Rights, 2010**)**. Most of these people often lack the physical strength that is required to fight or defend themselves from the perpetrators.

Research has shown that women are physically weaker than men (Warburton, 1998; Ireland and Company, 2002; Ebbe, 2005; Zeigler and Gunderson, 2005). For children and the mentally challenged, it is even worse because they can be easily tricked. Ebbe (2005) states that children can easily be deceived and made to believe that a certain act is normal. Predators who target children know that they offer little or no resistance, are innocent and have not yet reached the use of common reason (*Black Belt Magazine*, 2000; Ebbe, 2005). Just like children, older people have diminished physical strength and stamina, hence they are less able to defend themselves or escape from threatening situations (Levin and Bourne, 1999). The elderly are more likely to suffer from physical ailments such as loss of hearing or vision (*Ibid*) and this increases their vulnerability to ritual murder. Older people are more likely to live alone and social isolation increases their vulnerability to criminals (Smith, 1979). All these different groups of people who are vulnerable have been evident in cases of ritual killings in Zimbabwe.

Ritual murder as a human rights violation

From a human rights perspective, ritual murder is a violation of the right to life which is enshrined in the 1948 Universal Declaration of Human Rights. Closely related to the above, Article 5 of the African Charter on Human and People's Rights which Zimbabwe and many other African countries are signatories to, states that every individual shall be "entitled to respect for his life and the integrity of his person" (African Charter on Human and Peoples Rights, 1986). Article 8 of the same charter states that: "There should be freedom of conscience, the profession and free practice of religion shall be guaranteed and that no one may, subject to law and order, be submitted to measures restricting the exercise of these freedoms" (African Charter on Human and Peoples Rights, 1986).

However, the existence of this right does not render ritual killings legal. Thus, killing a human being for ritual purposes can be regarded as an abuse of religious freedom. While 'ritual' is a religious performance which cannot be regarded as a crime or something bad, 'ritual murder' is by contrast immoral and illegal (La Fontaine, 2011).

What even sounds awkward about the whole scenario is that the agents who kill people for rituals are promised money ranging from as little as US$4 000 to $20 000, yet there is nothing on earth that has a value equivalent to human life. Greed for money and wealth, therefore, sometimes forces people to do unimaginable things in Zimbabwe and many African countries.

In addition to the above, it is important to note that the ritual killing of people differs from that of animals primarily because of the significance we attach to human life (Steel, 1995). Even in the ancient world, it was again the most extreme form of sacrifice of a living creature (Kyle, 1998). Murder is ethically, religiously and morally wrong. In Christianity, murder in general and ritual killings in particular is also condemned. In the Bible, murder is condemned and it is the sixth out of the ten commandments that were given to Moses by God at Mount Sinai that were supposed to be obeyed by the Israelites (Exodus 20:13). Even in the modern day, the Ten Commandments still play an important role in shaping the norms and values of the Christian world. In the Old Testament, prophets denounced human sacrifice as one of the heinous sins that contributed to the fall of Israel and Judah (Jeremiah 7:31-34; Hosea 6:6-11). Bromiley (1988) avers that although human sacrifice did take place in Israel, it was considered an execrable aspect of Yahweh worship. Thus, ritual murder is a worst form of sacrifice which goes against the ethical and moral values of many societies.

Psychological and socio-economic impacts of ritual killings

Ritual killings have social, economic, emotional, psychological and cultural implications to the victims' families and friends as well as communities. Deakin *et al* (2012) assert that the unexpected death of a close relative or friend may cause post-traumatic stress disorder. In the same line of argument, (Miller, 2006) posits that the death of a parent or other close relative from any cause has a special impact on children. He further states that death that is sudden and unexpected leaves no chance to say goodbye or to take care of unfinished business and it leaves children with feelings of horror. As with all untimely death, children must cope with the loss of the parent and the disruptions in family routines, living standards and family roles that this entails (Ibid). In addition, the death of a parent or care-giver increases the incidents of child-headed households and foster parenting, thereby making children susceptible to poverty as well as emotional and physical abuse.

Ritual killings also have negative health repercussions on the victims' families. Research has shown that there is a correlation between stressful events and malignant diseases such as cancer (Dalton and Johansen, 2005; Walker *et al*, 2005). For instance, many studies have found an association between death of a husband or of close relative or friend and increased risk of breast cancer (Dalton and Johansen, 2005; Walker *et al*, 2005; Friis, 2010; Johansen, 2015). These studies suggest that such stressful life events may influence breast cancer onset through endocrinological and immunological mechanisms (Walker *et al*, 2005). Thus, given the painful, unexpected and untimely death caused by ritual murder, the stress may be severe to the bereaved families, implying that the chances of breast cancer may be high among the widows left behind as compared to death caused by sickness.

At the community level, the murder of a single person or many people may cause residents of that particular community to live in fear and horror. Ritual killings impede people from effectively participating in social and economic activities in their societies. For instance, since many children are kidnapped and killed on their way to and from school, some children will be afraid of going to school alone because they do not want to be victims as well. This scenario may lead to unnecessary absenteeism and drop outs. In certain circumstances, parents and guardians will be obliged to accompany their children to school, leaving behind other duties and activities which help to sustain their lives. In the rural areas, for example, farming activities which are the backbone of rural economies are negatively affected.

Furthermore, due to ritual killings, people (especially adults) may fail to efficiently execute their duties. Women, for example, may be afraid to fetch firewood or water for domestic use since they will be scared of falling prey to the murderers. By so doing, they will fail to perform their household chores effectively. From a social perspective, memories and fear of ritual killings in communities may lead to lack of participation in social gatherings and events such as church services, funerals and other ceremonies as people will be afraid of being murdered on the their way.

Conclusion

This chapter has looked at the causes and effects of ritual killings in Zimbabwe, drawing examples from different provinces and districts of the country. It started by tracing the history of ritual killings across the globe, citing specific regions in the world where such kind of murders were practiced during the ancient times. It also highlighted other African countries where cases of this practice are still rampant in the modern era. These countries include Nigeria, Uganda, Burundi, Tanzania, Malawi, Zambia, Lesotho and South Africa. The reasons why ritual killings were and/are practiced in Africa and beyond have been well articulated. The chapter has found out that in the present times, ritual murder is triggered by economic crises and the greed for sudden riches which are embedded in strong superstitious beliefs held by many African societies. The study argues that ritual killings are a gross violation of human rights, particularly the right to life.

Since incidents of ritual killings are increasing in Zimbabwe, there is need for awareness campaigns against ritual murder. Arresting the murderers alone is not a sufficient strategy. People need to be conscientised that business enhancement and riches cannot be brought about by killing fellow humans. Stiffer penalties should be applied to the perpetrators to convey a message that ritual murder is an inhuman and barbaric practice which is intolerable in the modern era. Harsh penalties should also be meted out to the traditional healers who provide people with wrong solutions to their problems. The business people and other groups of people who send their agents to kill innocent souls for rituals should also be arrested. Thus, the eradication of the prevalence of ritual killings in the country requires a holistic approach which does not only focus on the murderers but all the citizens.

References

African Commission on Human and People's Rights, (2010) *Ritual killing and human sacrifice in Africa*, African Commission on Human and People's Rights, Banjul.

Arp, R. (2013) *1001 ideas that changed the way we think*, Atria Books: New York.

Behrend, H. (2009) 'The rise of occult powers, AIDS and the Roman Catholic Church in western Uganda,' In: Becker, F. Geissler, P.W. (Eds.), *AIDS and religious practice in Africa*, Boston: BRILL.

Black Belt Magazine, 20-24 September 2000.

Bromiley, G.W. (1988) *The International Standard Bible Encyclopaedia*, Michigan: Eerdmans Publishing.

Carrasco, D. (2012) *The Aztecs: A very short introduction*, Oxford: Oxford University Press.

Carrosco, D. and Sessions, C. (1998) *Daily Life of the Aztecs: People of the Sun and Earth*, West Port: Greenwood Publishing Group.

Dalton, S. O. and Johansen, C. (2005) 'Stress and cancer: The critical research,' in: Cooper, C.L. (ed), *Handbook of stress medicine and health*, Second Edition, Boca Raton: CRC Press.

Daily News, (19 September 2012) 'Five killed in ritual murders', Available at: https://www.dailynews.co.zw/articles, Accessed 6 February 2017.

Deakin, S. *et al*, (2012) *Markesinis and Deakin's tort law*, Oxford University Press: Oxford.

Dube, L. (10 March 2017), 'Woman killed for rituals …Killers sleep with corpse…. move part of ritual murder, Available at: http://manicapost.co.zw, Accessed 10 April 2017.

Dube, S. (26 October 2013), 'Gruesome murder… Girl (6) killed for ritual purposes,' Available at: http://www.chronicle.co.zw, Accessed 12 April 2017.

Ebbe, O. N. I., (2009) 'Causes of criminal and non-criminal abuses of women and children,' in: Ebbe, O. N. I. and Das, D. K. (Eds.) *Criminal abuse of women and children: An international perspective,* Boca Raton: CRC Press.

Ezeh, A. J. (2011) *Secrets for endless wealth: Life-changing book*, Central Milton Keynes: Author House.

Friis, R. H. (2010) *Epidemiology 101*, Sudbury: Jones and Bartlett Learning.

Gaines, J. M. (2000) 'Birthing nations,' In: Hjort, M. and Mackenzie, S. (eds.) *Cinema and nation*, Routledge: New York.

Iadicola, P. and Shupe, A. (2013) *Violence, inequality and human freedom,* 3rd Edition, Lanham: Rowman and Littlefield Publication.

Ireland, J. L. and Company, J. W. T. (2002) *Bullying among prisoners: Evidence, research and intervention strategies*, Routledge: New York.

Jacob, I. (2013) *Higher truth*, Bloomington: Author House.

Jenkins, P. (1994) *Using murder: The social construction of serial homicide,* De Aldine Gruyter: Berlin.

Kansal, A. (2012) *The evolution of gods: The scientific origin of divinity and religion*, New York: Harper Collins.

Kastenbaum, R. (2016) *Death, society and human experience*, 11th Edition, New York: Routledge.

Kenya National Assembly Official Record (Hansard), Wednesday 18 November 2009.

Kyle, D. G. (1998) *Spectacles of death in ancient Rome*, New York: Routledge.

La Fontaine, J. (March 2011) 'Ritual Murder' Open Anthropology Cooperative Press, Interventions Series Number 3.

Laiton, C. (9 April 2016) 'Businessman killed for ritual purposes', Available at: https://www.newsday.co.zw, Accessed 21 June 2017.

Larr, F. (2013) *Africa's diabolical entrapment: Exploring the negative impact of Christianity, supervision and witchcraft on psychological structural and scientific growth in Black Africa*, Bloomington: Author House.

Lewis, B. R. (2001) *Ritual sacrifice: An illustrated history*, Stroud: Sutton.

Levin, J. and Bourme, R. (1999) *Social problems: Causes, consequences, interventions*, Boston: Roxbury.

Mangirazi, N., 19 July 2017. 'Tempers flare at Karoi ritual murder funeral', Available at: https://www.newsday.co.zw, Accessed 28 August 2017.

Maponga, G. (15 February 2012) 'Masvingo: Zim's murder capital', Available at: http://www.herald.co.zw/masvingo-zims-murder-capital/, Accessed 20 May 2017.

Masara, W. (15 February 2017) 'Jindu killed to harvest body parts on SA *inyanga's* instruction', Available at: http://www.chronicle.co.zw, Accessed 11 June 2017.

Masara, W. (18 May 2017) 'Body of missing 5-year-old found without private parts' Available at: http://www.chronicle.co.zw, Accessed 9 July 2017.

Mason, J. (2005) *An unnatural order: The roots of our destruction of nature*, Lantern Books: New York.

Mayor, J. S. and Cook, C.S. (2016) *Ancient China: A history*, Taylor and Francis: New York.

Mbogoni, L. E. Y. (2013) *Human sacrifice and the supernatural in Africa*, Mkuki na Nyota Publishers Ltd: Dar es Salaam.

Meyer, M. (2014) *Thicker than water: The origins of blood as symbol and ritual*, Routledge: New York.

Miller, L. (2006) *Practical police psychology: Stress management and crisis intervention for law enforcement*, Charles, C. Thomas Publishers Ltd: Illinois.

Moczar, D. (2013) *The church under attack: Five hundred years that split the church and scattered the flock*, Sophia Institute Press: Manchester.

Mswazie, W. (17 February 2017) 'Another ritual killing! Man kills brother to get rich', Available at: http://www.chronicle.co.zw, Accessed 7 May 2017.

Muponde, R. (26 June 2017) 'Gwanda 'ritual' murder. . .Suspect promised $25k for body parts, sends chilling SMS to SA number', Available at: http://www.chronicle.co.zw, Accessed 11 November 2017.

Ncube, L. (13 October 2014) 'Binga man could have killed wife for ritual purposes', Available at: http://www.chronicle.co.zw, Accessed 15 April 2017.

Nemet-Nejat, K.R. (1998) *Daily life in Ancient Mesopotamia*, London: Greenwood Press.

Newsday, (15 July 2011) 'Ritual murders rock Masvingo', Available at: https://www.newsday.co.zw, Accessed 6 February 2017.

NewZimbabwe, (21 April 2017) 'Duo in court over ritual killing of boy aged six', Available at: http://www.newzimbabwe.com/news-36813, Accessed 10 November 2017.

Ngwenya, N. (9 July 2016) 'Suspected body of missing Gweru boy found with missing parts', Available at: http://www.masvingomirror.com, Accessed 10 August 2017.

Nkala, S. (10 October 2016) 'Ritual' murder resumes', Available at: https://www.southerneye.co.zw, Accessed 22 November 2017.

Nwachindu, V and Ihediwa, N. (2017) 'Traditional burial rites and Christianity in culture clash: Focus on Mgbowo community, Enugu state,' in: Bewaji, J.A.I. *et al* (Eds.) *The humanities and the dynamics of African culture in the 21st century*, Cambridge Scholars Publishing, Newcastle.

Organisation of African Unity, (1986) African Charter on Human and Peoples Rights, Available at: http://www.achpr.org/files/instruments/achpr/banjul_charter.pdf, Accessed 23 March 2018.

Pearson, J. (2011) *Arena: The story of Colosseum*, Bloomsbury Reader: London.

Perlmutter, D. (2003) *Investigating religious terrorism and ritualistic crimes*, CRC Press: New York.

Quigley, C. (2013) *The corpse: A history,* McFarland and Company Publishers: North Carolina.

Sachiti, R. (13 June 2015). 'Shocking tale of a killer dad,' Available at: http://www.herald.co.zw, Accessed 22 May 2017.

Selin, H. (1997) *Encyclopaedia of the History of Science, Technology, and Medicine in Non-Western Cultures*, Springer Science and Business Media: New York.

Shelly, L. (2010) *Human trafficking: A global perspective*, Cambridge University Press: Cambridge.

Smith, J. R. (1979) *Crime against the elderly: Implications for policy makers and practitioners*, University of Michigan: Michigan.

Standard, (14 January 2012) 'Fear grips town as ritual murders rock Masvingo,' Available at: https://www.thestandard.co.zw, Accessed 22 June 2017.

Stapelberg, M. (2014) *Strange but true: A historical background to popular beliefs and traditions*, Crux Publishing Ltd: Horley.

Strenski, I. (2008) *Durkheim and the Jews of France*, University of Chicago Press: Chicago.

Te Velde, H. (2007) 'Human sacrifice in Ancient Egypt', in: Bremmer, J.N. (ed.) *The strange world of human sacrifice*, Peeters Publishers: Leuven.

Todaro, M. P. and Smith S. C. (2011) *Economic development,* 10th Edition, Essex: Pearson Education Limited.

Tort, C. (2017) *Day of wrath*, Morrisville: Lulu.com.

Tshili, N. (24 July 2015) 'Ritual murder…Grade Zero girl, 4, found with body parts missing', Available at: http://www.chronicle.co.zw/ritual-murder-grade-zero-girl-4-found-with-body-parts-missing/, Accessed 11 April 2017.

Vincent, L. (2008) 'New magic for new times: *Muti* murder in Democratic South Africa,' in: *Tribes and Tribals*, Special Volume, Number 2, pp. 43-53.

Walker, L.G. *et al*, (2005) 'Psychoneuroimmunology and chronic malignment: cancer,' in: Vedhara, K. and Irwin, M. R. (Eds.) *Human psychoneuroimmunology,* Oxford University Press: Oxford.

Warburton, N. (1998) *Thinking from A to Z,* Routledge: New York.

Wasyliw, P. H. (2008) *Martyrdom, murder and magic: Child saints and their cults in Medieval Europe*, New York: Peter Lang: New York.

Woolf, G. (2015) 'Ritual traditions of non-Mediterranean Europe', in: Raja, R. and Rupke, J. (Eds.) *A companion to the archaeology of religion in the ancient world,* John Wiley and Sons: West Sussex.

Xiong, H. (2015) *Urban crime and social disorganization in China: A case study of three communities in Guangzhou*, Springer: New York.

Zeigler, S. L. and Gunderson, G. G. (2005) *Moving beyond G.I. Jane: Women and the U.S. Military*, University Press of America: Langham.

Chapter 7

Victims of Frelimo and Renamo Brutality: The Ndau People of Mossurize District of Mozambique, 1976-2017

James Hlongwana

Introduction

In 1975, Mozambicans jumped skywards in celebration of the country's independence from Portuguese colonial rule. The independence followed a bloody and protracted liberation struggle prosecuted largely by the Front for the Liberation of Mozambique (FRELIMO) under the leadership of Eduardo Chivambo Mondlane and later Samora Moises Machel. However, the independence euphoria quickly ended when the Resistencia Nacional Mocambicana (RENAMO), a political outfit trained and armed by the Rhodesian Government, declared war on Mozambique's ruling FRELIMO government in 1976 (Hlongwana, 2018) .

Despite the Rome Accord of 1992 which brought FRELIMO and RENAMO to the negotiation table and ended the war, there has been a resurgence of civil war since 2012. Among other things, RENAMO demands to exercise authority at local levels in all the areas where it won majority votes (Hanlon, 2015). The civilian population has been in a dilemma as the belligerents have taken the war to the countryside. While RENAMO employs terror to force the civilian population into submissive posture, FRELIMO implements counter-insurgency tactics against the same population. It is alleged that FRELIMO has committed more human rights violations than RENAMO (Dingane, 2017).

Both parties have resorted to murder, looting and destruction of homes and animals. To avoid capture and subsequent loss of life, many people have taken refuge either in forests, mountains and steep-sided river valleys or in neighbouring Zimbabwe, leaving their property and animals at the mercy of FRELIMO and RENAMO soldiers (Mafika, 2017). By 2017, the Mossurize District countryside resembled a virtually deserted region with sporadic gunfire as part of the order of the day (Mutukweni, 2016). The chapter traces the origins of the Mozambican civil war and highlights the FRELIMO-RENAMO reign of terror against the civilian Ndau population in the Mossurize District. In the final analysis the study argues that the Ndau people have needlessly been caught in the crossfire of a political conflict between FRELIMO and RENAMO.

The study employed qualitative research techniques to collect data. These were oral interviews and textual analysis. Semi-structured interviews were conducted with displaced Mozambicans currently living in Zimbabwe. Document analysis involved the study of secondary sources of information such as published books, journal articles and electronic media sources. The data that was collected was interpreted and analysed qualitatively.

The historical dimensions of the FRELIMO-NDAU political conflict

This section discusses the growth of political tension between the FRELIMO (both as a liberation movement and later as a ruling party) with the Ndau people found to the north of the Save River in Mozambique. This helps to situate the growth patterns of the political tension between the two. Mozambicans fought a vicious ten-year long liberation war and gained independence in1975 from the Portuguese who had ruled the country for about 500 years (Turshen, 2001). Following estranged relations between Mozambique and Rhodesia, the Ian Smith-led Rhodesian government created a bandit movement known as RENAMO to attack Mozambique which had offered bases to the Zimbabwe African National Liberation Army (ZANLA) (Finnegarn, 1992). ZANLA was the military wing of the Zimbabwe African National Union (ZANU), one of the two largest African nationalist movements for the liberation of Zimbabwe. Mozambique's support for Zimbabwe's freedom fighters included the closure of the border with Rhodesia, training of ZANLA combatants, provision of weapons as FRELIMO had just concluded its war with the Portuguese and active participation in the Rhodesian war against Rhodesia(Pandya,1987). In addition to training and arming, the Rhodesians used to pay RENAMO rebels a regular monthly salary and an additional bonus for every successful operation against either FRELIMO or ZANLA (Taju, 1988).

RENAMO was initially under the command of Andre Matsangaisse who died when he attempted to attack a FRELIMO fortress in 1979 and was replaced by Afonso Dhlakama (Morgan, 1990). After Zimbabwe had gained independence in 1980, RENAMO relocated to South Africa where it received sponsorship in the form of training and logistical support from the Apartheid government of that country. South Africa was opposed to Mozambique's adoption of socialism and the support it was giving to South African liberation movements such as the African Nation Congress (ANC) (Turshen 2001). In its early days, RENAMO carried out sabotage activities, while occasionally it attacked both FRELIMO and ZANLA positions (Young, 1989)

To gain domestic and international sympathy, Dhlakama and RENAMO portrayed themselves as nationalists who were fighting to liberate Mozambicans from communist domination and oppression (*Renamo Bulletin*, 1983: Number 14). RENAMO also blamed the Mozambican Government for excluding other groups in governance and for pursuing policies that were ethnically biased (*Ibid*). It, therefore, argued for proportional representation in government, the holding of regular, free and fair elections and the abandonment of a command economy (Young, 1989).

RENAMO further exploited people's grievances with the FRELIMO government. Hoile, quoted in Chingono (1996) argues that FRELIMO's miscalculations contributed to the outbreak and progression of the civil war. He further contends that RENAMO was/is a genuine popular movement and the civil war was a *bona fide* war (Chingono, 1996). In support of RENAMO were some traditional chiefs who had a bone to chew with FRELIMO after being forced to relinquish their authority to government-appointed officials who in many cases were not familiar with local customs (Morgan, 1990). Further, compulsory villagisation (*aldeiacommunais*) alienated FRELIMO from the ordinary people in Mozambique (Hlongwana, 2018). Broadly, many people were less willing to leave their traditional home areas for the *aldeiacommunais* (Dinerman, 1994). Perreira argues that FRELIMO adopted villagisation as a ploy to exercise political control over the people rather than to initiate an agricultural revolution through collective agriculture (Perreira, 1999). However, Lorgen (1999) contends that the government set up communal villages in order to manage the redistribution of scarce resources and services to the peasants. However, Machel, who wanted to please his communist handlers such as China and Russia, adopted socialism as a guiding ideology. The result was chaos in the country's economy (Daniel, 2016). The new currency (*meticais*) was rendered useless by high-inflation while commodities disappeared from government-owned shops (Hlongwana, 2018, Mudhaniso, 2016).

Given these prevailing post-independence socio-economic challenges, Mozambican Ndau resorted to crossing the border to Rhodesia to get basic commodities as the country's populist policies had destroyed the economy. However, many of the Ndau people who attempted to survive through these cross-border pursuits were killed in the border area by landmines which had been planted by the Rhodesian soldiers to minimise the infiltration of Zimbabwean freedom fighters into Zimbabwe from Mozambique during Zimbabwe's war of liberation (Hlongwana, 2018).

In addition to the above, RENAMO also capitalised on FRELIMO's attitude on religion and tradition (Morgan, 1990). FRELIMO's determination to oppose all types of religion, age-old practices such as polygamy was motivated by the desire to modernise "backward-looking" Mozambicans and to get rid of practices and institutions that were closely associated with the Portuguese colonial government (Morgan, 1990:613). It is important, however, to note that some of FRELIMO's post-independence policies were meant to effect positive transformation (Manyoni, 2016). Among others, were the government's efforts to force people to use toilets, to stop the wearing of traditional mini–skirts, popularly known among the Ndau as *Chichakati/girigidera,* and its opposition to alcoholism, which, however, found little purchase among the Ndau (Hlongwana, 2018).

President Machel became particularly unpopular among Ndau men who could not stomach attempts to ban the consumption of home-brewed beers notably, *kachasu*/*nipa, chikeke* and others (Mafika, 2017). In spite of the allegation that such beers were a danger to health and sexual fertility, the local population had no substitutes as the commercially-brewed beers such as *vinho* and *cerveja* were expensive to buy. Women on the other hand argued that *girigidera*, unlike other dress apparels, enhanced their beauty in the eyes of men. While the above policies were intended to transform the Mozambican society, some commentators suggest that they should have been gradually introduced to prevent a backlash from tradition (Hlongwana, 2018, Muzondi, 2016).

There is also an ethnic dimension to the Ndau-FRELIMO conflict. The southerners, who happened to dominate FRELIMO politics, blamed the Ndau for witchcraft and mental incorrigibility while on the other hand the Ndau accused the southerners of displaying a disdainful attitude towards them (Chingono, 1996). The Ndau appeared to have a case as provinces north of the Save River had/have not had many chances at leadership of FRELIMO. To this extent the first three leaders of FRELIMO, two of whom became Presidents of the Republic of Mozambique, all came from the south: Eduardo Chivambo (Inhambane), Samora Moises Machel (Gaza) and Joaquim Alberto Chissano (Gaza) (Hlongwana, 2018, Chisiwa, 2017). Undeniably, southerners tend to have an upper hand over other ethnic formations because they benefited more from the Portuguese colonial system (Sumich, 2005).

In addition, many Ndau people blamed Samora Machel and his compatriots from the south of hijacking the revolution from a deserving Ndau man, Urias Simango, who, according to the FRELIMO's hierarchical structure should have become the president of the liberation movement when Mondlane was killed by a parcel bomb in 1969 (Chichava, 2010). However, many Ndau alleged that Simango was falsely accused of complicity in the assassination and subsequently expelled from FRELIMO (Mubango, 2016). As if the expulsion was not enough, Simango was arrested in 1974, abducted and executed in secret together with his wife allegedly on the orders of FRELIMO (Guilengue, 2014). It is, thus, clear and undeniable that the expulsion and the subsequent assassination of Simango drove a wedge between the Ndauand FRELIMO (Cahen, 1999).

Furthermore, RENAMO exploited the perceived labour conflict between the FRELIMO government and the Ndau. Since the discovery of minerals in South Africa in the 1860s, the Ndau, like other Mozambicans, had been working in South African firms and mines (Harington, *et al*, 2004). However, immediately after Mozambique had become independent, South Africa reduced the number of workers it recruited from Mozambique. It was a calculated move to create economic problems since, in addition to providing employment to thousands of Mozambicans, the Mozambican economy benefitted from remittances from South Africa (Napoleao, 2008). The result was that many Ndau people lost their jobs in South Africa and most of them did not appreciate that the loss of employment was a consequence of regional political dynamics. However, as Napoleao (2008) argues, the decision to reduce the recruitment of workers from Mozambique had other causes such as internalisation of labour and mechanisation of mines (Napoleao, 2008).What irked the Ndau most was the realisation that in spite of the reduction of the number of Mozambican workers that South Africa could employ from Mozambique, Mozambicans from southern provinces such as Maputo, Inhambane and Gaza continued to work in South Africa with the blessing of the FRELIMO Government. The loss of jobs by the Ndau and preferential treatment regarding recruitment of job-seekers from the south motivated the Ndau to support RENAMO (Shabhani, 2017).

Regarding the resurgence of the conflict since 2010, RENAMO accuses FRELIMO of running a warped political and economic system which disadvantages all those outside FRELIMO structures. Dhlakama argues that FRELIMO's political and economic governance strategy since the 1992 Peace Accord systematically isolates RENAMO and the generality of Mozambican population (Shikani, 2012). Broadly, RENAMO demands three major reforms. First, it wants its members to have greater representation and participation in government institutions which are currently dominated by FRELIMO. In particular, it wants greater inclusion of its former combatants in the country's army (Azevedo-Harman, 2015). However, an observer commented that FRELIMO is unlikely to allow access to RENAMO to institutions of power and authority because of the latter's unpredictability (Mutendeni, 2016). Secondly, it alleges that the electoral system is not transparent enough to guarantee flawless democratic processes in the country. Here, it demands greater representation in government in order to veto election outcomes when FRELIMO tampers with electoral processes. Thirdly, RENAMO asks for an equitable share of the country's natural resources (Shikani, 2012). Renamo complains that FRELIMO is keeping spoils of the country's wealth to itself and Dhlakama once described the former President of Mozambique, Armando Guebuza, as "robber-in- chief of public funds" (Mambondiani, 2012: 1).

Closely related to the above RENAMO demands is the issue of autonomy in regions where it won majority votes (Brueno, 2015).The proposal carefully follows the current Mozambican practice of dual administration for the elected municipal governments, where there is an elected assembly and president (mayor) and district administrators. While FRELIMO argues that devolution of power would undermine national unity, RENAMO maintains that decentralisation would ensure justice as parties would exercise power where they command popularity (Hanlon, 2015). Moreover, RENAMO asserts that devolution of power would eliminate ills that are caused by the "the winner takes all" political model which divides the nation into winners and losers thereby sowing the seeds of conflict. RENAMO further attacks the "winner takes all" political paradigm because not only does it result in wasted votes but empowers the "winners" to introduce policies aimed at the pursuance of selfish political agendas at the expense of building national unity (Dingane, 2017). However, while devolution of powers could act as a panacea to the country's political ills, FRELIMO argues that the demand is a ploy by RENAMO to dominate provincial governments north of the Save River where it won majority votes (Dzinesa, *et al*, 2013).

RENAMO's reign of terror

This section examines RENAMO's *modus operandi* in the civil war. RENAMO's brutality has over the years been characterised by murder, rape, slavery, kidnapping of youngsters and looting of assets. Broadly, these acts of violence were deliberately designed to force the civilian population into submission and coerce FRELIMO to accept RENAMO's demands.

Despite its blunders in the 1970s, FRELIMO remained relatively popular in the rural areas where it maintained a strong presence through militia groups and a network of political cells (Watch, 2017). RENAMO was aware of the difficulties it would face to penetrate such well defended areas. Accordingly, RENAMO singled out FRELIMO party members, and those who worked for the government in these areas such as the army and police as well as collaborators as its main targets (Chitiki, 2017). The same strategy has been employed in the current war where villagers were assured of safety unless they supported FRELIMO (Kind, 2017).

RENAMO did not shrink at taking way people's lives and the methods used exposed the victim to prolonged pain. Instead of shooting the victim, the executioners usually used machetes and knives to kill. While RENAMO argued that it would not waste bullets by killing a civilian, it has been suggested that RENAMO did not in some instances use fire arms in killing civilians because it feared to alert government forces (Chakara, 2017). However, it is important to note that RENAMO got addicted to killing as many people were needlessly lost their lives. Load carriers who displayed signs of tiredness due to long distances and hunger were killed in the presence others and wailing babies were murdered immediately to ensure that government forces would not get wind of their presence in an area (Mulalen, 2016). Strangely, RENAMO killers in some cases pleaded with the victim not to make noise as he was being killed, telling him or her 'chunga' which literally meant to be brave in the face death (Mutukweni, 2016). A woman quoted by Chingono who witnessed cold blooded murder being perpetrated against the chairperson of a collective farm remarked thus:

> My mother with other women laboured so hard at the *shamba de povo* (collective farm) but never got anything out of it. They were always told that the money was being saved to buy new equipment. Meanwhile, the *chefe* (party boss) of the collective farm's belly was

growing bigger and bigger... But it (injustice) was righted when the boys [RENAMO fighters] arrived. They killed him and hacked off his wife's ears and nose (Chingono, 1992: 43).

More disturbing was the fact that in some cases, RENAMO prevented the community from burying bodies of FRELIMO's collaborators. To make matters worse for the few lucky ones who got 'light punishment' such as mutilation of fingers, noses, lips and ears were ordered to roast and eat their former organs (Magamura, 2017).

While FRELIMO party members and civil servants were targets of RENAMO's violence, parents or relatives of such people were not spared of brutality especially after they had managed to sneak away (Mapara, 2016). As punishment for being related to RENAMO's enemy, RENAMO combatants sometimes raped women in the presence of their husbands, relatives and brothers and in other cases, fathers were forced to rape their daughters or brothers were forced to have sex with their sisters (Thailer, 2003).

Concomitant with the above, RENAMO also conducted itself in a manner that seemed to suggest that it had a natural right to women irrespective of their marital status and viewed them as part of the war booty (Wilson,1992). While, Schafer (2001) opines that government soldiers and RENAMO combatants tended to abuse women mostly from areas that were controlled by the enemy and at the same time respected women in their own areas, women were generally raped in privacy and many RENAMO cadres had slave wives. A victim of rape cited in Turshen (2005: 5) remarked that:

They (RENAMO) were raping our people- we were seeing them. They were coming to us as husbands. Can you afford to face such a thing? At the camp I was chosen to be the wife of the commander. And others together with my children were given as wives to other soldiers. We feel it because RENAMO were showing us guns that if we do not do these things-sleep with them and cook for them - they will kill us. We did these things. So that was a terrible thing to happen to us.

RENAMO also violated the rights of children as young girls and boys were press-ganged into its ranks (Schafer, 1998). It recruited children in all areas especially where adult males were hard to come by (*Africa Watch*, 1992). In the study area of Moussurize, RENAMO resorted to recruiting child soldiers because many adult males were either working in the Republic of South Africa or Zimbabwe (Nox, 2016). To change the mindset of the youngsters into terror-loving warriors they were subjected to a period of terror and physical abuse (Goodwin-Gill *et al*, 1994). The curriculum involved among others components, physical abuse and humiliation, punishment for being sympathetic to victims, exposure to violence, drills and exercises and killing (Boothby, 1992). In many cases, RENAMO forced children to murder their own parents in order to sever links with their communities and tie them to the movement through shame and guilt. As well, "the new recruits were forced to smoke a substance made from marijuana and gun powder purportedly to enhance their courage and physical strength" (Schafer, 1998: 21).

In spite of worldwide condemnation of recruitment of children, RENAMO proceeded to recruit them because they added value to the movement. The boys were considered to possess more stamina and better survival skills than their adult counterparts. Also, they displayed more loyalty than adult cadres who did not readily accept instructions (*Africa Watch*, 1992). A former RENAMO fighter argued that the youngsters were better fighters because to them the war was an adventure and psychologically, they were more focused than their adult counterparts who had left families behind (Fred, 2017). Child soldiers, in addition to fighting, were instrumental in information gathering and reporting and in the collection of food from villages (Matemai, 2016). However, Honwana (2000) notes that some children voluntarily joined either RENAMO or FRELIMO for personal reasons ranging from lack of employment, the need to protect their religious beliefs to the desire to revenge for the deaths of their relatives. Barnes (1997) points out that FRELIMO also organised raids to kidnap young men for military service but also recruited children by force. The core claim of the argument above is that child soldiers were used by both FRELIMO and RENAMO. However, it is important to note that forced intake of drugs ruined the future of the former child soldiers as some of them many years after the first civil war remain aggressive, withdrawn and unassertive (Shorai, 2017).

Added to the above, RENAMO also caused food shortage within the local population in two main ways. Teams of young soldiers were always in the countryside collecting food for the movement (Bwerani, 2016). During the raids, valuables such as goats, chicken, cattle and grain were taken away (Liesegang, 1995). While everyone was a target, homes belonging to *magaisa,* that is, those worked in South Africa, were preferred targets since, by local standards, they were believed to be richer than the rest of the population (Liesegang, 1995).

However, as the organisation's food requirements increased, RENAMO began to produce its own food. Expansive fields were opened up where peasants residing near major military bases such as Mujiwambava in Chief Chaibva's area had to commit six days of work a week (Nordstorm, 1997). While the idea to produce food was a pragmatic move to avert hunger and starvation within its ranks, it had far-reaching results. As peasants had limited time to work on their plots, the production of food declined and subsequently food shortage became a chronic existential challenge (Chiyembo, 2017). Nevertheless, it is important to highlight that in the current conflict (2010-2017), RENAMO to a large measure has abandoned terror warfare. As was the case in the past, it targets government forces and FRELIMO party members (Gumangeyi, 2017)

FRELIMO's counter-insurgency strategy

This section examines measures which FRELIMO implemented to counter RENAMO activities. While scholarship on this subject has tended to blame RENAMO, this chapter argues that FRELIMO in its counter-RENAMO pursuits equally terrorised many sections of the civilian population.

Terror warfare by FRELIMO against Ndau civilians has been attributed to three reasons: the Ndau are known to be strong supporters of RENAMO; the majority of the villagers did not relocate to government-controlled areas and also it was difficult to distinguish between RENAMO and the civilian population (Thailer, 2012).On the whole, the government's conduct resonated well with President Machel's argument that, "Those who deal with bandits will die with the bandits" (Thailer, 2003:272). According to Thailer

(2003), rural civilians living outside FRELIMO-controlled areas were subjected to violence. Similarly, Nordstrom (1997) argues that FRELIMO committed gross human rights violations. Among others, men were shot on sight, while those captured were interrogated and later burnt live (Monase, 2017). Respondents from the Mossurize District argue that FRELIMO is still implementing terror warfare in the current civil war (2010-2017) (Albert, 2017). This accounts for the thousands of Mozambicans who have sought refuge in neighbouring Zimbabwe (Kuda, 2017).While the ill-treatment of the Ndau could be linked to their ethnic connection with RENAMO leadership, several respondents were of the view that government forces were implanting terror tactics to strike fear into the rural population so that they would relocate to government-controlled areas (Tsikwi, 2017).

Furthermore, government forces laid landmines in areas inhabited by civilians (Tanganda, 2017). While government officials claimed that their forces laid landmines to secure their positions when they camped during the night, no effort was made to remove the mines when leaving the sites (Human Rights Watch, 1995).While the preceding argument sounds plausible, the villagers, however, failed to understand the government forces' intention to plant landmines in pathways used by civilians. While it could have a defensive method to protect themselves from RENAMO rebels who were in the habit of attacking government forces from behind, the local population argued that it was calculated victimisation for their co-existence with RENAMO rebels in the countryside (Chena, 2017). On the whole, the planting of landmines posed serious security threats as several people lost their limbs and lives (Human Rights Watch, 1992).

Furthermore, and to show that the government forces have not abandoned terror warfare as a *modus operandi*, they have continued to burn down whole homes usually with people in them and granaries as part of the scotched earth technique meant to eradicate any possibility of feeding RENAMO combatants. Residents generally attribute the attacks to several reasons: either the government forces will have been defeated in battles by RENAMO; wanted to reassert power by attacking unarmed villagers or they suspected the villages of harbouring RENAMO rebels (Ngwenya, 2017). However, the majority of the respondents argue that FRELIMO's conduct was motivated by the desire to drive people to government-controlled areas such as Espungabera, Dongi Redhuna and Post Machaze in order to deprive RENAMO of shelter and food. However, some respondents argued that government forces were venting their anger on the wrong people as the communities had not invited RENAMO to join them (Gadazi, 2017).

Conclusion

The chapter examined the underlying causes of the war and analysed the tactics that were employed by the belligerent forces in the execution of the war. The chapter established that both parties used violence against the civilian population as punishment for cooperating with one of them. It has further been demonstrated that while the two forces were more brutal in unleashing violence in the earlier conflict, FRELIMO is the main perpetrator of terror in the ongoing conflict (2010-2017). It has also been established that in both cases, violence caused irreparable damage ranging from death, loss of property to perpetual psychological trauma. As FRELIMO soldiers have developed a tendency of coming to RENAMO-controlled areas during the night in order to carry out surprise attacks in the morning, people have resorted to sleeping in the bush. Also as crops are routinely slashed down or burnt, the communities are facing severe food shortages.

Furthermore the reign of terror caused massive displacement of people with some seeking protection in government-controlled areas such as Espungabera, Dhongi Redhuna and Post Machaze while others sought refuge in neighbouring Zimbabwe. The chapter further indicated that in both conflicts, Mozambicans who sought refuge in Zimbabwe either lived in refugee camps like Tongogara or were given places to stay by local chiefs and farmers. However, those living in farms were and are exposed to exploitation by Zimbabwean farmers who demand unpaid labour from the refugees in return for safe refuge. In summation, the chapter argued that both RENAMO and FRELIMO have needlessly perpetrated violence against the Ndau people living in Mossurize District.

References

Africa Watch, (1992) *Conspicuous destruction: War, famine and the reform process in Mozambique*, New York: Africa Watch.

Albert, M. Interview, Muzite, Chipinge, 3 January, 2017.

Arndt, C. (1999) *Stabilisation and structural adjustment in Mozambique: An appraisal*, Indiana: West Lafayette.

Azevedo- Harman, E. (2015) "Patching things up in Mozambique", *Journal of Democracy*, 26(2): 139-150.

Barnes, S. (1997) *The socio-economic reintegration of demobilised soldiers in Mozambique*, Maputo: The Soldiers View, 1997.

Boothby, N. Upton, P. & Sultan, B. (1992) *Boy soldiers of Mozambique*, Oxford: Refugee Children, Refugee Studies Programme.

Brueno, N. Plageman, J. & Strashem, J. (2015) 'Provincial autonomy: The territorial dimension of peace in Mozambique,' in: *German Institute of Global and Area Studies*, Focus Number 10, pp. 1-8.

Bwerani, J. Interview, Zamchiya, Chipinge, 23 December 2016.

Cahen, M. (1999) 'The Mueda case and Maconde political ethnicity: Some notes on work in progress,' in: *Africana Studia*, Number 2. pp. 29-46

Chakara, P. Interview, Beacon, Chipinge, 4 January 2017.

Chena, M. Interview, Jersey, Chipinge, 5 January 2017.

Chichava, S. (2010) 'MDM: A new political force in Mozambique,' in: *Instituto de EstudosSociais e Economicos (ESE)*, Maputo.

Chingono, F. M. (1996) *The state, violence and development: The political economy of war in Mozambique, 1975-1992*, Aldershot: Arebury.

Chisiwa, B., Interview, Mashaishai (Border region), Mozambique, 5 January, 2017.

Chitiki, Z. Interview, Chichita (Border region), Chipinge, 6 January 2017.

Chiyembo, T. Interview, Gwenzi, Chipinge, 3 January 2017.

Daniel, I. D. (2016) 'Socialist ideas of Samora in Mozambique,' in: *International Journal of Humanities and Social Science Studies (IJHSSS)*, Volume 2, Number (6), pp.281-226.

Dekeya, L. Interview, Gwenzi, 28 December 2016.

Dinerman, A. (1994) 'In search of Mozambique: The imaginings of Christian Geffray in Lacause des Armes du Mozambique. Anthropologie d'une Guerre Civile,' in: *Journal of Southern African Studies,* Volume 20, Number, pp 569-586.

Dingane, T. Interview, Mupingo (Border region Mozambique), 7 January 2017.

Dzinesa, G. A. and Motsamai, D. (2013) 'Renamo's war talk and Mozambique's peace prospects,' *Institute for Security Studies,* pp.1-4.

Finnegarn, F. W. A. 1992.*Complicated war: The harrowing of Mozambique,* London: Berkeley.

Fred, M. Interview, Gwenzi, Chipinge, 3 January 2017.

Gadazi, V. Interview, Beacon Chipinge, 4 January 2017.

Goodwin-Gill, G. and Cohn, I. (1994) *Child soldiers: The role of children in armed conflicts,* Oxford University Press: New York.

Guilengue, F. (2014) 'A new Mozambican political system in the making: An interview with MDM politician Lutero Simango,' in: *International Politics, Rosa, Luxemburg Stiflung Southern Africa*, pp.1-7.

Gumangeyi B. Interview, Beacon, Chipinge, 4 January 2017.

Hanlon, J. 19 March 2015. Mozambique News Reports and Clippings 282.

Harington, J. S., McGlashan N. D. & Chelkowska, E. Z., A century of migrant labour in the gold mines of South Africa,' in: *Journal of Mining and Metallurgy*, pp. 64-71.

Hlongwana, Z. Interview, Veneka Village, Chipinge, 29 December 2016

Hlongwana, J. (2018) "Old habits die hard: Resistensia Nacional Mozambicana (Renamo)'s propensity for military confrontation against its professed embracement of peaceful conflict resolution, 1976-2017, *African Journal of Political Science and International Relations,* 12(2): 22-32.

Honwana, A. (2000) 'War cleansing in Mozambique and Angola,' Paper presented at the University of Chicago's *Council on Advanced Studies in Humanities and Special Sciences,* 28 November 2000.

Human Rights Watch, 11 April 1995, Maputo,' London: Human Rights Watch.

Human Rights Watch, (1992) 'Arms protocol,' London: Human Rights Watch.

Kind, M. Interview, Shishita (Border region), Chipinge, 6 January 2017.

Kuda, M. Interview, Gwenzi, Chipinge, 28 January 2017.

Liesegang, G, Der Burgekrieg, (1995) *Mozambikca 1980-1992, Ablaufe und Struktureller Wandeldes Landes,* Maputo.

Lorgen, C. C. (1999) 'The experience of villagisation: Lessons from Ethiopia, Mozambique and Tanzania,' in: *Oxfam.* GB.

Mafika, C. Interview, Shishita (Border region), Chipinge, 6 January 2017.

Magamura, T. Interview, Rimbi, Chipinge, 29 December 2017.

Manyoni, N. Interview, Rimbi, Chipinge, 29 December 2016.

Mapara, G. Interview, Cheche, Chipinge, 29 December 2016.

Matemai, R. Interview Manzvire, Chipinge, 29 December 2016.

Morgan, G. (1990) 'Violence in Mozambique: Towards an understanding of RENAMO,' in: *The Journal of Modern African Studies,* Volume 28, Number 4, pp.605-619.

Mubango, T. Interview, Mabeye, Chipinge, 30 December 2016.

Mudhanisso, J. Interview, Mabeye, Chipinge, 30 December 2016.

Mulalen, S. Interview, Mabeye, Chipinge, 30 December 2016.

Mutendeni, B. Gwenzi, Chipinge, 31 December 2016.

Mutukweni, L. Mundanda, Chipinge, 31 December 2016.

Muzondi, A. Interview, Mundanda, Chipinge, 30 December 2016.

Napoleao, D. (2008) 'The reduction of Mozambican workers in South African mines, 1975-1992: A case study of the consequences for Gaza Province-District of Chibuto,' in: *WIRED Space,* Johannesburg: Wits Institutional Repository Environment on Space.

Ngwenya, P. Interview, Jersey Tea Estate, 5 January 2017.

Nordstorm, C. (1997) *A different kind of war story,* Philadelphia: University of Pennsylvania Press.

Nox, C. Interview, Mundanda, Chipinge 30 December2016.

Pandya, P. (1987) 'Foreign support to ZANU and ZANLA during the Rhodesian war,' in: *ISSUP Strategic Review,* pp.46-57.

Perreira, J. C. G. (1999) 'The politics of survival: Peasants, chiefs and Renamo in Meringue District, Mocambique, 1982-1992', MA Thesis, Johannesburg: University of the Witwatersrand.

Renamo Bulletin, (1983) Number 14.

Schafer, J. (1998) 'A baby who does not cry will not be suckled: AMODEG and the reintegration of demobilised soldiers,' in: *Journal of Southern African Studies,* Volume 24, Number 1, pp 207-222.

Schafer, J. (2001) 'Guerrillas and violence in the war in Mozambique: Desocialization or Resocialisation,' in: *African Affairs,* Volume 100 Number 399, pp. 215-237.

Shabhani, M. Interview, Gwenzi, 31 January 2017.

Shikani, R. 24 April 2012. 'Mozambique: Post-war socio-economic and political challenges,' in: *ISS Situation Report.*

Sumich, J. M. (2005) *Elites and modernity in Mozambique,* PhD Thesis, London School of Economics.

Taju, G. (1988) 'Renamo: Osfactos que Conhecemos,' in: *Cadernos de Historia Boletin do Departmento de historia,* 7, du Universidade Eduardo Mondlane.

Tanganda, T. Interview, Mugondi, Chipinge, 2 January 2017.

Abbink, J. De Bruijkn, M. and van Walraven, K. (Eds.), (2003) *Rethinking resistance: Revolt and violence in African History,* Brill: Boston.

Thailer, K. (2012) 'Ideology and violence in civil wars: Theory and evidence from Mozambique and Angola,' in: *Civil Wars,* 14 (4):546-567.

Tsikwi, F. Interview, Gwenzi, Chipinge, 1 January 2017.

Turshen, M. (2001) *The political economy of rape: An analysis of systematic rape and sexual abuse of women during armed conflict in Africa,* London: Zed Books.

Watch, F. Interview, Tongogara, Chipinge, 29 December 2016.

Wilson, K. B. (1992) 'Cults of violence and counter violence in Mozambique,' in: *Journal of Southern African Studies,* 18(3): 527-582.

Young, T., (1989) 'The MNR (RENAMO): External and internal dynamics,' in: *African Affairs, 89* (357):495-505.

Chapter 8

Social Media, Infidelity and Domestic Violence in Zimbabwe

Nancy Mazuru

Introduction

This chapter examines the nexus between social media, infidelity and domestic violence in Zimbabwe, specifically in the second decade of the new millennium. The contemporary world has seen the gigantic proliferation of social media in various spheres of life. The digital epoch has been growing the interest in designing technologies that mediate and create a feeling of relatedness within interpersonal relationships beyond the explicit verbal communication (Hertlein and Ancheta, 2014). Communication technologies such as cell phones, the internet, and social networking sites have become a central feature in people's lives as tools for establishing and maintaining these relationships (*Ibid*). Through several types of social media platforms such as WhatsApp, Facebook, Twitter and Skype, communication has been made easy and cheaper, thereby increasing the interconnectedness of the world. Social media has made the lives of many people easy, for example, by facilitating business communication and transactions, circulating advertisements, disseminating information about social events such as weddings, funerals, parties as well as sending greetings and jokes to friends and relatives.

While social media can be applauded for bringing positive changes in people's lives, it is important to note that in certain circumstances, these platforms have been misused by some people. Often, this has resulted in negative repercussions to the people concerned together with their families. Recently, social media has become one of the most used methods of finding out former and new love partners as well as sending love messages and "sexting". These platforms are used by both married and unmarried people.

Many social networks also provide an online environment for people to communicate and exchange personal information for dating purposes (Ayodele, 2012). Of paramount importance to note is the fact that social media has rapidly heightened the rates of infidelity among couples, thereby increasing marital disputes, divorce and domestic violence in the country.

This chapter argues that there is a strong interrelationship between social media, infidelity and domestic violence in Zimbabwe. Although there are different forms of domestic violence, this chapter is much concerned with intimate partner violence and its undesirable consequences.

Social media and infidelity: Some cases and insights

Almost all individuals, married or cohabiting, expect sexual and emotional restrictedness of their partners (Madathil and Sandhu, 2008). Nevertheless, this exclusivity is not always guaranteed in every relationship due to the infidelity of one or both partners. Infidelity refers to an action taken by a partner in a committed love relationship that violates the agreement of sexual and/ or emotional exclusivity (Solomon and Teagno, 2006). This definition applies equally to marital, non-marital, heterosexual and homosexual relationships (Ibid). Infidelity, also commonly referred to as adultery or cheating, traditionally involves a person willingly engaging in sexual physical activity with a person other than one's spouse or committed relationship partner (O'Brien, 2009).

However, more recently, the definition of infidelity has been expanded to include other forms of behaviour such as cybersex (sex over the computer using words), viewing pornography, varying degrees of physical intimacy such as kissing and holding hands, and even emotional intimacy with another person to the detriment of the primary relationship (Hertlein *et al*, 2013). Nevertheless, what is complex about this broad definition of infidelity is that two different people in the same relationship might have different ideas about what represents infidelity or what constitutes an affair (Ibid). Therefore, due to these different opinions, couples are often at loggerheads, accusing one another of breaking their love contract. This scenario is increasingly causing domestic violence in Zimbabwe, as in many societies across the world.

Nonetheless, infidelity must be taken to include any behaviour that breaks the contract that two people have with each other (Tarrant, 2016). It constitutes the classic erosion of trust in a relationship and/ or marriage and it entails lying, the breaking of promises, and the infliction of emotional pain (Pfeiffer, 2012). Research has shown that approximately, 20% of women (about 1 in 5) and approximately 30% of men (about 1 in 3) have committed sexual infidelity (O'Brien, 2009). While the exact rates of infidelity vary, studies consistently show that men report a greater rate of infidelity compared to women (*Ibid*). It is, however, instructive to highlight that infidelity is not a new practice in the world, as it has been in existence since time immemorial. Nevertheless, it is important to note that the incidences of infidelity have increased in the modern era in many countries due to an expansion in the use of social media, and Zimbabwe is not an exception. As Nelson and Salawu, (2017) have demonstrated, the advent of social media networks has heightened an alarming rate of emotional and sexual infidelity across the globe. Today, the world is faced with rapidly evolving and profound technologically-driven changes in social connection and human intimate and sexual interactions (Schneider *et al*, 2012).

On the whole, it must be admitted that technology can help to develop relationships. It helps people to meet new colleagues, allowing those with similar beliefs, hobbies, and habits to find each other more easily (Hertlein and Ancheta, 2014). However, as people reach out to each other through new technology, new types of relationships and conflicts occur (*Ibid*). One of my informants, a young married woman from the Zimbabwean city of Masvingo, explained how her Facebook friendship with her former high school boyfriend left her with bruises on the face after her husband discovered the friendship (Interview with Muchena, 2 June 2017). She stated that: "even though I explained to my husband that it was just a Facebook friendship and not a love affair, he did not believe me. He was very angry and he slapped me several times on the face."

This, therefore, validates Hertlein and Ancheta's (2014) assertion that in the digital era, it is difficult to be clear about unacceptable relationship behaviour when the opportunities for connection and betrayal escalate so quickly. In the same line of argument, Nelson and Salawu (2017) avow that while social media is supposed to help build friendships and reconnect old friends, it has become a disadvantage to many married couples and youths in relationships. Facebook, Twitter and other social media provide a never-ending stream of updates about partners involved in an affair (Marshal, 2015). Mobile phones allow someone to ping a message into your home at any time of the day or night (Ibid). Thus, technology provides private methods by which to talk to one another as it is easier to be intimate on texts because they are not heard by everyone around you (Hertlein and Ancheta, 2014). One informant from the Zimbabwean city of Mutare reiterated during an interview as follows: "Social media has come to the advantage of spouse-cheaters because you can easily communicate with the person whom you are having an extra-marital affair with, as well as sending one another photographs and videos to spice-up the relationship" (Interview with Muchineyi, 28 June 2017).

In the same line of thought, Hertlein and Ancheta (2014) argue that through technology, those who are in a relationship are able to find videos and online resources that they can use to better support their relationships such as date-night ideas. Schneider *et al* (2014) also share the same view arguing that prior to the 1990s, a period that brought about a sea change of interpersonal communication driven by the arrival of the internet, someone wishing to have a sexual experience whether in or outside of a committed relationship had to negotiate and meet a potential affair-partner before starting that relationship.

However, with the introduction of online networks, life brought with it both unlimited computer-based admission to film and live sexual acts, and unrestricted access to flirtation and sexualised interaction, without the need for close proximity to another person (*Ibid*). The same technology also allows the discoverer of the affair to read all the messages between the affair partners, which means that particularly hurtful phrases get stuck into their minds (Marshal,

2015). This increases the risk of continuous physical and emotional abuse between the spouses concerned.

The link between infidelity and domestic violence

The term 'domestic violence' is used in many countries to refer to violence between partners but the term can also encompass the abuse of children or elders, or ill-treatment by any member of a household (World Health Organisation, 2012). To the above, Walsh and Hemmens (2008) add that it refers to any abusive act, be it physical, sexual or psychological that occurs within the family. Although any member of the family can be a victim of domestic violence, this study is much concerned with intimate partner violence that is triggered by infidelity.

Adultery has a plethora of negative implications on the perpetrators as well as their spouses. Disloyalty in marriages does not only cause break of trust but may also lead to different forms of abuse. According to Jain and Sahni (2016), infidelity has the potential to cause and aggravate intimate partner violence particularly in the form of physical, emotional and psychological abuse. Sharing the same view, Buss and Duntley (2013) argue that the detection or suspicion of infidelity is one of the key predictors of intimate partner violence. Thus, whether actual or suspected, infidelity has a significant contribution to domestic violence or spouse homicide (Daly and Wilson, 1988). The different ways in which infidelity may cause psychological/emotional abuse, physical abuse and homicide are explained below.

Infidelity as a form of psychological abuse

According to Hall and Fincham (2006), infidelity occurs in 20% to 25% of all marriages in the world and it can have a number of deleterious effects on a relationship and the individuals involved. The impact of infidelity on a romantic relationship can be quite complex and multi-dimensional (Ibid). Since domestic violence can be psychological, physical or sexual, it is therefore important to note that infidelity can cause emotional pain which may take time to heal. In an interview, one Masvingo woman who had an adulterous husband lamented:

> There is nothing that is emotionally painful as having a spouse who is adulterous. Being betrayed by the person you love is so stressful especially when you are faithful to him/her. When I discovered that my husband of 14 years was having affairs with other women, I could not bear the pain. I have not yet forgiven him and I have completely lost trust in him (Interview with Mujena, 2 June 2017).

From the foregoing, the act of adultery in itself is a form of domestic violence (Stuart, 2005). According to Stuart (2005), the violated person suffers emotional abuse that leaves deep invisible wounds. It is the effect of emotional abuse and the scars that are left on people's memories that lead to low self-esteem, especially in women (Ibid). In the same vein, Ravindra (2013) posits that a spouse who feels the need to find love on the side has completely abused the trust of his or her spouse. Therefore, it is important to note that while many people think that domestic violence has more to do with physical abuse, in the case of infidelity, the abuse starts with the violation of emotional and sexual exclusivity which may lead to stress and loss of self-esteem.

Schneider *et al* (2014) concur with the above and posit that either sudden or protracted discoveries of sexual and/or romantic betrayal by a long-term partner represents a profound and recurring psychological trauma for those who endure it, similar to suddenly losing a job, child or home. According to Hales and Hales (2017), psychological trauma increases the risk of developing (and dying from) cardiovascular disease. What is worse is that stress may be as great a threat for cardiovascular disease as smoking, hypertension, and other major risk factors, depending on how individuals respond to a stressor. Anger, fear, self-doubt, pain over the loss of past perceptions of the relationship, distrust, shame, self-blame, and depression can be emotionally overwhelming to partners and spouses, causing symptoms such as intrusive thoughts, depression, and preoccupation (Schneider *et al*, 2014). Therefore, infidelity should be equated with other forms of domestic violence such as physical and sexual abuse because they can all trigger health problems to the victims. Critically, for this chapter, infidelity should also be considered as a key factor in causing domestic violence and abuse.

As Ravindra (2013) rightly observes, a spouse is entitled to dignity and self-respect. Nevertheless, when one partner commits adultery, it entails that the dignity and self-respect of the affected partner is not guaranteed. Some of the women who were interviewed revealed that when they discovered their husbands' extra-marital relationships on social media, their husbands tried to be defensive using threatening and uncaring language to prevent them from asking about the same issue (Interviews with Mamvura, 7 June 2017; Masimba, 7 June 2017). This affirms Schneider *et al*'s (2014) assertion that the woman who remains with her unfaithful husband may have to put up with her husband's foul language, frequent absences, verbal threats, various forms of abuses, along with his insulting behaviour if she dares to challenge him about his adulterous escapades. They further state that, for these partners, repeated dishonesty on the part of their user/sex addict mate, who often denies the spouse's questions, gut reactions, and instincts, is indeed traumatizing and traumatic (Schneider *et al*, 2014). Many women find psychological, verbal, and emotional abuse more harmful and of far greater duration than physical abuse (Buzawa *et al*, 2012). Therefore, given the psychological consequences of infidelity and the discourteous behaviour of the cheating spouses, adultery and domestic violence should be seen as two interwoven issues.

Infidelity and spouse physical abuse

Building on Pfeiffer's (2012) contention that increases in the use of social media have enabled adulterous relationships to occur almost anywhere, and in many cases this has caused several forms of domestic abuse, this section argues that in addition to causing emotional trauma, infidelity can also lead to physical abuse due to anger, jealousy and misunderstanding that may arise between the couple. Many people who are cheated retain recorded messages of their spouse on WhatsApp, Facebook, Twitter chats, among others, as evidence of infidelity (Jain and Sahni, 2017). In many cases, women who commit adultery usually end up being victims of domestic violence. However, this does not necessarily mean that women do not exert violence on their spouses when they discover their infidelity. As will be demonstrated in the forthcoming paragraphs, some women also become violent to their husbands when they discover their adultery. However, cases of male-exerted violence seem to outweigh female-exerted violence.

As already been highlighted, wife-battering is a common practice among men who discover the infidelity of their wives. In January 2016, for instance, a 36-year-old man from the Zimbabwean city of Chitungwiza man was slapped with a sixth-month prison term because he had physically abused his wife after he discovered a WhatsApp conversation between her and an alleged boyfriend (Meya, 2016). The husband told the court that he could not control his emotions after unearthing the truth between his wife and her boyfriend (Ibid). He also asserted that what worsened his anger was the fact that his wife had saved the contact name of her boyfriend in her phone bearing the name of her female friend (*Ibid*).

In another similar event, in January 2017, a woman from Glen View Suburb in Harare, the Zimbabwean capital, was hospitalised at the Harare Central Hospital after she was attacked with an empty beer bottle by her husband because he had discovered through WhatsApp messages that she was cheating on him with two men (Nyamayaro, 2017). Her husband stated that he discovered from her WhatsApp conservations that she was planning to visit her boyfriend in South Africa after having another quality time with her local lover at a lodge (Ibid). He further stated that he went through her mobile phone while she was taking a bath and that was when he discovered her illicit affairs with the two men (Ibid). The two cases cited above buttress Buss and Duntley's (2013) findings that female sexual infidelity may dramatically increase a woman's risk of being battered.

Stieglitz *et al* (2012) also aver that men's jealousy over women's infidelity is the strongest impetus to lethal and non-lethal violence against female partners. Sharing the same view, Goetz and Shackelford (2008) posit that male sexual jealousy is one of the most frequently cited cause of intimate-partner violence. To them, jealousy is an emotion that is experienced when a valued relationship is threatened by a real or imagined rival, and generates responses aimed at stifling the threat (*Ibid*). It functions to maintain relationships by motivating behaviours that deter rivals from mate-poaching and prevent intimate partners from infidelity or outright departure from the relationship (*Ibid*). A man may afford his partner many freedoms, but these freedoms only rarely include sexual liberty with other men (*Ibid*). Therefore, in the event of a wife committing adultery, men usually beat their wives or engage in many other forms of physical and emotional abuse. On the whole, physical aggression in response to infidelity may serve specific purposes, such as to punish the partner for her infidelity, discourage the partner from future infidelities or from relationship defection, and/or signal to rivals that one is capable of violence, which may deter potential mate-poachers (Buss, 2005). In the final analysis, as the World Health Organisation (2012) reports, intimate partner violence is one of the most common forms of violence against women and includes physical, sexual, and emotional abuse and controlling behaviours by an intimate partner.

In addition to jealousy, the other reason why men in Zimbabwe beat up their wives for infidelity stems from the fact that most indigenous societies, just like in many other African countries, are patriarchal. In many such societies, there are fears that wife infidelity may interrupt family genealogies. Family genealogies in a patriarchal society go hand in glove with fathers' lineages/ancestry. Among the Shona people of Zimbabwe, for example, if a woman commits adultery, it is feared that she will give birth to an illegitimate child (*gora*) and this disturbs family tree (Interview with Mandove, 2 June 2017). Furthermore, cultural beliefs that see women as men's property especially due to lobola payment have seen many women being victims of domestic violence when their husbands discover their adultery. Culturally, it may be deemed acceptable for a man to have an affair or relationships with other women while he is married, but that dishonours his wife and his marriage vows (Ravindra, 2013). In an interview, one man stated that:

> We are black people and not whites, we have our own unique culture. It is acceptable in our culture for a man to have an extra-marital affair or even to have a second wife. However, a woman cannot do

that. There is no man who wants to share his wife with another man. As men, we pay lobola to get our wives and that gives us the 'ownership' of women (Interview with Zungayi, 2 June 2017).

These cultural perceptions are in sync with certain biblical verses which some men actually quote to support the notion that women should be faithful to their husbands. In the Old Testament, for example in Genesis (2: 18), a married woman was not only seen as a companion and helper of her husband but also as his property (Onwuka, 2007). It was from this perspective that the woman was bound to be faithful to her husband without the corresponding fidelity required of the husband (*Ibid*). Adultery in this case is seen as a violation of the right of the husband to whom the wife belongs but not of the wife (*Ibid*).

It is these beliefs that often lead to wife beating and other forms of physical abuse in the event of the wife having an extra-marital relationship. Stieglitz (2012) asserts that given men's greater size and physical strength, violence against wives may be used as a "bargaining" tool to strategically leverage a selfish outcome, despite potential costs to the victim, aggressor and offspring. Therefore, cultural perceptions about male superiority over women when combined with the discovery of wife infidelity through social media can fuel wife battering together with other forms of physical abuse.

Infidelity and spouse homicide

Infidelity can also lead to spouse homicide. As Erickson (2011) argues, in some cases, domestic violence can escalate to murder when husbands become angry after their wives step out of their prescribed role as submissive and dependent helpmates. In September 2015, for example, a man from the mining town of Hwange went berserk and allegedly stabbed his wife to death after finding WhatsApp messages from her boyfriend in her phone (Moyana, 2015). In a similar incident, in January 2014, a 41-year-old man from Kwekwe Town appeared in court facing a murder charge after he allegedly fatally assaulted his wife accusing her of receiving a WhatsApp message accompanied by images of male sexual organs (Muhlanga, 2014).

Correspondingly, a study conducted by Eriksson and Mazerolle (2013) about the general strain theory of intimate partner homicide reveals that men who kill their partners report experiences of losing control, suspecting infidelity, involuntary separation, jealousy, and rage. Fearing sexual competition and infidelity, men experience jealousy, which is the psychological link between the perceived threat of sexual infidelity and the violent act (*Ibid*). Hence, the discovery of spousal infidelity on social media does not only trigger physical abuse but can also cause unnecessary fatalities.

It is crucial to note that even in circumstances where men commit adultery, they can still physically abuse their spouses in a bid to silence them. Unfortunately, some of these corporal abuses may cause deaths. In April 2016, a 48-year-old man from New Magwegwe Suburb in the City of Bulawayo was arrested for allegedly killing his wife in front of their 22-year-old daughter following a row over WhatsApp messages he had received from his girlfriend (Masara, 2016).

As has been highlighted earlier, it is also important to note that it is not only men who beat up or kill their spouses when they come across the infidelities of their partners on social media. There are also cases of women who engage in similar acts after finding out the illicit relationships of their partners on WhatsApp or Facebook. In January 2016, for instance, a 22-year-old woman from Inyathi Village in south-western Zimbabwe was fined US$50 at the Magistrate's Court for assaulting her husband after she caught him sending a WhatsApp message to his ex-girlfriend (Moyo, 2016).

Similarly, in November 2016, a 27-year-old woman from Harare's Warren Park Suburb was charged with capable homicide after she scalded her husband with boiling water which spilled and killed her six-month-old son (Charumbira, 2016). The incident occurred after the wife had come across a video of a naked woman in her husband's laptop (*Ibid*). The woman became furious after seeing the video and poured a pot of hot water on her husband who reacted swiftly but got burnt on the right arm and left foot and the bulk of the boiling water burnt the infant that was sleeping on the sofa (*Ibid*).

In another similar event in April 2016, a 36-year-old Chitungwiza woman was sentenced to eight years in jail for killing her husband with a knife after he had refused to show her a 'suspicious' WhatsApp message that he had received on his phone (*Bulawayo Bureau*, 2016). Taking the above cases into consideration, Wilson and Daly's (2016) assertion that men kill in response to revelations of wifely infidelity and women almost never respond similarly, although their mates are more often adulterous becomes less valid. Some women can become violent just the same as men when they discover their husbands' extra-marital affairs. This is the reason why many women in Zimbabwe scald their cheating spouses with hot substances such as water or cooking oil due to anger. Sharing a similar view, in an interview, a certain man stated that:

> It is quite surprising that women are regarded as more susceptible to domestic violence just because they are biologically weaker than men yet of late they have turned into real criminals especially on matters relating to domestic violence. They are actually taking advantage of the fact that they are always seen as victims of domestic violence yet they can be perpetrators as well (Interview with Charehwa, 2 June 2017).

Therefore, the violent actions taken by some women after discovering their husbands' extra-marital affair validate Stieglitz *et al's* (2012) assertion that men and women have a similar frequency and intensity of jealous emotions during recalls of potential infidelity. Hertlein *et al* (2014) also hold a similar opinion and they argue that those whose partners have had affairs feel a sense of betrayal and anger at their partners. Studies also acknowledge that women, just as their male counterparts, can commit violence and that it can also occur equally in same-sex and heterosexual relationships (Queensland Government Report, 2012). Thus, given the fact that both men and women can be angry at their spouses when they break their matrimonial bond, both are capable of engaging in violent acts against their intimate partners. Hence, both men and women can be victims as well as perpetrators of domestic violence.

The costs of domestic violence

Domestic violence has serious negative repercussions on the victims, the perpetrators and the family (children at large). According to Fisher and Lab (2010), the impacts of domestic violence are considerable for victims, their children and other people in their lives, including family, neighbours, co-workers and members of the general community. Victims of domestic violence experience a host of physical, psychological and social effects resulting from the abuse (Jackson 2006). Physical effects include high rates of medical problems such as injuries (broken bones, hearing impairments, vision loss, and injuries to internal organs, severe burns, disability, and premature death). In addition to the above physical costs, Green and Roberts (2008) point out that in women, domestic violence, especially wife–battering, may result in miscarriages, abortions and increased rates of rape. This study has already highlighted cases of physical abuse that were triggered by the discovery of spousal infidelity on social media platforms which include spouse-battering, scalding spouses with hot substances, attacking spouses with empty beer bottles and stabbing spouses with knives. As well, incidences of physical abuses which resulted in death have also been discussed above. Taking these incidences into consideration, it becomes very clear that domestic violence causes unbearable physical damages on the victims.

Psychologically, domestic violence often results in low self-esteem, post-traumatic stress disorder, mental disorders, alcohol and drug abuse as well as suicide attempts (Green and Roberts, 2008). Domestic violence deprives victims as well as family members, friends, the community, and even the broader society of their sense of emotional well-being (Jackson, 2007).

Economically, the costs of domestic violence include expenditures on medical treatment (emergency room care, hospitalisation, costs of treatment), psychological counselling, police services (police spend time on arrests and responding to calls), activities in the criminal justice system (prison and detention costs as well as prosecution and other court costs) as well as other social services for the victims, especially women and children (Buvinic, *et al,* 1999). Cases of perpetrators who were arrested and imprisoned after physically abusing or killing their spouses because of WhatsApp messages have also been discussed above. Furthermore, the abuse that victims endure at home affects them in the workplace, impairing their ability to do their job (Lee 2005). Domestic violence causes absenteeism and lack of concentration at workplaces, thereby reducing workforce production. The victim's inability to take his/her mind off the abuse results in mistakes in calculation, difficulty in working with peers or customers, and even compromises in workplace safety, depending on the employee's responsibilities (Ibid). One informant, a victim of domestic violence, stated that:

> When I confronted my husband over suspicious WhatsApp messages in his phone, he became very rude and we ended up exchanging harsh words. He then started being hostile to me before he bashed me and uttered all sorts of bad names. I spent the whole week at home enduring the pain. I was also ashamed of the visible injuries. In fact, I did not want my workmates to see me in that state (Interview with Kasirai, 3 June 2017, Masvingo).

This, therefore, clearly shows that the costs of domestic violence go beyond physical damages on the victims as they also affect their work performance and may even cost some their jobs or sources of livelihood sustenance.

The repercussions of domestic violence also adversely affect children in different ways. Children in abusive families appear to be the most susceptible to the effects of domestic violence (Buzawa and Buzawa, 2003). Green and Roberts (2008) assert that each year, more than 10 million children witness domestic violence, especially women battering in the privacy of their own homes worldwide. The impact of growing up in a violent home often results in an intergenerational cycle of violence and poverty (Ibid). Children who regularly witness domestic violence may also take the abuse to school and become aggressive to their peers and teachers (Mcgee, 2000). Living with domestic violence may affect children's school performance and emotional development (Jackson, 2006). Besides witnessing domestic violence, some children may end up being targets of physical, sexual and verbal abuse by the perpetrator (Ibid). Children's psychological problems precipitated by domestic violence may include bed-wetting, nightmares, withdrawals, loss of confidence, lack of self-esteem, tantrums and emotional outbursts (Ibid). Thus, domestic violence has severe adverse effects on the children and other family members.

Way forward

Given the adverse effects of the correlation between social media, infidelity and domestic violence, and the subsequent costs, one important question which may arise is: what then should be done? In 2016, a Zimbabwean High Court judge ruled that it is illegal for spouses to pry into each other's cell phones without permission (*Bulawayo Bureau*, 2016). The High Court judge ruled that evidence obtained through prying into a cell phone should not stand in court as it would have been obtained illegally (Chara, 2016). The judge said snooping into someone's phone contravenes Section 57(d) of the Constitution, which guarantees every person the right not to have the privacy of their communication infringed (Ibid). The magistrate further stated that there is no law which provides that a husband or wife has a right to infringe on the privacy of the other's communications (*Ibid*).

However, while the judgement seems to be plausible, it can be seen as solving a problem by creating another. Some lawyers and marriage counsellors asserted that although the ruling was correct since it was backed by constitutional provisions, it was however not workable in a "proper" marriage set-up (Ibid). The ruling also attracted public debate with some people criticising it arguing that spouses should not hide phone messages from one another. Thus, while the ruling was correct especially because it helps to prevent conflicts between spouses, it indirectly gives unfaithful partners the green light to have extra-marital affairs, thereby worsening domestic disputes.

This chapter, therefore, suggests that spouses should be allowed access to their partners' cell phones. However, emphasis should be placed on the point that if spouses come across evidence of cheating, they should not exert violence to their partners. There is also need for more awareness campaigns in the country about the negative effects of domestic violence to the victims, perpetrators and family members. There is also need to criminalise spouses who allow children to witness acts of domestic violence, that is, either to hear or see acts of domestic violence as this may have many long term impacts on the children.

Conclusion

This chapter has analysed the detrimental nexus between social media, infidelity and domestic violence in Zimbabwe. It has been ably demonstrated that the increase in the use of social media in the contemporary world has led to an increase in the rate of infidelity among couples which in turn heightens cases of domestic violence in the country. Many spouses discover the infidelity of their partners through social media platforms such as WhatsApp and Facebook and due to anger and jealousy, most of them end up physically abusing their partners. In certain circumstances, the abuse may culminate into homicide and this may lead to an increase in the number of orphans and child-headed families.

References

Ayodele, O. P. (2012) 'Facebook love on online social networking platforms: An analysis of the linguistic expression and portrayal of love in a selected Nigerian Hip-Hop track' in: *International Journal of Linguistics*, Volume 4, Number 1, pp. 254-273.

Buvinic M. *et al*, (1999) 'Violence in the Americas: A framework for action' in: A. R. Morrison and M.L. Biehl (Eds.), *Too close to home: Domestic violence in the Americas*, Washington D C: Inter-American Development Bank.

Buzawa, E. S. *et al*, (2012) *Responding to domestic violence: The integration of criminal justice and human services*, Thousand Oaks: Sage Publications.

Buss, D. M. (2005) *The murderer next door: Why the mind is designed to kill*, New York: Penguin Press.

Buss, D. M. and Duntley, J. D. (2013) 'Intimate partner violence in evolutionary perspectives', in: T.K. Shackelford and R.D. Hansen (Eds.) *The evolution of intimate partner violence*, New York: Springer.

Chara, T. 10 April 2016. 'Thou shall not touch thy partner's phone', Available at: http://www.sundaymail.co.zw, Accessed 4 July 2017.

Charehwa, A., Interview, Masvingo, 2 June 2017.

Charumbira, S., 7 April 2016. 'Woman scalds hubby, kills baby with hot water', Available at: https://www.newsday.co.zw, Accessed 10 June 2017.

Daly, M. & Wilson, M. 1988. *Homicide*. New York: Airline de Gruyter.

Erickson, L. (2011) *Westward-bound: Sex, violence, the law, and the making of a settler society*, Toronto: UBC Press.

Erikssson, L. and Mazerolle, P. (2013) 'A general strain theory of intimate partner homicide' in: *Aggression and Violent Behaviour*, 18(5): 1-33.

Fisher, B.S. and Lab, S.P. (2010) *Encyclopaedia of victimology and crime prevention*, Thousand Oaks: Sage Publications.

Gandadza, J., Interview, Mutare, 28 June 2017.

Green, D.L. and Roberts, A.R. (2008) *Helping victims of violent crime: Assessment, treatment and evidence-based practice*, New York: Springer.

Goetz, A. T. and Shackelford, T. K. (2008) 'Evolutionary psychological perspective on men's violence against intimate-partners' In: J. Keeling, and T. Mason (Eds.), *Domestic violence: A multi-professional approach for healthcare practitioners*, Berkshire: McGraw Hill Press.

Hales, D. and Hales, J. (2017) *Personal stress management: Surviving to thriving*, Boston: Cengage Learning.

Hall, J. H. and Fincham, F. D. (2006) 'Relationship dissolution following infidelity, in Fine, M.A. and Harvey, J.H. (Eds.), *Handbook of divorce and relationship dissolution*, New York: Routledge.

Hertlein, K. M. *et al*, (2013) 'Infidelity: An overview' in: K.M. Hertlein *et al* (Ed.) *Handbook of the clinical treatment of infidelity*, Routledge: New York.

Hertlein, K.M. and Ancheta, K. (2014) 'Advantages and disadvantages of technology in relationships: Findings from an open-ended survey' in: *The Qualitative Report*, 19(22): 1-11.

Jackson, N.A. (2007) *Encyclopedia of domestic violence*, Routledge: New York.

Jackson, Y. (2006) *Encyclopedia of multicultural psychology*, Thousand Oaks: Sage Publications.

Jain, G. and Sahni, S. P. (2017) 'Understanding attribution bias and reasons behind internet Infidelity in India' in: E.C. Viano (Ed.), *Cybercrime, Organised crime, and societal responses: International approaches*, Springer: New York.

Lee, J. (2005) *Addressing domestic violence in the workplace*, Massachusetts: SRD Press.

Machafa, M. Interview, Masvingo, 3 June 2017.

Madathil, J. and Sandhu, D. S. (2008) 'Infidelity in Asian Indian marriages: Implications for counselling and psychotherapy' in: *The Family Journal: Counselling and Therapy for Couples and Families*, Volume 16, Number 4, pp. 338-343.

Majoni, G. Interview, Masvingo, 12 May 2017.

Mandove, M. Interview, Masvingo, 2 June 2017

Marshal, A.G. (2015) *I can't get over my partner's affair: 50 questions about recovering from extreme betrayal and the long term impact of infidelity*, Marshal Method Publishing: London.

Masara, W. (14 April 2016) 'WhatsApp murder…Message from small house sparks fight… Big silver knife used to 'cut wife's throat', Available at: http://www.chronicle.co.zw, Accessed 10 August 2017.

McGee, C. (2000) *Childhood experiences of domestic violence*, London and New York: Jessica Kingsley Publishers.

Meya, L. (11 January 2016) 'Hubby jailed for bashing cheating wife', Available at: http://www.herald.co.zw, Accessed 2 May 2016.

Masiiwa, C. Interview, Masvingo, 12 May 2017.

Masimba, N. Interview, Harare, 7 June 2017.

Mamvura, R. Interview, Harare, 7 June 2017.

Moyana, F. (15 September 2015) 'Man stabs wife to death in WhatsApp message row', Available at: http://www.chronicle.co.zw, Accessed 7 April 2017.

Moyo, A. (20 January 2016) 'Woman intercepts husband's WhatsApp message to lover, beats him up', Available at: http://www.chronicle.co.zw, Accessed 3 May 2017.

Muchena, T. Interview, Masvingo, 2 June 2017.

Muchineyi, A. Interview, Mutare, 28 June 2017.

Muchokore, M. Interview, Masvingo, 3 June 2017.

Muhlanga, B. (10 January 2014) 'Man kills wife over WhatsApp pictures', Available at: https://www.newsday.co.zw, Accessed 17 July 2017.

Mujena, R. Interview, Masvingo, 2 June 2017.

Nelson, O. and Salawu, A. (2017) 'Can my wife be virtual-adulterous? An experiential study on Facebook, emotional infidelity and self-disclosure, in: *Journal of International Women's Studies,* Volume 18, Number 2, pp.166-179.

Nyamayaro, A. (12 January 2017) 'Woman beds three men …attacked by crazy hubby,' Available at: http://hmetro.co.zw, Accessed 12 May 2017.

O'Brien, J. (2009) *Encyclopaedia of gender and society*, London: Sage Publications.

Onwuka, P. C. (2007) *The law, redemption and freedom in Christ: An exegetical-theological study of Galatians 3, 10-14 and Romans 7, 1-6*, Rome: Gregorian Biblical Bookshop.

Pfeiffer, K. (2012) 'Virtual adultery: No physical harm, no foul? In: *University of Richmond Law Review*, Volume 46(2): 667-690.

Ravindra, G. (2013) *Transforming the traditional Indian marriage*, Tucson: Wheatmark.

Schneider, J. P. *et al*, (2012) 'Is it really cheating? Understanding the emotional reactions and clinical treatment of spouses and partners affected by cybersex infidelity,' in: *Sexual Addiction and Compulsivity*, 19 (1-2): 123–139.

Solomon, S.D. and Teagno, L. J. (2006) *Intimacy after infidelity: How to rebuild and affair-proof your marriage*, Oakland: New Harbinger Publications.

Stieglitz, J. *et al*, (2012) 'Infidelity, jealousy and wife abuse among Tsimane forager farmers: Testing evolutionary hypotheses of marital conflict', in: *Evolutionary Human Behaviour*, 33(5): 438-448.

Stuart, B. Y. (2005) *Betrayal of sacred trust: Living with an unfaithful husband*, New York: iUniverse.

Tarrant, S. (2016) 'Sex and social media' in: Tarrant, S. (Ed.) *Gender, sex and politics: In the streets and between the sheets in the 21st Century,* New York and London: Routledge.

Walsh, A. and Hemmens, C. (2008) *Introduction to criminology: A text/reader,* London: Sage Publications.

Wilson, M. and Daly, M. (2016) 'The evolutionary psychology of couple conflict in registered versus defacto marital unions' In: A. Booths *et* al, *Couples in conflict,* Routledge: New York and London.

World Health Organisation, (2012) *Understanding and addressing violence against women*, United Nations: World Health Organisation.

Zungayi, N. Interview, Masvingo, 2 June 2017.

Part II

In Pursuit of Peace through Everyday Modes of Justice and Healing

Chapter 9

Political Violence and "Common Sense" Justice: *Kuripa Ngozi* as a Transitional Justice Mechanism among the Shona People in Zimbabwe's Rural Areas

Ngonidzashe Marongwe

Introduction

This chapter discusses how the rural Shona people of Zimbabwe's "common sense" beliefs in avenging spirits (*ngozi*) and paying restitution to appease avenging spirits (*kuripa ngozi*) may inform the search for a lasting transitional justice (TJ) mechanism following the 2000-2008 countrywide violence. It responds to the question of how non-state actors can aid in the search for a lasting TJ. It also responds to the calls by the government-instituted Organ for National Healing, Reconciliation and Integration (ONHRI) to Zimbabweans to participate in the search for a TJ for Zimbabwe that has been rocked by cycles of violence and impunity dating back to the pre-colonial period. Outside the ONHRI initiative there have also been calls, from individual victims, human rights non-governmental organisations (NGOs) and some politicians, demanding victim-based TJs to stamp out the culture of violence and impunity.

Using a combination of cases of pervasive political violence, alleged witchcraft and other occult practices reported in news items and an ethnographic study in Shurugwi District, emanating from the 2000-2008 era, this chapter explores the value and potential for the adoption of the indigenous Shona practice of *kuripa ngozi* as a possible alternative TJ method for Zimbabwe's rural areas. However, this is not to reduce its potential usage in urban areas. It is also not to discount the role the state can play in the TJ. To begin with, ideally, the concept of the state, in the Hobbesian sense, emanates from the desire for justice and common good of its citizens who share a common history, culture and destiny (Skaria, 2002). This is also not an attempt to reduce the potential contribution of the 'modern' prosecutorial transitional justice mechanisms that may deal a blow to the state and party agents' impunity. In fact, as illustrated in Rwanda and Sierra Leone, the 'traditional' methods can be used in combination with the 'modern ones' (Sriram, 2009). Primarily, this chapter posits that there is a possibility for TJ by utilising the intersections between political violence, and the locals' beliefs in *ngozi*.

Besides transcending the binary between peace and justice, *kuripa ngozi* would be suitable for rural areas because it is a well-known practice, cost-effective, quick, is supportive of socio-economic rights, and is less encumbered technically. Its potential usage also undercuts the thread of passiveness of communities in T J that has been marked by blanket amnesties. *Kuripa ngozi* is also informed by pragmatic concerns under Zimbabwe's conditions of severe political polarity.

ONHRI and the search for transitional justice

TJ involves "a range of approaches that societies undertake to deal with diverse past political situations such as authoritarianism, totalitarianism, or conflicted democracies to a stable democratic state" (Zimbabwe Human Rights (ZHR) NGO Forum, June 2009: 18). It encompasses "criminal justice, restorative justice, social justice and economic justice" (Ibid). At the core of any TJ is the need to establish the truth in redressing the wrongs of the past to help prevent the recurrence of similar violations of human rights. The other guiding principle "is ensuring justice and fairness in dealing with past offences and crimes in a period of movement from an unwanted post-conflict situation to a desired situation that restores normalcy, equity, peace and social cohesion" (CCSF, 2009).

From the above, a comprehensive TJ system plays two critical roles. Firstly, it seeks justice for past wrongs and charts a better and more democratic future. Secondly, it seeks peace, national unity and reconciliation (Alaquett cited in SSoka, 2009). For it to be able to perform these two roles, a comprehensive TJ system should be rooted in five cornerstones, which are: trials, truth-seeking, reparations, institutional reform and memorialisation (CCSF, 2010).

Whilst there have been earlier calls for a comprehensive TJ mechanism that transcends an amnesty in post-colonial Zimbabwe (CCJP and LRF, 1997), these were reinforced following the end of the 2000-2008 violence, the signing of the Global Political Agreement (GPA) and the formation of the Government of National Unity (GNU). This latter search for a TJ mechanism was premised on Articles 7 and 18 of the GPA (2008) which called the government to set up a body to spearhead national healing and unity and where possible to arrest and/ or prosecute perpetrators. In an unprecedented and historic move, the nation was simultaneously called to participate in the search for a TJ framework.

Pursuant to this, the GNU launched the ONHRI in July 2009 "to facilitate the creation of a society imbued with values of mutual respect, tolerance and development [and] … freedoms enshrined in the Constitution" (ONHRI, 2009: 3). However, because "the exact character, scope and parameters of a process of national healing being in question" there was need to "consult widely and seek best practices to make the process credible and legitimate and above all […] Zimbabwean" (Ibid). Above this, the ONHRI was supposed to offer "oversight, monitoring, facilitation and evaluation of the national healing programme" (Ibid). In addition, the ONHRI's *Concept paper,* which is the Government's 'Green Paper,' alludes to the possible adoption of *kuripa ngozi* as a local strategy rooted in "culture" and "tradition" of Zimbabweans that guarantees the long term healing of the country (ONHRI, 2009: 22-25).

However, the ONHRI remained fraught with severe challenges. First, it tended to gravitate towards healing without justice (Machakanja, 2010) possibly reflecting the triumph of the ruling Zimbabwe African National Union-Patriotic Front (ZANU-PF) preferred position of peace/reconciliation over the two Movement for Democratic Change (MDC) formations' preference for justice. This dissonance created a polarity at the civic society and individual levels. Both paradigms, however, have fatal weaknesses. On one hand, emphasising peace over justice has in the past spurred cyclic patterns of violence and impunity in post-independence Zimbabwe (Ibid). On the other hand, the call for unfettered justice failed due to "the continued political tensions, the non-reformed judiciary and security sectors, the continued existence of a partisan media," and the continued reign of ZANU-PF which opposed it (CCSF, 2009).

The ONHRI mandate to consider both pre-independence and post- independence violence was also nebulous (Mashingaidze, 2010) rendering possible different "interpretations and prescriptions" regarding its mandate (ONHRI, 2009: 17). The above challenges were compounded by the fact that when the tenure of the GNU drew nigh the work of the ONHRI was relegated in preference for the constitution-making process and the envisaged elections that determined the immediate political survival for the major political parties. Because of these challenges, the achievements of the ONHRI remained marginal with the notable exception being the production of a "reconciliation" film (*Newsday*, 20 November 2013). Critically, however, the ONHRI's calls presented an official platform for the society to discuss the need for a comprehensive TJ framework for Zimbabwe.

"Common sense" conceptual framework

Common sense, spontaneous or everyday philosophy, refers to the "conception of the world which is uncritically absorbed by the various social and cultural environments in which the moral individuality of the average man is developed" (Gramsci, 1998: 419). At face value and because it is philosophy by the "man on the street", and is a product of superstition, folklore, religious beliefs and hegemonic thoughts of the rulers, common sense, is dynamic, deeply penetrative, "fragmentary, incoherent and inconsequential, in conformity with the social and cultural position of those masses whose philosophy it is" (Ibid). This makes it "an ambiguous, contradictory and multiform concept" that is incoherent but entrenched in commonly-held belief systems in a particular community (Ibid: 423).

However, as Geertz (1975: 8) contends, common sense is a "relatively organised body of considered thought rather than just what anyone clothed and in his right mind knows," whose major function is the "immediate deliverance of experience, and not deliberated reflections upon it". Furthermore, common sense is equal to a cultural system that has a genealogy, hence, it can be put through epistemological discursive framing that "can be questioned, disputed, affirmed, developed, formalised, contemplated, even taught..." (Ibid: 8). It also contains "good sense" or "practical empirical common sense" (Gramsci, 1998: 323), out of which, and in an important genealogy, emerges "philosophy and science" (Gencarella, 2010: 231).

On the whole, common sense framework enables an understanding of the power of common sense in re/shaping society, sometimes outside the realms of political and economic structures that are always thought to be the strangleholds of transforming societies (Pandian, 1992). It is also crucial to highlight that because it contains "good sense," it is not necessarily retrogressive hence it is an important site for the subaltern classes to contest hegemonic narratives and ideologies (Pandian, 1992: 6). Working in the Geertzian mode, the chapter evokes the good sense in the common sense belief of *kuripa ngozi*-based TJ, because ultimately "a people are the ideas they believe and practise- the worldviews they embody and around which they construct identities" (Gencarella, 2010: 223).

What is *ngozi*?

Ngozi are spirits that come from relatives or strangers, that were murdered, were wronged or offended, those with a vendetta to make, or those who were improperly buried which cause serious misfortunes, and which require the living to make sacrifices to appease them (Mbiti, 1969). This notion is based on the belief that the dead or living-dead acquire more power and metamorphose into super-spiritual beings who can become interlocutors between the living and God (Tirivangana, 2010). While *ngozi* may be retributive, it largely seeks redress for wrongs committed through revealing a concealed crime, the perpetrator, the victim and their bloodlines (Mahoso, 2012). It also seeks restoration through pushing the wrongdoer to restore the value of the loss for the victim/victims' family (Muwati, *et al*, 2006).

Ngozi usually manifests itself through death of family members of the murderer until the wrongdoer pays compensation (*The*

Standard, 22 May 2010). *Ngozi* affects the other family members because in the traditional set up, all assets, both material/tangible and intangible (including ancestors and life), were shared by the family. In like manner, a deprivation of any asset, either through murder, injury or loss, was a loss to the whole family. Similarly, compensation also signified compensation to the whole family (Tirivangana, 2010). Compensation also restored both the production and reproduction lost (Andersson, 2002) to the family.

However, *ngozi* manifests itself in several other ways, for example, perpetrators may go mad and others lose property mysteriously. Others suffer innumerable misfortunes, like divorces, ill luck, sickness, and loss of jobs and wealth. For some, their children may fail to find marriage partners. Others are beset by bad dreams and visions. At other times *ngozi* manifests itself through possessing a relative of the perpetrator who then re-enacts the murder, which leads the families into negotiations over compensation (Tirivangana, 2010; Muwati, *et al*, 2006).

More broadly, however, as Chivaura says, *ngozi* also refers to any crime that requires redress (*The Standard*, 22 May 2010). As Tirivangana (2010) observes, in addition to referring to sanguinary crimes, "*ngozi* is essentially a crime of depriving one group of their asset or assets (tangible or intangible)". In further qualification, Tirivangana (Ibid) highlights five types of *ngozi*: archetypal *ngozi*, which is directly linked to murder; marital *ngozi*, which occurs when a woman commits suicide in her marital home; transactional *ngozi*, which is related to credits. Fourth, is political *ngozi*, where territorial spirits encouraged guerrillas to fight during the Zimbabwe's liberation war; and, ethical *ngozi*, which occurs when children abuse their mother *(kutanda botso)*.

If *ngozi* exists, why cannot all people who were murdered haunt their killers? As Nyati avers, medicine is used to invoke the *ngozi* spirit (*The Standard*, 22 May 2010). This argument however, has its own limitations as there have been cases where avenging spirits have wreaked havoc in the perpetrators' families without being invoked. The case of Rudo's *ngozi* that beset Munashe leading Munashe's family to seek out Rudo's relatives settled some 500 kilometres away and 23 years after the murder, in Kanengoni's novel (1997), best illustrates this. Also, *the Sunday Mail* (12-18 February 2012), in the Gilbert Kupemba case reported that some relatives of the perpetrators had been possessed by the slain's *ngozi* spirit leading to the exposure of the *ngozi*. A similar case comes from Buhera District where Sosana Mhongoyo discovered her son's murderers through one of the murderers' sister being possessed by her son's spirit (Marwizi and Chimhete, 2010). Together with other occult beliefs: witchcraft and sorcery, *ngozi*, is argued to be at the heart of indigenous African "life forces", that is fertility, sex, disease and death in Zimbabwe (Andersson, 2002: 425).

Kuripa ngozi justice and the everyday

The adage *"mushonga wengozi kuripa"* literally, avenging spirits have to be appeased, is common in the everyday Shona peoples' language. It also defines their social relations. While *ngozi* primarily targets murders, its meaning is extendable to any kind of crime or transgression that people commit. This is the *ngozi*, defined earlier as all those crimes that require redress that this chapter argues for as the basis of the TJ for rural areas. When extended, it means that "all crimes must be atoned" (ONHRI, 2009: 25). In this way, it compels individuals to own up to their wrongs by accepting liability and paying restitution for crimes. This is based on the indigenous Shona principle of restorative justice that centralises material compensation in agreed value as an acknowledgement of the damage or loss caused as the basis for lasting peace. Thus, while *kuripa ngozi* focuses largely on the satisfaction of the victim's needs, it also concerns itself with the "building of bridges" that enable the wrongdoer and the aggrieved to co-exist peacefully and re-establish relations through "cooperative and participatory efforts" (Muwati, *et al*, 2006: 4).

In the case of murder among the pre-colonial Shona, for example, the family of the deceased was usually compensated by social and economic [re]productive items, notably livestock and/or unmarried women. The young women, helped with the procreation, which helped to extend the deceased family line. As Schmidt, (1992) argues, women among the Shona constituted the symbolic and biological reproducers of states because the continuation of lineages and states depended on their fertility. Simultaneously, the cattle and the children born would extend the productive and reproductive lines of the deceased. The children born of the woman "belonged" to the deceased, who was assumed to continue living. This was based on the Shona thinking that *munhu haarovi*, signifying that death is not final, but a transition into a higher and purer spiritual life that could protect the living (Tirivangana, 2010). This also completes the *ubuntu* transformation stages, from the unborn, the living and the living-dead (Nabudere, 2008). Overall, this form of *kuripa ngozi* justice potentially appeased both the living and the living-dead because it rendered various possibilities for restorative justice. First, it enabled dialogue and material compensation between the victims and perpetrators as well as their families. Secondly, it allowed the two parties involved, and the larger community, material and spiritual healing. It, also, afforded the perpetrators the opportunity to be reintegrated into their communities.

From Shurugwi, I observed that the tradition of dialoguing towards restorative justice still happens, especially over civil cases such as, *inter alia*, lobola disputes, *ngozi*, land disputes, and village leadership wrangles. The feuding parties, and other interested community members gather for mediation at village gatherings on rest days (*chisi*). The mediation is presided over by village heads, headmen or chiefs. The complainant lays his/her claim to which the accused responds. Other community members or witnesses are called upon to speak. In the process the issues are laid out and it leads the perpetrator accepting or rejecting the crime. People also ask for forgiveness, others are made to compensate their victims, which in Muwat, *et al*'s words, cited earlier, enables the "building of bridges" between the aggrieving parties. In the case of archetypal *ngozi*, there is the performance of some cleansing rituals which ensures that the *ngozi* spirit is brought to its family to rest whence from it begins to look after the living, thus reuniting the hitherto avenging spirit with the living (Muwati *et al*, 2006: 14).

The justice *kuripa ngozi*, in terms of socio-economic restoration, is relevant in the context of a country that is recently emerging from the horror of political intolerance, the targeting of opponents, and intimidation that had cascaded to the lower tiers of society including neighbours and family members (ONHRI, 2009). Of significance is that while the violence might have been engineered centrally by the major political parties, it was executed at the community/village and individual levels. This mechanism of *kuripa ngozi* seems suitable because it targets the provision of TJ at the level most violence was executed, and potentially where more violence might be played out in the future.

Why *kuripa ngozi?*

The choice of *kuripa ngozi* TJ is informed by the nature of cases including archetypal *ngozi,* and perpetrators who sought forgiveness in the post-violence period. *The Standard (*22 May 2010), reported that a prominent war veteran from Buhera District had been terrorised by *ngozi* of the people he had killed between 2000 and 2008. *African Crisis* (2010) also reported that Sosana Mhongoyo, also from Buhera, established her son's murderers after one of the suspects' sister had been possessed by her son's avenging spirit leading to a settlement.

Still from Buhera, it was also alleged that another prominent national war veterans' leader together with his supporters were being haunted by the *ngozi* of their victim, Nyoka Chokuse, and had consulted numerous spirit mediums to ward off the angry spirit (*Nehanda Radio*, 03 June 2010). Yet another case is that of ZANU-PF's Peter Mabangure who allegedly abandoned his home after being haunted by MDC activist Dickson Chibamba's *ngozi* that also caused the death of his father (Ibid). From Harare, it was also reported that the alleged killers of Tonderai Ndira of the MDC-T visited his grave to pacify his spirit (Ibid). From Gokwe District came the case of Trymore Chokuda's *ngozi* that was settled when the Machaya family paid 35 herd of cattle and US$15 000 (*The Herald*, 19 October 2011).

There were also cases where alleged perpetrators sought forgiveness claiming coercion by their political parties to engage in the violence. They further alleged that they had been abandoned by their respective political parties and were left to rebuild their social relations with their neighbours in the post-violence period (Eppel, 2009). Solidarity Peace Trust (July 2008), and *The Zimbabwean* (6 May 2009), respectively, reported that some war veterans, from Masvingo and Mberengwa had sought forgiveness from their former victims after being haunted by avenging spirits.

From Shurugwi, Marongwe (2013) established that the 2000-2008 violence was one of widespread participation by the low-level community members. This led to allegations of numerous cases in which people participated in the violation of their neighbours. These cases involved people who kept lists of those who did not support their preferred political party and cases of petty-jealousies that were fought on the political stage. While small, these were numerous and involved close relations. They also reveal situations where villagers, neighbours and families, in various degrees, were caught up in the intricate web of the new millennium violence.

Furthermore, there was also evidence from Shurugwi District that some of the alleged victims looked forward to some form of compensation, for the injuries, and for economic and social losses they had sustained (Ibid). Some relations in the district remained ruptured, and there was a strong need to heal the wounds of the violence that occurred between close relatives and work-mates. These findings speak to those of the ZHR NGO Forum (in *Zimonline*, 10 September 2011) that established that up to 76% of the 2000-2008 violence victims were still bitter or failing to cope. In addition, 49% of the victims wanted compensation in addition to calling for a "broad-based truth, recovery and reparation programme as the lasting solution to the national problem" (Ibid). The model for this emerges from the cases where some perpetrators initiated compensation to their victims. An example is from Bindura where the MDC-T chairperson for Bindura North Constituency, Tongai Jack, received a written apology and US$1 500 as compensation by four jailed ZANU-PF supporters for his house they had damaged (*Newsday*, 7 June 2010). There are also instances where some Zimbabwean soldiers and state security operatives sought out their victims/victims' families in an effort to seek forgiveness for atrocities they committed against civilians in Matabeleland and Midlands provinces during the period 1983-1984 (CCJP/LRF, 1997). From the above cases, it is thus necessary to open avenues for the villagers to negotiate peace and possibly organise healing and token compensation through village-based leadership structures.

Traditional justice, *unhu* and *kuripa ngozi*

Lessons on the possibility of adopting a tradition-based TJ for local communities is evinced by the adoption of *magamba* (liberation heroes) spirits in Mozambique, the *mato oputi* in Northern Uganda, and also the *gacaca* in Rwanda (Sriram and Pillay, 2009). Locally, there was the use of similar traditional methods in Zimbabwe including the exhumation and reburials in Matebeleland for the liberation warcombatants and victims of the Matabeleland massacres of the early 1980s sponsored by the Amani Trust in the early 2000s. Despite using Latin American forensic expertise, the reburials relied heavily on African spirit-appeasing practices (Eppel, 2001). Maxwell (1995) also established practices of venerating and appeasing of spirits, including avenging spirits, by the Hwesa of Manicaland Province in Zimbabwe. However, it has been observed that increased references to occult beliefs heighten in moments of hopelessness and increased challenges including war, HIV and AIDS, poverty and economic challenges, among others, symbolising heightened insecurities (Andersson, 2002; Geschiere and Fisiy, 1994; Ashforth, 2005). Notwithstanding the above, it ought to be noted that the cases, however, improve our understanding of the role occult fears play in highlighting societal challenges (Geschiere and Fisiy, 1994). It also compels us "to think about connections between living in a world without justice and living in a world with [occult beliefs] and how these two features of life might affect the cause of democracy", (Ashforth, 2005: XIV) and also what "justice means in a spiritually insecure world" (Ibid: 86).

As such, whilst there could be limitations and criticisms in the above-cited models, they point to some possibility. Arguably as noted by the ONHRI (2009: 22) there is need to recognise and reinforce "traditional means and cultural mechanisms of settling disputes/conflicts" because "long-lasting healing may not take root without national and local ceremonies by the people and their leaders, consistent with cultural timetables, practices and community participation".

In most of Zimbabwe's rural areas, people still live in varied forms of *ubuntu (unhu* in Shona), where members' worth is relational and measured against a collective and members have a duty to the common good of their communities. *Ubuntu* has been defined as "I am because you are, and without you there can be no me" (ONHRI, 2009: 8). This encapsulates the African collective identification, shared humanity and communal destiny. Importantly *ubuntu's* ethos informs the search for the closure of the violence in Zimbabwe because that violence is seen in terms of violating the community at large that, according to the Shona, is against *unhu hwedu* (our humanity). This is because, as Tutu avers, "When I dehumanise you, I inexorably dehumanise myself" (Nabudere, 2008: 5). *Kuripa ngozi*, while placing greater emphasis on the victim, also recognises the wrongdoer's and community's needs in an effort to foster continued mutual existence. As such, "once committed, violence and its consequences cannot be ignored for political expediency. It needs to be addressed in order for individuals, communities and the nation to realise peace and meaningful development" (Muwati *et al*, 2006:10).

The case for a traditional TJ mechanism for Shurugwi District was highlighted at the ZHR NGO Forum TJ consultative meeting at Makusha Community Hall on 3 February 2010 (Zimbabwe Human Rights NGO Forum, 2010). It was suggested that "survivor justice", in the Mamdani (2001: 271-272) formulation, had to be through the payment of restitution by the individual perpetrators to their victims. In addition, the other cases from the district, and cases of alleged *ngozi* from other parts of Zimbabwe, referred to earlier also point to the need for restoration. *Kuripa ngozi* fits the survivor justice billing because its mediation looks at restoration and at the future relations for the two parties bound by a shared humanity and, as Mamdani (Ibid) posits, who have the common blessing of a life after a violent epoch and who have to seek a shared future. This is through the various processes undertaken: mutually inclusive dialogue, forgiveness, cleansing and reparations (Muwati *et al*, 2006: 4; 14), which help the restoration of socio-economic relations between the parties involved.

Furthermore, during interviews conducted in Shurugwi District, for example, many informants kept referring to the need for *kugeza ropa mudunhu redu*/cleansing "our" district of the effects of the violence. This concept of a communal "our", where everything belongs to all comes from the fact that among the Shona, assets, that is, both tangible (material) and intangible (spiritual), are always collectively shared emphasising mutual-coexistence (Tirivangana, 2010). In like manner, success or loss, damage and death, to any of these assets are also shared (Ibid) as communities constitute larger families.

In this *ubuntu* worldview, conflicts "are brought before courts but are resolved through reconciliation. If there is a trial, each party has to make reciprocal concessions so that it can, eventually, be terminated amicably" (Van Hoecke and Warrington, 1998:506). Particular emphasis in the justice system is placed in the "arbitration and mutual concessions" (Ibid: 508) than in the final acquisition of one's rights, with the ultimate aim being survivor justice and restoration through agreed compensation (Ibid). As Muwati *et al* (2006: 5) note, there is "emphasis on harmony, balance, peace, inclusion, restoration and participation."

By articulating survivor justice*, kuripa ngozi* also opens up the opportunity for comprehensively healing the communities affected by violence. Reference is here made to Maxwell's (1995: 327) definition of healing, which is the "totality of activities and ideas which help both individuals and the wider community to come to terms with the experience of violence and bereavement caused by [violence] in a manner which allows them to continue their daily existence". As outlined already, under *kuripa ngozi* this will be through dialogue, cleansing and reparations, which help to restore the physical, emotional and spiritual well-being of the grieving families. Further, by centralising restoring lost economic and social values, *kuripa ngozi* will help foster a culture of individual accountability which helps to restrain potential perpetrators.

The Amani Trust also established that many people in rural Matabeleland had little knowledge of, and little regard for, Western concepts of post-traumatic counselling but preferred the age-old tradition of appeasing spirits (Eppel, 2001). Also, the appeasing of spirits is not an esoteric tradition. Rather, it is one of the metaphysical foundations for a universal and constantive practice in Zimbabwe in the cosmology that links the living with the "living-dead". Following a spate of vehicular accidents at Boterekwa Pass, the Shurugwi Local

Government officials and traditional authorities organised a cleansing ceremony at the site in August 2008 to appease district spirits. A similar ceremony was also held at the National Sports Stadium in Harare in 2003 following the death of 13 soccer fans during the Zimbabwe-South Africa match led by the Zimbabwe Football Association (ZIFA), the Ministry of Education, Sports and Culture. Also in the 1990s and early 2000s, the Zimbabwe government embarked on the reburials and reconstructions of former guerrilla camps in Zambia, Tanzania and Mozambique, for similar reasons (Marongwe, 2013).

I also established from Shurugwi even in 2017 that the practice of appeasing spirits is still common at the household level. For example, when a person dies, before burial, the locals conduct a spiritual autopsy, to establish "who" was responsible for the death (Andersson, 2002), a process called *kurova gata or kuvhunzira* where they consult traditional healers (*n'angas*) or Christian diviners. If the deceased was reportedly bewitched, his or her spirit is invoked to avenge the death. After a year, usually in August, another process called *magadziro* is performed to "bring" the dead person's spirit home, similar to the Ndebele practice of *umbuyiso* (Eppel, 2001). *Magadziro* is preceded by *kubvunzira,* meant to ascertain whether or not someone aggrieved the spirit of the deceased. People still believe strongly that if they do not perform these rituals they risk the wrath of spirits, resulting in misfortunes. Thus, despite the pervasiveness of Christianity and a subscription to "modernity" in Shurugwi, people are still linked to the practice of respecting their ancestral spirits in a discourse of the "traditional".

The above recalls the words of Nabudere (2008: 4) who asserts that, "through these invisible forces, Africans seek explanations to certain happenings which cannot be explained by 'normal' or rational means." The case of the spiritual autopsy in Shurugwi certainly shows that although death is a common everyday occurrence, it is still an "extra ordinary" event beyond "normal" explanation. Related conflicts are also a part of the "uncertainties of existence" (Ibid) that demand supernatural forces in the reconciliation process.

As such, the practice of *kuripa ngozi* is a part of the locals' common sense with the payment of restitution constituting the rock upon which social and other relations in Shurugwi are ballasted. Indeed, as Muwati *et al* (2006: 11) say, "[A]mong the Shona people, restorative justice in the form of restitution and the payment of other reparations is indispensable. *Ngozi* becomes an effective instrument in the full realisation and concretisation of the philosophy of restorative justice." In this cosmogony, while material compensation is paid at the physical level, the *ngozi* spirit "fights from the metaphysical front for truth, restoration and justice" (Ibid). As Nabudere (2008: 5) avers, the twinning of the metaphysical and the real-life forces should be understood in terms of the *ubuntu* philosophy where there is an "inextricable bond between *Umuntu* (individual), the Ancestors and the Supreme Being". In this way, spirits are supposed to play a pivotal role among the living. What we have to note is that these should not be taken as simply useless superstitions, but rather as parts of African philosophy and lived experiences that define the complex cosmogony of the indigenous Zimbabweans.

In arguing for *kuripa ngozi,* this paper is not, however, averse to the calls that senior officials and serious cases be prosecuted and made accountable (*Solidarity Peace Trust*, July 2008). However, as elsewhere, the current political dispensation where one of the perpetrator parties, ZANU-PF, with its control of the state media, the security arms and the judiciary, make such calls premature.

Other pragmatic reasons also inform the choice of this traditional method. There have been about 25 truth and/or reconciliation commissions of inquiry globally since 1974 which have failed to stem violence (Eppel and Raftopoulos, 2008). In Zimbabwe, there have been two government-sponsored commissions of inquiry in the post-independence violence. These were the Dumbutshena, 1981, and the Chihambakwe, 1984, commissions, into the Entumbane disturbances and the Matabeleland atrocities, respectively (Ibid). Strikingly, none of the findings of the commissions were made public, with the government, for example, claiming that the Chihambakwe Commission Report had been lost (Gutu, 2009). Furthermore, the scale and pace of related trials as recorded elsewhere on the continent is worryingly low where only 40 and 10 cases from the Rwandan genocide and the Sierra Leonean conflict, respectively, had been concluded by 2009 (Sriram, 2009).

Civil society organisations have also been calling, without much success, for the establishment of some kind of body to account for Zimbabwe's post-colonial violence (Eppel and Raftopoulos, 2008). In the end, the calling for prosecution or a truth and reconciliation commission at this point of incomplete transformation has proved to be based on a "combination of strong moral fervour and weak political analysis" (Mamdani, 1996, in Eppel and Raftopoulos 2008: 4). Mamdani's analysis seems cogent as the ruling ZANU-PF party prefers unconditional reconciliation to any other methods. As well, the costs of undertaking a TRC, for instance, may be prohibitive for a country that is struggling financially.

Traditional authorities who are still powerful in the districts can be used as Justices of Peace to supervise *kuripa ngozi* programmes. In this role they may be asked, as community leaders, to lead in the mediation of political disputes between feuding members of their societies. It is imperative to note that chiefs and headmen have for long been presiding over civil disputes at their courts, been intercessors between the living and the dead, and led their communities in rainmaking ceremonies, conserving the environments and in communicating with district spirits. It was also on the basis of their long held authority and leadership of their communities that chiefs were chosen to head Ward Centres in the ONHRI hierarchical structure (ONHRI, 2009).These roles are close to what may be expected under *kuripa ngozi* TJ where they will be expected to preside over political cases involving their communities. As such, the addition of political cases to their duties may not constitute a complete disjuncture with their other roles, but simply one more role.

As already stated, this author established from Shurugwi District that most of these village/rural courts sit on '*chisi*' or rest days, which are Thursdays. At these traditional courts I found that people are given the platform to present their case, to respond, and to call upon their witnesses. The other villagers also participate during the mediation. Under this varied form of Family Group Conferencing, where the aggrieved, the perpetrator and the larger community interface and dialogue (Muwati *et al*, 2006), the traditional authorities invite victims and perpetrators to their courts for arbitration. As established from Shurugwi traditional courts, the major arguments and evidence are presented, and the witnesses are called upon. Lastly, chief's or headman's councils consult and pronounce the verdict. In cases where one is found guilty the council then sets the restoration value to be instituted in line with the provisions of the Traditional Leader's Act. What may be needed is the setting of parameters for these courts, regularisation and standardisation of the procedures of these courts to minimise the abuse of privilege and vigilantism (Bizos, 2009). As Bizos (2009: n.p) said:

> I have heard that communities [of Zimbabwe] will start talking to one another. Yes, people within a divided community must start talking but they require, I think, some sort of structure in order to control the dialogue between them and offer some sort of apology, some sort of compensation for loss in order for the process to work.

These parameters should be able to deal decisively with cases of multiple and false accusations that may inadvertently crop up and complicate the TJ method. Lessons could be drawn from the mandate, flaws and strengths of the *gacaca* courts of Rwanda. As well, there might also be need to empower the traditional courts to give their mediations legal force. As Derrida (1992: 11) says, justice is not justice "if it does not have the force to be 'enforced'; a powerless justice is also not justice in the sense of *droit* … justice without force is contradictory, as there are always the wicked … so it is necessary to put justice and force together; and, for this, to make sure that what is justice is strong …"

However, the close association of the traditional leaders with ZANU-PF might compromise their efficacy. They are viewed as functionaries of the ZANU-PF regime because they have continued to receive patronage goods from the state and, because the leadership of the Council of Chiefs, are openly aligned to ZANU-PF, which has led to allegations of the forced deposition of anti-ZANU-PF chiefs Source? Because of this, some of them may have a somewhat vested interest in the cases they are supposed to superintend, which might potentially result in compromised adjudications. Indeed, Scharf's (2003) work in Botswana, established that the outcomes of cases adjudicated by traditional courts largely mirrored ties with the chiefs.

Whilst the above might be an indictment for the chiefs, we ought to realise that few structures were left untainted by political patronisation including the judiciary. Allegations have been made that senior appointments have been influenced by political patronage, that judges have received rewards from ZANU-PF violence including farms, cars and household goods, which makes them invested (*Zimeye*, 28 November 2010). At another level, most of the cases on political violence brought before the judiciary since 2000 have not been finalised, including, the 38 MDC election petitions to the High Court in 2000, and the 2002 election petition by Morgan Tsvangirai. All of these cases were delayed into the next elections rendering them academic (Reeler, 2009). Thus, the case against the traditional leaders, while extreme, is one of degree. If empowered, they can still help mediate many cases. Interestingly, chiefs have had this sort of relationship with the colonial government from the late 1960s and the 1970s (Lan, 1985), but managed to transform into allies of the post-colonial state.

Traditional mediation is also cheaper and more accessible compared to the Western-style courts. In Shurugwi, one needs only US$5 to have their case heard by the headman or the chief. This is much more favourable when looked at against the conventional judicial system where the process is expensive and complicated with the need for police reports, technical processes and legal jargon, and the need for lawyers. Besides, such courts are mostly found in towns and cities. While the Magistrates' courts are located in local towns, the High Court is located in Harare and Bulawayo with occasional sessions in the provincial capitals. The Western-style justice system in Zimbabwe is also fraught with challenges, including, staff shortages, corruption, delays and postponements which leads to increased costs as well as repetitive visits to the courts (*Newsday*, 17 January 2011). Because of this limited reach of the Western justice system, traditional authorities then can have a bigger stake in the TJ.

In arguing for *kuripa ngozi,* the chapter is not calling for an extra-legal transitional justice mechanism. It is using *kuripa ngozi* in the widest sense that seeks the restoration of equilibrium between the victims and perpetrators of the violence, and not necessarily the traditional use of using young women or girls for the appeasements. In this regard, the role of aggrieved spirits can be interchanged with aggrieved living victims seeking justice. Also, whilst the Zimbabwean constitution is silent on the use of women and girls in *kuripa ngozi*, the practice is technically illegal if we consider the Sexual Offences Act, 9, 21; Criminal Law (Codification and Reform) Act, which criminalises sexual relations with minors; Section 14 of the Constitution which is against holding people in slavery or servitude or to perform forced labour; and, the Domestic Violence Act (*Constitution of Zimbabwe,* 2013).

Additionally, such abuses would not continue in the face of a strong lobby by women and gender equality groups in the country such as Msasa Project, Girl Child Network, and Women and Law in Southern Africa. Indeed, the Girl Child Network and the police at one time stopped the transference of five young girls who had been pledged by their families to appease Gibson Kupemba's *ngozi* (The *Sunday Mail*, 12-18 February 2012). Furthermore, as in the past, even in the archetypal *ngozi,* such abuses were limited because of the interventions of the spirits, spirit mediums and the *ngozi* spirits which mediated between the families in disputes and offered checks and balances (Maxwell, 1995).

Conclusion

Drawing on several cases of alleged *ngozi* from across the country, this chapter has argued for the adoption of the historically-rooted practice of *kuripa ngozi* as a TJ method for rural areas of Zimbabwe. It contended that the fear of *ngozi* in the rural areas provides an opportunity for restorative transitional justice, and the potential to reduce impunity. The method seems most feasible as it forms an integral part of rural Zimbabwe people's common sense, is widely known, will not target big political cases that can potentially scuttle the attainment of peace, is cost-effective, quick and is less encumbered technically.

References

Andersson, J.A. (2002) "Sorcery, in the era of 'Henry IV'": Kinship, mobility and mortality in Buhera District, Zimbabwe" in: *Journal of the Royal Anthropological Institute*, Volume 8, (3): 425-449.

Ashforth, A. (2005) *Witchcraft, violence and democracy in South Africa*, Chicago: Chicago University Press.

Catholic Commission for Justice and Peace and The Legal Resources Foundation, (1997) *Breaking the silence, building true peace: A report on the disturbances in Matebeleland and the Midlands 1980-1988*, Harare: CCJP/LRF.

Church and Civil Society Forum, 12-15 May 2009, "Zimbabwe National Reconciliation and Healing Framework: A Proposal Developed at the FORUM'S Consultative Meeting", Kariba, Zimbabwe.

Church and Civil Society Forum, (2010) "Initial national healing discussion paper", Harare.

Derrida, J. (1992) "Force of law: The mystical foundation of authority", in: Cornell, D., *et al*, eds., *Deconstruction and the possibility of justice*, New York and London: Routledge.

Eppel, S. (2009) "A tale of three dinner plates: Truth and challenges of Human Rights Reports in Zimbabwe", in: *Journal of Southern African Studies*, Volume 35, Number 4.

Eppel, S. 26-27 April 2001. "Healing the dead to transform the living: Exhumation and reburial in Zimbabwe", Paper presented at the *Regional and Human Rights' Contexts and DNA*, University of California, Berkeley.

Eppel, S., and Raftopoulos, B. (2008) "Political crisis, mediation and the prospects for transitional justice in Zimbabwe", *IDASA*, Available at: www.zimbabweinstitute.net/File*, Accessed 11 June 2011.*

Geertz, C. (1975) "Common sense as a cultural system", in: *The Antioch Review*, Volume 33, Number 1.

Gencarella, S.O. (2010) "Gramsci, good sense, and critical folklore studies", in: *Journal of Folklore Studies*, Volume 47, Number 3.

Geschiere, P and C. Fisiy, (1994) "Domesticating personal violence: Witchcraft, courts and confessions in Cameroon", *Africa: Journal of the International African Institute*, Volume 64, Number 3. .

Global Political Agreement, (2008) Ministry of Constitutional and Parliamentary Affairs, Harare.

Gramsci, A. (1998) *Selections from the prison notebooks*, edited by Quintin Hoare and Geoffrey Nowell Smith, Chennai: Orient Longman.

Gutu, O., (2009) "National healing impossible without truth commission", Available at: http://www.zimbabwemetro.com/news, Accessed 18 April 2011.

Kanengoni, A. (1997) *Echoing silences*, Sandton: Heinemann.

Lan, D. (1985) *Guns and rain: Guerrillas and spirit mediums in Zimbabwe*, London: James Currey.

Machakanja, P. (2010) "National healing and reconciliation in Zimbabwe: Challenges and opportunities", in: *Zimbabwe Monograph Series*, Number 1, Institute for Justice and Reconciliation Africa Programme.

Mahoso, T. (5-11 February 2012) "*Ngozi*: The philosophical foundation of African Living Law", in: *The Sunday Mail*, Harare: Zimbabwe.

Mamdani, M. (2001) *When victims become killers: Colonialism, nativism, and the genocide in Rwanda*, Princeton University Press: Princeton.

Marongwe, N. 2013) Rural women as victims of militarised political violence: The case of Shurugwi, 2000-2009, *Unpublished PhD thesis*, University of the Western Cape, Cape Town.

Marwizi, W. and Chimhete, C. (15 May 2010) "Avenging spirits torment Zanu PF terror militia", in: *The Standard*, Harare: Zimbabwe.

Mashingaidze, T. (2010) "Zimbabwe's illusive national healing and reconciliation processes: From independence to the inclusive government, 1980-2009, in: *Conflict Trends*, Issue 1.

Maxwell, D. (1995) "Witches, prophets and avenging spirits: The Second Christian movement in North East Zimbabwe" in: *Journal of Religion in Africa*, Volume 25, Number 3 pages?

Mbiti, J. S. (1969) *African religion and philosophy*, London: Heinemann.

Muvingi, I., (2011) "Transitional justice and political pre-transition in Zimbabwe," in: *Conflict Trends*, Issue 1.

Muwati, I., *et al*, (2006) "Echoing Silences as a paradigm for restorative justice in post-conflict Zimbabwe: A philosophical discourse", in: *Zambezia,* Volume XXXIII.

Nabudere, D.W., (2008) "Ubuntu philosophy: Memory and reconciliation", Available at: http://www.doc-txt.com/Ubuntu-Themes.pdf, Accessed 12 March 2012.

Nehanda Radio, 3 June 2010. "*Ngozi* haunts ZANU-PF killers", Available at: http://nehandaradio.com, Accessed 5 August 2011.

Newsday, 17 January 2011. "Magistrate, prosecutor breathe fire", Harare: Zimbabwe.

Newsday, 7 June 2010. "ZANU-PF dumps arrested cadres", Harare: Zimbabwe.

ONHRI, 2009. "Concept paper," Harare: Government of Zimbabwe.

Pandian, M.S.S. (1992) *The image trap: MG Ramachandran in film and politics,* New Delhi: Sage Publications.

Reeler, T. (2009) "Sublimal terror? Human rights violence and torture in Zimbabwe during 2008", Cape Town: Centre for the study of violence and reconciliation.

Scharf, W. (2003) "Non-state justice systems in Southern Africa: How should governments respond?" Paper delivered at workshop on "Working with Non-State Justice Systems held at the Overseas Development Institute held 6-7 March, Institute of Development Studies, Available at: www.ids.ac.uk/ids/law/pdfs/scharf.pdf, Accessed 12 December 2010.

Skaria, A. (2002) "Gandhi's politics: Liberalism and the question of the Ashram", in: *South Atlantic Quarterly*, Volume 101, Number 4.

Sriram, C.L., and Pillay, S. eds. (2009) *Peace vs Justice: The dilemma of transitional justice in Africa*, Scottsville: UKZN Press.

SSoka, Y. L., (2009) "The politics of transitional justice" in: Chandra Lekka Sriram and Suren Pillay, eds, *Peace vs Justice: The dilemma of transitional justice in Africa*, Scottsville: UKZN Press.

SW Radio Africa, 10 April 2009 "Hot seat interview with George Bizos, Sekai Holland, Glen Mpani and Mary Ndlovu: Reconciliation, justice and national healing", in:

http://kubatana.net/html/archive/demgg090410swradio.asp? Accessed 21 May 2011.

The Herald, 19 October 2011. "Governor pays US$15 000, 35 cattle compensation to deceased family", Harare: Zimbabwe.

The Herald, 20 May 2011. "Summit dissolves tribunal", Harare: Zimbabwe.

The Herald, 26 July 2011. "Parties' differences disrupt Bill hearing", Harare: Zimbabwe.

The Standard, 22 May 2010. "*Ngozi*: Primitive superstition or reality?" Harare: Zimbabwe.

The Sunday Mail, 12-18 February 2012. "Kupemba's lone battle," Harare, Zimbabwean.

The Zimbabwean, 6 May 2009. "I need forgiveness-Chitoro," London: United Kingdom.

Tirivangana, A., 29 May 2010. "The metaphysical scope of *Ngozi*", in: *The Standard*, Harare: Zimbabwe.

Van Hoecke, M. and Warrington, M. (1998) "Legal cultures, legal paradigms and legal doctrine: Towards a new model for comparative law", in: *International and Comparative Law Quarterly*, Volume 47, Available at: http://www.jstor.org, Accessed 12 March 2011.

Zimbabwe Human Rights NGO Forum, (2009) 'Outreach Report,' June 2009.

Zimbabwe Human Rights NGO Forum, (2010) "Who will dare begin the process of recovering the truth", Volume 2, cited in http://www.hrforum.com/special_hrru/outreach-report-07-10.pdf, Accessed 19 May 2011.

Zimeye, 28 November 2010. "Bennett asks judge to disclose farms", Available at: http://www.zimeye.org/?p=24633, Accessed 31 July 2011.

Chapter 10

Appeasing the Dead and Cleansing the Living: the Pursuit of Peace in the Aftermath of Political Violence in 21ˢᵗ Century Zimbabwe

Fidelis Peter Thomas Duri

Introduction

The culture of violence became deeply embedded in Zimbabwe's political fabric during the new millennium. Since 2000, most incidents of political violence which left many people dead involved the ruling Zimbabwe African National Union Patriotic Front (ZANU-PF) under Robert Mugabe and the Movement for Democratic Change (MDC) under the leadership of Morgan Tsvangirai. It should be noted that the MDC split into three factions in 2005 which went on to name themselves after their respective leaders. The parties that resulted from the split were the MDC-Tsvangirai (MDC-T), the main faction under the leadership of Morgan Tsvangirai; the MDC Ncube (MDC-N) led by Welshman Ncube; and the MDC Mutambara (MDC-M) under Arthur Mutambara (*Nehanda Radio*, 11 June 2015). Since its formation the MDC and later the MDC-T was most involved in incidents of political violence with ZANU-PF than other factions. Zimbabwe's history of political violence shows that ZANU-PF had an advantage over the opposition because as the ruling party, it controlled various aspects of state machinery such as finances, secret service, police force, army, judiciary and the media (Machaya, 20 June 2016; Makumbe, 2006).

Concerns have been raised in various quarters about the ability of Zimbabwe's criminal justice system in handling murder cases in general and those related to politically-motivated violence in particular in a manner that brings about reconciliation and lasting peace to the generality of the population. The impartiality of Zimbabwe's judiciary when handling cases of politically-motivated murders has also been questioned by various critics (*Financial Gazette*, 19 January 2017; Human Rights Watch, 3 November 2008; Johnson, 5 March 2001; *New Zimbabwe*, 30 July 2014). This scepticism arose because, since 2000, the Zimbabwean government appointed judges and magistrates who were known to be sympathetic to ZANU-PF (Human Rights Watch, 3 November 2008). Godfrey Chidyausiku, Zimbabwe's late Chief Justice, George Chiweshe, the Judge President of the High Court, during the period 2001 to 2017, were cited as examples by various analysts. When Zimbabwe became independent in 1980, Chidyausiku, for example, was elected into the first parliament on a ZANU-PF ticket and was immediately appointed Deputy Minister of Local Government by Robert Mugabe, the then Prime Minister. He went on to assume the powerful position of Attorney General before being appointed Chief Justice in 2001. Regarding Chiweshe, he served in the armed forces before he was appointed to be a High Court Judge and later Judge President of the High Court (Muzulu, 21 January 2017).

Such burning concerns that interrogate the impartiality, credibility and effectiveness of 'modern' criminal justice systems in general and the Zimbabwean judiciary in particular in handling cases of politically-motivated murder call for serious consideration of alternative or complementary non-prosecutorial transitional justice mechanisms that guarantee social healing and lasting peace. This chapter, therefore, examines some of the African indigenous justice mechanisms employed mostly by the rural Shona and Ndebele people of Zimbabwe in an effort to achieve peace and reconciliation in conflict and post-conflict communities that were decimated by political violence during the new millennium. Focusing specifically on the institution of avenging spirits, *ngozi* in Shona and *uzimu* in Ndebele (Masaka and Chemhuru, 2011; Zambara, 2015), the chapter underlines the importance of "a ritual resolution of the history of violence" (Alexander, 2006: 109). The chapter argues that the institution of avenging spirits can be a viable mechanism of transitional justice that heals social fissures and guarantees lasting peace in post-conflict societies.

Conceptualisation of *ngozi* as a transitional justice mechanism

The belief in the existence of avenging spirits of deceased persons that haunt the living has its origins in many parts of pre-colonial Africa and continues to constitute an important aspect of the socio-cultural landscape among post-colonial African societies such as the Shona and the Ndebele in Zimbabwe (Bourdillon, 1982). Scholars generally agree that *ngozi/uzimu* is the angry and disgruntled spirit of a person who is ether dies after experiencing a lifetime of ill-treatment, or is murdered in cold blood, that returns to haunt its tormentors. A few definitions from some scholars will be examined in this section.

According to Benyera (2014: 21), *ngozi* is "a traditional justice system used predominantly by the Shona people in Zimbabwe and Mozambique, in which the deceased person returns in spirit to haunt his/her murderer's family until the members admit to committing the crime. This leads to their subsequent payment of compensation to the deceased's family, usually in the form of cattle and money." Once restitution has been paid, peace and normalcy return to the perpetrators, their families and relatives (Muwati, Gambahaya and Mangena, 2006). Tabona Shoko, a Zimbabwean writer, quoted by Guma (18 July 2012: 1) describes *ngozi* as "the spirit of a person whose death came as a result of foul play or who has been wronged and dies harbouring feelings of being mistreated." Muwati, Gambahaya and Mangena (2006: 5) state that *ngozi* is "the ravaging spirit of a wronged person who dies before the wrong is corrected. In most instances, *ngozi* is a result of justified or unjustified violent murder of another person…"

Mutekwa (2010: 162) provides a very informative definition of *ngozi* (avenging spirits) as:

> Avenging spirits, as the name implies, are spirits questing for revenge for some wrong perpetrated on them, and unrectified, during their lifetime. The quest for retribution and justice is the reason for the malevolence of the avenging spirits, and they should not be confused with any evil spirit… In the context of the avenging spirits the word is

also an indication of the danger posed by these spirits, and the havoc they are capable of bringing about...

It should be noted, therefore, that *ngozi* is a form of restorative justice which, according to McLaughlin, Fergusson and Hughes (2003), seeks to appease the victims and cleanse the offenders. Restorative justice therefore differs from retributive justice which involves "the use of criminal courts to bring punishment on (the) perpetrators of human rights abuse" (Church and Civil Society Forum, 2012: 4). In the words of Muwati, Gambahaya and Mangena (2006: 4):

> Restorative justice is a concept or philosophy of justice that emphasises first and foremost, the need to repair damage, loss or harm engendered by criminal behaviour, of which politically-motivated violence is a part. The most critical aspect in restorative justice is restoration rather than retribution or mere punishment. Restorative justice is not meant to benefit only the justice system, as retributive justice often does; it benefits both the victim and the offender, ensuring that the two parties continue to live together in peace and harmony...Mere punishment or retribution does not benefit the offended particularly in a context where he or she has lost material possessions or even life. The reason is that with retributive justice, the emphasis is on the offender, that is, the offender must receive appropriate punishment and the punishment must mirror the crime committed. Attention is not given to the victim. On the other hand, restorative justice requires cooperative and participatory efforts that involve both the offenders and the aggrieved with a view to compensate the victim.

Benyera (2014) outlines some of the advantages of 'traditional justice' mechanisms such as *ngozi*. Among other things, the avenging spirit causes various calamities which force offenders to confess their commission of a crime. Thus, *ngozi* exposes crimes such as murder that may not have been detected by the police and the general public. In addition, *ngozi* is didactic to the general community on the consequences of committing murder by causing suffering on the perpetrator's family members and relatives. The payment of restitution also serves an important social function of reconciling the families of the perpetrator and the bereaved.

It should be emphasised that *ngozi* is not a demon but an aggrieved spirit that seeks to heal the dead and positively transform the living (Eppel, 2006; Nhemachena, 2014). As Mupeperekwi (26 February 2015: 1) rightly noted:

> …*Ngozi* is the spirit of a wronged person seeking justice. This must be viewed against the wrong general public notion that *ngozi* is an evil spirit that seeks to destroy life and property…Today many church-going people and others who have become alienated from their African roots want to dismiss *ngozi* as…evil spirits.

As a restorative justice mechanism, *ngozi* "restores the dignity of the offender, the humanity of the victim and the solidarity of the community" (Benyera, 2014: 202). It is "a theory of social repair" that "engage(s) the participation of the victims, offenders and their respective communities" (Church and Civil Society Forum, 2012: 5).

Politically-motivated murder in 21st century Zimbabwe: An overview of selected cases

From the year 2000, political violence pervaded Zimbabwe's political landscape. Most incidents of political violence were perpetrated by the ruling ZANU-PF party as it sought to cling to power at all costs in the face of the rising popularity of the MDC that had been formed in 1999 (Bond and Manyanya, 2001; Duri, 2010; Hammar and Raftopoulos, 2003; Raftopoulos, 2003). The Amani Trust, a non-governmental organisation which monitored incidents of political violence from mid-February 2000 to the time of elections in June, observed that around 35 000 politically-motivated incidents of violence occurred and ZANU-PF supporters were behind 91.2% of them (Feltoe, 2004). During the same period, more than 30 people were killed and around 18 000 were subjected to human rights abuses, with most of the victims reported to be MDC supporters and sympathisers (Masunungure, 2004). More than 120 lives were lost during the pre-election violence (Hill, 2003). The Human Rights Non-Governmental Organisations Forum noted that between January and September 2004, 12 MDC supporters lost their lives during incidents of politically-motivated violence (Chimhete, 8 January 2005). Political violence during the year 2008 resulted in the death of more than 200 people, mostly opposition party supporters (Human Rights Watch, 8 March 2011). The 2013 pre-election period was also characterised by incidents of political violence. According to the Heal Zimbabwe Trust, a non-governmental organisation, 83.3% of the recorded cases of political violence during this period were instigated by ZANU-PF supporters (Heal Zimbabwe Trust, 28 July 2013).

It is not the intention of this chapter to demonise ZANU-PF and exonerate opposition parties such as the MDC from incidents of political violence. Indeed, some MDC supporters and officials were implicated in some cases of political violence. In December 2001, for example, a group of suspected MDC supporters reportedly killed Wills Dhliwayo, a war veteran and ZANU-PF member, near Chako Business Centre in Chipinge District. Local reports stated that he was found murdered a day after quarrelling with MDC supporters (*News 24 Archives*, 28 December 2001). On 29 May 2011, MDC-T supporters under the leadership of Tungamirai Madzokere, Yvonne Musarurwa and Last Maengahama, allegedly murdered Petros Mutedzi, a ZRP Inspector, at Glen View 3 Shopping Centre in Harare. The three were each sentenced to 20 years in prison by the High Court in December 2016 (Munyoro, 13 December 2016). In late October 2011, MDC-T youths reportedly attacked ZANU-PF officials who were carrying out a provincial audit exercise in Harare's Hatcliffe Suburb. They went on to besiege a local police station where they smashed vehicles and assaulted people (*Zimbabwe Broadcasting Corporation News Online*, 31 October 2011). On 24 August 2016, MDC-T youths who were demonstrating in Harare looted supermarkets and put to flame two vehicles belonging to the ZRP and the Zimbabwe Broadcasting Corporation (Razemba, 25 August 2016).

It can be noted that opposition parties such as the MDC were sometimes implicated in cases of political violence. For reasons mentioned earlier on in this chapter, ZANU-PF, as the ruling party, often had the advantage in most of the violent contestations. This section examines selected incidents of political violence during which the people were murdered and their avenging spirits reportedly 'returned' to torment the perpetrators together with their families. It will be noted from these selected cases that ZANU-PF members were the perpetrators while MDC supporters were the victims.

During the March 2002 presidential elections, Tedious Chokuda, an MDC activist and Headmaster of Murowe School in Buhera District, was murdered by suspected ZANU-PF assailants (Marwizi and Chimhete, 15 May 2010; Movement for Democratic Change, 1 June 2010). Chokuda was firstly abducted from his school before being murdered. His body was later found hanging from a tree at Chiurwi School where he was the Presiding Officer during the elections. The police informed the Chokuda family that the headmaster had committed suicide for undisclosed reasons (Marwizi and Chimhete, 15 May 2010).

In 2004, Misheck Busangavanye, the then Chipinge Rural District Council Vice-Chairman and also ZANU-PF Ward 26 Councillor, together with his sons Jairos and Brighton, allegedly murdered Philemon Nyamunda, an MDC party member. In committing the crime, they were also assisted by Erisha Tomu, Sugar Gondoma, Richard Matikwa, James Mapamha and Tackson Tenda. Nyamunda was reportedly killed at the councillor's shop at Matikwa Business Centre. Busangavanye and his accomplices allegedly handcuffed Nyamunda to a pole at the shop. They reportedly flogged him and pulled his private parts throughout the night (Bishi, 3 March 2017). They allegedly hung him upside-down during the nightlong assault (*TellZim News*, 10 February 2017). Nyamunda died at Chisumbanje Police Station where Busangavanye had gone to get a police report so that they could rush Nyamunda to seek medical treatment after sustaining severe injuries. It was reported that Busangavanye gave his accomplices beer while they assaulted Nyamunda throughout the night (Bishi, 3 March 2017).

In 2007, Alois Chandisarewa Sangare, the then MDC-T Councillor for Ward 16 in Murewa North District, was murdered by suspected ZANU-PF supporters. The dead body was discovered in his house at Chinake Village. His hands were tied with a rope and a woman's inner garment (petticoat) was stuffed in his mouth (Makoni, 5 July 2011; *Zimbabwean*, 7 August 2012).

In May 2008, Mupango Chokuse, the MDC-T Chairperson for Ward 27 in the Buhera South District of Manicaland Province, was allegedly murdered by ZANU-PF supporters. On 17 May 2008, about 600 ZANU-PF sympathisers comprising civilian activists, soldiers and members of the Zimbabwe Republic Police (ZRP) besieged Ward 27 to terrorise the local MDC-T supporters ahead of the June Presidential run-off election. During the orgy of terror, Chokuse, who had hidden in a toilet, was allegedly abducted by two ZRP officers named Dick and Chitima. They force-marched him to a local ZANU-PF camp where a senior member of the Zimbabwe National Liberation War Veterans Association (ZNLWVA) and alleged leader of the 'operation', was stationed. At the camp, Chokuse was severely assaulted. When the ZNLWVA official realised that Chokuse's life was in danger as a result of the injuries sustained during the assault, he allegedly sought to rush him to a local clinic for treatment. Chokuse died in the official's car before they reached the clinic. They then ferried Chokuse's body to the Birchenough Bridge Hospital where they left it in the mortuary (Benyera, 2014; *Shortwave Radio Africa*, 20 May 2008). For three months, Chokuse's body lay in the mortuary as the police were unsure of what to do. They then dumped the corpse in the nearby crocodile-infested Save River (Benyera, 2014).

On 21 March 2009, Moses Chokuda, the MDC-T's Organising Secretary for Gokwe District in the Midlands Province, was allegedly waylaid and murdered by four ZANU-PF activists while on his way to the party's District Council meeting. The names of the four assailants were later reported as Farai Machaya, the son of the then ZANU-PF Midlands Provincial Governor; Abel Maphosa, a ZANU-PF activist; Edmore Gama, a Zimbabwe National Army (ZNA) soldier and ZANU-PF's Midlands Province Youth Secretary; and Bothwell Gama, a brother to Edmore and also a member of the ZNA. The father of Edmore and Bothwell was Ignatius Gama, the then ZANU-PF Gokwe District Coordinating Chairperson (Benyera, 2014; *Standard*, 30 October 2011).

Tawengwa Chokuda, the deceased's father, refused to bury the body until the perpetrators had been brought to book. The police threatened to arrest him for not burying his son (Benyera, 2014). To add insult to injury on the Chokuda family, it took almost three years for the murder case to be heard in court while the Machaya family refused to admit guilt (Benyera, 2014). In September 2011, the High Court found the accused persons guilty of murder and sentenced each one of them to 18 years in prison. Despite the sentence, Tawengwa Chokuda refused to bury his son until the families of the perpetrators had come to see him to admit guilt and pay restitution (Benyera, 2014). The deceased remained in the mortuary for close to three years and was only buried on 22 October 2011 after restitution had been paid (Benyera, 2014; *Standard*, 30 October 2011; Zambara, 2015).

On 26 May 2012, Cephas Magura, the then MDC Mudzi North District Ward 1 Chairperson, was murdered by a crowd of ZANU-PF supporters at Chimukoko Business Centre. The mob, which numbered about 300 ZANU-PF supporters, drawn from the villages of Makaha, Chikwizo, Nyamatawa and Goromonzi in Mudzi District, was mobilised by the local ZANU-PF Members of Parliament to disrupt an MDC rally, attended by about 70 people, that was underway at the business centre (*Bulawayo 24 News*, 1 August 2012; Guma, 18 July 2012). The ZANU-PF assailants who were directly implicated in the murder were led by David Chimukoko and included Uyandipi, Chimukoko's mother-in-law; Eric Chatiza, a teacher at Chimukoko Primary School; Tangwe Chionerwa, Chatiza's uncle; Loveness Chipuriro, Pedzisai Jumbe, Gilbert Chionerwa and another supporter only reported as Better (*Bulawayo 24 News*, 1 August 2012).

According to a young boy who was herding cattle and managed to witness the event, skirmishes began when ZANU-PF supporters arrived to disrupt an MDC rally that was taking place at Chimukoko Business Centre. Magura fell to the ground after being hit by a stone on the head. A group of ZANU-PF supporters continued to assault Magura. They dragged him to the roadside and left him lying helplessly on the ground. Seven other MDC supporters were injured during the incident and had to be rushed to the Avenues Clinic in Harare for treatment (Guma, 18 July 2012).

Without exonerating those opposition party officials and sympathisers who sometimes engaged in violence, this section has demonstrated that ZANU-PF members allegedly perpetrated most of the incidents of politically-motivated murder in which many MDC supporters fell victim. What seems to lend credence to this observation, as will be noted later on in this chapter, is that most of the perpetrators later confessed to the families of the deceased, and sometimes at public fora, after experiencing mysterious happenings and went on to pay restitution in accordance with the procedures laid out by local traditional courts.

Manifestations of *ngozi*

Avenging spirits are believed to manifest themselves in a number of mysterious happenings. In some cases, the dead express their concerns through a possessed medium (Gelfand, 1973). In many instances, *ngozi* causes illness, death and a plethora of misfortunes on the perpetrator's family members and close relatives (Bourdillon, 1982; Tatira, 2014). Such manifestations continue until the perpetrator admits guilt and pays restitution; thus, the Shona proverb *mushonga wengozi kuripa* (avenging spirits can only be appeased by payment of restitution) (Benyera, 2014; Moyo, 2015; Shoko, 2013). This section looks at how the avenging spirits of some victims of politically-motivated murders reportedly manifested themselves to the murderers and their family members as a way of pressing them to confess, show remorse and pay reparations.

On 3 July 2008, in Matenga Village in Buhera South District, Dickson Chibamba, an MDC activist, was murdered at his home by a group of ZANU-PF supporters led by Peter Mabangure. Within a few months, Chibamba's avenging spirit allegedly began terrorising Peter Mabangure's family. Peter Mabangure's father, for example, reportedly woke up every morning while in the house of the deceased Chibamba. Peter Mabangure died in 2010 and reports from the village community indicated the avenging spirit as the cause of death. In addition, there were numerous reports that the ghost of Dickson often 'visited' Peter Mabangure asking him why he had murdered him. In May 2010, Peter Mabangure fled from his home in fear of

Dickson's ghost which he said frequently visited him (Movement for Democratic Change, 1 June 2010).

In early 2010, Patrick Basopo, a police constabulary and a ZANU-PF activist who had played part in the murder of Tedious Chokuda, an MDC activist and Headmaster of Murowe School in Buhera District, during the 2002 presidential elections, publicly confessed that he had been involved in the murder of Tedious Chokuda. He was forced to make the confession after mysterious happenings had begun taking place. Reports indicated that Basopo's sister from Mutiusinazita Village became possessed with Chokuda's avenging spirit from September 2009 (Marwizi and Chimhete, 15 May 2010; Movement for Democratic Change, 1 June 2010).

The woman is reported to have confronted Patrick, her brother, inquiring why he had murdered Chokuda. She also disclosed to Basopo's relatives how, in the middle of the night, a group of ZANU-PF thugs led by Patrick abducted Chokuda from the house in which he was sleeping and brutally killed him. In order to conceal evidence of the murder, they tied him with shoelaces and left him hanging from a tree to give the impression that he had committed suicide. The possessed woman went on to warn the Basopo family that Chokuda's angry spirit would not rest until reparations had been paid in full. In late 2009, the Basopo family approached Cuthias Mahachi Chapanduka, the then Headman Mashumba, to convene a traditional court in order to organise the payment of restitution. During the court proceedings, the woman became possessed again and narrated how Patrick Basopo and four accomplices murdered Chokuda. Patrick then confessed murdering Chokuda after his sister had finished narrating. The possessed woman ordered Patrick to pay 65 cattle as restitution. When Patrick tried to disclose the names of the other four killers, the possessed woman stopped him and stated that the spirit of Chokuda would tackle each of the assailants one by one. The possessed woman added that Patrick had been paid for the murder and used the proceeds to construct an asbestos-roofed house. She then ordered him to remove the asbestos sheets, windows and nails and hand them to the Chokuda family. The woman also demanded that Patrick pay the Chokuda family an additional cow to compensate for the groceries he bought from some of the money he

201

was paid for committing the murder (Marwizi and Chimhete, 15 May 2010).

Strange happenings were reported soon after the murder of Mupango Chokuse, the MDC-T Chairperson for Ward 27 in the Buhera South District of Manicaland Province, by ZANU-PF supporters on 17 May 2008. Reports circulated that, in the Birchenough Bridge Hospital mortuary, the police found Chokuse "seated on his coffin and raising his hand in the MDC-T slogan. Those who tried to move his body reported strange events such as hearing Chokuse's voice demanding to know why he had been killed" (Benyera, 2014: 243-244). In June 2010, Naison Nemadziva, the then MDC Buhera South Member of Parliament, revealed that a senior ZANU-PF official, also a ZNLWVA leader, who had been implicated in the murder, was being tormented by Chokuse's spirit together with his accomplices:

> (He) has become a constant visitor to spirit mediums as Chokuse's ghost has been terrorising him. Even the youths who were sent by Chinotimba have not been spared in this ordeal (Movement for Democratic Change, 1 June 2010: 1).

Unusual happenings were reported following the murder of Moses Chokuda, the MDC's Organising Secretary for Gokwe District in the Midlands Province, on 21 March 2009 by four ZANU-PF activists under the command of Farai Machaya, the son of ZANU-PF's Governor for the Midlands Province. When the Chokuda family refused to bury Moses until the perpetrators had paid them restitution through a traditional court, a group of 10 policemen took matters into their own hands and organised a pauper's burial but they reportedly failed to lift his coffin out of the Gokwe District Hospital mortuary (Benyera, 2014; *My Zimbabwe*, 21 June 2016). Meanwhile, mysterious happenings were taking place within the Machaya family. Governor Machaya's daughter, for example, reportedly fled the family home and took refuge in a graveyard (Benyera, 2014).

As Moses' body lay in the mortuary over the years, state officials who tried to intervene also underwent unusual experiences allegedly instigated by the avenging spirit of the deceased. Three officials from the Attorney General's Office who visited the Chokuda homestead to persuade the family to withdraw murder charges against the Governor's son allegedly saw the deceased Moses in person forcing them to flee from the village leaving their vehicle behind (Benyera, 2014). When the Moses Chokuda's murder was first heard at the criminal court, the magistrate who granted the accused persons bail reportedly began to experience mental challenges that forced him to retire on medical grounds. He only became well again after the murder case had been settled at the High Court (Benyera, 2014). Reports also circulated that the staff at the Gokwe District Hospital often saw the deceased Moses sitting on top of his metal coffin in the mortuary (*My Zimbabwe*, 21 June 2016).

In early July 2012, some of the ZANU-PF supporters accused of murdering Cephas Magura, the MDC Mudzi North District Ward 1 Chairperson, in May earlier during the year were reported to be dying under mysterious circumstances while others were living uncomfortable and haunted lives. Eric Chatiza, for example, collapsed and died in his cell at Mutoko Prison on 12 July 2012. During Chatiza's funeral, his uncle, Tangwe Chionerwa, who was also implicated in the death of Magura but was not arrested, collapsed and died. They were both buried the next day (*Bulawayo 24 News*, 1 August 2012; Guma, 18 July 2012). Commenting on these deaths that happened within two days of each other, Kubvoruno Choga, the MDC-T Mudzi North District Spokesman said: "We really suspect that (they) died because of what we call in Shona *ngozi*" (Guma, 18 July 2012: 1). David Chimukoko, the gang leader of Magura's murderers, was reported to be critically ill at the Mutoko Remand Prison while Uyandipi, his mother-in-law who was also involved in Magura's murder, collapsed and died at Chirova Village on 18 July. Local villagers also noted that other assailants such as Loveness Chipuriro, Pedzisai Jumbe, Gilbert Chionerwa and Better had developed mental challenges bordering on madness (*Bulawayo 24 News*, 1 August 2012; Guma, 18 July 2012). Fungai Mahachi, the then Mudzi North District Ward 1 Councillor, confirmed these developments attributed to the avenging spirit of Cephas Magura: "The stories might sound unreal but they are true. I can confirm reports on an avenging spirit that has been haunting those responsible for Magura's death asking them why they killed him" (*Bulawayo 24 News*, 1 August 2012: 1). Among other things, these incidents from Mudzi District show that avenging spirits can kill the perpetrators themselves if there are no hopes that restitution would be paid. In Shona traditional beliefs, *ngozi* is "capable of causing disease and hardship and may haunt the perpetrators to death if they are not appeased" (*Insider Zimbabwe*, 11 February 2013: 1).

During August 2012, the families of ZANU-PF thugs who allegedly murdered Alois Chandisarewa Sangare, the MDC-T Councillor for Ward 16 in Murewa North District, in 2007 were reportedly besieged by avenging spirits. Villagers from the area reported that family members of the alleged murderers were "perishing mysteriously. Some have reportedly lost their sanity" (*Zimbabwean*, 7 August 2012).

In February 2013, Cairo Mhandu, the ZANU-PF Member of Parliament for Mazowe North Constituency, was reported to have become mentally deranged as a result of his involvement in various murders committed during the run-up to the June 2008 presidential election run-off. Shepherd Mushonga, the then MDC Member of Parliament for Mazowe Central Constituency, and Martin Musemwa, the then MDC local councillor, informed United States embassy officials that Mhandu had become mentally incapacitated because of avenging spirits that were tormenting him. Mushonga appraised that Mhandu approached Makope, the local chief, for assistance in resolving the matter. Mhandu told Chief Makope that he was prepared to offer a cow to the family of one of the victims of the 2008 violence in Chaona Village where six people had died as a result of serious injuries. Chief Makope refused to serve as an arbiter and told him to go it alone which Mhandu never did (*Insider Zimbabwe*, 11 February 2013).

Up to February 2017, when he paid restitution for the murder of Philemon Nyamunda, an MDC supporter, in 2004, Misheck Busangavanye, the Chipinge Rural District Council Vice-Chairman and also ZANU-PF Ward 26 Councillor, was reportedly tormented by *ngozi*. During this period, Busangavanye reportedly saw the deceased sitting in his bedroom on many occasions. The Councillor is also alleged to have fled his car several times after seeing the deceased seated next to him. The baby of one of Busangavanye's wives reportedly drowned in a bucket of water one night. These unusual happenings forced him to abandon his home and relocate to Checheche Growth Point some 20 kilometres away (Bishi, 3 March 2017). In 2013, 2014 and 2015, Busangavanye's brothers died under mysterious circumstances together with his sons who were working in South Africa (Bishi, 3 March 2017; *TellZim News*, 10 February 2017). These terrifying developments forced Busangavanye to approach Village Head Lameck Matikwa in February 2017 seeking assistance to resolve the issue with the Nyamunda family, leading to the payment of restitution (Mawawa, 6 February 2017).

This section illustrated the various manifestations of avenging spirits of deceased persons on their murderers and family members. In some cases, as noted in this section, these manifestations show up soon after the commission of murder. In other cases, it has been shown that the manifestations show up a number of years after the murder as if to give the murderers adequate time to reflect on their wrongdoing, confess, show remorse and pay restitution. Such manifestations that appear after lengthy periods of time offer enough lessons to the perpetrators and the society at large that a crime can never be brushed aside by the passage of time; hence the Shona proverb: *mhosva hairovi*, implying that a criminal offence is never concealed forever until it is properly brought to its final conclusion (Gappah, 2016).

Arbitration, restitution and cleansing

In accordance with indigenous African jurisprudence, an avenging spirit of a murdered or wronged person can be appeased after certain procedures are followed. The perpetrator has to show remorse, confess and pay restitution in order to be cleansed. In most cases, as shall be noted in this section, these formalities are mediated by traditional leaders such as chiefs, headmen/women and village heads assisted by spirit mediums. This arbitration process, which results in the payment of restitution, is normally conducted at a traditional court where people from the local communities are allowed to attend.

It is generally believed that avenging spirits cannot be appeased through shortcuts. Those who have sought to calm them by conducting cleansing ceremonies without paying restitution through the proper procedures have reportedly failed to bring normalcy back into their lives. In October 2011, for example, more than 700 perpetrators of political violence, most of them ZANU-PF war veterans who had murdered opposition supporters during the 2008 elections, were reportedly trekking to Njelele Shrine "in vain attempts to cleanse their bloodied hands and to find peace with the dead and the maimed victims of their 'valiant' deeds" (*Newsday*, 21 October 2011: 1). Haunted by the avenging spirits of their victims, many of these "pilgrims" slaughtered cattle at the Njelele Shrine "in a bid to get national ancestors to wash blood off their hands and cleanse their cursed spirits" (*Newsday*, 21 October 2011: 1).

This section discusses some incidents in 21st century Zimbabwe that illustrate the belief among most African societies that the procedure of appeasing avenging spirits van neither be short-circuited nor suppressed by cleansing ceremonies without restitution being paid through the formal protocol of traditional courts. As some of the examples also demonstrate, 'modern' criminal justice systems only serve the purpose of punishing the offenders but do not appease the dead.

The murder of Moses Chokuda, the MDC's Organising Secretary for Gokwe District in the Midlands Province, by a group of assailants led by Farai Machaya, the son of the ZANU-PF Midlands Provincial Governor, on 21 March 2009, for example, was only settled after close to three years in October 2011 by a traditional court despite an earlier High Court ruling that had sentenced each of the perpetrators to 18 years in prison. The mediation by Chief Njelele, the local traditional leader, brought the case to its final conclusion when he convened a meeting between the Chokuda and Machaya families (Benyera, 2014). At the traditional court, the Machaya family members admitted guilt and Chief Njelele ordered them to pay the Chokuda family US$15 000 and 35 herd of cattle as restitution (Benyera, 2014; *Standard*, 30 October 2011). The traditional court session was concluded by a reconciliatory process during which the two families shared a meal while apologies were being offered (Benyera, 2014). After two years and seven months (*Newsday*, 26 October 2011), Moses was finally laid to rest on 22 October 2011 following the payment of restitution (*Standard*, 30 October 2011; Zambara, 2015).

It becomes quite apparent that the institution of *ngozi* as a restorative justice mechanism serves the important social function of restoring peace and harmony between the families of the perpetrators and the bereaved. Commenting on the conclusion of the Chokuda case, Phathisa Nyathi, a Zimbabwean historian, observed:

> The traditional system worked in this case because in our African culture imprisoning a culprit does not help at all. When such things happen in our culture, what is important is to reestablish the lost equilibrium, the lost harmony: the injured social relations. The Shona have the best solution to this; the operation of *ngozi* where the murderer has to pay (*Standard*, 30 October 2011: 1).

In addition, the ravages of *ngozi* serve as a deterrent to the general community from committing acts of murder. As Kally Mashizha, a headman from Gokwe District, noted in late October 2011: "You don't just kill a human being like that. Life has to be respected. And truly, the fight by Moses was painful, but necessary to teach our people a lesson. I hope they have learnt" (*Newsday*, 26 October 2011: 1). These sentiments were echoed by Obert Chinyama, a councillor from the same district:

> People here in Ndlele, Ward 16, have rested after his (Moses's) spirit has been appeased. We even blamed his death for droughts. Everything bad which happened around here was blamed on the avenging spirit. Now we are resting. We are happy that this matter which troubled the people of Gokwe has come to a closure (*Newsday*, 26 October 2011: 1).

In early 2010, Patrick Basopo, a ZANU-PF supporter who had been involved in the murder of Tedious Chokuda, an MDC activist and headmaster of Murowe School in Buhera District in 2002, fled from his home after surrendering only a few herd of cattle out of the 65 that a traditional court had instructed him to pay as restitution. A few months later in May 2010, he died under mysterious circumstances in the town of Marondera where he had gone to seek assistance from the Mwazha Apostolic sect where he had converted to an Elder (*Madzibaba*) in an attempt to pacify the avenging spirit. Villagers reported that he was suffering from severe mental stress during the few days preceding his death (Marwizi and Chimhete, 15 May 2010; Movement for Democratic Change, 1 June 2010). This incident is fascinatingly illuminating on the dynamics of the avenging spirit as an institution. It illustrates the futility of shortcuts in addressing the ravages of *ngozi*. This case also reinforces the cosmological discourses that avenging spirits can effectively be appeased by the payment of restitution that is processed in accordance with the dictates of indigenous African jurisprudence.

Another case in point pertains to the manner in which Misheck Busangavanye settled a murder case by paying restitution in 2017. From 2004 when Busangavanye, the then Chipinge Rural District Council Vice-Chairman and also ZANU-PF Ward 26 Councillor, together with his sons Jairos and Brighton, reportedly murdered Philemon Nyamunda, an MDC party supporter, the case was heard several times at the Mutare Magistrate's Court and the Mutare High Court for more than a decade without a final verdict being reached. During all the court hearings, the accused pleaded not guilty. Despite pleading his innocence at the criminal courts for 13 years, Busangavanye approached the Nyamunda family at Matikwa Village on 3 January 2017 to confess to the murder and appease the avenging spirit of the deceased which he said had been haunting him over the years (Bishi, 3 March 2017).

He went on to approach Village Head Matikwa to arbitrate (Mawawa, 6 February 2017). The Village Head convened a traditional court at the deceased's home which was attended by more than 200 villagers. Through the mediation of the village head and a spirit medium, Busangavanye paid 12 herd of cattle as restitution to the Nyamunda family. Six of the beasts were alive while the rest were paid in cash at a cost of US$700 each. During the court session,

Busangavanye was also ordered to avail a goat for purposes of dramatising how they had murdered the deceased (Bishi, 3 March 2017). Narrating how the perpetrators demonstrated the murder, one of the deceased's brothers said,

> Busangavanye tied the goat to a pole and together with his sons started beating the animal with all sorts of weapons and sometimes pulled the goat's scrotum until it died. There was drama at the ceremony when the father (Busangavanye) pulled the goat's testicles while his sons were hitting it with logs until it died. After its death, they prepared the meat and cooked sadza for everyone who was at the ceremony (Bishi, 3 March 2017: 1).

In addition to the 12 herd of cattle he paid as restitution, Busangavanye reportedly paid four beasts just to be granted permission to enter the deceased's homestead. Reports also indicated that he had earlier on paid another seven beasts after the Nyamunda family had threatened to rebury the deceased's body at his homestead. Busangavanye therefore paid a total of 23 beasts to the Nyamunda family. He was also ordered to buy seven drums of beer for all the villagers who attended the traditional court session (Bishi, 3 March 2017; *TellZim News*, 10 February 2017). During an interview with *TellZim News* in February 2017, Busangavanye admitted paying restitution to the Nyamunda family and hoped that he would live a normal life from then on. He said: "I paid out of my own free will. This is a matter of tradition. I realised that I would have more problems in the future if I had not paid" (*TellZim News*, 10 February 2017: 1).

This section has illustrated that avenging spirits can only be appeased through the payment of restitution in accordance with the protocol of indigenous African jurisprudence stipulated by traditional courts. It has demonstrated that the 'modern' criminal justice system can only punish offenders but cannot appease avenging spirits. The section has also shown that *ngozi*, as a mechanism of justice, does not discriminate on the grounds of one's socio-economic or political status in society. Those who commit crimes and hope to be immune from prosecution in the criminal courts because of their position of power and influence in society cannot escape from the wrath of avenging spirits until the pay restitution.

Official instrumentalisation of *ngozi* in efforts to curb political violence in Zimbabwe

Despite the fact that *ngozi* is a spiritual phenomenon, officials from various quarters never underestimated its potential as a transitional justice mechanism that inculcated the values of tolerance, peace and restraint. Some officials from the government, various political parties, civil organisations and the traditional leadership warned people in their constituencies about the ravages of avenging spirits if they tortured, maimed or killed their political opponents.

Even though the ZANU-PF party was implicated in most of the cases of politically-motivated violence and murder, as noted earlier on in this chapter, some of its officials engaged in the rhetoric of instrumentalising *ngozi* in an attempt to instil peace and tolerance. In October 2011, for example, Joyce Mujuru, the then Vice-President of both ZANU-PF and Zimbabwe, warned political zealots who engaged in violence that they would stand alone when avenging spirits of their victims returned to haunt them (*Newsday*, 21 October 2011). During the same month, Martin Dinha, the ZANU-PF Mashonaland Central Governor advised villagers around Nzvimbo Growth Point in Chiweshe District about the dangers of *ngozi* if they involved themselves in violent contestations with their political opponents (*Newsday*, 21 October 2011).

In late January 2013, John Mafa, the then ZANU-PF Mashonaland West Provincial Chairman, urged party supporters to desist from political violence in the run-up to the local government, parliamentary and presidential elections that were to be held later during the year, arguing that the avenging spirits of the people they would have murdered would return to haunt them. He warned:

> Elections are around the corner and some political leaders will be tempted to employ violence in order to win votes. My appeal to youths, who are mostly used by politicians to perpetrate violence, is to refrain from these heinous acts as avenging spirits won't attack the politician

who sent you or the party, but would haunt you for the rest of your lives. Avenging spirits are there, they are real (*Newsday*, 5 February 2013: 1).

The MDC-T also added its voice by enlightening political activists on the realities of *ngozi*. Addressing diplomats and villagers at his rural home in Humanikwa Village in Buhera District in November 2012, Morgan Tsvangirai, the then Zimbabwean Prime Minister and MDC-T leader, warned that avenging spirits would torment perpetrators of political violence:

> Perpetrators of violence are inviting avenging spirits by killing each other. Our voices are now getting hoarse as we condemn violence. President (Robert) Mugabe is also saying it every day. We say no to violence in the forthcoming elections. If we heed this message, our country will develop and God will help us go through this transition (Matenga, 17 November 2012: 1).

Civil organisations also weighed in by enlightening people on the dynamics of avenging spirits. In October 2011, for instance, Zimrights, a human rights organisation, printed T-shirts warning the youths on the dire consequences of being hired to inflict harm on political opponents. The message printed on the T-shirts read: *Ngozi haiteveri akutuma, inotevera iwe* (An avenging spirit does not torment those who sent you, but pursues you who has been sent) (*Newsday*, 26 October 2011: 1).

Commenting on the Zimbabwe Republic Police (ZRP) brutality on protestors from civil organisations and opposition parties, Nhlanhla Khumalo, a member of the Mthwakazi Cultural Association, a Zimbabwean Non-Governmental Organisation, warned in March 2016:

> In our culture, love and respect are very important values of the society. If you pretend to be cleverer and kill someone, the spirit of the dead person will always follow you wherever you are. It might not be now, but it will surely happen. Those who can be sent by anyone to kill must know that it is not those who sent them who suffer spiritual

attack, but those who participate in the killing of innocent people. The one you are killing sees you and not the one who sent you hence you become that person's target (*Zim Eye*, 30 August 2016: 1).

These sentiments were reiterated by Iphithule Maphosa, the spokesperson of the opposition Zimbabwe African National Union (ZAPU):

The police and military officers, while they carry out orders to brutalise citizens, should remember that they will face the consequences alone with their families. Those issuing out orders will still be enjoying their luxurious good lives free of the backlash from avenging spirits. Besides fear of avenging spirits, police and the military must respect both human life and human rights. People of this country have a constitutional right to display dissatisfaction and displeasure with the regime and nobody should take that right away through brutality (*Zim Eye*, 30 August 2016: 1).

Some traditional leaders convened gatherings where they cautioned their subjects about the ravages of avenging spirits if they committed acts of political violence. One such ceremony was convened on 4 December 2010 in Zaka District by Ward 24 village heads under Chief Bota in the aftermath of the 2008 political violence. During the occasion, the traditional leaders advised local communities that formal court procedures up to the Supreme Court cannot handle cases of spiritual appeasement which, if not settled, would result in misfortunes on both the perpetrators in particular and the community in general. Villagers contributed millet after which they brewed beer for the ceremony whose proceedings included confessions, apologies and pleas for peace. The ceremony was presided over by local spirit mediums who led the villagers in dance (*Zimbabwean*, 8 December 2010).

This section has shown that even though *ngozi* is a spiritual phenomenon, it has often been instrumentalised in various official circles to instil fear, restraint and tolerance among would-be perpetrators of political violence in an effort to bring about a harmonious social order. The instrumentalisation of *ngozi* in the pleas for peace by various officials from government, political parties, civil organisations and the traditional leadership signify attempts to co-opt localised African indigenous jurisprudential systems into the national framework of transitional justice.

Conclusion

This chapter has demonstrated that avenging spirits (*ngozi/uzimu*) are not demons and should not be associated with evil. They constitute a spiritual agent or medium that manifests itself in various ways in an attempt to seek justice among the living. In other words, the manifestations of *ngozi/uzimu* illustrate the presence of the spiritual world in the daily earthly world. As a mechanism of transitional justice, the institution of *ngozi/uzimu* has the constructive potential to resolve conflicts and heal societal fissures. As an enforcer of a harmonious social order, avenging spirits cause untold suffering to the family members of perpetrators thereby offering useful lessons to the community in general to desist from ill-treating others. This didacticism is also conveyed at public gatherings convened by traditional leaders where perpetrators make confessions, show remorse and pay restitution.

Thus, the institution of *ngozi* is a typical example of cosmological values of the past help to positively (re)shape the society in the present: what Morreira (2016: 64) refers to as "the past in the present." It is a spiritual phenomenon, an African reality and "a major cornerstone of the spiritual dimension of the African justice system" (Mupeperekwi, 26 February 2015: 1) that can complement the other mechanisms in addressing issues of conflict prevention, conflict resolution, reconciliation and lasting peace.

References

Alexander, J. (2006) 'Legacies of violence in Matabeleland, Zimbabwe,' in: P. Kaarsholm (ed.) *Violence, political culture and development in Africa,* Oxford: James Currey, pp.105-121.

Benyera, E. (2014) 'Debating the efficacy of transitional justice mechanisms: the case of national healing in Zimbabwe, 1980-2011,' D.Phil. Thesis, University of South Africa.

Bishi, M. (3 March 2017) 'Avenging spirits: Chipinge ZANU-PF councillor pays 23 beasts,' in: *The Mirror*, Masvingo: Zimbabwe, Available at: http://www.masvingomirror.com, Accessed 13 March 2017.

Bond, P. and Manyanya, M. (2001) *Zimbabwe's plunge: Exhausted nationalism, neoliberalism and the search for social justice*, Asmara: Africa World Press.

Bourdillon, M. F. C. (1982) *The Shona peoples: An ethnography of the contemporary Shona, with special reference to their religion*, Gweru: Mambo Press.

Bulawayo 24 News, (1 August 2012), 'MDC-T turns to *ngozi* to haunt ZANU-PF murderers,' Available at: http://bulawayo24.com/index, Accessed 13 March 2017.

Bulawayo 24 News, (5 February 2013), 'ZANU-PF members warned of avenging spirits,' Bulawayo: Zimbabwe.

Chimhete, C. (1 May 2005), 'MDC decries ZANU-PF retribution,' in: *The Standard*, Harare: Zimbabwe.

Church and Civil Society Forum (CCSF), (2012) *Traditional mechanisms in transitional justice*, Harare: CCSF.

Duri, F. (2010) *The relentless governance by the sword: Situating Operation Murambatsvina in Zimbabwean history*, Saarbrucken: VDM Verlag.

Eppel, S. (2006) 'Healing the dead: Exhumations and reburials as a truth-telling and peace-building activity in rural Zimbabwe,' in: T. Borer (ed.) *Truth-telling and peace-building in post-conflict societies*, Notre Dame: University of Notre Dame Press, pp.1-23.

Feltoe, G. (2004) 'The onslaught against democracy, and the rule of law in Zimbabwe in 2000,' in: D. Harold-Barry (ed.) *Zimbabwe: The past is the future: Rethinking land, state and nation in the context of crisis*, Harare: Weaver Press, pp.199-203.

Financial Gazette, (19 January 2017) 'Myth of judicial independence in Zimbabwe,' Available at: www.financiagazette.co.zw, Accessed 14 March 2017.

Gappah, P. (2016) *The book of memory*, New York: Farrar, Straus and Giroux.

Gelfand, M. (1973) *The genuine Shona: Survival values of an African culture*, Gwelo: Mambo Press.

Guma, L. (18 July 2012), 'Two suspected killers of MDC-T official die within two days,' Available at: https://nzcn.wordpress.com, Accessed 13 March 2017.

Hammar, A. and Raftopoulos, B. (2003). 'Zimbabwe's unfinished business: Rethinking land, state and nation,' in: A. Hammar, B. Raftopoulos and S. Jensen (eds.) *Zimbabwe's unfinished business: Rethinking land, state and nation in the context of crisis*, Harare: Weaver Press, pp.1-47.

Heal Zimbabwe Trust, (28 July 2013), 'The 2013 pre-election political environment analysis,' Available at: www.healzimbabwe.co.zw, Accessed 10 January 2016.

Hill, G. (2003) *The battle for Zimbabwe: The final countdown*, Cape Town: Zebra Press.

Human Rights Watch, (3 November 2008) 'Our hands are tied: Erosion of the rule of law in Zimbabwe,' Available at: www.hrw.org/reports, Accessed 14 March 2017.

Human Rights Watch, (8 March 2011), 'Perpetual fear: Impunity and cycles of violence in Zimbabwe,' Johannesburg: Human Rights Watch, Available at: http://www.refworld.org/docid, Accessed 14 March 2017.

Insider Zimbabwe, (11 February 2013), 'MP haunted by *ngozi* after election violence,' Available at: http://www.insiderzim.com, Accessed 13 March 2017.

Johnson, R.W. (5 March 2001), 'Zimbabwe's rule of law ousted,' Available at: www.upi.com/Archives, Accessed 14 March 2017.

Los Angeles Times, (24 July 2008), 'Fearsome Zimbabwe militias are also afraid,' Available at: http://articles.latimes.com, Accessed 6 December 2016.

Machaya, S. (20 June 2016) 'Beyond violence and intimidation: Explaining possible ZANU-PF victory in 2018- The role of third parties,' Available at: www.africanpoliticsandpolicy.com, Accessed 14 March 2017.

Makoni, J. (5 July 2011) 'MDC district chairperson in court for calling a spade a spade,' Available at: http://thezimbabwean.co, Accessed 13 March 2017.

Makumbe, J. (2006) 'Electoral politics in Zimbabwe: Authoritarianism versus the people,' in: *Africa Development*, Volume 31, Number 3, Available at: www.jstor.org/stable, Accessed 14 March 2017.

Marwizi, W. and Chimhete, C. (15 May 2010) 'Avenging spirits torment ZANU-PF terror militia,' in: The Standard, Harare: Zimbabwe, Available at: http://www.thestandard.co.zw, Accessed 6 December 2016.

Masaka, D. and Chemhuru, M. (2011) 'Moral dimensions of some Shona taboos (*zviera*),' in: *Journal of Sustainable Development in Africa*, Volume 13, Number 3, pp.132-148.

Masunungure, E. (2004) 'Travails of opposition politics in Zimbabwe since independence,' in: D. Harold-Barry (ed.) *Zimbabwe: The past is the future: Rethinking land, state and nation in the context of crisis*, Harare: Weaver Press, pp.147-192.

Matenga, M. (17 November 2012) 'Beware of avenging spirits: Tsvangirai,' in: *The Newsday*, Harare: Zimbabwe.

Mawawa, T. (6 February 2017) 'Mugabe terror activist haunted by avenging spirits,' Available at: www.zimeye.net, Accessed 13 March 1017.

McLaughlin, E. Fergusson, R. and Hughes, G. (2003) 'Introduction: Justice in the round: Contextualising restorative justice,' in: McLaughlin, E. Fergusson, R. Hughes, G. and Westmorland, L. (Eds.) *Restorative justice: Critical issues*, London: Sage, pp 1-19.

Morreira, S. (2016) *Rights after wrongs: Local knowledge and human rights in Zimbabwe*, Stanford: Stanford University Press.

Movement for Democratic Change (MDC), (1 June 2010), '*Ngozi* haunts ZANU-PF killers,' in: *The Changing Times*, Issue 038, Harare: MDC Information and Publicity Department.

Moyo, H. (2015) 'Pastoral care in the healing of moral injury: A case of the Zimbabwe National Liberation War Veterans,' in: HTS Teologiese Studies/Theological Studies, Volume 71, Number 2, Available at: http://www.hts.org.za/index, Accessed 6 December 2016.

Munyoro, F. (13 December 2016) 'MDC-T cop killers jailed 20 years each,' in: *The Herald*, Harare: Zimbabwe.

Mupeperekwi, S. (26 February 2015) 'Reclaiming our spiritual independence: *Ngozi* spirits: Seeking justice and restitution,' Available at: http://www.thepatriot.co.zw, Accessed 15 March 2017.

Mutekwa, A. (2010) 'The avenging spirit: Mapping an ambivalent spirituality in Zimbabwean literature in English,' in: *African Studies*, 69 (1): 161-176.

Muwati, I. Gambahaya, Z. and Mangena, F. (2006) 'Echoing Silences as a paradigm for restorative justice in post-conflict Zimbabwe: A philosophical discourse,' in: *Zambezia*, Volume XXXIII, Number i/ii, pp.1-18.

Muzulu, P. (21 January 2017) 'Chidyausiku's legacy: Pioneer or ZANU-PF's point-man?' in: *The Newsday*, Harare: Zimbabwe.

My Zimbabwe, (21 June 2016) 'MDC activist buried three years after he was murdered by ZANU-PF members,' Available at http://www.myzimbabwe.co.zw/news, Accessed 9 March 2017.

Nehanda Radio, (11 June 2015) 'Why do Zimbabwe's opposition parties split so much? (Part 2),' Available at: http://www.zimbabwesituation.com/news, Accessed 14 March 2017.

New Zimbabwe, (30 July 2014) 'Top judges still pro-ZANU-PF: Madhuku,' Available at: www.newzimbabwe.com/news, Accessed 14 March 2017.

News 24 Archives, (28 December 2001) 'MDC supporters killed war vet,' Available At: www.news24.co/Archives, Accessed 21 March 2017.

Newsday, (21 October 2011) 'Avenging spirits: no better lesson for political zealots,' in: *The Newsday*, Harare: Zimbabwe.

Newsday, (26 October 2011) 'Chokuda: The man who fought his own battle?' in: *The Newsday*, Harare: Zimbabwe.

Nhemachena, A. (2014) 'Knowledge, *chivanhu* and struggles for survival in conflict-torn Manicaland, Zimbabwe, D.Phil. Thesis, University of Cape Town.

Raftopoulos, B. (2003) 'The state in crisis: Authoritarian nationalism, selective citizenship and distortions of democracy in Zimbabwe,'

217

in: A. Hammar, B. Raftopoulos and S. Jensen (Eds.) *Zimbabwe's unfinished business: Rethinking land, state and nation in the context of crisis*, Harare: Weaver Press, pp. 217-241.

Razemba, F. (25 August 2016) 'Violence, looting in MDC-T demo,' in: *The Herald*, Harare: Zimbabwe.

Shoko, J. (20 February 2013) 'Zimbabwe war veterans demand compensation,' in: *The Africa Report*, pp.18–56

Shortwave Radio Africa, (20 May 2008) 'Chinotimba implicated in MDC's activist's murder in Buhera,' Available at: http://www.swradioafrica.com/news, Accessed 8 March 2017.

Standard, (30 October 2011) 'Chokuda case: Avenging spirits exact justice?' in: *The Standard*, Harare: Zimbabwe.

Tatira, L. (2014) 'Shona belief systems: Finding relevancy for a new generation,' in: *Journal of Pan African Studies*, Available at: https://www.thefreelibrary.com, Accessed 6 December 2016.

TellZim News, (10 February 2017), 'Haunted ZANU-PF councillor pays cattle to appease avenging spirits,' Available at: http://www.radiovop.com, Accessed 13 March 2017.

Zambara, W. (Ed.) (2015) *Community healing manual: A training manual for Zimbabwe*, Cape Town: Institute for Justice and Reconciliation / Peacebuilding Network of Zimbabwe.

Zim Eye, (30 August 2016) 'Chihuri's murderous cops hit by furious avenging spirits soon,' Available at: www.zimeye.net/org, Accessed 9 March 2016.

Zim Eye, (13 December 2016) 'Outrage as justice is murdered,' Available at: www.zimeye.net, Accessed 14 March 2017.

Zimbabwe Broadcasting Corporation News Online, (31 October 2011) 'MDC-T violence condemned,' Available at: www.zbc.co.zw, Accessed 21 March 2017.

Zimbabwean, (8 December 2010) Perpetrator apologises to community at Zaka traditional cleansing ceremony,' in: *The Zimbabwean*, London: United Kingdom.

Zimbabwean, (7 August 2012), 'Avenging spirit causes havoc,' Available at: http://thezimbabwean.co, Accessed 13 March 2017.

Chapter 11

Healing Zimbabwe: Impact of the Catholic Church's Response to political Violence on People at Grassroots Level

Conrad Chibango

Introduction

Due to its prolonged history of political violence stretching from the pre-colonial era to date (Ndlovu-Gatsheni, 2009), Zimbabwe has remained a wounded society in need of healing. Works such as *Breaking the Silence* by the Catholic Commission for Justice and Peace (CCJP) and the Legal Resources Foundation (LRF) provide ample evidence of state-sponsored violence. The Church and Civil Society Forum (CCSF) (2012) has classified this violence as functionalist meant to sustain the ruling Zimbabwe African National Union-Patriotic Front (ZANU-PF) regime's grip on power, no matter the wounds inflicted on the society. Scholars, such as Chitando (2011) and Matikiti (2012) have provided theological perspectives on this culture of violence while churches have responded through pastoral documents and engagements with political leaders. However, Zimbabwe's political intolerance has persisted. This chapter has used the term 'healing' to refer to the attempt to eliminate violence by taking measures that promote justice and peace in the society, transforming it for the better.

The main aim of this chapter is to assess the impact of the Catholic Church's pastoral documents on healing the society at grassroots level. As a result, the chapter explores the nature and extent to which Zimbabwe is a wounded society and the efficacy of the Catholic Church's documents on healing. The chapter employed a qualitative case study methodology to gather and analyse data from Ruwa Urban Parish community, following the post-elections violence of 2008. It employed the Catholic Social Justice Theory as its conceptual framework, a body of knowledge that offers a way of

219

thinking about social reality and how people should ethically respond to it.

The chapter argues that although the Catholic Church's pastoral documents have empowered people with knowledge and skills to assess the moral position on the use of political violence, their impact on grassroots communities has remained compromised, largely due to fear. The chapter also argues that the approach to ending political violence via the education of the people at grassroots level is in line with bottom-up approaches to peace-building and in particular, that of Lederach (1997), who argues that all levels of the society should participate in promoting peace. The chapter concludes that by educating people at the grassroots level, the pastoral documents empower the ordinary people to transform the wounded society of Zimbabwe.

A wounded society

> Action on behalf of justice and participation in the transformation of the world fully appear to us as a constitutive dimension of the preaching of the Gospel or in other words, of the Church's mission for the redemption of the human race and its liberation from every oppressive situation, (World Synod of Bishops, 1971).

The above citation of Catholic bishops demonstrates that promoting justice and peace and participating in transforming the society for the better is part of the core business of the Catholic Church. In his work on Ireland entitled *A Wounded Church: Religion, Politics and Justice in Ireland*, Joseph McVeigh (1989) posited that by promoting peace and fighting against oppression, the Church was capable of healing the wounded society. Zimbabwe too is a wounded society in need of healing due to the long genealogy and intensity of violence and conflict that it has gone through over the years and continues to experience.

While violence can be political, social or economic (Church and Civil Society Forum, 2012), this chapter limits itself to politically-motivated violence. In general, it refers to the commission of destructive, cruel, pitiless, unsympathetic and forceful acts motivated

220

by a desire, conscious or unconscious, to obtain or maintain power (Aolin, 2006), be it political, social or economic. This chapter focuses on political violence by both state and non-state actors. Such violence occurs in the context of a group such that members of a particular group act violently against persons they perceive as belonging to a different political group or as having differing political views. The violence is characterised, among others, by assaults, murder, sexual abuse such as rape and destruction of property (Moser and Clark, cited in Church and Civil Society Forum, 2012), torture and destruction of property.

Politically-motivated violence in Zimbabwe has become so common that it has become justifiable to consider the Southern African country as characterised by a culture of violence. There is a lot of literature that addresses this culture of violence. The Catholic Commission for Justice and Peace (CCJP) of the Catholic Church in Zimbabwe, for instance, has published several documents on state-sponsored violence in the country. In 1975, in conjunction with the Catholic Institute for International Relations, CCJP published two reports, namely, *The Man in the Middle: Torture, Resettlement* and *Eviction and Civil War in Rhodesia*, both of which exposed the plight of civilians during the liberation war. *Breaking the Silence: Building True Peace: A Report on the Disturbances in Matabeleland and the Midlands, 1980 to 1988* (CCJP Zimbabwe, 1997), was a report which gave intriguing insights into what transpired during the tragic moment in the history of post-colonial Zimbabwe whereby over 20 000 people in Matabeleland were massacred in a state-led operation called *Gukurahundi* (remove chaff). Whilst a lot of evidence points to a blatant violation of people's rights in the pogrom, the state and its then leader, Robert Mugabe, the country's leader from independence to 2017, refused to apologize to victims and their relatives. Mugabe lamely accepted the blame by referring to the sad episode as 'a moment of madness' (Murambadoro, 2015). However, in his autobiography, Msipa (2015), the late ZANU-PF Governor for the Midlands Province, questioned whether such a pogrom of over five years could be reduced to 'a moment of madness'.

There is also vast documentation on several other 'moments of madness.' The CCJP's *Crisis of Governance* (CCJP, 2001) gave detailed accounts on political violence in the country and so too did Makumbe and Compagnon (2000). For instance, the CCJP (2001) presented thick descriptions of tortures and murders committed during the controversial Fast Track Land Reform Programme that started in 2000. The programme involved the violent seizure of white-owned commercial farms. Other works such as that by Tibaijuka (2005) critique *Operation Murambatsvina,* which saw many urban informal houses erased to the ground after a directive from Government. Following incidences of state-sponsored political violence after the 2008 harmonised elections, the CCJP also released *Graveyard Governance: A Report on Political Violence following the March Harmonised 2008 Elections.*

Various works analyse the political violence in Zimbabwe in an attempt to understand the roots of this violence as well as provide solutions. Scholars such as Ezra Chitando (2011), David Kaulemu (2006), Robert Matikiti (2012), among many others, have reflected on the place and role of religion, Christianity, in particular, in the context of a society experiencing a culture of violence. Several works also show that Christian churches have also played and continue to play a critical part in ending the culture of violence in the country. Some of these include Gundani (2002), Churches of Zimbabwe (2006) and Dombo (2014). The work by Hove (2013), who approaches the topic of political violence from an Early Warning Systems Perspective, is also relevant to this discussion. Works by Sachikonye (2011), who provides a genealogy of violence in Zimbabwe from the 1960s, and Huyse (2003), whose study on reconciliation focuses on why reconciliation failed in Zimbabwe, provide analyses pertinent to the focus of this chapter. Below, the chapter gives brief overviews of some of these works.

Luc Huyse (2003) argued that the presence of violence in Zimbabwe is mainly due to its failure to achieve true reconciliation. He observed that the post-colonial government made little effort to bridge the differences between the white minority and the black majority. There was also little effort to address the differences among the blacks themselves. According to Huyse, the post-colonial government put little emphasis on the question of reconciliation within the black community, where two political groups (namely the

Zimbabwe African National Union, Patriotic Front [ZANU PF] and the Zimbabwe African People's Union, Patriotic Front [ZAPU PF]) had fought bitter conflicts, both in the far past and as rivals in the liberation movement. For Huyse, the inter-black division is based on three interrelated divisions: ethnic (majority Shona versus minority Ndebele); regional (North and South Matabeleland, which is predominantly Ndebele country, versus most of the other regions; political (diverging visions of how to build the country after independence) (Huyse, 2003).

Arguing from the discourse of transitional justice, Huyse (2003) considers violence in both colonial and post-colonial Zimbabwe to be a result of both amnesia (failure to address past memories of committed atrocities) and impunity, which is characterised by failure to reach some degree of retributive, restorative and economic justice. For instance, Huyse argues that Mugabe's policy of reconciliation soon after independence promoted amnesia, an officially imposed form of forgetting as it allowed Rhodesian perpetrators of human rights violations to go unpunished. The assumption was that seeking truth and justice regarding the war atrocities was going to disturb the newly acquired peace at independence. This route of political reconciliation was good news to many perpetrators of violence from both the Smith regime and the liberation war political parties.

In the colonial period, impunity was in form of curfew laws (both written and unwritten), which simply gave the security forces and officers of the regime the licence to kill civilians with impunity and to carry out any form of punishment they deemed necessary (Mushonga, 2005). The CCJP and the Catholic Institute for International Relations' work entitled *The Man in the Middle: Torture, Resettlement and Eviction and Civil War in Rhodesia (1975)*, gives a narration of many atrocities against the majority blacks committed by the oppressive colonial State machinery. According to Huyse (2003), impunity in post-colonial Zimbabwe has often been characterised by the erosion of the independence of the judiciary, political manipulation of the police, and silencing independent media and human rights organizations. Huyse's analysis seems to explain why perpetrators of the Matabeleland *Gukurahundi* atrocities were never punished and relatives of victims were never compensated (Teute,

2015). It also explains why Government did not seem to have any problem with driving out white commercial farmers without any compensation (Chilunjika and Uwizeyimana, 2015). The analysis by Huyse also explains why perpetrators of the post-2008 elections violence have not faced any judiciary reprimand (CCJP, 2009).

According to Sachikonye (2011), political leaders in Zimbabwe have often used violence as a vehicle for either attaining power or holding on to it. The Smith Regime, for instance, used violence to maintain its grip on power. As Sachikonye (2011) observed, the colonial state used weapons such as *sjamboks*, dogs, guns and even poison to torture and suppress nationalist activists and liberation fighters. The liberation war was a form of counter-violence by groups aspiring to power. Liberation war songs such as 'Zimbabwe *ndeye ropa*' (Zimbabwe was born out of the fires of a bloody revolution) indicated that Zimbabweans had to resort to war in order to attain their freedom (Church and Civil Society Forum 2012, 14). Thus, people perceived violence as an acceptable way of solving problems.

Once in power, ZANU PF, like its colonial predecessor, employed violent means to hang onto power. Logically, it retained some of the arsenal and repressive techniques it inherited from its colonial master (Sachikonye, 2011). It thwarted threats to its power through violent means. Incidents such as the *gukurahundi* and during or after elections can be understood in this context. After over 30 years of perfecting the use of violence as an instrument for hanging onto power, the ZANU-PF government has managed to interweave violence into its ideology (Matikiti, 2012). The Church and Civil Society Forum (2012, 3) lamented that 'violence has sadly become an accepted culture affecting present-day Zimbabwean politics, particularly when the country is facing an election'. Given the existence of a culture of impunity alluded to by Huyse (2003), perpetrators of violence would, in many a cases, consider themselves untouchable (Church and Civil Society Forum, 2012). Inevitably, such an environment has gradually turned the country into a society traumatised by fear, withdrawal, and collective depression based on past memories of violence, intimidation, harassment and forced amnesia (Matikiti, 2012).

The Catholic Church's response to violence

The response to violence by the Catholic Church in Zimbabwe is inspired by the Catholic Social Theory, popularly referred to as the Catholic Social Teaching (hereafter referred to as CST). This body of knowledge, which reflects on critical contemporary issues, is derived from the teaching of Catholic leaders, namely popes and bishops. The Catholic Bishops jointly published several pastoral letters since the colonial period to date. Individual bishops have also released pastoral documents addressing contemporary social issues affecting the society. Before considering a couple of these pastoral documents in this chapter, a brief examination of the CST framework shall help clarify the context of this discussion.

Catholic Social Teaching (CST)

The history of CST stretches as far back as the 19th century when Pope Pius IX wrote an encyclical letter condemning socialism, communism and godless secular liberalism. However, the often-cited document and the one recognized as having created the framework for CST is *Rerum Novarum* by Pope Leo XIII (1891), which addressed the rights and duties of employers and workers. Since then, popes and bishops have come up with documents or pastoral letters addressing critical social issues of their times. Some of these documents included the following: *Gaudium et Spes* (1965), a Vatican II pastoral document on the constitution of the church in the modern world; *Justice in the World* (1971) by the World Synod of Bishops; *On Concern for the Social Order* (John Paul II, 1987); and *The Compendium of the Social Doctrine of the Church* (2004). At regional, national, metropolitan and diocesan levels, bishops also issue pastoral documents of CST nature, addressing current social issues in the context of their societies. It is in this context that the Catholic leadership's response to its concrete and current pastoral challenges by way of pastoral letters is also a version of CST.

There are several social themes based on gospel values associated with CST. As a social doctrine, CST provides principles of reflection, criteria for judgement as well as guidelines regarding several themes related to social life. As a social analysis method, it also emphasises the 'see, judge, act' approach to social action (African Forum for Catholic Social Training [AFCAST], 2009: 19), such that a critical observation of realities culminates in action that brings about the common good. CST considers the goal of society and social life as that of developing the human person in community in order to enhance the common good (Ibid). Justice is also a central social theme to the framework of CST. According to Pope John Paul II (2002), peace without justice is inconceivable in any given society. For Pope John Paul II (2002), peace is not merely the absence of war but it also involves mutual respect and confidence between peoples and nations. Some of the social themes that define CST include human freedom, equality, love of neighbour, participation, subsidiarity and the common good.

According to AFCAST (2009), there are critical foundational pillars upon which CST stands. These include the following: human dignity; relation with community; relation with creation; and option for the poor. The African perspective of CST has often included *Ubuntu* and the social nature of human beings as another pillar. The principle of human dignity derives from the belief that God created people equally and in his image (*Gaudium et Spes*, 1965, Number 26). It is from this belief that human rights emanate, while duties are the other side of the rights. CST also assumes that people should live in harmony, not only with one another (relation with community) but also with the environment (relation with community). In societies that have experienced violence, CST advocates for peace and restorative justice as it underlines the need for respecting the human dignity and importance of properly relating with each other in the community. It also encourages participation, democracy and subsidiarity (AFCAST, 2009). It is in this context that one has to understand the pastoral letters of the Zimbabwe Catholic Bishops' Conference and the various documents and forms of activism promoted through CCJP, its commission for justice and peace.

Pastoral letters and violence

The pastoral letters of the Catholic leadership have not only invited people to reflect on the plight of the country, but have also challenged the society to do something about it – a call to action.

Below we consider two of these letters as a case study, namely the one by Archbishop Pius Ncube of Bulawayo Archdiocese and *God Hears the Cry of the Oppressed*, a joint pastoral letter by the Zimbabwe Catholic Bishops' Conference (ZCBC) (2007).

On 26th April 2000, the then Archbishop Pius Ncube of Bulawayo Archdiocese published a pastoral letter entitled *A Prayer of Hope for Zimbabwe: A Concern on the Present Situation in Zimbabwe* (CCJP, 2001). Taking personal risk, Pius Ncube clearly condemned the government for the socioeconomic crisis that led the ordinary citizen into abject poverty. He clearly stated that all this was due to the government's notorious use of terror to cause fear among the people solely to remain in power. However, he stated that people could overcome state intimidation through prayer, fasting, voting according to their conscience and unity of purpose. After the release of this letter, Pius Ncube received death threats and relations between him and the then President Robert Mugabe became very constrained as the latter accused him of having influenced people in Matabeleland to vote against his party, an accusation that Ncube categorically denied (CCJP, 2001). Ncube also stated that he would not stop speaking out arguing that: "I will be just as critical of MDC (Movement of Democratic Change, an opposition political party) as of any party because I stand for Christian ethics and for justice and respect for every person. If these are not respected, I will speak out" (CCJP, 2001: 102).

God Hears the Cry of the Oppressed, A Letter on the Current Crisis in Zimbabwe (2007), was an unequivocal document which not only spelt out and defined the nature of the crisis in the country but also articulated its roots and then reminded the society that God was always on the side of the poor. According to the bishops, one of the characteristics of the crisis was a divided Christian community. They observed that:

> …Committed office-bearers of [both the ruling and] opposition parties actively support church activities in every parish and diocese…They are all baptised, sit and pray and sing together in the same church, take part in the same celebration of the Eucharist and partake of the same Body and Blood of Christ. While the next day,

outside the church, a few steps away, Christian State Agents, policemen and soldiers assault and beat peaceful, unarmed demonstrators and torture detainees. This is the unacceptable reality on the ground, which shows much disrespect for human life and falls far below the dignity of both the perpetrator and the victim, (Zimbabwe Catholic Bishops' Conference (ZCBC), 2007: para. 3).

Pope John Paul II (1987), who emphasised the importance of identifying and naming the root of individual evil leading to social sin, appears to have influenced the bishops' approach in this pastoral letter. Pope John Paul II pointed out that since structures of sin were rooted in individual sin, it was important to deal with this individual sin first before addressing the social one. In doing so, he viewed it as important to 'give a name to the root of the evils which afflict us' in order to understand the reality that confronts us. In this context, the bishops named the nature of crisis that Zimbabwe was confronting. According to them, the country was facing various crises: crisis of governance, crisis of moral leadership and crisis of spiritual and moral nature. The roots of the crisis as per this document resonated with the view of Hayse (2003) as it states that:

> Despite the rhetoric of a glorious socialist revolution brought about by the armed struggle, the colonial structures and institutions of pre-independent Zimbabwe continue to persist in our society. None of the unjust and oppressive security laws of the Rhodesian state have been repealed; in fact, they have been reinforced by even more repressive legislation, the *Public Order and Security Act and the Access to Information and Protection of Privacy Act*, in particular,' (ZCBC, 2007: para. 3).

The letter went further to cite some biblical texts that showed that God was always on the side of the oppressed and that oppressors were cruel, ruthless and violent. However, to the oppressed, God was revealed as compassionate and as one who hears the cry of the oppressed and liberates them from the oppressor (ZCBC, 2007: para. 22). The pastoral letter also challenged those responsible for the crisis to repent and listen to the cry of the oppressed. To the majority of citizens, the bishops appealed for peace and restraint in the expression of their justified grievances and claims for their human rights. Concerning violence, the bishops were loud and clear, pointing out that "we say…No to power through violence, oppression and intimidation" (ZCBC, 2007: para. 26).

Through this letter and their other documents, the Catholics bishops portrayed themselves as leaders that were not co-opted by political authorities, but as leaders who could firmly stand by the message of the gospel as they guided their faithful to redemption. As demonstrated in the comparative study on the relations between churches and government by Sylvester Dombo (2014), resisting co-option by political authorities is a difficult task for many churches. Hence, church leaders that manage to do so merit commendation. In contrast, churches led by leaders such as Pastor Obediah Musindo fully identified themselves as partisan, siding with the ruling party, ZANU PF, and inadvertently became complicit in the oppression of the generality of the people (Dombo, 2014).

Typical of CST, the documents by the Catholic bishops reflected on the contemporary social issues, judged the situations and gave guidance in terms of social action. The CST themes of justice, human dignity and option for the poor are also addressed but in a way unique to the Zimbabwean society. Most of these documents are a call to social transformation meant to heal Zimbabwe's wounds of violence. However, the persistence of violence seemed to suggest that there were challenges concerning the impact of these documents on the Zimbabwean society.

Just a year after the release of *God Hears the Cry of the Oppressed*, a new wave of political violence was ushered soon after the 2008 harmonised elections. *Graveyard Governance*, a CCJP (2009) report on this wave of violence, which analysed the nature and extent of the atrocities committed during this operation, stated that some victims had their hands cut off, their houses burnt and some lives lost. While the 2013 harmonised elections in which Robert Mugabe and his ZANU PF party overwhelmingly won were judged as peaceful, intimidation still reigned as ZANU PF threatened that it would go back to war if it lost the elections (CCJP Zimbabwe, 2013). The overall problem, therefore, is that, regardless of the bishops' efforts to social change based on gospel values, Zimbabwe remained a wounded society as political violence continued to reign.

Peace-building at grassroots level

Inspired by peace-building literature, which emphasises the critical role of all parts of the society, including local people, in transforming societies experiencing conflict (Lederach, 1997; Saunders; Davies and Kaufman; Netabay 2007; Wallace 2010), this chapter focuses on the impact of the pastoral letters on the grassroots or local communities. It uses a case study of St. Charles Lwanga Parish located in Ruwa, about 30 kilometres east of Harare. According to Lederach (1997), effective peace-building involves simultaneously paying attention to three levels of society: the leaders, the grassroots, and the middle level. Leaders mainly focus on policy issues and are the most publicly visible. The grassroots level involves the largest and least visible aspects of society. In the middle, people often struggle to find a role that may influence the leaders or elites above them and draw on the grassroots below them in order to advance peace building. Lederach contends that there should be coordinated relationships across the levels and most importantly, coordinated and responsive relationships between the levels. He argues that peace efforts often become futile due to poor coordination (vertical capacity) between the various levels (Lederach, 1997). A study by Nuredin Netabay (2007), for instance, suggested that a bottom-up approach was more viable in promoting peace in Sudan than the top-down approach, whereby leaders came up with policies and agreements that related little to the situation on the ground. According to the approach of Lederach, failure to involve the majority at the bottom level of the society as in the case of Sudan signified a poor vertical capacity. Authors such as Leonardsson and Rudd (2015) and Wallace (2010) have argued for a peace-building process that is essentially local.

However, involvement of the people at grassroots level but without equipping them with proper knowledge to influence change would not improve the situation. According to Saunders (1999), educating the people at the grassroots level is a practical and effective way of promoting change in a society experiencing conflict. It is in this context that this chapter considers the pastoral letters of the Zimbabwe Catholic Bishops Conference as potentially powerful instruments for building the capacity of local communities in Zimbabwe.

Grassroots perspectives on the pastoral letters – The case of Ruwa Parish

Data collected from eight semi-interviews and one Focus Group Discussion carried out in Ruwa at St. Charles Lwanga's Catholic Parish revealed various views concerning the effectiveness of the ZCBC pastoral letters in communities. Several themes ranging from the method of disseminating the pastoral letters to the necessary steps to take in order to end violence in the society emerged from the collected data, leading to lessons learnt.

How do Christians access the pastoral letters?

The parish employs various methods to disseminate the pastoral letters. The main one is whereby the parish distributes copies of the pastoral letters to its various Small Christian Communities so that these would read the letter during their weekly bible sharing and prayer meetings. Father Luis Guerrero (22 May 2016) acknowledged that since there was no feedback mechanism, it was difficult to establish the extent to which Christians read these pastoral documents. Evidence revealed that there was selective reading of the pastoral letters. At other times, as Phiri (22 May 2016) posited 'If the document is a hot potato, we do not read it for fear of political victimisation.' In some cases, a priest may replace his homily with a summary of the critical issues addressed in a certain pastoral letter. In other cases, depending on the directive from bishops, Christians read the pastoral letters after the Holy Mass on Sundays. One parish executive member who had read one of the pastoral letters ran into trouble as some secret government agents visited him for questioning (Shoko, 23 May 2016). Other methods of dissemination included the posting of pastoral letters on the parish notice board.

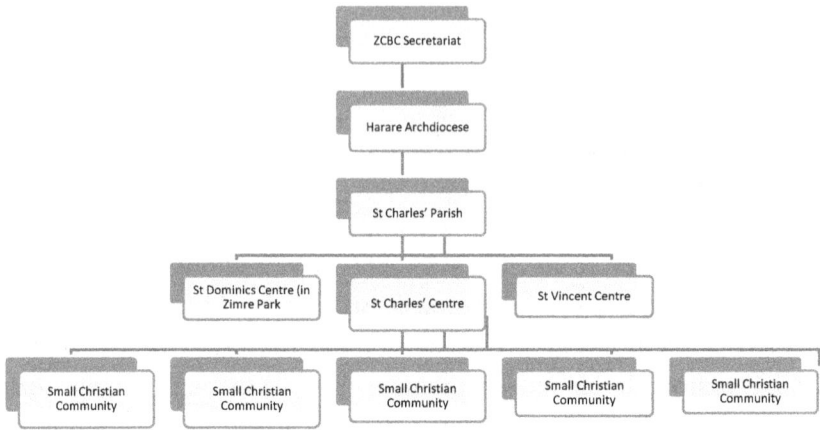

Figure 1: Church structure from ZCBC to Small Christian Communities

How have the letters helped the communities?

The pastoral letters empowered communities in various ways. They have helped to open space for dialogue and peace-building initiatives at community level. One such initiative was a CCJP organised workshop, which attracted participants from various sectors of the Ruwa community. Participants included representatives from various political affiliations, church members, council representatives and ordinary community members (Nguwi, 22 May 2016). According to the Chairperson of the CCJP Ruwa, Masvaya (3 April 2017), "Our local workshop participants from both the ruling party and opposition parties appreciate a forum that accommodates various different views." According to Fr. Luis Guerrero (22 May 2016), some people felt encouraged in faith as the letters gave them hope during difficult moments. The pastoral letters gave people hope since they addressed issues normally regarded as 'taboo' in Zimbabwe's volatile political environment. As Shoko puts it, "The truth is said openly, helping us to see things more clearly and make decisions informed by gospel values," (Shoko, 23 May 2016). The pastoral letters have also empowered Christians with basic knowledge regarding human rights, procedures to take in the event

232

of rights violation as well as the realisation that Christians had a duty to actively participate in politics and thereby bring about social transformation in their society (Phiri, 22 May 2016). For Fr. Guerrero (22 May 2016), the complaint usually levelled against the bishops that they meddled in politics through their pastoral letters was absurd. For him, "Everything one touches is politics and whatever position one takes is political".

Why has political violence persisted?

Fear is one of the factors that facilitate the perpetuation of violence in Zimbabwean communities. Due to the political polarisation in communities, any church message addressing issues related to political violence is interpreted as either for or against a certain political party in Zimbabwe (Nguwi, 22 May 2016). This fear is real because some Christians in Ruwa got into trouble for reading the pastoral letters (Guerrero, 22 May 2016). Some Small Christian Communities in Ruwa dared not read one letter because it was too politically sensitive. "We never read it but preferred to pass it from one family to another, without attracting the attention of outsiders lest we were victimised," said Shoko (23 May 2016).

According to David Muvindi (22 May 2016), the then Ruwa Parish Executive Chairperson, pastoral letters and activities of the CCJP would have reduced violence in the community if the society was free from fear and intimidation. For him, fear was an inevitable consequence of an environment that lacked the rule of law (Muvindi, 22 May 2016). People who assaulted teachers in Ruwa, for allegedly "allowing people to vote wrongly," were never arrested. Such a situation encourages impunity in the community (Guerrero, 22 May 2016).

In the absence of fear, Christians would speak more openly about the critical social issues discussed in the pastoral letters from the Catholic leadership. As a result, Christians tended to shun any church activities or programmes that addressed political matters. The CCJP for long had existed at parish level but very few people wanted to have anything to do with it because of the wrong stigma it carried (Muvindi, 22 May 2016). It took the courage of a few charismatic leaders to re-launch the CCJP in the parish and rectify the mistaken understanding that the CCJP was synonymous with politics, but was there simply to promote justice and build peace in the community through the cooperation of every community member (Nguwi, 22 May 2016).

Poverty and unemployment were some of the factors suggested as perpetuating violence in the community. The young people constituted the majority of agents of violence. In most cases, they would be hired by politically powerful figures in the community. Most of these youths hardly resisted, as they would have been promised employment. Some would simply carry out violent missions only to get drugs as payment (FGD, 23 May 2016; Masvaya, 3 April 2017). The government also purposely orchestrated poverty as a means of hanging on to power. It used poverty and unemployment to create a conducive environment for supplying labour for political violence (Muvindi, 22 May 2016).

Some people in the community take advantage of an environment of political violence in order to settle their own scores. As a result, they victimise their targets in the name of politics as they can even go to the extent of falsely accusing them of committing incriminating acts. Their real agenda may be vengeance against a wrong deed or pure evil intentions against a member of the community. Political slogans such as *pasi naye* (down with - literally meaning s/he deserves to die) teach the society to take no prisoners. They also encourage people to take the law into their hands (Masvaya, 3 April 2017).

How can the message of the bishops be more effective?

The dissemination and sensitisation of the pastoral letters needs diversification so that it reaches as many people as possible. One of the most powerful ways of spreading the message of pastoral letters was packaging them in homilies, summarising the main message of the pastoral letter. Homilies are powerful because they provide both information and formation (Guerrero, 22 May 2016). The Focus Group Discussion (FGD) (23 May 2016) consisting of youths observed that the process of distribution and sensitisation of the pastoral letters did little to target them and yet they constituted the majority of the population, not only in the community but also in the nation at large. They argued that by engaging the youths more, a large number of the community members is reached. More so, involving the youths was quite strategic because they would effectively influence change among their peers (Ibid). Disseminating the pastoral letters through the social media such as the WhatsApp and Facebook would also be effective especially in terms of speed and cost effectiveness (Ibid). The Catholic Church should also appreciate and adopt the aggressiveness displayed by local Pentecostal Churches in spreading their message through television stations. According to Maphosa (25 May 2016), it was high time the Catholic Church launched a television station and community radio stations for evangelisation purposes.

Finally, since violence is a phenomenon that cuts across the whole community, the pastoral letters should also be disseminated to various stakeholders of the community, and if possible, hold all-stakeholder sensitisation workshops. Some of these stakeholders would include leaders of various political affiliations, local government officials, schools, clinics, the business community, youths, police and various faith communities (Nguwi, 22 May 2016).

Findings from Ruwa parishioners also indicated the need for, not only proper understanding but also putting the message into concrete action. Before attempting to influence people of other faiths in the community, Christians should internalise the pastoral letters and be ready to take action for social change in their community (Boterekwa, 22 May 2016). However, the fact that most of the parishioners do not read the pastoral letters compromises the positive impact of the pastoral letters on reducing political violence (FGD, 23 May 2016). According to Muvindi (22 May 2016), part of the social action to end political violence would be simply withdrawing labour for violence (Muvindi, 22 May 2016). Put differently, people should simply refuse to collaborate on issues that perpetuate political violence. This would paralyse political violence attempts since, as Shoko (23 May 2016) observed, those who normally hire such labour have no power to execute it on their own.

Other forms of action include making use of available resources and mechanisms that promote peace in the community such as use of legal routes whenever violent crimes are committed, even in the context of a compromised judiciary system (Guerrero, 22 May 2016). According to Father Guerrero, it would also be important to make use of available means to arrive at forgiveness and reconciliation, for instance, through traditional courts, mediation through community elders and the sacrament of reconciliation.

Whither healing Zimbabwe?

Based on the above findings, this chapter draws four main conclusions in relation to the pastoral letters and political violence. First, pastoral documents have the potential to empower the people at grassroots level. Second, poor dissemination methods have reduced the positive impact of the pastoral letters. Third, fear is one of the greatest hurdles to societal transformation. Fourth, the bottom-up approach employed by the Ruwa CCJP enhances coordination and interaction among the various levels of the society, thereby showing hope for healing Zimbabwe.

Empowerment

Through the pastoral letters and initiatives from the CCJP at parish level, Christians have come to appreciate that violence is not the solution to social problems in the society. Documents such as *Breaking the Silence*, *God Hears the Cry of the Poor* and the pastoral letter published by Archbishop Pius Ncube challenged Christians and the community at large to 'see and judge' critical social issues in their present-day society. The pastoral letters also re-package the CST values as they remind both Christians and non-Christians in the society that, as Pope John Paul II (2002) averred, peace is not merely the absence of war but is the promotion of justice. The pastoral documents also underline the importance of promoting and protecting people's human dignity, given that they were created in the image of God (*Gaudium et Spes*, 1965). It is upon this foundation that the various human rights emanate. Violence inflicted on the human person is denounced on the grounds of human dignity.

Ruwa parishioners also attested to the empowering effect of the pastoral letters. As Fr. Luis Guerrero (22 May 2016), the then Priest-in-Charge of Ruwa, pointed out, the pastoral letters helped parishioners to discuss issues previously regarded as too politically sensitive. Masvaya (3 April 2017), the then Chairperson of the Ruwa Parish CCJP, noted that through the *see-judge-act* principle, the pastoral documents equipped Church members in the various Small Christian Communities with skills to observe and analyse local issues related to social justice. The *see-judge-act* concept is an effective CST tool for equipping young people with critical thinking, thereby empowering them to resist being involved in political violence which barely benefits them except the political leaders who manipulate them (FGD, 23 May 2016; Muvindi, 22 May 2016; Shoko, 23 May 2016). The observation by Phiri (22 May 2016) also demonstrates the extent to which the pastoral documents empowered the Christians in Ruwa and especially in the area of human rights violation. He noted that discussion related to the CST led Ruwa church members to the realisation that Christians had a duty to actively participate in politics, thereby bringing about social transformation in their society.

Dissemination

However, in order to increase the impact in terms of empowering people with knowledge and skills of analysing critical social issues that affect them, dissemination and sensitisation methods need improvement. This would ensure that the social teaching of the Church reaches as many people as possible. According to ZimStat (2012: 18), an estimated 82.8% of the Zimbabwean population was below the age of 35 years in 2012. As the Focus Group Discussion (2016) rightly highlighted, since the youths in the country did not only constitute the bulk majority of the total population but were also the majority of the people hired to carry out violent activities. Most of the challenges related to dissemination and sensitisation mentioned by various respondents need serious attention in order to empower people with skills of how to assess and deal with violence in their communities. As indicated in the Focus Group Discussion (2016), the young people generally observed that there was little effort in targeting them, even though they represented the majority of Ruwa parishioners. The views by some parishioners such as Maphosa (25 May 2016) that the church should be more aggressive in distributing the pastoral letters by way of both social media and even electronic media such as a Church TV or radio station can help to step up the fight against political violence.

The fear factor

"I learned that courage was not the absence of fear, but the triumph over it. The brave man is not he who does not feel afraid, but he who conquers that fear" Nelson Mandela (inspirational quote).

The fear factor is the main reason compromising the effectiveness of the pastoral letters in reducing political violence, according to evidence from Ruwa. Findings suggest that while people have been generally empowered to *see-and-judge*, they have not gathered enough courage to *act* as demanded by the *see-judge-act* principle of the CST. As Shoko (23 May 2016) observed, their fear is not due to some imagined danger, but to a concrete historical experience whereby one can get into serious problems of assault, torture and even death for merely expressing one's opinion. Events elsewhere confirm that this fear is real. It is alleged, for instance, that some secret state agents abducted Itai Dzamara, a journalist and outspoken human rights activist, who has been missing since 2015 (Manayiti, 2016).

The fear is also exacerbated by a culture of impunity (Huyse, 2003), as the arm of justice always seems to leave the perpetrators scot-free. The *Gukurahundi* atrocities in Matabeleland serve as one good example (Teuten, 2015). As stated by Huyse (2003), impunity perpetuates violence. By suppressing action (related to the see-judge-act principle) on the part of the Christians, fear has led to the lack of integrity on the part of Christians as they literally 'talk right and walk left', almost as depicted in Patrick Bond's work entitled *Talk Left, Walk Right: South Africa's Frustrated Global Reforms* (2006). According to Muvindi (22 May 2016), the then Chairperson of St Charles' Parish, Ruwa, Christians understood the demands of what their bishops taught but did not have the courage to implement what they believed due to political intimidation and violence. The phenomenon of fear, therefore, signifies the extent to which Zimbabwe remained unhealed, regardless of the efforts of church leadership. Church leaders should therefore go beyond the issuing of pastoral documents and, in God's name, directly confront the princes of political violence in the society (Shoko, 23 May 2016). Such a move would demonstrate prophetic leadership in the fold of canonical prophets such as Amos, who were courageous enough to challenge people in high places as they advocated for justice in defence of the vulnerable.

Even so, prophetic leaders have not been totally lacking but would need reinforcement through collective effort and vision. One example of prophetic leadership is that of Pius Ncube who was courageous enough to denounce injustices amidst death threats (CCJP, 2001). However, his resignation, following a court case regarding his alleged affair with a married woman, affirmed the observation of Ezra Chitando *et al* (2014) that the prophetic mission in Zimbabwe was a costly one. Nonetheless, the fearlessness demonstrated by Pius Ncube as he stood by the CST values managed to shake the state establishment that funnelled political violence. This indicates the huge impact that pro-activeness can have on ending violence if more Christians were as determined as Archbishop Pius Ncube. There may be some Christians of his calibre in the society but as long as they act in isolation, there will always be little hope of improvement (Shoko, 23 May 2016). According to Father Guerrero (22 May 2016), the Small Christian Communities are there to encourage unity of purpose in witnessing gospel values, some of which include the promotion of human dignity. In addition, the workshops frequently held by the Ruwa CCJP often created a healthy atmosphere for dialogue as participants usually discussed issues that were usually considered as sensitive.

Bottom-up approach

The approach by the local CCJP in dealing with political violence in the community by way of holding multi-stakeholder workshops is in line with the bottom-up approaches to peace-building (Netabay 2007; Saunders 1999; Netabay 2007). According to Netabay (2007), whose work focuses on the conflict in Sudan, a bottom-up approach is a people-centred approach that advocates for peace from within the affected societies and requires changing hearts and minds of the local people to get them to work for peace and reconciliation wholeheartedly. Such is the approach that the CCJP in Ruwa adopted as it used the CST to convert the minds of the local people. As pointed by parishioners and CCJP activists during interviews (Nguwi, 22 May 2016; Phiri, 22 May 2016), the Ruwa CCJP invited participants from various sectors of the community inclusive of political parties such that there was proper representation of the community. Such forums are ideal for addressing differences and charting a way forward in an effort to create a better community. This approach also concurs with Lederach's argument that effective peace initiatives should seriously consider the contribution of the people at grassroots level.

Saunders (1999) adds that the capacity of the people at grassroots level should be enhanced through education. The approach of educating people at grassroots level through workshops and pastoral documents in order to influence transformation from below is in tandem with the general literature on peace-building, which advocates for the involvement of people at the grassroots level (Lederach 1997; Saunders 1999 and Netabay 2007). This approach moves away from decision-making processes that alienate citizens from participating in making decisions that affect their lives. Typical of such a scenario was the Zimbabwe's 2009 Government of National Unity formation (Mapuva, 2011), which was the product of a top-down approach to decision-making. Since ordinary people were not consulted, the peace arrived at was inevitably short-lived.

Members of the Ruwa CCJP believed that their method of involving all community stakeholders in peace-building workshops inspired by the pastoral documents could effectively reduce violence in the community. As Masvaya (3 April 2017) pointed out, the local CCJP workshops provided a forum for local community leaders, political representatives from various political parties included, to express themselves freely, without fear of victimisation. However, these same local structures (wards and districts) were responsible for perpetrating political violence (CCJP, 2009). Nonetheless, in the case of Ruwa, Masvaya (3 April 2017) argued that the approach of involving local community leaders, politicians and local government officials included, facilitated the building of trust in the community. Hove (2013) also contended that the involvement of all stakeholders also helped to avoid any suspicion by the state. Many critics considered the ZANU PF government as suspicious of its citizens. Mendel and Mukundu (2004), for instance, argue that the enactment of repressive laws such as Access to Information and Protection of Privacy Act (AIPPA) and Public Order and Security Act (POSA) was a result of this suspicion.

This approach by the Ruwa CCJP is also in line with an early warning system suggested by Hove (2013), adopted from Sierra Leone's format of the District Code Monitoring Communities, whereby members from various sectors of the districts participated in peace monitoring. Hove (2013) maintains that Zimbabwe could take advantage of its already existing ward structures to form committees for monitoring peace. They would consist of representatives of local groups such as traditional leaders, community leaders, local religious leaders, teachers, nurses, police, youths, and representatives of political parties. For him, involving both these lower structures of governance and other non-governmental bodies at the local level would facilitate in re-building trust and unity of purpose and preventing political violence in Zimbabwe. Likewise, the CCJP peace-building workshops by the Ruwa CCJP opened a platform for dialogue and especially for sensitising the community about peace. The workshops also provided an opportunity for the community members to study various approaches to ending violence, including that of the CST as well as those derived from other Christian denominations, African Traditional Religions and best practices of peace-building elsewhere (Masvaya, 3 April 2017; Nguwi, 22 May 2016). Such an approach could provide an opportunity to heal the Zimbabwean society from the roots since it would be a bottom-up initiative, taking cognisance of the views of the people on the ground and at the receiving end of the political violence.

Furthermore, the workshop model promoted by the Ruwa CCJP fits in well with the approach of Lederach (1997) to peace-building. As discussed above, Lederach (1997) argues that effective transformation of society can only be realised if there is coordination within and interaction among the three levels of the society (grassroots, middle and top levels). Without this vertical axis (interaction of the various levels), peace-building efforts remain compromised, argues Lederach (1997). The CCJP-driven workshops encouraged coordination within the community in Ruwa by promoting dialogue among community members from different backgrounds. According to Nguwi (22 May 2016) and Boterekwa (22 May 2016), these workshops cover a variety of topics such as human rights, social justice, retribution and responsible citizenship. By ensuring that there is the local government representation at these forums, this church-driven process also promoted the interaction between the Ruwa community and government (the top level), which was in charge of policy formulation. The presence of law enforcers at these workshops, for instance, facilitated discussions on why there was poor law enforcement and impunity (Masvaya, 3 April 2017). In this way, the workshops, in a small but significant way, addressed the problem of impunity pointed out by both Sachikonye (2011) and Huyse (2003) and the use of political violence to settle personal vendettas (Masvaya, 3 April 2017). The emphasis on educating the people at the grassroots level (Saunders 1999) through the pastoral documents improved the quality of interaction between this level and the two other upper levels, thereby increasing the chances of transforming the society.

Conclusion

This chapter has considered some dimensions of how Zimbabwe is a wounded country in dire need of healing. The Southern African country has experienced politically-motivated violence that has tormented the civilians in both the colonial and post-colonial periods. To date, Zimbabwe's citizenry still lives in fear of state-sponsored torture, harassment and even killings, regardless of the call by church leaders to end violence. Using the case of the Ruwa Parish, the study has assessed how the Catholic Church's pastoral documents influenced the society at grassroots level. The chapter has established that the church's pastoral documents constitute a gospel-based social analysis method called the Catholic Social Teaching (CST). Based on fieldwork findings, the chapter argued that the teaching of the Catholic leaders empowers the people with knowledge of the current situation. They have also empowered Christians with skills to make their own judgements, empowering them to be proactive in the face of political violence. The chapter also observed that Zimbabwe may never effectively heal as long as fear dominates in the society. It is this fear that has significantly reduced the positive impact of the bishops' pastoral letters on the society.

Nonetheless, a bottom-up approach, spearheaded by the Ruwa CCJP by way of workshops, is a positive impact of the pastoral letters. Such a forum is conducive for dialogue and charting Zimbabwe along a path of healing. Based on evidence from St Charles' Parish in Ruwa, the chapter has argued that the approach to ending political violence via the education of the people at grassroots level is in line with bottom-up approaches to peace building. Lederach (1997), for instance, posits that effective peace-building entails both the coordination and interaction of all levels of the society. Interaction between the grassroots level with the top level of policymaking is more effective when the former is well educated (Saunders, 1999). The chapter has argued that despite their shortcomings, the pastoral documents have the potential to empower people at grassroots level in order to transform the wounded society of Zimbabwe.

References

AFCAST. (2009) *Four levels of Catholic Social Teaching: A guide to teaching CST in seminaries and formation houses in Africa,* Harare: The African Forum for Catholic Social Teaching (AFCAST).

Aolin, F. N. (2006) 'Political violence and gender during times of transition,' in: *Columbia Journal of Gender and Law,* Volume 15, Number 3, pp.829-849.

Bond, P. (2006) *Talk left, walk right: South Africa's frustrated global reforms.* Available at: ccs.ukzn.ac.za/files/BondTalkLeftWalkRight2ndedn.pdf, Accessed 13 March 2017.

Boterekwa, S. 22 May 2016, Interview, Harare.

CCJP Zimbabwe, (1997) *Breaking the silence: Building true peace: A report on the disturbances in Matabeleland and the Midlands 1980 to 1988,* Harare: CCJP and Legal Resource Foundation (LRF).

CCJP Zimbabwe, (2001) *Crisis of governance: A report on political violence in Zimbabwe - An account of events highlighting efforts to subvert the popular will in parliamentary elections held in June 2000*, Volume 1, Harare: CCJP.

CCJP Zimbabwe, (2009) *Graveyard governance: A report on political violence following the March harmonised 2008 elections,* Harare: CCJP.

CCJP Zimbabwe and the Catholic Institute for International Relations, (1975) *The man in the middle: Torture, resettlement and eviction and civil war in Rhodesia,* Harare: CCJP.

CCJP Zimbabwe, (1997) *Breaking the Silence: Building true peace: A report on the disturbances in Matabeleland and the Midlands 1980 to 1988,* Harare: The Legal Resources Foundation.

CCJP Zimbabwe, (2013) *The Catholic Observer: Election Observation Report for 2013 harmonised elections, Zimbabwe,* Harare: CCJP, CPLO and SOCCOM.

Chilunjika, A. and Uwizeyimana, D. E. (2015). 'Shifts in the Zimbabwean land reform discourse from 1980 to the present', in: *African Journal of Public Affairs,* Volume 8, Number 3, pp.130-144.

Chitando, E., Taringa, N. T. and Mapuranga, T. P. (2014) 'Zimbabwean theology and religious studies during the crisis years (2000-2008): a preliminary study' in: *Studio Historiae Ecclesiasticae,* Volume 40, Number 1, pp.173-189.

Chitando, E. (2011) 'Prayers, politics and peace: The church's role in Zimbabwe's crisis', in: *Open Space,* Volumen 1, pp.43-48.

Church and Civil Society Forum, (2012) *A study on the role of the church in violence in Zimbabwe,* Harare: The Church and Civil Society Forum (CCSF).

Churches of Zimbabwe, (2006) *The Zimbabwe we want: Towards a national vision of Zimbabwe,* Harare: Barnaby Printing and Publishers.

Dombo, S. (2014) 'Refusing to be co-opted? Church organizations and reconciliation in Zimbabwe, with special reference to the Christian Alliance of Zimbabwe 2005-2013', in: *Journal for the Study of Religion,* Volume 27, Number 2, pp.137-171.

Focus Group Discusions. 23 May 2016, Harare.

Guerrero, L. 22 May 2016, Interview, Harare.

Gundani, P. (2002) 'The land crisis in Zimbabwe and the role of the churches towards its resolution, in: *Studia Historiae Ecclesiasticae,* Volume 28, Number 2, pp.122-169.

Hove, I. (2013). 'Preventing violence in future elections: Moving towards an early warning system for Zimbabwe,' in: *Journal of Peacebuilding and Development,* Volume 8, Number 1, pp.79-83.

Huyse, L. (2003). 'Zimbabwe: Why reconciliation failed,' in: T. B. David Bloomfield (ed.), *Reconciliation after violent conflict,* Stockholm: International IDEA, pp.34-39.

John Paul II, (1987) *Sollicitudo Rei Socialis (On concern for the social order),* Available at:
http://www.catholiceducation.org.uk/images/Election_resouce s/SOLLICITUDO_REI_SOCIALIS.pdf, Accessed 20 December 2017.

John Paul II, 1 January 2002. *Message of His Holiness Pope John Paul II for the celebration of the World Day of Peace,* Available at: http://w2.vatican.va/content/john-paul, Accesed 13 April 2017.

Kaulemu, D. (2006) 'The role of the church in society,' in: Churches in Manicaland, 2006. *The truth will make you free: A compendium of Christian Social Teaching,* Mutare: Churches in Manicaland, pp.vii-xii.

Lederach, J. P. (1997) *Building peace: Sustainable reconciliation in divided societies,* Washington DC: Institute of Peace Press.

Leo XIII, (1891) *Rerum novarum: Encyclical of Pope Leo XIII on capital and labor.* Vatican Archive.

Leonardsson, H. and Rudd, G. (2015) 'The 'Local Turn' in peacebuilding: A literature review of effective and emancipatory local peacebuilding,' In: *Third World Quarterly,* pp.825-839.

Makumbe, M. J. and Compagnon, D. (2000) *Behind the smokescreen: The politics of Zimbabwe's 1995 general elections,* Harare: University of Zimbabwe Publications.

Manayiti, O. (16 October 2016) 'Activists 'name' Dzamara's abductors' Available at: https://www.thestandard.co.zw, Accessed 14 March 2017.

Maphosa, S. (25 May 2016), Interview, Harare.

Mapuva, J. (7 April 2011), 'Safeguarding citizen participation through Government of National Unity (GNU) or is democracy being violated?,' in: *Peace and Conflict Monitor*, 7 April 2011.

Masvaya, V. (3 April 2017), Interview, Harare.

Matikiti, R. (2012) 'Christian theological perspectives on political violence in Zimbabwe: The case of the United Church of Christ in Zimbabwe', Thesis submitted to the Department of Religious Studies, Classics and Philosophy of the University of Zimbabwe in fulfilment of the requirements for the Degree of Doctor of Philosophy.

McVeigh, J. (1989) *A wounded church : Religion, politics, and justice in Ireland,* Chester Springs, PA: Mercier Press; U.S. Distributor Dufour Cork.

Mendel, T. and Mukundu, R. (2004) *Access to Information and Protection of Privacy Act: Two years on,* London and Harare: ARTICLE 19 and MISA-Zimbabwe.

Msipa, C. G. (2015) *In pursuit of freedom and justice: A memoir,* Harare: Weaver Press.

Murambadoro, R. (2015) "We cannot reconcile until the past has been acknowledged': Perspectives on Gukurahundi from Matabeleland, Zimbabwe' in: *African Journal on Conflict Resolution,* Volume 15, Number 1, pp.33-57.

Mushonga, M. (2005) 'Curfew and the 'Man in the Middle' in Zimbabwe's war of liberation with special reference to the eastern areas of Zimbabwe, 1977-1980,' in: C. A. Hendricks (Ed.) *From national liberation to democratic renaissance in Southern Africa,* Dakar: CODESRIA, pp.171-190.

Muvindi, D. (22 May 2016) Interview, Harare: Zimbabwe.

Ndlovu-Gatsheni, S. (2009) *Do 'Zimbabweans' exist?: Trajectories of nationalism, national identity-formation and crisis in a post-colonial state, Volume 3*, city of publication missing. Peter Lan.

Netabay, N. (2007) 'Bottom-Up approach: A viable strategy in solving the Somali conflict,' MA Thesis in Peace Studies, Notre Dame: Joan B. Kroc Institute for International Peace Studies, University of Notre Dame.

Nguwi, R. 22 May 2016. Interview, Harare: Zimbabwe.

Phiri, L. 22 May 2016. Interview, Harare: Zimbabwe.

246

Pontifical Council for Justice and Peace, (2004) *Compendium of the social doctrine of the church*, Vatican: Libreria Editrice Vaticana.

Sachikonye, L. (2011) *When a state turns on its citizens: Institutionalized violence and political culture*, Auckland Park: Jacana Media.

Saunders, H. H. (1999) *A public peace process*, New York: Palgrave.

Second Vatican Council, (1965) *Pastoral constitution on the church in the modern world (Gaudium et Spes)*, Vatican.

Shoko, P. (23 May 2016) Interview, Harare: Zimbabwe.

Teute, B. (2015) "A recipe for another war of revenge": The lasting impacts of the Gukurahundi on Matabeleland, Zimbabwe, *Herald*, Harare: Zimbabwe.

Tibaijuka, A. K (2005) 'Report of the fact-finding mission to Zimbabwe to assess the scope and impact of Operation Murambatsvina,' Available at:. http://www.un.org/News/dh/infocus/zimbabwe/zimbabwe_rpt.pdf, Accessed 7 December 2016.

Wallace, R. (2010) 'Grassroots community-based peace-building: Critical narratives on peacebuilding and collaboration from the locality of indigenous and non-indigenous activists in Canada,' Doctoral dissertation, Bradford, West Yorkshire: University of Bradford.

World Synod of Bishops, (1971) *Justice in the world*, Libreria: Vatican.

Zimbabwe Catholic Bishops' Conference, (2007) *God hears the cry of the oppressed: A pastoral letter on the current crisis in Zimbabwe*, Harare: Social Communications Department.

ZimStats, (2012) *Population Census National Report*, UNICEF: Harare.

Chapter 12

Vanishing Traditions? Girl Children as Sacrificial Lambs in the Context of Shona Indigenous Transitional Justice Mechanisms in 21ˢᵗ Century Zimbabwe

Fidelis Peter Thomas Duri

Introduction

This chapter examines an indigenous transitional justice mechanism among the Shona people of Zimbabwe known as *kuripa ngozi* (appeasing avenging spirits) paying particular attention to the practice of marrying off young girls to the families of murdered persons. This institution has its origins in the pre-colonial period and has persisted into the post-colonial era, albeit at a less prevalent rate due to some socio-economic developments such as urbanisation, the spread of Christianity as well as interventions from various stakeholders including governments, churches and civil society groups (Bourdillon, 1998). In 2015, global statistics on child marriages indicated that an estimated 39 000 girls were married off each day and 14 million each year (*Herald*, 27 February 2015).

    The Shona jurisprudential tradition of appeasing the avenging spirit of a murdered person obliged the perpetrators to pay restitution in the form of livestock, mostly cattle, and at times a girl, to the bereaved family (Benyera, 2014; Tagwireyi, 5 May 2013; Thorpe, 1991). In the purported pursuit of 'justice', the innocent girl who is surrendered becomes "a slave and wife to a member of the deceased's family" (Sithole, 20 December 2016: 1). In most cases, the girl was married off to an adult man but at times to a boy (Kachere, 29 September 2009). The negative generational dynamics of the institution of *kuripa ngozi* involved family and community elders violating the rights and liberties of children. Gender insensitivity is also evidenced by the fact that girls were in most cases given husbands who were not of their own choice. Instead of delivering justice and achieving lasting peace, societal discord emerges. The flight of girls from forced marriages and the reports that some of them made to the police since the pre-colonial period, among other things, attest to this betrayal of justice.

This chapter argues that the cultural practice of marrying off a young girl in order to appease the avenging spirit of a murdered person is both ambivalent and self-defeating in that it sacrifices the rights and liberties of girl children, and at times boy children, under the guise of seeking peace and justice. As a jurisprudential institution, it causes societal discord by appeasing the dead and their bereaved families at the expense of innocent young people whose childhood and adulthood are both compromised.

Situating the study in academic discourse

Considerable research on Shona indigenous cultural practices has been undertaken by many Zimbabwean scholars during the new millennium. Most of the scholars, it should be noted, are 'nationalist'/ 'Africanist' in orientation or approach and tend to glorify and celebrate the African past and its traditions. To most of these scholars, indigenous African cultural values and practices inculcated moral, responsible and commendable behaviour within individuals that helped to enhance social order not only in the past, but also in the present. This section will sample a few of these scholarly works against which this chapter seeks to mark a significant departure.

Mutekwa's (2010) work, for example, is silent on the manner in which some Shona indigenous socio-cultural practices such as the handing over of girl children to appease avenging spirits subordinated and marginalised women and girls. His overlooking of gender insensitivities associated with this indigenous Shona transitional justice mechanism is not by omission, but by commission. In actual fact, he deliberately avoids delving into the issue on grounds that doing so would be "problematic as it denies the existence of female subjectivities" and that "it is a negation of reality to construct the pre-colonial African woman as no more than a victim of patriarchy. This victim construction of women can ultimately be detrimental to moves to emancipate the African woman" (Mutekwa, 2010, 168-169).

Masaka and Chemhuru (2011: 132) studied Shona taboos and emphasised their "moral dimensions" in a wholly positive sense, noting the critical role they played, and still play, "in shaping human conduct and fostering eco-friendly behaviour." They also insist that Shona cultural practices "forbid people from behaving in such manners that are a threat to the welfare and wellbeing of fellow human beings" (Masaka and Chemhuru, 2011: 147).

Similarly, Tatira's (2014) work is basically a eulogy of the African past and how it constructively shapes the present. Among other things, he argues that Shona socio-cultural beliefs were gender sensitive and upheld the status of women in several ways. He argues:

> Contrary to the popularised view that Africans, Shona people included, have a proclivity to abusing women, the Shona people through their belief protect women against abuse. This does not mean that there are no abusers of women among the Shona, what we want to clearly articulate is that there are beliefs which protect women against abusers. The woman members are believed to be physically weaker than their male members in Shona society thus we have beliefs which protect them against men (Tatira, 2014: 4-5).

In concluding, Tatira (2014: 9) finds no weaknesses in the African past and its socio-cultural beliefs and practices:

> This paper has discussed three basic Shona belief systems which are ancestral belief, avenging spirits and witchcraft. Yet, despite all the thinking postures in which the Shona value trust or confidence, these three have been singled out because they are fairly capable of representing Shona philosophical, sociological psychological and anthropological world-views. Thus, this presentation has managed to show that the selected belief systems of the Shona are neither retrogressive nor irrelevant because they provide important lessons that can be used today, because it helps people cope with their day-to-day challenges. Through the values, as espoused in the beliefs, the present generation can derive important lessons for life on human dignity,

respect of each other, peaceful co-existence with each other and the environment, perseverance and humility. All such attributes are vital for a healthy society.

It is quite apparent that these views are characteristic of those Afrocentric discourses that were particularly intended to counter the sentiments colonial apologists. Their common weakness lies in their unrelenting defence of the African cause at all costs to the extent that they degenerate into mere polemic. As discussed elsewhere in this book, there is no doubt that the institution of *kuripa ngozi* was, and is still, an important indigenous transitional justice mechanism but its shortcomings also need to be examined in order to reform the institution as part of the endeavours to achieve lasting societal peace and justice. One such weakness, which this chapter is preoccupied with, is the handing over of girl children as compensation to appease avenging sprits. It is not the intention of this chapter to demonise African indigenous cultural values and practices in general and those pertaining to the Shona in particular, but to highlight some of their shortcomings with the hope of reforming them in an attempt to deliver true justice and attain lasting peace.

The tradition of forced marriages among the Shona since the pre-colonial period

The practice of forcing girls and women into marriages in order to settle societal disputes and family hardships took various forms in many African communities since the pre-colonial period. Among the Chopi of southern Mozambique, for example, women and girls were sometimes handed over to resolve disputes between members of clans since the 16th century (Young, 1977). Even though this chapter is primarily concerned with the marrying off of girls to appease the avenging spirit of a murdered person, it is necessary to explore other forms of forced child marriages in order to contextualise the discussion.

The traditional marriage practice of widow inheritance or the levirate system (Mair, 1969), known as *kugara nhaka* among the Shona, was prevalent in many pre-colonial African societies

(Bourdillon, 1998). In this system, a widow was expected, or even obliged, to cohabit with the brother of her deceased husband. The living brother of the deceased person thus inherited the widow and became her husband (Bourdillon, 1998; Radcliffe-Brown, 1950; Thorpe, 1991). Similar practices took place in other parts of pre-colonial Africa among societies such as the Lozi of present-day Zambia, the Zulu of South Africa (Gluckman, 1950), the Nuba of Sudan (Nadel, 1947), the Nyakyusa of southern Tanzania and northern Malawi (Wilson, 1950) and the Mende of Sierra Leone (Little, 1976).

Another forced marriage practice was the sororate system in which a girl was ordered to marry the husband of her deceased sister (Mair, 1969). Among the pre-colonial Shona, the substitute wife was known as *bondwe* or *chigadzamapfihwa* (Hannan, 1959). It was also a fairly widespread practice among the Shona for family members and kin to force a barren woman's younger sister, or another female relative, to become a co-wife (Masasire, 1996).

Child betrothal, the custom of pledging a young daughter in marriage, usually in order to repay a debt or to obtain material benefits from those who were relatively well off (Mair, 1969), was also widely practised. Known as *kuzvarira* by the Shona (Hannan, 1959), this institution was widespread in pre-colonial Africa and persisted well into the colonial period among societies such as the Ila (Smith and Dale, 1920) and Bemba (Richards, 1940) in Zambia; the Fingo (Thomson, 1898) and the Venda (Schapera, 1937) in South Africa; the Swazi in Swaziland (Kuper, 1947) and the Kongo in the present Democratic Republic of Congo (Mair, 1969). In the majority of cases, the practice involved pledging girls to older men, but was at times arranged for two children (Mair, 1969). Poor parents sometimes pledged their daughters to rich men in return for assistance in the form of grain in times of drought and the temporary use of cattle for ploughing fields. In such cases, the betrothed girl was a form of pawn married away to repay a debt. Bourdillon (1998: 41) articulated how this institution operated among the pre-colonial Shona people:

…It was possible for a man to favour a friend or an associate with the promise of a small daughter in marriage…Particularly after a bad harvest, a family without enough to live on may try to relieve the situation by marrying off a small girl and using the bride price to buy food for the family. In such a case, the girl stays with her parents until she reaches a marriageable age…

During the 1930s, one European observer in Rhodesia noted that child-pledging was on the rise owing to wage employment which empowered a considerable number of men to obtain young daughters from poor parents in exchange for financial and other material benefits (Schmidt, 1992). One Mrs Manhenga, an African woman who had come to Salisbury, the Rhodesian capital, during the 1950s, explained to Teresa Barnes (1992: 68) how she was pledged by her father at a very young age:

I left school because I had been pledged by my father. My father gave me to a man who had three wives and I went on to become the fourth one. The law during those days was so oppressive, saying, "If your father says do this, don't refuse!" I was very young, I don't know the years, if they were 12, or whatever, I was very young, with breasts just coming out. So, I was given to him…It went like this: say a baby was born in that village, so a man would go and look for firewood and come and drop it at the door where the child had been born, to claim a wife, if it was a girl. So our fathers went to work in the farms where *chirungu* (westernisation) started, and became sort of friends with people there. So when that happened he would say, "You don't visit others, I have daughters." So they think of coming to look for wives. These would be old men of the same age.

I left home on that old man's bicycle, with his beard fanning me, that man's beard, and I was so frightened…The hair went fu-fu-fu on my mouth, while I was on the crossbar, not the carrier. I was put in the middle, with his hands clutching the handles and his beard fanning me, on the crossbar of the bicycle. And people at his home said, "Why have you brought this child?"

In Shona cultural practices dating back to the pre-colonial period, young girls, specifically virgins, were also married off to appease avenging spirits in a practice known as *kuripa ngozi* (Tagwireyi, 5 May 2013; Thorpe, 1991). This happened when one committed murder and the bereaved family demanded compensation in the form of a girl and livestock to calm the avenging spirits. The virgin girls could be as young as six years old (Kachere, 29 September 2009. In some cases, the girl could be as young as five years (Sithole, 20 December 2016). The surrendered girl had to live with the deceased person's family, regardless of how young she was. When she reached puberty, she was forcibly married to one of the male members of the deceased's family (Kachere, 29 September 2009). The virgin girl was given away specifically to bear children purportedly "to allow the victim to be resuscitated by the replacement" (Benyera, 2014: 248). If restitution was not paid, it was believed that the perpetrator's family would experience untold misfortunes such as unpredictable deaths and illnesses (*Herald*, 27 February 2015).

Girls who refused to consent to pre-arranged marriages were sometimes intimidated and flogged by their parents and kin (Schmidt, 1992). As the Chief Native Commissioner (CNC) for Mashonaland Province in colonial Zimbabwe (Rhodesia) noted in 1911:

> It is no uncommon occurrence for parents to inflict torture on their daughters to compel them to marry against their will. Cases are always coming to light of native girls running away to missions, or drifting on to the mines, rather than submit to the hardships inflicted at home to compel them to marry (National Archives of Zimbabwe, 1911, File N9/I/14).

The colonial government passed various pieces of legislation in an effort to stop child marriages. Rhodesia's Native Marriages Ordinance of 1901 and subsequent amendments in 1905 and 1912, for example, were attempts to curb this practice (Southern Rhodesia Government, 1939). The Native Marriages Ordinance of 1917 made it a criminal offence punishable by a fine of up to £50, or a year's imprisonment with hard labour, for a man to marry a girl aged 12 years and below (National Archives of Zimbabwe, 1917: File

N3/17/4/2; Peaden, 1970). In colonial Zimbabwe, most of the cases involving forced marriages were handled by the Native Commissioner's (NC) Courts. In the Goromonzi District, for example, 95 out of the 345 cases heard at the NC Court during the period October 1899 to February 1905 involved young girls who had refused to become wives of men forced upon them by their parents and relatives (Schmidt, 1992).

During the colonial period, some women and girls deserted their homes after husbands had been forced upon them. In addition, the influence of urbanisation, Christian missionaries and colonial administrations resulted in many African women and girls resisting forced marriages and some African communities abandoning the practice. Some girls fled to become nuns at mission stations (Dachs and Rea, 1979). Commenting in 1923 on girls who rejected being betrothed resulting in them seeking refuge at mission stations, a reverend of the Wesleyan Methodist Church in Rhodesia, quoted by Schmidt (1992: 140), stated that, "naturally we do not teach disobedience to parents, but we are thankful to see that with some encouragement, the girls are likely to strike a blow at those heathen customs of marriage which are so disgusting." At St. Paul's Mission, north-west of the capital, Salisbury, a Dominican nun recalled that by 1926, the Catholic establishment had become "a place of refuge for girls whose pagan parents insisted on their marrying a pagan youth and in some places even an old man" (Schmidt, 1992: 220).

Commenting on the rise of prostitution in Rhodesian towns, the *African Weekly* of 25 July 1945, quoted by Barnes (1992: 119), noted the flight from the rural areas of African girls who had been forcibly married as one of the major causes:

> What are the causes of prostitution? First, the pledging of daughters. A girl is given to a husband before she 'wants' a man, because her father envies that man's cattle or produce. When she grows older she thinks of choosing for herself, but she is forced because her parents have already used the lobola. So she runs away to town. Whose fault is this?

The presence in Rhodesian towns of women and girls, particularly those who had come without the consent of their family members and kin, increasingly became a worry to colonial officials and some sections of the African population which included traditional leaders and male family heads (Barnes, 1997). In 1931, for example, the Native Commissioner for Umtali suggested the introduction of residential passes for females who came to settle permanently, and temporary passes for those who visited as a way of monitoring the movement of African women and girls into the town (National Archives of Zimbabwe, 4 June 1931: File S2584/73). In August 1932, an all-male African delegation from the so-called Native Association of Umtali urged the government to strictly monitor the movement of African women and girls into the town. They advised the government to demand from girls who came to the town of Umtali a letter of consent from their parents, failure for which they would be returned to their homes (National Archives of Zimbabwe, 15-17 August 1932: File S235/475). During the same year, the Advisory Committee of the Umtali Native Girls' Hostel urged the government to oblige all African women and girls working in Umtali to have registration certificates (National Archives of Zimbabwe, 15 August 1932: File S235/475). Despite these concerns, African women and girls continued to enter towns largely because of domestic challenges at their rural homes most of which emanated from patriarchal chauvinism and various socio-cultural constraints. In addition, the Rhodesian government did not take immediate action to address these concerns because a great deal of material and financial resources was required to implement such measures (Barnes, 1997).

The institution of forcing women and girls to marry men who were not of their choice was a clear manifestation of the violation of basic human rights and liberties. In such cultural practices, patriarchal interests and those of collectivities such as families and kin groups overrode and curtailed the wishes and freedoms of women and girls. Consequently, some women and girls fled to towns, mission stations, mines and across national borders during the colonial period as they sought freedom from such socio-cultural constraints imposed upon them by their rural communities. In particular, the indigenous Shona practice of surrendering young girls to appease angry spirits reflected "gender insensitivity" (Benyera, 2014: 248). As the next section illustrates, this deplorable practice persisted into the post-colonial period, albeit at a lower rate owing to various developments such as urbanisation, the spread of Christianity and prohibitions brought about by the 'modern' criminal justice system.

Selected cases of girl children surrendered to appease *ngozi* in independent Zimbabwe

This section examines selected cases of girl children who were married off to appease avenging spirits in independent Zimbabwe. The section demonstrates that the giving away of human beings in general and girls in particular in order to settle disputes is a gross violation of human rights and a form of slavery. The institution is a retrogressive cultural practice characterised by patriarchal chauvinism and gender insensitivity.

In 1999, in the Honde Valley of Manicaland Province, for example, Felicitas Nyakama, Nesta Maromo, Juliet Muranganwa, Precious Maboreke and Perseverance Ndarangwa, who were then young girls aged between seven and 15 years, were surrendered by their parents to the family of Gibson Kupemba as part of the reparations for the man's murder (Kachere, 29 September 2009). Consequently, the girls dropped out of school and became "under-age wives and mothers" who lived "an impoverished life as vegetable vendors to contribute to their new families' household income" (Kachere, 29 September 2009: 1). Kupemba's grandson, who was 28 years old, married Precious Maboreke, one of the surrendered girls, who was then aged 15 years. In September 2009, the couple had three children (Kachere, 29 September 2009).

It was alleged that the relatives of the girls killed Kupemba to prepare a traditional medicine (*muti*), which was made up from parts of the human body. Following Kupemba's murder, reports from local villagers stated that his avenging spirit began to cause sudden illnesses and fatalities in the families of the perpetrators. As a result, some of the murderers confessed to murdering him. The businessmen, who had orchestrated the murder, for example, also confessed that they had severed his genitals, tongue, little fingers and some hair to prepare traditional medicines for ritual purposes to enhance their entrepreneurial fortunes. Despite the confessions, the perpetrators were not apprehended and the deceased's relatives believed that they had bribed the police (*Ibid*).

The deceased's grandson also stated that his murdered grandfather 'approached' him in his sleep, ordering that a virgin girl and 22 herd of cattle be surrendered as restitution by each of the families that had been involved in killing him. He emphasised that the girls were not forcefully surrendered but did so out of their own volition in order to save their families from the ravages of the avenging spirit (Kachere, 29 September 2009). This explanation from the deceased's grandson that all the girls voluntarily surrendered themselves is highly improbable considering that some of them were as young as seven years of age and could not have possibly made such independent decisions. It is most likely that Kupemba's grandson was fully aware that child marriages were criminalised under Zimbabwean law and therefore sought to formulate such statements in an effort to avoid being prosecuted by the criminal justice system.

In another case of child pledging in 2009, Maira Gwati, a 14-year-old girl, from Guruve District, had to drop out of school after her parents had forcibly married her to a 60-year-old man in order to appease the avenging spirit of a murdered person (*IRIN News*, 7 November 2011). Narrating her ordeal in 2011, Maira Gwati told *IRIN News* (7 November 2011: 1):

> My grandfather killed a woman who had refused to be married to him many years ago and her family wanted a virgin as compensation to appease her spirit. I was chosen and given to an old man in marriage, but he often beat me up and even though I fell pregnant I could not stand the abuse.

This case clearly demonstrates the resistance by some members of the young generation to some age-old indigenous cultural practices that infringed upon their rights and liberties as human beings. The flight of girls who had been forcibly married in order to appease avenging spirits illustrates the change of times when the suppressed voices of the marginalised and downtrodden sections of the society cannot always be silenced forever.

In some cases, a girl was forcibly married to a boy from the family of a murdered person in an attempt to appease an avenging spirit. In May 2012, in Mberikwazo Village under Chief Mazungunye in Bikita District, for example, the Macheke family married off their 14-year old daughter who was doing Form Three at Gwindigwi High School to a 15-year old boy from the Chireya family during a ritual to appease avenging spirits. The murder case took place in August 1998 in the Bikita District of Masvingo Province when Masimba Macheke of Bengura Village under Chief Mazungunye allegedly stabbed and killed Kudzai Chireya of Mberikwazvo Village under Chief Mukanganwi. The two fought over contracts to dig wells in the district. When Macheke realised that he was being overpowered, he took a knife and stabbed Chireya several times on the body, leading to his death (Gunda, 7 May 2012). Such cases of *kuripa ngozi* illustrate how the young generation (boy and girl children) was sometimes sacrificed in order to settle the scores of adults.

Another case of a forced child marriage took place on 1 May 2013 when Raymond Nyakarange, a 40-year-old man from Nyanga District in north-eastern Zimbabwe, gave away his 14-year-old daughter to Mutava Jairosi Mukanga to compensate for the murder he had committed on his relative some years before. Mysterious deaths had begun taking place in Nyakarange's family forcing him to approach Mukanga to arrange the payment of reparations for the murder. The Mukanga family demanded that Nyakarange pay 10 herd of cattle as restitution. Since Nyakarange did not have the cattle, he decided to hand over his daughter as compensation (Zhakata, 4 April 2014). In this case, an innocent girl was used as a pawn to settle disputes involving adults. Such pursuits of justice involving the sacrificing of human beings in an attempt to appease the avenging spirit of a murdered person only manage to appease the bereaved family and afford the adult perpetrators some relief but antagonise those who would have been sacrificed.

The cases examined in this section demonstrate that forced child marriages violated the rights, freedom and liberties of girl children and at times boys. The section has illustrated how young girls were

260

forced into marriage unions with adult men in most cases, and boys in some. Their childhood, during which they were supposed to attend school while being groomed and socialised into adulthood by their parents and guardians, was terminated abruptly. In addition to having been deprived of their right to choose a spouse, some girls suffered from numerous health ailments as a result of giving birth at a young age. Again, being forced out of school at an early age shattered their future livelihood prospects thereby jeopardising their adulthood. Above all, the institution of appeasing avenging spirits by surrendering girls to the families of murdered persons is not an effective mechanism of achieving justice and lasting peace considering that it appeases other sections of the society while antagonising the others, particularly those girls who would have been married off against their wish.

Vanishing traditions: Interventions against the pledging of girl children in appeasing *ngozi*

The Shona indigenous institution of forcibly marrying off girls in order to appease spirits is becoming less prevalent in independent Zimbabwe owing to the efforts of various stakeholders. There have been vigorous efforts from several quarters, both national and international, to stop the practice. In Zimbabwe, the major players are the government, civil rights groups and traditional leaders while the United Nations (UN) has played a leading role in the campaign.

In Zimbabwe, the pledging of girls in order to appease avenging spirits is a criminal offence under the Domestic Violence Act, Chapter 5, of 2006 (Kachere, 29 September 2009; UN Committee on the Elimination of Discrimination against Women, 1 March 2012). The Anti-Domestic Violence Council was also set up to oversee the implementation of the Act (UN Committee on the Elimination of Discrimination against Women, 1 March 2012). Chapter 5(16) of the Act specifically provides for protection and relief of women and children from domestic violence. In addition, Section 80 of the 2013 Constitution particularly provides for the rights and liberties of women and protection of their dignity and worth as equal persons in the society. In particular, Section 80(3) criminalises laws, customs, traditions and other cultural practices that deprive women of their rights and personal safety. The cultural practices outlawed by the Act include virginity testing, female genital mutilation, pledging of women or girls for the purposes of appeasing avenging spirits, forced marriage, child marriage and forced wife inheritance (Majome, 3 December 2016).

In a number of instances, the Zimbabwean police arrested people who gave away their daughters to bereaved families as compensation for murder. In March 2014, Raymond Nyakarange, a 41-year-old man from Nyanga District, for example, appeared before the Nyanga Magistrates' Court to answer charges of handing over his 14-year-old daughter to the Mukanga family for the murder of their relative some years before. After Nyakarange had surrendered the girl to the Mukanga family on 1 May 2013, the police rescued her on 31 October during the same year and placed her under the custody of a Social Welfare centre. The court accused him of breaching Section 94(1) of the Criminal Law (Codification and Reform) Act which criminalises the pledging of a female person (Zhakata, 4 April 2014). Nyakarange pleaded guilty to the charges of giving away his daughter, saying an avenging spirit was causing many deaths in his family. In addition, he stated that he had no other option besides handing over his daughter since he did not have the 10 cattle which the bereaved family had demanded as restitution. The Magistrate found Nyakarange guilty and fined him US$200 or three months in prison. A further six months of Nyakarange's sentence were suspended on condition that he did not commit a similar offence within the next five years. The Magistrate castigated Nyakarange for giving away his daughter and stated that girls have their own liberties and rights to decide who to marry (Zhakata, 4 April 2014).

A considerable number of traditional leaders also condemned the practice of surrendering young girls in order to appease spirits. From 2012, in the Bindura District, for instance, Chief Musana and his headmen embarked on a campaign to end some cultural practices that upheld child marriages such as *kuripa ngozi*. Chief Musana tasked all his headmen to compile registers of all boys and girls of school-going age in their areas in order to monitor how they were raised in their families. The registers were to be submitted to Chief Musana who would check with teachers and headmasters in the area whether the children were attending school. After picking up that some girls were not attending school because they had been married off, the chief reported the cases to the police. During the period 2012-2015, there was a drastic decline in cases of child marriages in Chief Musana's area as a result of the efforts of local traditional leaders to end the practice (*Herald*, 27 February 2015). As Chiveso, one of Chief Musana's headmen, confirmed in February 2015:

> We have put an end to all that in our area. We no longer settle cases involving child marriages at our courts. Marrying off young girls is now history in my area. I ended all those practices. I now actually want to visit those areas which are still marrying off young girls on traditional grounds to really understand why they are still violating the rights of young girls in this day and age where there are many diseases such as HIV (*Herald*, 27 February 2015: 1).

Similarly, in October 2012, Headman Medzani Mandeya of Mutasa District in Manicaland Province stated that the use of virgin girls to appease avenging spirits was a thing of the past in his area: "This is very real and it is happening. As traditional leaders, we are against that. We have introduced a new law where all those found guilty of perpetuating child marriages would be heavily fined and at the same time arrested by police to appear at the magistrates' court" (Masekesa, 21 October 2012: 1).

Some local non-governmental organisations played a considerable role in complementing the efforts of the Zimbabwean government and some traditional leaders to end child marriages. In 2006, for example, the Girl Child Network (GCN) requested the police and the Department of Social Welfare to investigate the matter in which five girls from Honde Valley in Manicaland Province were surrendered to the family of Gibson Kupemba as restitution by people who had been involved in his murder in 1999. Since 1999, the perpetrators' families had surrendered five virgin girls and the bereaved family was still demanding 14 more. The GCN ordered a halt to the practice and demanded that the five girls be returned to their families. The police managed to rescue four of the girls from the Kupemba family and placed them under the custody of the GCN, which later on returned them to their families (Kachere, 29 September 2009). Anna Ndarangwa, one of the girls who had already been married into the Kupemba family, refused to return home (Kachere, 29 September 2009). Her mother, however, vowed to fight on until her daughter returned home when she declared: "I don't want my daughter to pay for a crime she did not commit. I will die fighting for her" (Kachere, 29 September 2009: 1). Anna Ndarangwa's case illuminates that some indigenous jurisprudential practices can bifurcate the society along gender lines. It also shows how patriarchal machinations of seeking to resolve disputes by pledging girls sometimes provoked protest during which mothers fought on behalf of their daughters who had been forcibly married off.

In 2015, the Family Aids Counselling Trust (FACT), another local non-governmental organisation, launched the End Child Marriages Campaign in the Nyanga District of north-eastern Zimbabwe. Various stakeholders in the district were urged to play an active role in ending cultural practices such as the pledging of girl children. Watch groups were formed to safeguard girls from being forcibly married. WhatsApp platforms, which were organised by FACT, and managed by the Zimbabwe Republic Police (ZRP) Victim Friendly Unit, were set up to enable communities to report cases of child marriage to the authorities such as the police and the Ministries of Women's Affairs and Social Welfare. Rural women's assemblies made up of local women were also formed to educate communities on the retrogressive effects of child marriages (Sithole, 20 December 2016).

Some non-governmental organisations operating in Zimbabwe jointly organised campaigns in local communities to discourage some cultural practices such as the pledging of girl children to appease avenging spirits. On 8 and 9 December 2016, for example, four non-governmental organisations organised two such events, one in the small town of Nyanga in north-eastern Zimbabwe and the other in the surrounding rural areas, to commemorate 16 Days of Activism against Gender-based Violence. The events, whose theme was 'Ending Child Marriages,' was jointly organised by ActionAid

Zimbabwe, FACT, Simukai Child Protection and the Diocese of Mutare Community Care Programme (DOMCCP). The events were attended by various stakeholders who included traditional leaders, rural women, teenage mothers and government officials (Sithole, 20 December 2016).

Both events started off with those in attendance watching a video on child marriages titled *Voices* which was produced by an organisation called African Women Film Festival. The film dwells on the causes of child marriages and highlights their health and psychological effects on girl children. After viewing the film, the participants engaged in discussion during which some women recounted their personal experiences when they were forced to marry at a young age. One woman stated that she had been married off at the age of 15 and within five years, she had given birth to five children. In addition to the negative health effects of giving birth every year, she revealed, she was also harassed by her in-laws (Sithole, 20 December 2016). Another woman, in her mid-50s, recalled:

> This film is a true reflection of my life. I got married at the age of 15 and had no clue what marriage was all about. After delivering my baby, I remember playing with other girls leaving the child unattended. Fortunately my mother in-law understood that I was a child and took over my responsibilities (Sithole, 20 December 2016: 1).

During the events, government officials and traditional leaders also gave presentations on the challenges faced by girl children. The government officials were from the ZRP Victim Friendly Unit; and the Ministries of Primary and Secondary Education, Public Service Labour and Social Welfare; and Health and Child Care. The traditional leaders who were present also declared an end to child pledging in Nyanga District (Sithole, 20 December 2016). Chief Katerere, for example, said,

> In Nyanga District we have declared that there will be no more child pledging! The girl child will never be used to appease avenging spirits ever again! Avenging spirits will be negotiated with and told to

accept livestock instead of the girl child (Sithole, 20 December 2016: 1).

Chief Katerere's speech did not condemn the institution of *kuripa ngozi* altogether. Instead, it can be noted that he was highlighting the need to reform the cultural practice by putting an end to marrying off girls and that restitution be paid only in the form of livestock and other material goods. His speech demonstrates the active role played by Zimbabwean traditional leaders in seeking to transform indigenous transitional justice mechanisms in a manner that upholds human rights and liberties in order to achieve lasting peace in the society as a whole.

The UN and other international human rights organisations were actively involved in safeguarding and upholding the rights of women, girls and children against a background of infringements and violations from some pervasive socio-cultural practices prevailing in some societies around the world, including Zimbabwe. The UN, for example, set aside 11 October of every year as the International Day of the Girl Child. Among other things, the annual commemorations seek to illuminate the unique challenges of girl children across the world, safeguard their rights and reduce cases of abuse such as child marriages. During the commemorations, the UN raises awareness that child marriages deny girl children their childhood, disrupt their education, jeopardise their health, limit their opportunities and expose them to risks of being victims of violence and abuse (Masekesa, 21 October 2012).

The UN also sent observers to various countries around the world, including Zimbabwe, to identify incidents of child abuse, such as pledging girls to appease avenging spirits, and make recommendations to respective governments. In its June 1996 report on Zimbabwe, for example, the UN Committee on the Rights of the Child (1996: 1) noted "the persistence of behavioural attitudes in the society as well as cultural and religious practices which, as recognised by the State party, hamper the implementation of children's rights...such as *ngozi* (girl child pledging)...and early marriage..." In April 1998, the UN Human Rights Committee's (6 April 1998: 1) observation team to Zimbabwe also expressed concern about

266

"…continued practices…such as *kuzvarira* (pledging of girls for economic gain), *kuripa ngozi* (appeasement to the spirits of a murdered person)…" and recommended to the Zimbabwean government that "these and other practices…be prohibited by legislation (and)…adequate measures to prevent and eliminate prevailing social attitudes and cultural and religious practices hampering the realisation of human rights by women."

Some international human rights groups also played their part in combating harmful socio-cultural institutions that violated the rights and liberties of girls and women. In 1991, the Women's Global Leadership Institute, coordinated by the Centre for Women's Global Leadership, for example, launched the 16 Days of Activism Against Gender-based Violence. The 16 Days of Activism Against Gender-based Violence is a 16-day global campaign held annually from 25 November to 10 December to sensitise people on the need to safeguard and uphold the rights and dignity of women and children. The annual 16-day event starts off on 25 November, which is the International Day for the Elimination of Violence against women, and ends on 10 December, which is Human Rights Day. The 16 days are derived from the number of days between the two days. Since its launch in 1991, the campaign has been commemorated annually by many countries in the world including Zimbabwe. The 16-day period also encompasses two other important international days which are the Universal Children's Day and World Aids Day (Majome, 3 December 2016).

From 2014, the World Association for Christian Communication (WACC) became actively involved in curbing child marriages in Zimbabwe. Among other notable achievements, the organisation founded and funded the Creative Centre for Communication and Development (CCCD), a civil rights group in Zimbabwe that has its headquarters in the city of Bulawayo (Jabson, 30 January 2015). Since 2014, the CCCD undertook programmes to capture the experiences of child brides. In addition, the CCCD publishes the cases of child abuse including forced marriages and mobilises communities to report and condemn such practices (Jabson, 30 January 2015). As part of its campaign against child marriages in Zimbabwe, a CCCD report, quoted by WACC (23 October 2014: 1) stated:

Child marriage robs girls of their girlhood, entrenching them and their future families in poverty, limiting their life choices and generating high development costs for communities. Child marriage brings an abrupt and unnatural end to a girl's childhood and adolescence through imposing adult roles and responsibilities before she is physically, psychologically and emotionally prepared.

There is evidence from post-independence Zimbabwe that some girls who were forcibly married in order to appease the spirits of murdered persons were not always hopeless victims who only waited for interventions from various stakeholders to have their plight addressed. Some girls who were forcibly married off to adult men sometimes took matters into their own hands and fled to seek refuge elsewhere. An example can be drawn from the case of Maira Gwati, a girl from Guruve District in northern Zimbabwe, who at the age of 14 years in 2009, was married off to a 60-year-old man in order to calm the avenging spirit of a murdered person. Even though she fell pregnant, she fled to Harare where she sought refuge at a centre that accommodated abandoned pregnant girls. She stayed there until she gave birth to a baby girl. Her daughter, however, died after six months. Gwati did not return to school but joined an athletics club in Harare with the hope of earning a living through sport (*IRIN News*, 7 November 2011). This shows that, having been abused, some girls sought to rid themselves of their predicament of victimhood by striving to become agents of their own destiny.

It is quite apparent that the institution of marrying off girls in order to appease the avenging spirits of murdered persons is now a vanishing tradition owing to the vigorous efforts of various stakeholders. This section has examined the efforts of the Zimbabwean government, traditional leaders, the UN and various local and international civil rights groups to curb the practice. In addition, some girls became agents of their own destiny by refusing to be married off to men who were not of their choice.

Conclusion

The duality of the legal statutory law and the African indigenous jurisprudence (customary law) in Zimbabwe should be institutionalised, regularised and harmonised in a way that safeguards and upholds the rights and liberties of all sections of the society, particularly women and girls. The harmonisation of the two institutions will go a long way in eliminating contradictions within the justice-delivery system in order to achieve gender parity, social harmony and lasting peace for the nation at large.

The pledging of girls in order to appease avenging spirits is a patriarchal stereotype that discriminates against women and violates their rights and liberties. It is indeed a harmful cultural tradition that regards women as second-class citizens who can be commodified and given away as compensation for crimes such as murder, most of which were committed by men. Such practices are self-defeating because instead of achieving peace and justice, they create societal discord characterised by conflict along gender lines among other ills. In short, the pledging of young girls as a justice mechanism is both ambivalent and awkwardly one-sided by appeasing the bereaved families and abusing innocent young girls.

The giving away of young girls as a form of compensation for murder is a retrogressive cultural practice characterised by female victimhood to patriarchal machinations. It is a manifestation of male chauvinism and the marginalisation of female subjectivities in society. Thus, gender parity has to be taken seriously as an indispensable dynamic in the struggles for peace, justice and development.

References

Barnes, T. (1997) 'Am I a man? Gender and the pass laws in colonial Zimbabwe,' in: *African Studies Review*, Volume 40, Number 1, pp.59-81.

Barnes, T. and Win, E. (1992) *To live a better life: An oral history of women in the city of Harare, 1930-70*, Harare: Baobab Books.

Benyera, E. (2014) 'Debating the efficacy of transitional justice mechanisms: the case of national healing in Zimbabwe, 1980-2011,' D.Phil. Thesis, University of South Africa.

Child Rights International Network, (1996) 'Zimbabwe: Persistent violations of children's rights,' Available at: https://www.crin.org/en/library/publications/zimbabwe, Accessed 23 March 2017.

Dachs, A. J. and Rea, W. F. (1979) *The Catholic Church and Zimbabwe, 1879-1979*, Mambo Press: Gwelo.

Gluckman, M. (1950) 'Kinship and marriage among the Lozi in northern Rhodesia and the Zulu of Natal,' In: A.R. Radcliffe-Brown and D. Forde (eds.) *African systems of kinship and marriage*, Oxford: Oxford University Press.

Gunda, T. (7 May 2012), 'Girl, 14, marries boy, 15, to appease avenging spirits,' Available at: http://zimdiaspora.com/index, Accessed 23 March 2017.

Hannan, M. 1959. *Standard Shona dictionary*, Salisbury: College Press.

Herald, 27 February 2015, 'War to end child marriages,' Available at: http://www.zimbabweonlinenews.com, Accessed 22 March 2017.

IRIN News, 7 November 2011, 'Thousands of girls forced out of education,' Available at: http://www.irinnews.org/news, Accessed 23 March 2017.

Jabson, F. 30 January 2015, 'Young girls in Zimbabwe opt for marriage to escape poverty,' Available at: www.waccglobal.org/articles, Accessed 28 March 2017.

Kachere, N., 29 September 2009. 'Zimbabwe: Virgins forced into marriage to 'appease' evil spirits,' Available at: http://www.ipsnews.net/2009/09/zimbabwe, Accessed 22 March 2017.

Kachere, P. 29 May 2011. 'Avenging spirit (*ngozi*) demands three virgins,' Available at: http://chibhebhi.blogspot.com, Accessed 22 March 2017.

Kuper, H. (1947) *The African aristocracy*, London: Oxford University Press.

Little, K. (1976) 'The Mende in Sierra Leone,' in: D. Forde (ed.) *African worlds: Studies in the cosmological values of African peoples*, International African Institute: Oxford University Press.

Mair, L. (1969) *African marriage and social change*, London: Frank Cass and Company.

Majome, M. T. 3 December 2016. 'Gender-based violence,' Available at: https://www.newsday.co.zw, Accessed 23 March 2017.

Makoni, B. (16 June 2014), 'Thirty most violent sexual harmful cultural practices the world must protect girls from,' Available at: http://www.girlchildnetworkworldwide.org, Accessed 23 March 2017.

Masaka, D, and Chemhuru, M. (2011) 'Moral dimensions of some Shona taboos (*zviera*)' in: *Journal of Sustainable Development in Africa*, Volume 13, Number 3, pp.132-148.

Masasire, A. (1996) 'Kinship and marriage,' in: S. Mutswairo, N.E. Mberi, A. Masasire and M. Furusa (Eds.) *Introduction to Shona culture*, Eiffel Flats: Juta Zimbabwe Limited.

Masekesa, C. 21 October 2012, 'Child marriages on the rise in Manicaland Province,' Available at: www.thestandard.co.zw, Accessed 22 March 2016.

Mutekwa, A. (2010) 'The avenging spirit: Mapping an ambivalent spirituality in Zimbabwean literature in English,' in: *African Studies*, Volume 69, Number 1, pp.161-176.

Nadel, S. F. (1947) *The Nuba*, London: Oxford University Press.

National Archives of Zimbabwe (NAZ), 1911. File N9/1/14. 'Report of the CNC, Mashonaland, for the year 1911,' Harare: NAZ.

NAZ, 1917. File NS/17/4/2. 'Native Marriages Ordinance, Number 5 of 1917,' Harare: NAZ.

NAZ, 4 June 1931. File S2584/73. 'NC Umtali to CNC, correspondence,' Harare: NAZ.

NAZ, 15 August 1932. File S235/475. 'Departmental committee on native female domestic service: Evidence taken from members of the Advisory Committee of the Umtali Native Girls' Hostel, 15 August 1932,' Harare: NAZ.

NAZ, 15-17 August 1932, File S235/475. 'Departmental committee on native female domestic service: Evidence taken from Umtali, 15-17 August 1932,' Harare: NAZ.

Peaden, W.R., (1970) *Missionary attitudes to Shona culture, 1890-1923*, Salisbury: Central African Historical Association.

Radcliffe-Brown, A.R. (1950) 'Introduction,' in: A.R. Radcliffe-Brown and D. Forde (eds.) *African systems of kinship and marriage*, Oxford: Oxford University Press.

Richards, A.1. (1940) 'Bantu marriage and present economic conditions,' Rhodes-Livingstone Paper Number 4.

Schapera, I. (1937) 'Law and justice,' in: I. Schapera (ed.) *The Bantu-speaking people of South Africa*, London: Routledge.

Schmidt, E. (1992) *Peasants, traders and wives: Shona women in the history of Zimbabwe, 1870-1939*, Harare: Baobab.

Sithole, B. (20 December 2016) 'Nyanga scores a first in ending girl child pledging,' Available at: http://www.actionaid.org/zimbabwe, Accessed 23 March 2017.

Smith, E. W. and Dale, A. (1920) *The Ila-speaking people of Northern Rhodesia*, London.

Southern Rhodesia Government, (1939) *Statute law of Southern Rhodesia Volume IV*, Salisbury: Southern Rhodesia Government.

Tagwireyi, D. (5 May 2013), 'Spiritual husbands terrorise women,' Available at: https://www.thestandard.co.zw, Accessed 22 March 2017.

Tatira, L., (2014) 'Shona belief systems: Finding relevancy for a new generation,' in: *Journal of Pan African Studies*, Available at: https://www.thefreelibrary.com, Accessed 6 December 2016.

Thomson, H.C. (1898) *Rhodesia and its government*, London: Smith, Elder and Company.

Thorpe, S.A., (1991) *African traditional religions*, Pretoria: University of South Africa Press.

UN Committee on the Elimination of Discrimination against Women, 1 March 2012. 'Concluding observations,' In: Child Rights International Network, 2012. 'Zimbabwe: Persistent violations of children's rights,' Available at: www.crin.org/en/library/publications/zimbabwe, Accessed 23 March 2017.

UN Committee on the Rights of the Child, (1996) 'Harmful traditional practices; Concluding observations, June 1996,' in: Child Rights International Network, 2012. 'Zimbabwe: Persistent violations of children's rights,' Available at: www.crin.org/en/library/publications/zimbabwe, Accessed 23 March 2017.

UN Human Rights Committee, (6 April 1998), 'Concluding observations,' in: Child Rights International Network, 2012. 'Zimbabwe: Persistent violations of children's rights,' Available at: www.crin.org/en/library/publications/zimbabwe, Accessed 23 March 2017.

Wilson, M. (1950) 'Nyakyusa kinship,' In: A.R. Radcliffe-Brown and D. Forde (eds.) *African systems of kinship and marriage*, Oxford: Oxford University Press.

World Association for Christian Communication, 23 October 2014. 'Working to end child marriage Zimbabwe,' Available at: www.waccglobal.org/articles, Accessed 28 March 2017.

Young, S. (1977). 'Fertility and famine: Women's agricultural history in southern Mozambique,' in: R. Palmer and N. Parsons (eds.) *The roots of rural poverty in Central and Southern Africa*, London: Heinemann.

Zhakata, A. (4 April 2014) 'Man uses daughter to appease avenging spirit,' in: *The Manica Post*, Mutare: Zimbabwe, Available at: http://bulawayo24.com/index-id-news, Accessed 23 March 2017.

Chapter 13

Cultural Interpersonal Communication and Naming: The Case of Peri-urban Beitbridge in Zimbabwe

Prosper Hellen Tlou

Introduction

The aim of this work is to show how the Vhavenḓa people in the Beitbridge peri-urban area of Zimbabwe near the border with South Africa have deployed names for the dual role of identification and as a tool to send different coded messages that advocate for peace. In many cases, the names convey bad messages in an ironic way. To this end, the chapter demonstrates how the Vhavenda have appropriated a 'newer role' to the naming of objects, possessions and property. In this regard, instead of merely using names as forms of identification, the Vhavenḓa have introduced a communication element to it. Shops, taxis and domestic animals, among others things, are given names that not only identify them but also communicate different messages to perceived enemies, jealous friends/relatives or people in general. The names vary from protests to advice with the sole aim of maintaining peace. They are also used as a way of reprimanding those whose behaviour is considered unacceptable without direct confrontation. The Vhavenḓa see this as a better option to dealing with conflicts as it minimizes open friction and animosity.

In Zimbabwe, most of Vhavenda people are situated in the southern part of the country, mostly in the Beitbridge District of Matabeland South Province. Tshivenḓa language was one of the once marginalised languages in Zimbabwe before the 2013 Constitution was adopted. The marginalisation of the Venda language, like others elsewhere, was premised on the erroneous thinking that it was spoken by very few people. What has to be considered is that this is a debatable issue because more often than not, such languages may be minority languages in a specific country whilst they may be spoken across several countries. In the case of the Venda language, it is spoken in both Zimbabwe and South Africa. Like many other African people in Zimbabwe, the Venda also suffered from land alienation when the white settlers acquired their land (Hachipola, 1998). Inconsiderate colonizers drew up national boundaries, dividing ethnic groups into smaller units and this has seen fewer Vhavenda remaining in Zimbabwe while the majorities were left out on the other side of the country in South Africa. What is worse is that sociolinguistically, a minority language is defined not only by its relative demographic inferiority but also, and more so, by its limited public functions. Thus, a minority language can be identified horizontally by looking at its weak or non-dominant position in relation to other languages in the region or nation, and vertically on the basis of its low status and absence of use in public or official areas (Batibo, 2005).

Humanity and good relations are considered to be of great importance among many Africans ethnic groups. To this extent, the Vhavenḓa strive to do well and live a desirable life through maintaining peace. According to the Tshivenḓa culture, humanity rests on an Ubuntu variant that says '*Muthu ndi muthu nga vhañwe*' (Milubi, 2004: 163) shortened to '*vhuthu*', meaning 'a person is defined and becomes what s/he is by the influence of others.' The adage proves that the Vhavenḓa seek to always uphold good relations among themselves. To keep relationships intact even if misunderstandings arise within families, communities and societies, the Vhavenḓa had an intelligent way of addressing those without direct confrontation as a way of upholding peace and harmony. Secrecy and indirect communication was and is still used in naming property as this preserves one's identity and dignity for a good name or reputation is better than sacrifice. Such is portrayed by proverbs such as '*Muḓi ndi vhathu, maṱanzu ndi maḓagala*' (Ibid) meaning that 'a home is made up of people and dirty things are rubbish explaining that humanity is of importance than property,' 'U *naka a hu fani na u ḓihwa*' (Ibid), that is, 'Beauty cannot be compared to popularity' meaning honour surpasses outward appearance. This chapter will therefore give special attention to dog names, business names for shops and commuter omnibuses in order to showcase how names are deployed to reprimand some, correct deeds and maintain peace.

Names coined during and after the Zimbabwean 2008 crisis are to be used in this study. The morph-syntactic composition of the given names will be looked at. The chapter argues in the Ngugi wa Thiong'o (1998) sense that a person's language is the vehicle of their particular culture. People are identified by their own culture and language is also part of an individual's distinct identity. Language, according to Ngugi wa Thiong'o (1998) plays a key role in a society worldwide as he postulates that a language has a dual character in that it is both a means of communication and a carrier of culture. Ngugi's contention shows that every language is important to its concerned speakers as it has many functions that it provides that are needed by its users. Language, thus, equals culture and culture equals identity for men and women. It is therefore, the contention of this chapter to look at Tshivenda names and the role they play in maintaining harmony and peace for names are more than a name by which a person, animal, place or thing is known (Guma, 2001).

Lastly, in as much as the Vhavenḓa objects, possessions and property names serve as modes of communication, the concept of individualism is also portrayed. Some names advocate for self-centeredness whereas in some, people are advised against the practice. Individualism is a contemporary mentality among Africans who have been influenced by Western practices.

Data collection for this chapter was done through the use of the triangulation methodology scheme of observations, interviews and reading of onomastic literature. The approach used was thus qualitative. The qualitative approach was useful in the study since it deliberated on the motives and attitudes of people (namers and consumers) with regard to names and their role in peace-maintenance in Beitbridge which is the study of social phenomenon. Different people from various areas were contacted and relevant information was gathered. Interpersonal relations, personal values, meanings and beliefs towards names which exist among members of the Beitbridge community were easily perceived by the researcher.

In light of the subject of discussion here, the chapter seeks to use the tacit of Ubuntu/ *Vhuthu* in showing how names as an African indigenous tradition can be used to advocate for peace. The major aim of this section, therefore, is to historically contextualise the chapter.

Ubuntu, Vhavenda naming and communication mechanisms in the Zimbabwean crisis, 2000-2008

Ubuntu is a South African tacit principle which helps in peace-building. Research reveals that the concept originates in pre-colonial African rural setting and is linked with indigenous ways of conflict resolution (Swanson, 2008). Masina (2000) notes that, Ubuntu places emphasis on cooperation with one another for the common good as opposed to competition. Tutu (1999) emphasizes that a person with Ubuntu is the one who is open and lives peacefully with one another, and does not feel threatened when others achieve success because he or she recognizes that they belong to a greater whole. This therefore makes the theory to be relevant to the study. Zartman (2000) argues that, Africa is a heterogeneous society with diverse cultures, but certain features of African indigenous culture, such as 'traditional' conflict-resolution mechanisms, have survived the onslaught of colonialism.

As such, this section briefly examines the Zimbabwean socio-economic crisis during the period 2000-2008. It illustrates how the socio-economic meltdown, characterized by unemployment, starvation and extreme poverty among many other ills (Raftopoulos, 2009), bred a dispensation of despondency, agitation and the propensity to violence in many sections of the Zimbabwean population. It was in this volatile situation that the Vhavenda crafted nomenclature both as a coping mechanism and as a way of advocating for peace. Zimbabwe's socio-economic hardships can be traced back to the 1990s when the Economic Structural Adjustment Programme (ESAP) was introduced (Duri, 2016; Mazuru, 2016). One of the most negative consequences of ESAP was the skyrocketing of unemployment in the country. During the new millennium, Zimbabwe's indigenisation and empowerment statutes further eroded foreign investor confidence and aggravated the unemployment crisis (Duri, 2016). The Indigenisation and Empowerment Act of 2007, for instance, obliged all foreign companies to surrender 51% shares to local entrepreneurs (*Ibid*). As a result, deindustrialization crept in as many investors quit the country and this further hiked the unemployment rate (*Ibid*). Hyperinflation further impoverished the majority of Zimbabweans. Natural calamities in the form of persistent droughts worsened the situation. In addition, supermarket shelves across the country were empties as the country was hit by severe shortages of basic commodities. As many citizens became agitated due to poverty, the government employed extremely violent measures to suppress dissent (*Ibid*).

Many Zimbabweans engaged various strategies in an effort to mitigate the situation. Large numbers left the country as a result of political violence while others sought employment and other livelihood opportunities across the border. Within the country, many Zimbabweans embarked on informal economic activities to salvage sustenance. Within Zimbabwe, such informal livelihood pursuits included vending and the unlicensed transportation of goods and people from one point to the other. By far the most popular cross-border livelihood activities were the smuggling of goods into the country for domestic consumption or resale (*Ibid*).

A fledging informal cross-border transport business also emerged to ferry various wares into the country for resale in unlicensed shops (tuck-shops) that sprouted across the country. Other informal means of transport were involved in ferrying people across the border. Among other things, this chapter examines the different naming and communication mechanisms used to refer to various informal aspects, such as shops and taxis, which emerged as a response to the crisis. Most importantly, the chapter will demonstrate how Vhavenda naming and communication spread the gospel of peace during this volatile period in Zimbabwe.

Morph-Syntactic composition

Traditionally, the Vhavenda anthroponyms (people names) have existed in the form of a word, phrase or sentence though only a part of it can be used so often. At this point in time, it is noted that the same style has been adopted to naming dogs and businesses. Indeed,

African names, as symbols of language, can be divided into two morph-syntactical categories. They can be nominal that is, they are constituted of single words. They can also be syntagmatic, meaning that they are made up of sentences or parts thereof (Batoma, 2009). According to this criterion, Vhavenda names fall into two subcategories: nominal and syntagmatic and their choice/form are determined by the purpose they have to serve because many a time they are not meant for identification only.

Examples of names in the nominal category

1. *Lotsha* (Sunrise)
2. *Thusanani* (Help each other)
3. *Faranani* (Unite/Unity)
4. *Mulalo* (Peace)

The above are nominal examples used for the identification of shops as well as conveying the cultural values and traditions of the people's daily experiences. *Lotsha* (sunrise) as a name promotes peace in the sense that people are asked to forget about what transpired the previous day even if it was so agonising. It is believed that sorrow can last for a night but joy comes in the morning. More to that, the element of forgiving and forgetting is also advocated for, thus names can be used as peace mechanisms. *Thusanani,* which means helping each other, is another name again which is famous among the Vhavenda people, which also promote peace. *Faranani* is a term urging people to unite despite the differences which exist among them, thus peace if promoted. *Mulalo* means peace thus as people use it, they are reminded to maintain peace.

Examples of syntactical names:

1. *Shaka ndi zwanda* - relatives are hands
2. *Vha funa vhe vhone* - It is well when it is done by them
3. *Maita zwitoma* - Doer of little things
4. *Sedzani zwanu* - Mind your own business
5. **Vha do neta** - They will get weary

Polemic names

Polemic names are those with a strong and attacking meaning and these among Vhavenḓa have stood the test of time and still surface. Some of the names may be construed to have a negative connotation or meaning and some can be categorised as insults. However, whenever they are used, the intention is not to hurt one's feeling but to correct those who offend others. They are used as a corrective measure to unite the community for it is important and desirable to uphold peaceful relations with everyone in most African ethnic groups, in particular Vhavenda. Although this at times can be difficult to attain, one has to strive to do so. Asante (1987) posits that in customary African law, the primary consideration is not the establishment of guilt but, the restoration of communal balance and, therefore peace. This, however, does not rule out that people do cross each other's path but in such a case there are diligent ways of dealing with it which are meant to come up with peaceful resolutions for the parties involved. One of the philosophies used is naming, where a name is used for identification and sending messages which resolve a conflict.

Domestic animals like dogs are sometimes given polemic names which are insultive and which, if referred to a certain individual, will be very provocative because of their strong sentiment. If given to an animal, no one can claim that the message conveyed is directed at him or her. Meiring (2010), in agreement with this idea, says this onomastic system is aimed at repairing what is considered to be a wrong or an infringement on the right of the name-giver and the offender. It should, however, be noted that it is not done randomly but in a tactful and diplomatic way. As a result, therefore one can stipulate that this onomastic practice is a useful and corrective tool that can be employed by both the offender and the offended to call back one to his/her senses thereby maintaining peace.

Examples of such names are:

1. *Zwiyafana* (it is still the same)
2. *Ndozwivhona* (I can see it/ I am aware of your shennanigans)
3. *Avhathakhei* (they cannot be honoured)

4. *Zwimalofhani* (it runs in the blood)
5. *Vhadoneta* (they will get weary)
6. *Mafela* (dying for)

Names derived from proverbs and idioms

Tshivenḓa names are derived from various lexical items or word categories. Sources for name-taking stretch back to the philosophy of Africans which existed from times immemorial which among them are proverbs and idioms. The source of a name is influenced by the role it has to play which is not only identification but also includes the embedded message in the name.

Linguistically, every noun has a literal meaning attached to it, whereby semantically the term 'noun' can have many meanings. It is common knowledge that proverbs and sayings are tools of telling or conveying messages in a hidden and hard way but which can easily be accepted without straining relationships between the involved parties. As such dogs, taxis and businesses have been named from proverbs and sayings as a way of relaying coded messages. Many times, segments instead of whole proverbs or sayings are used; it can be one word or a shortened phrase taken from it. The following are examples of taxi and shop names extracted from proverbs and idioms:

1. *Tsetsetse* - the full proverb reads: *'Tse tse tse i vhidza luvhilo'* (Slow speed leads to high speed) meaning that something can start at a low pace but as it goes the speed accelerates.

2. *Iremangaluṅwe* - the full proverb reads: *'I rema nga luṅwe mbevhana mulindi wa vhuya wa ḓala'* (A mouse carries its food in small portions until it fills the hole) meaning that things have to be done slowly but surely.

The above proverbs put across the point that in everything that one does no matter how small, it does not mean that it will remain as such, with time it will grow big (Mbedzi, 2017). The beginning of something can be small but that does not determine its destiny. In business, given the magnitude of Zimbabwe's socio-economic meltdown, many people experienced discouragements, criticism, challenges and competitors and some of these proverbs should be understood in the context of such challenges.

From the two proverbs cited above, it can be noted that Africans, and in particular the Vhavenḍa, have their own philosophy which clearly shows that no business blooms overnight but one has to work his/her way up to the top through hard work, persistence, patience, endurance, perseverance and courage. The aforementioned values then help one to grow big in terms of wealth. More to that, in as much as the proverbs mould one's character or behaviour, the notion of patience, which is very important towards peace–building, is upheld.

One of the commonest names that appeared on taxis was *Mphemphe*. The name *Mphemphe* was derived from a proverb '*Mphemphe i a netisa*' (begging is so tiresome). The message portrayed by the full proverb shows that begging annoys, is tiresome and something which is not desirable among the Vhavenḍa people. This name was therefore used for identification and sending a message to people to refrain from begging as well as discouraging those who were emulating the practice. It is quite apparent that this proverb was crafted after the realisation that some people had developed parasitic tendencies such as panhandling instead of working hard to earn a living as the Zimbabwean crisis worsened. (Interview with Muleya, 30 September 2017). Indeed, begging by local communities and people, both the abled and the disabled, from various parts of the country became banal at the Beitbridge Border Post as the Zimbabwean crisis worsened (Marongwe and Moyo, 2015).

Maita zwitoma (doing little things) is a name used for shops as identification as well as a diplomatic way of sending messages to targeted people. It is an idiom that delivers a message that little things lead to greater achievements. The giver of the name, who in this case is the owner of the shop, was advising those with the tendency of looking down upon other people's to refrain from doing so and instead appreciate that small beginnings may develop into remarkable achievements (Interview with Manyiki, 29 September 2017).

Another expression widely used by people who use scotchcarts as a mode of transport in and around Beitbridge is *Vha funa vha vhone* (it is well when it is done by them. Most people in Beitbridge Town and its peri-urban area still use scotchcarts as a mode of transport mostly to ferry domestic goods and building material. More so instead of using trucks to transport gravel, pit sand and bricks for building purposes, carts are used and thus it is another key livelihood mechanism in the district. Carts are also used for other domestic chores like fetching firewood, water and taking grain to the market. A cart is still valuable among Vhavenda people and as part of the property that one owns, it is also named like other assets. *Vha funa vhe vhone,* among other references, is related to a proverb which reads '*Didingwe ḽi ri mavhala anga,*' meaning that some people may consider the reliance on carts as demeaning, but when they themselves are plunged into severe hardships and resort to the same practices, they would not consider them in derogatory terms. This proverb, therefore, sends a strong message of tolerance, that one should appreciate the informal non-criminal pursuits that some people embark on in order to eke livelihoods.

The name *Mashaka*, meaning relatives, is given to dogs with the intention of sending a message. It is derived from a proverb *Mutsinda ndi khwine shaka ndi bulayo* meaning 'a neighbour is better off than a relative.' One gives such a name after realising that s/he gets assistance or help from neighbours only, when those who are close to him or her celebrate his/her hardships or downfall (Interview with Shoko, 30 September 2017). People craft such references in times of severe crisis, such as the one experienced in Zimbabwe between 2000 and 2008, as a diplomatic way of revealing their feelings and emotions towards their jealousy, unsympathetic and unhelpful relatives.

Tshamato is another name used by the Vhavenda of Beitbridge. It is a name derived from the idiom '*Tsha mato ndi u vhona*' (Eyes are meant for seeing) which means that one just has to watch, see things and leave them like that without commenting or taking action, if one cannot help in a positive manner. Criticising other people's work is discouraged and in so doing conflicts is avoided. Peace is thereby maintained broadly because people will refrain from poking their nose into other's business given that they have nothing positive to offer.

The individualist perspective as portrayed in names

Among many African communities the spirit of working together is inculcated as one grows up from childhood to adulthood. This also holds true for the Vhavenda, where the proverb *munwe muthihi a u tusi mathuthu* (Milubi, 2004: 163) encapsulates the essence of working together for the good of the community. The willingness of helping each other is planted and nurtured to every individual for one to qualify to be considered a social human being. Being human in the African perspective is something which has to be achieved and not given simply because one is born of human seed. Igboin (2011) notes that the willingness to help others for the development of the community is reciprocal. It is the duty of every member of the community to care for each other for one represents all in that what befalls one affects the whole community. It is within this communality that personhood is fulfilled. This is aptly expressed by Mbiti (1969:106), when he wrote: 'I am because we are and since we are therefore, I am,' literally in Tshivenda being: *ndi zwine nda vha zwone ngauri ro ralo ngazwo u nga ro ralo ndi ngazwo ndi zwine nda vha zwone.*

However, because of contact with other cultures, particularly Western influences such as capitalism, the spirit of a whole gradually became replaced by self-centeredness which is commonly known as individualism. Communal practices like working as an extended family had so much value before the coming of the Westerners to Africa but in the contemporary world, they have been denigrated as backward as many people adopt individualism. Communal ways of living are taken to be irrelevant in the contemporary world and are seen to be discouraging competition and individual ambitions in life. This is, however, opposed by (Gyekye, 1996) who posits that individualistic values are not necessarily contradictory to those shared by a community but are in most cases closely linked.

From the foregoing discussion, it stands to reason that interdependence is encouraged and should be the norm among Africans, particularly the Vhavenda. Anything that one does should be meant for the promotion of the greater and cumulative good of the entire community because collectivity brings people together and unites them resulting in a peaceful dispensation. Collectivistic societies value family cohesion, cooperation, solidarity, and conformity (Skillman, 2000).Thus, people in these societies tend to make more references to others, emphasize group goals, and follow the expectations and regulations of the group (Desai, 2007). However, from the names given to dogs, shops and taxis these days, a different personality among the Vhavenḓa is being noted. People are losing the concept of collectiveness and are resorting to individualism. People believe in that one becomes successful through hard working as an individual or as a family excluding the extended family and the community. More to that, relatives are taken to be of no help and are instead viewed as enemies. This observation was also made by Fanon (1967) who noted that African culture is becoming more and more cut off from the events of today. It finds its refuge beside a hearth that glows with passionate emotion. Asante (1987) has further argued that if we have lost anything, it is our cultural centeredness, that is, we have been moved off our platforms. The contemporary motto in most communities, therefore, is to mind one's own business. Below are such examples:

1. *Sedzani zwanu* - Mind your own business
2. *Shaka ndi zwanda* – True relatives are one's hands
3. *Vha ḓo neta* - They will get weary

In a way, the idea of not indulging into other people's business minimises friction or conflicts. If laziness is also discouraged, then everyone will be a hard worker who is ever occupied to the extent that he/she will neither afford to waste time in envying other people's achievements nor find space to antagonize others. As a result, the chances of a peaceful dispensation within the community become brighter.

Positivity embedded in names

The discussion will end on a positive note, by discussing names which encourage and denote good morals. Though it has been highlighted that many names are used as mechanism for peaceful or diplomatic protest to express grievances and concerns, some

Vhavenda names are loaded with affirmatives. All dreary names of sending messages of animosity and harsh emotions already discussed above can be balanced by names that express peace, love, hope, oneness and working together which are attributes that every society cherishes. Below are a few examples that reflect positivity.

1. *Faranani* - Unite/unity
2. *Thusanani* - Help each other
3. *Lotsha* - Sunrise

Conclusion

Giving names to businesses and animals, just like naming human beings, is a basic activity that portrays how people view the world around them, showing how they value their life experience and remember the past. It is through naming that Africans define their relationships between individuals and within families, communities and societies at large. The relationship is that of reciprocity for one cannot live without the other thus, if something emerges that can ruin that relationship it is addressed through naming, among other strategies. This chapter has also argued that besides being used for identification purposes, naming can be a diplomatic way of expressing emotions and protest. By doing so, direct confrontation that causes animosity is avoided thereby preventing overt forms of violence within communities. In addition, the chapter has also noted some Vhavenda nomenclature that directly promotes peace, love, hope and oneness in times of severe crises.

References

Asante, K.M. (1987) The Afrocentric Idea, Temple University Press: Philadelphia.

Batibo, H.M., (2005) *Language decline and death in Africa: Cause, consequences and challenges*, Multilingual Matters: Clevedon.

Duri F. P. T. (Ed.) (2016) *Resilience amid adversity: Informal coping mechanisms to the Zimbabwean crisis during the new millennium*, Gweru: Booklove Publishers: Gweru.

Fanon, F. (1967) *The wretched of the earth*, Mac Gibbon and Lee: Great Britain.

Guma, M. (2001) The cultural meaning of names among Basotho of Southern Africa: A Historical and Linguistic Analysis in Nordic Journal of African Studies 10(3): 265-279.

Gyekye, K. (1996) *African cultural values: An introduction*, Sankofa Publishing Company: Accra.

Hachipola, S. J. (1998) *A survey of the minority languages of Zimbabwe*, Harare: University of Zimbabwe Publications.

Igboin, B.O. (2011) Colonialism and African cultural values: *African Journal of History and Culture*, Volume 3, Number 6, pp 96-103.

Makoni, S. *et al* (2003) *Black linguistics: Language, society and politics in Africa and America,* London and New York: Routledge.

Masina, N. (2000) 'Xhosa practices of Ubuntu for South Africa,' in: I.W Zartman (Ed) Traditional cures for modern conflicts: African conflict "medicine". Boulder: Lynne Rienner Publishers

Meiring, B. (2010) 'Aspects of violence reflected in South African geographical names,' in: Werkwinkel, Volume 5, Number 2, pp 95-112

Mbedzi, P. Interview, Beitbridge, 30 September 2017.

Mbiti, J. S. (1969) *African religion and philosophy*. Oxford: Heinemann Education Publishers.

Milubi, N.A. (2004) *Ngoma Ya Vhatei,* NAM Publishers: Polokwane.

Mukwena, F. Interview, Beitbridge, 2 October 2017.

Muleya, F. Interview, Beitbridge, 2 October 2017.

Ndou S. N. Interview, Beitbridge, 30 September 2017.

Ngugi wa Thiong'o, (1981) *Decolonising the mind: The politics of language in African literature*, Zimbabwe Publishing House: Harare.

Raftopoulos, B. and Mlambo, A. (Eds.) (2009) *Becoming Zimbabwe: A history from the pre-colonial period to 2008*, Harare: Weaver Press.

Sibanda S., Interview, Beitbridge, 30 September 2017.

Swanson, D.M. (2008) Ubuntu: An African contribution to research for with a humble togetherness, *Journal of Contemporary Issues in Education*, 2 (2): 53-67.

Tutu, D. (1999) *No future without forgiveness*, Pinter: London.

Chapter 14

The Moral Significance of the *Dare* System in Seeking Justice and Peace among the Shona People of Zimbabwe

Erasmus Masitera

Introduction

This chapter seeks to tackle the Shona people's use of the *Dare* (a 'traditional' court gathering) as a moral tool for moulding good and humane behaviour and conduct. In this sense the *Dare* is necessary for the moral grounding through which right and good are pursued. Broadly speaking, the traditional Shona people's *Dare* system expresses the Ubuntu moral expectations that combine a number of ethical doctrines that include virtue and deontological ethical theories. Apart from expressing the virtue and deontological ethical practices, the *Dare* system also expresses the Shona people's preoccupation of achieving social justice and common good. The argument forwarded here is that the *Dare* is one of the best ways through which social justice and common good are advanced. In that regard, the *Dare* system is a channel that is utilized to influence behaviour among the Shona people. Besides influencing behaviour, the system also helps in establishing peace, justice and the principle of equality among the Shona people. Thus, this 'traditional' system is a way through which psychologically, the Shona people are influenced into a particular way of thinking and behaving. Noteworthy, though, is that the influence is mostly positive, for the good of the community at large, a common good approach.

The chapter will also establish that the individual rights are not thwarted within the execution of the good that the community reaps. In other words through the *Dare* system, human dignity is established. Thus, it is not only for the community's good but that everyone in that community benefits. Apart from the mentioned, the chapter also focuses on the composition of the *Dare* among the

Shona people. The structure, in other words, is not imposed upon the people but emanates from the community itself, and this makes it acceptable and eventually making its discussions binding and respected by the people.

To fully expose the above ideas, the chapter will proceed by first understanding who the Shona people are, then second, seek to understand their morality expressed through the Ubuntu worldview. Third, focus will be on the process of attaining and sustaining justice and peace via the *Dare* system which includes in-depth discussion on the justice process within the Shona communities.

The Shona people

The aim of this section is to clearly expose who the Shona people are. In other words, the focus is on the identity of the people who are known as or who refer to themselves as the Shona people. Thus, the focus of this section is on the question of identity with regards to the Shona people. In order to clearly present the identity of the Shona people, it is necessary to articulate some of the major characteristics that are related to this group of people and the main areas of occupation in which they are located.

Concerning their location, the Shona people mostly inhabit the Mashonaland area (Dodo and Nyoni, 2016). In the view of Masitera (2015) and as a confirmation of Dodo and Nyoni's (2016) position, the Shona groups occupy large parts modern Zimbabwe and are widely dispersed in the Zimbabwean state. Of the 13-14 million Zimbabwean population, 75% belong to the Shona group (Gwaravanda, 2011). According to Chemhuru and Masaka (2010) the Shona language "is a conglomeration of a number of linguistic groupings ... namely the Korekore, Karanga, Zezuru, Ndau, Kalanga, and the Manyika." Noteworthy is the fact that these groups share similarities in traditions, cultures, language, and philosophy of living among other characters.

Among the similarities that are shared by the Shona groups are practices of living and morals. Some of these living practices and morals are exhibited in beliefs systems, myths, social practices and social teachings in the form of proverbs, idioms and idiophones

(Masitera, 2015). Among the Shona people, the living practices and morals are important in as much as they form part of identity for the people. Not only is identity key, but also the fact that it is important in fostering a particular kind of behaviour and thinking that is expected of the group.

For the Shona people, living in peace and pursuing peace is one of the expected ways of living which members of society should uphold. As such, practices that lead to the achievement of the stated are based upon and arrived at through communal practices. Communal practices connected to these, as Gwaravanda (2011) noted, are mostly achieved through court systems. The court system, known as the *Dare* system among the Shona, is a routine practice that aims at solving social problems that could lead to social disharmony if not attended to. In this regard *Dares* (the plural of *Dare*) can be found at family, village and community levels. More on the *Dare* system will be discussed latter in the chapter. Important to note here though is that the *Dare* institution is a place for maintaining and developing social harmony and developing peace.

Another important form of identity among the Shona is their moral system, referred to as *Ubuntu/Unhu*. Scholars such as Ramose (2014), Chuwa (2014) and van Nierkek (2013) have alluded to the fact that *Ubuntu* is a set of ethical practice that is dominant within Southern Africa. However, the term *Ubuntu* is referred to differently by other Southern African groups. For instance, the Shona use the term *Unhu* to refer to *Ubuntu*. Thus, *Unhu* is a Shona word for *Ubuntu*. The Shona people share in the *Unhu/Ubuntu* ethical practices and the two terms will be used interchangeably as well. *Unhu* is a lived and living tradition that the Shona people adhere to. Furthermore, *Unhu* is but an extension and extrapolation of *Ubuntu*. The chapter now proceeds by defining the *Dare* system. Thereafter, it will provide the working definition of *Ubuntu/Unhu* and afterwards make an in-depth analysis of the *Dare* system. This will include its uses and functions.

Dare: The court system

Among the Shona people, the *Dare* is important in the day to day organization of the community. The *Dare* is the backbone and wellspring of the Shona social and political life. This means that through the *Dare*, social organisation, laws, morality and resolving of day to day conflicts are done. Beyond the stated, the *Dare* was/is also very useful in advancing justice within the Shona way of living. Of importance is the fact that the *Dare* is a place of rational discussion and negotiations that aim at fostering humane relations in society.

According to Gwaravanda (2011), there are three kinds or forms of *Dare*. These are the family, village and community courts. These courts deal with matters that pertain to human life at the different levels. The gravity of a matter determines where it will be discussed. The family court deals with minor day to day conflicts that emanate in families or among family members. The resolutions reached are always binding and result in the development or establishment of family cultures which eventually develop into family traditions. This is also the beginning of establishing family morals. In most cases, the family court is presided over by the family head or eldest members of the family.

The village court deals with issues that could not been resolved at family level and also for resolving conflicts between two or more families. The idea expressed here is that in some instances conflicts between families may be volatile and resolving them demands the immediate neighbours' (village) intervention. Just like the family courts, the ultimate result is that existing norms are emphasised and upheld, and in some cases, new forms of interaction and organisation between or among members of society are developed. The village court is presided over by the village head (Gwaravanda: 2011; Masitera: 2015).

The community court (also popularly known as the chief's court) is the highest court among the Shona people. This court addresses matters that exist or erupt between feuding villages who cannot resolve their conflicts among themselves. It also acts as the referral court as it is also used in addressing issues that have not been resolved at village level (Gwaravanda: 2011; Masitera: 2015)). Most importantly the court system was, and still is, an effective way of advancing justice, peace and reconciliation, and resolving conflicts.

Unhu worldview

Unhu/Ubuntu is an African moral tradition (van Niekerk, 2013; Chuwa, 2014) that is concerned with human relations and in particular with the cultivation of positive human interactions (Hapanyengwi-Chemhuru and Makuvaza, 2014; Mangena, 2016). Furthermore, *Unhu* is a reflection of the authentic existential history of the people that permeates the epistemological, axiological and ontological lives of the Shona people (Hapanyengwi-Chemhuru and Makuvaza, 2014; Mangena: 2016). It is from this perspective, the axiological or moral perspective, that van Niekerk (2013) argues that *Unhu/Ubuntu* is a tradition that reveals the value(s), the normative expectation(s) or requirement(s) of people's lives that are drawn from the African tradition. In definitive words, Magobe Ramose (2014) avers that *Ubuntu* is "the lived and living experience of human beings" of Southern Africa. This implies that *Ubuntu* is a philosophy that has a past, a philosophy relevant in the present and a project for the future as well (Ramose, 2014).

Ubuntu is neither ahistorical nor a hypothetical situation as is the case with some philosophical thought experiments of how to live together (these are not under consideration in this paper). *Ubuntu* as a project from the past and relevant in the present and future as well, implying that, it is a worthwhile project that has practical implications in different facets of human living (Furman, 2014). The facets include the social, political and economic lives of people. In that regard, *Ubuntu* is thus a principle of living which should be taken seriously; it should be recognized, promoted, and protected from vanquishing into oblivion.

The term *Unhu* is synonymous with the terms *Ubuntu, Botho, Vunhu* and *Hunhu* (Hapanyengwi-Chemhuru and Makuvaza, 2014; Mangena, 2016). These terms refer and mean the same. Their difference is their origins which vary with the ethnic origins within the Southern African region. For this chapter, the term *Unhu* will mostly be used. The main thrust of using the term *Unhu* is that it helps in establishing the identity of concerned communities (Hapanyengwi-Chemhuru and Makuvaza, 2014). Thus, it identifies the particular people or groups under discussion.

Unhu has a number of attributes. *Unhu* emphasises or puts imperative upon the communal existence as opposed to the Western imperative or occidental thinking of emphasising on the individual existence and rights (Mangena, 2016). In other words, this means that community interests always come before the individual interests (Mangena, 2016). This position assumes that the individual interests and rights are subsumed within the communal interests. A critical reflection on the preceding statement is that the individual interests and rights and the communal interests are not at variance. Rather, the community is a reflection of the individual though in a form of the general rather than particular. The idea expressed here is that the community always acts for its good and inevitably that of the individuals who are within it. The community does not seek to disadvantage any of its members for doing so breeds animosity. Animosity is a threat to communal peace and harmony. Common good is achieved through consensus that is reached through dialogue that leads communal beneficiation. Such a position is achieved through the dialogical nature of reaching positions in communities (Eze, 2008).

Noteworthy is the fact that the discussions or the dialogic nature of the *Unhu* system aims at achieving and enhancing interdependence (Hapanyengwi-Chemhuru and Makuvaza, 2014; Mangena, 2016). The interdependence expresses the axiological thinking that exists among the Shona people that is founded upon the thinking that all are related and that human life is sacred. In the philosophical world, this thinking was well captured by the Kenyan philosopher Mbiti (1970) in the statement: "I am because we are, and because we are I am." Basically, the statement shows the interconnectedness and interdependence that exists within the Shona societies. Mangena (2016) goes on to interpret this as meaning that the interdependence and interconnectedness are reflected in the working together and sharing of benefits and burdens of the community without prejudice. This is done for a reason. The reason has to do with ensuring community stability, harmony and to some extent prosperity. There is, thus, a sense in which *Unhu* is a mixture of virtue and deontological thinking. These are Western categories that are being applied to African thinking because the categorisation helps in explaining and

296

defining some moral concepts in a universally understood philosophical framework. This has its own difficulties which are beyond the scope of this chapter.

I now turn to discuss the moral connection between *Dare* system and virtue ethics. Virtue ethics is a branch of moral philosophy that upholds or emphasises on uprightness of a moral character. In this sense, a virtue is a disposition of excellent character trait of valuing doing the right thing (Sreenivasan, 2002). Beyond the stated, doing a right thing is always underlined by reason for thinking, acting and doing a virtuous deed (Hursthouse and Pettigrove, 2016). The reason for acting in a virtuous manner is always guided by the interest of promoting happiness and flourishing of the human kind. By saying this, virtue ethics as a moral theory recognises that human thinking and acting should, by and large, promote human life and living. In short, virtue ethics emphasises excellence or good character, on human happiness and flourishing and on having a moral or practical reason for acting in a particular manner. These are the reasons that make virtue ethics a necessary component in life.

In connection with the *Dare* system then, virtue ethics is relevant. The relevance lies in that the *Dare* system is more of a platform whereby people exhibit their virtues through expressing their interconnectedness and always doing that which is good for the human species. The interconnectedness reflects the disposition of people in ensuring and encouraging human flourishing through setting out conditions or rules that encourage peaceful co-existence. Beyond that, the *Dare* was/is also useful in showing the right or correct emotions and character of the people that is through feeling and acting in a manner that is empathetic and sympathetic towards others. By showing these emotions the Shona people at the same time act according to the expectations of the *Unhu* philosophy of 'being there for each other.'

Interdependence and interconnectedness reflect the deontological dimension of the *Unhu* system. On their own, interdependence and interconnectedness symbolise collectivism that is characterised by cooperation, working together, teamwork, sharing and helping others (Eze, 2006). By deontological is meant those kinds of duties that are required, forbidden or permitted, or what is required of people to do (Alexander and Moore, 2016). A deontological ethical theory concerns itself with making choices that conform to moral norms and not to the results or consequences that are achieved by choosing a particular action or choice, this belongs to the consequential or utilitarian thinking (Alexander and Moore, 2016). In other words, this means making choices that accord individuals the right to be ends in themselves and not as means to an end (freedom to choose and act as one wills and not be used by others to achieve their own ends). What this translates to is that the deontological dimension of *Unhu* relates to obligations and duties that individuals have to execute in society. In that regard, *Unhu* stresses that individuals are obligated to or have to act according to the dictates and requirements of their society (social norms). That is, individuals are required to be there for each other, this is because it is a social dictate. However, the obligations are followed for a reason, the reason being to achieve stability and harmony in society, this is something which the society had long reflected upon and reasoned out and realized is important for human progress and therefore something to be strived for.

Deontic thinking in some sense aims at advancing justice in society. The kind of justice advocated for in *Unhu* thinking relates to common good. It is prudent to highlight that justice is an elusive concept. However, in this chapter we consider justice as relating to the establishment of expected or proper relations among individuals themselves and with material goods (Gule, 2015; Moyo, 2015). This entails that among individuals, justice pertains to giving each individual what he or she deserves (Kanu, 2015). In this regard if one transgresses social expectations of the society, he or she ought to be punished according to the dictates of that particular society. At the same time if an individual does what is expected, he or she receives commensurate respect from the community.

Etymologically, the term justice comes from the Latin word *justicia* which means giving to each according to what he or she deserves (Barry and Matravers, 2011). In technical understanding, justice refers, among others, to a wide range of connected versions which include understanding justice as fairness (Rawl, 1971), justice as what we owe each other (Leontsini: 2015), justice as restitution, justice as deterrence, justice as equality, justice as punishing, justice as impartiality, justice as retribution, justice as common good (Catholic and African thinking). There is a sense in which justice is achieved through punishing and banishing 'other' individuals as is the case when individuals have transgressed societal norms. This kind of justice has more to do with negative justice. It is justice achieved by punishment or deterrence in order to teach or encourage good behaviour among members of society. Most important here is to note the observation made by Olagunju (2014) that in most African traditional justice systems, the aim was not to punish for the sake of punishing, as is the case with other traditions yonder Africa such as the European traditions however, but reconcile. As Olagunju (2014) notes:

> The goal was never to punish *per se*, although wrong-doers got convicted and punished. The ultimate aim of adjudication was always to promote the unity of the community as opposed to concern with individuals; in other words, the restoration of social equilibrium is the paramount factor and consideration.

The same observation was also made by Glaukman (1955) concerning the Lozi of Zambia. Glaukman notes that the Lozi traditional justice system aimed at promoting social equilibrium and unity among members of the community. These observations are important for advancing and supporting my argument that justice among the Shona always aimed at achieving common good. As reflected upon earlier, the Shona people encouraged *Unhu* so as to foster a kind of behaviour that promotes the good of all. This was for practical reasons. Justice that punished without reconnecting was discouraged because it was thought to lead to disgruntlement and fragmentation of the society. When punished and not reconnected to the society, individuals may feel alienated from the community thereby leading to resentment, anger and frustration in a system. The argument here is that once the mentioned feelings exist in societal members, it is easy to turn against the community thereby leading to a kind of social violence. This was not expected in the African society.

Dare and the common good

The argument presented in this section is that common good as a form of justice was the aim in the *Dare* system, which always aimed at reconciling and restoring the social equilibrium, and establishing social satisfaction rather than fragmentation among members of the community. Common good as a form of justice follows the thinking that good for all does not just happen; rather it is built by the people concerned. This is the kind of thinking that guides and underlie the philosophy behind the *Dare* system among the Shona. Most importantly as well is that the concept of common good is inclusive and recognises and respects all the people in a particular society (Velasquez *et al*, 1992; Gyekye, 2010). In other words, common good seeks to establish equality and unity among the people. These principles of justice –equality and unity – are to be considered as derived from the people's expectations and not something that just comes naturally to them. The kind of equality that is being discussed, as in the Velasquez's *et al* (1992) sense, pertains to equality of opportunities, equality before the law, equality of welfare and equality of recognition. These are the main ideas that the *Dare* system aims at establishing. Furthermore, these ideas of equality are the key tenets in discussing issues that deal with human dignity of which the Shona political system exhorts highly. The foregoing is notwithstanding that such political practices also lead to general satisfaction and happiness of the people, hence encouraging social cohesion, stability and satisfaction.

Dare and the search for justice

The process of achieving justice among the Shona people of Zimbabwe was also done through the *Dare* system. The same justice system is found among other Bantu speaking people such as the Zulu and Ndebele, among others (Gwaravanda, 2011; Letseka, 2014). The principle behind the *Dare* was that discussions and mutual agreements (which were in the form of concessions and consensus) were necessary for solving communal mishaps such as violation of rights. This helped to build the society's cohesion and inspire collective aspirations and hopes. Above all, the *Dare* was necessary for correcting offenses committed in the community. Justice, therefore, was basically people-generated, that is, it was a process reached through and a result of people's input and not something imposed upon the people. Justice in this sense meant re/establishing cordial relations in the society (relations that respect human dignity, equality and fairness acceptable to all).

During the *Dare* meetings, members of society were given chance to contribute their views without any form of discrimination. In the final stages of making up a decision, all the inputs would be put into perspective, though the final decision was/is made by the chief and his advisors (Gwaravanda: 2011). During discussions at the *Dare*, the views of the people were not taken for granted. Rather, they were put through critical analysis not only from the chief and his advisors, but even from other members of the society. In so doing, the chief and his advisors acted in accordance with people's expectations thus upholding and producing justice in the process. In a sense, the principle of equality was also achieved through equal participation, recognition and consideration of people's ideas.

Additionally, the communal dimension of living together and promoting harmony is again shown here. This was achieved through the fact that the equal participation was a communal effort aimed at solving problems and violations of rights of communal members. The idea of engaging in dialogue and reaching mutual agreement was meant to encourage social cooperation and cohesion thus promoting the working together of people while at the same time discouraging resentment and unnecessary conflicts as is the matter when verdicts or decisions are made without the involvement of people. In a sense, the Shona *Dare* system reflects the democratic approach to court sessions and even in governance. The system also reflects the bottom–to-top approach that considers the will and interests of the citizens rather than imposition of the will of the ruling elite.

Notwithstanding the foregoing, it is essential to note that traditionally, among the Shona, women were regarded as minors and as such, did not play much of a role in the court system. The basis of this emanated from the common argument among the Shona that says '*vakadzi varipo kuonekwa kwete kunzwikwa*' –translated as 'women are there to be seen not to be heard'. The same kind of thinking relates to children as well. However, this thinking was flawed in that it did not fully reflect the Shona people's respect for roles that were neutral to biological appearance of individuals. Nzwengu (2004) attests to this by stating that the distinction of roles according to biological make-up was not so much pronounced in traditional African societies. In the traditional African system, roles defined people. Yet the roles were not sacrosanct; they were always changing such that a male figure could take on the role of the mother figure and vice-versa. For instance, among the Shona people, in particular, a brother to one's mother is also considered a mother to the children of his sister (a relationship commonly referred to as the *sekuru-muzukuru* relationship [uncle – nephew relationship]). A sister to a father is considered a father by the children of her brother. In other words, there are roles that are not defined by biological make-up among the Shona people and indeed this is characteristic of most African traditions (Nzwengu, 2004). Basing on the distinction proffered above, the chapter proceeds to argue that while in the traditional setup, gender profiling between men and women determined non-participation of women at the *Dare*, but at the same time the role of the individual determined participation as well.

However, in 'modern' political set-ups established after the colonial period or in the independence period, the distinction between women and men and their participation at court sessions or *Dare* no longer exists. Men and women participate equally (Gwaravanda: 2011), none is discriminated against on grounds of gender in society. This goes to show that the *Dare* concept has transcended the traditional set-up which in some sense was discriminatory. The *Dare* concept has also adopted the contemporary political and legal thinking and practice that respects human dignity and that upholds equality of people despite their gender.

Reconciliation or conflict resolution?

This section attempts to answer the question: what is the real aim of *Dare* system? In this endeavour the section makes use of two key phrases that always appear whenever the discussions on traditional court systems occur. These are reconciliation and conflict resolution. It is important to note that the court systems always endeavour to bring justice, equality and unity among members of the community. These endeavours can only be achieved through processes that satisfy, and are agreeable to, all members especially feuding parties. In that regard, reconciliation and conflict resolution are the ideal means through which these endeavours are realised. For that reason, attention now turns to the terms reconciliation and conflict resolution as the processes that the *Dare* embarks on so as to promote peace and harmony in the community.

Conflict resolution is a process through which different forms of conflicts are resolved within communities and/or the world at large. Wallensteen (2015: 8) contends that, "Conflict resolution is a situation where the conflicting parties enter into an agreement that solves their central incompatibilities, accept each other's continued existence as parties and cease all violent action against each other." The thinking behind Wallensteen is that conflict resolution is made up of two processes which are: the formal part which includes agreement between warring parties and the second one which involves the actual implementation of the resolution. On the whole, the crux of the matter is that conflict resolution involves various strategies that are designed to end the many forms of disagreement between states, people, and groups.

Questions may arise in relation to the form of the resolution. From the definition provided by Wallensteen, it is implied that the resolution is one that advocates for peace. Indeed, peaceful resolutions have been advocated for since time immemorial within African communities (Gwaravanda, 2011; Olagunju, 2014). For the two philosophers, the conflict resolution was always reached through a communal approach aimed at attaining social solidarity. Just like Wallensteen, Gwaravanda (2011) and Olagunju (2014) aver that the success of a conflict resolution method always rested with the implementation of the agreement. However, in the traditional system the implementation rested on achieving peace and unity among the communal members and this was achievable since the communal members always aimed at achieving social equilibrium rather than individual satisfaction.

Furthermore, conflicts were viewed as inevitably providing chances for bettering the community rather than as obstacles to social growth. According to Gwaravanda (2011), disagreements provide the community with an opportunity for introspection and for moving forward together through discussions. Conflicts in the Shona system are a social reality that have to be dealt with. The best way to address the conflicts is by having the conflicting parties coming together and resolve their differences with the mediation of the community. The presumption is that resolutions that come from the people themselves are accepted by the people rather than those that are imposed from above.

It is worth mentioning that the ideas of social harmony and social equilibrium discussed in the above discussion on conflict resolution are deeply embedded in the *Unhu* concept. Among the different principles that *Unhu* emphasises is the idea of communalism. Communalism is a system whereby collectivism abounds. Collectivism among the Shona people is deeply steeped in the *Unhu* thinking of togetherness, peace and harmony. The idea stems from the Shona saying '*munhu munhu navanhu*', translated as 'a personhood is meaningless without others'. This is close to the English saying: 'no man is an island.' Another saying that guides the Shona moral life is '*kugara hunzwana*'. Meaning that living together is the key to human livelihood. These moral teachings are all part of the moral teachings that Shona people receive from childhood through adulthood. These moral teachings are also guidelines which inform local court systems when resolving disputes.

Reconciliation on the other hand is the healing of broken-down relationships. The healing of the relationships takes the form of a social therapy. In the Shona 'traditional' sense, the social therapy targeted the whole community (Gwaravanda, 2011). As Gwaravanda (2011) points out, social disagreements or conflicts are a social anomaly that affect the whole community, including individuals. In addition, the therapy also targets individuals are hurt within the society. In the end, therefore, the healing process also involves the whole community and it is not an individual or isolated process. This means that members of the community participate in the healing process. In technical terms, the healing process is a therapeutic mechanism of correcting past wrongs through reconciliation and agreements that necessitate social harmony and ultimately social development (Mangena, 20156; Tshuma, 2015). The reformulation of social values and interests is important in the reconciliation process. Most important though, is the fact that the compromises made are founded on and through communal therapy. Communal therapy is an attempt by a society to understand itself through events that have occurred. Furthermore, communal therapy is a process by which society intervenes by coming together to correct wrongs that have occurred and at the same time ensure that no social dislocation and disharmony occurs (Murungi, 2004; Idowu, 2006; Gwaravanda, 2011; Tshuma, 2015). The therapeutic process involves addressing the deep divisions that society has already encountered. Beyond that, the therapy attempts to map the future by suggesting better ways for coexistence. In this regard, Mangena (2015) and Moyo (2015) view this system as a useful tool for crafting new beginnings to mend ruptured societies.

Challenges in applying the *Unhu/ Ubuntu* philosophy

As much as the *Unhu* philosophy sounds very impressing, it is worthy to note that it has its own challenges which will be discussed below. The challenges also have negative impacts on the *Dare* system. The first challenge is that there is insufficient dissemination and sensitisation of information on *Unhu*. It is not a surprise that although *Unhu* is a philosophy associated with positive attributes, it is not well known by people within the Zimbabwean society. The attributes are little known especially among the generality of the people. And, at times it is the people, particularly the youngsters, who confuse the attributes of *Unhu* by limiting it to how, for example, one dresses or greets others. The major cause of such misconceptions is that there is no adequate space in the education curriculum to disseminate this philosophy. The educational system is dominated by foreign ideologies which are largely reflected in the day to day practices of people. In particular the individualism has become the dominant force in the people's way of life at the expense of communal culture (Lutz, 2009). In relation to the *Dare*, the challenge is that the system has been negatively affected by Western influences in the form of urbanisation which has promoted individualism in many sections of the society, particularly the young generation.

Closely connected to the first challenge, is the proliferation of foreign ideologies. Noteworthy is the fact that 'modern' societies are constituted by people from different and varying cultures and backgrounds. The coming together of different people has somehow caused cultural exchanges and dilution of different cultures in the name of multiculturalism. The cultural dilution has dealt a heavy blow upon the concept and practice of *Unhu*, in that some individuals compromise the *Unhu* practise by taking on other ideologies so as to fit into the new societies that they find themselves in. The exchange of cultures has also brought foreign ideas which appeal to people differently, especially the idea of individual rights and freedom over and above communalism's conformity to the group. In illustrating the effects of multiculturalism on *Unhu*, it is fair to say that multiculturalism demands reconciling *Unhu* with some aspects of foreign cultures. This process compromises the fundamental principles of *Unhu*.

New cultures have also affected the *Dare* system. The foreign (Western) court system has established itself, presided over by magistrates, lawyers, and some other 'qualified' individuals in the area of 'law.' Furthermore, the new system is alien to the traditional system in that communal participation is no more because only individuals summoned to court participate while others are mere onlookers. More importantly is the fact that there is now a dual legal system, with the 'traditional' system handling mostly civil cases, mainly in the rural areas while the 'modern' judicial system has a monopoly over criminal cases and is more popular with urban dwellers. In addition, the powers of the family-heads, village-heads and chiefs in the traditional court system have been severely limited by Western legal systems. This renders some roles of the traditional system out of sync and eventually rendering them irrelevant.

The third challenge is that some of the rituals, customs and practices associated with *Unhu* are obsolete. For example, the emphasis of *Unhu* on group prosperity through upgrading and working together has been overtaken by capitalism and individualism. In addition, *Unhu*'s emphasis on sentimentalism (group over individual interests) may be misconstrued on the labour market as nepotism, favouritism and corruption which are criminal offence in the courts of Nepotism, for example, is favouring those that are close to you, particularly from your ethnic group or community, and discriminating against those who are not. In this sense then, *Unhu*'s idea of community prosperity runs the danger of being associated with discrimination and favouritism.

In the 21st century dispensation in which capitalism is the dominant mode of production, *Unhu* may be construed as discouraging personal achievement. *Unhu/Ubuntu* emphasises social achievement rather than individual pursuits (Afrocentric Alliance, 2001). This stems from the fact that an individual who seems to aspire and excel above the community is considered as going against the communal expectations and hence considered an enemy. Such thinking sounds retrogressive as it deprives individuals the right to fully express themselves through their ingenuity and initiatives.

It is quite apparent that the implementation of *Unhu* is fraught with a plethora of challenges. There is need for serious sensitisation, dissemination and teaching of *Unhu* throughout the different social facets of Zimbabwe. This will include discussions on *Unhu* at the political, social, economic and scientific levels. There is also need to focus on this concept through the different forms of media. Media is essential in disseminating the ideas of *Unhu* since it is accessible in one form or the other to all people. Another important disseminator of the concept will be the education system. The proposition here is that in the education programmes, *Unhu* ideas and ideals should be incorporated and applied since they are important facets of human living.

Conclusion

This chapter has revealed the importance of the *Dare* system among the Shona societies of Zimbabwe. In particular, the chapter showed that the *Dare* is a pertinent component in the social and political lives of the Shona people. In the social realm, the *Dare* is useful as a tool for social cohesion by helping to foster acceptable behaviour in many Shona communities. In this regard, through the *Dare* system the community forms its own moral system which informs and influences how people should behave. At the *Dare*, the thinking and behaviour of the people is always directed towards the common good. The system operates through discussions and negotiations among the people. In this regard, the *Dare* system promotes the rights and responsibilities of the people towards each other. On the political front, the *Dare* system is an essential tool for forging reconciliation, peace and tolerance in Shona communities. The reconciliation process is expressed through the idea of social therapy whereby communal ills and disagreements are settled through rational communal discussions that aim at ending social dislocations and disharmonies. It is through the process of solving the communal mishaps that tolerance and harmony are also established.

References

Alexander, L. and Moore, M. (2016) 'Deontological Ethics' In: *Stanford Encyclopedia of Philosophy*, Available at: https://plato.stanford.edu/entries/ethics-deontological/, Accessed 30 August 2017.

Barry, B. and Matravers, M. (2011) 'Justice,' in: E. Craig (ed.) *Routledge Encyclopaedia of Philosophy*, London: Routledge.

Chemhuru, M. and Masaka, D. (2010) 'Taboos as source of Shona people's environmental ethics,' in: *Journal of Sustainable Development in Africa*, Volume 12, Number 7, pp.121 – 133.

Chuwa L. T. (2014) *African indigenous ethics in global bioethics*, Pennsylvania: Springer.

Dodo, O. and Nyoni, C. (2016) 'Stepmother and stepson relationship within the Shona people, Zimbabwe,' in: *Journal of Divorce and Remarriage*, Volume 57, Number 8, pp.542 – 552.

Eze, M. O. (2008) 'What is African communitarianism? Against consensus as a regulative ideal,' in: *Southern African Journal of Philosophy*, Volume 27, Number 14, pp. 106 – 119.

Furman, K. (2014) 'Ubuntu and the law: Some lessons for the practical application of

Ubuntu,' In: Praeg, L. and Magadla, S. (eds.) *Ubuntu: Curating the archive,* Grahamstown: University of KwaZulu-Natal Press, pp.150 – 166.

Gluckman, M. (1955) *The judicial process among the Barotse of Northern Rhodesia,* Manchester University Press: Manchester.

Gule, L. (2015) 'Ibn Khaldun: Law and justice in the science of civilization,' in: Fløistad, G. (ed.) *Contemporary philosophy: A new survey Volume 12: Philosophy of justice.* Oslo: Springer.

Gwaravanda, E. T. (2011) Philosophical principles in the Shona traditional court system, *International Journal of Peace and Development Studies,* 2(5): 148 – 155.

Gyekye, K. (2010) 'African Ethics,' in: *Stanford Encyclopaedia of Philosophy,* Available at: https://plato.stanford.edu/entries/, Accessed 6 August 2017.

Hapanyengwi-Chemhuru, O. and Makuvaza, N. (2014) '*Hunhu*: In search of an indigenous philosophy for the Zimbabwean education system,' in: *Journal of Indigenous Social Development,* Volume 3, Issue 1, pp.1 – 15.

Hursthouse, R. and Pettigrovela, G. (2016) 'Virtue ethics,' In: *Stanford Encyclopaedia of Philosophy.,* Available at: https://plato.stanford.edu/entries/, Accessed 12 August 2017.

Idowu, W. (2006. 'Against the skeptical argument and the Absence Thesis: African jurisprudence and the challenge of Positivist Historiography,' in: *The Journal of Philosophy, Science and Law,* Volume 6, pp.34 - 49.

Kanu, A. M. (2015) 'A philosophical appraisal of John Rawls' Difference Principle in the context of the Quorta System of Nigeria,' in: *Philosophy Study,* 5 (2): 78 – 85.

Leontsini, E. (2015) 'Justice and moderation in the state: Aristotle and beyond,' in: Fløistad, G. (Ed.) *Contemporary philosophy: A new survey Volume 12: Philosophy of justice,* Oslo: Springer.

Letseka, M. (2014) 'Ubuntu and justice as fairness,' in: *Mediterranean Journal of Social Science,* 5 (9): 544 – 551.

Lutz, D., (2009) 'African Ubuntu philosophy and global management,' in: *Journal of Business Ubuntu*, Volume 84, pp. 313 – 328.

Mangena, F. (2015) Restorative justice's deep roots in Africa, *South African Journal of Philosophy*, 34(1): 1 - 12.

Mangena, F. (2016) 'Hunhu/Ubuntu in the traditional thought of Southern Africa,' in: *Internet Encyclopaedia of Philosophy*, Available at: www.iep.utm.edu/hunhu/, Accessed 10 August 2017.

Masitera, E. (2015) 'Proverbial jurisprudence: A Shona social teaching for social cohesion in a multicultural society,' in: Mapara, J. and Mazuru, M. (Eds.) *Indigenous knowledge in Zimbabwe: Laying foundations for sustainable livelihoods*, Diaspora Publishers: Gloucestershire.

Mazarire, G. C. (2003) 'The politics of the womb: Women, politics and the environment in pre-colonial Chivi, Southern Zimbabwe, c 1840 – 1900,' in: *Zambezia*, Volume XXX, Number I, pp 35 – 50.

Moyo, K. (2015) Mimicry, transitional justice and the land question in racially divided former settler colonies, *The International Journal of Transitional Justice*, 9(1): 70 – 89.

Murungi, J. (2004) 'The question of an African jurisprudence: Some hermeneutical reflections,' In: Wiredu, K. (Ed.) *A Companion to African Philosophy*, Blackwell Publishing Ltd: Malden.

Nzwengu, N. (2004) 'Feminism and Africa: Impact and limits of the metaphysics of gender,' in: Wiredu K. (Ed.) *A companion to African philosophy*, Blackwell Publishing Ltd: Malden.

Olagunju, O. (2014) 'Traditional African Dispute Resolution (TADR) mechanisms,' Available at: https://www.linkedin.com/pulse, Accessed 20 August 2017.

Ramose, M. B. (2014) 'Ubuntu: Affirming a right and seeking remedies in South Africa,' In: Praeg, L. and Magadla, S. (Ed.) *Ubuntu: Curating the archive,* Pietermaritzburg: University of KwaZulu-Natal Press, pp.121 – 136.

Rawls, J. (1971) *A theory of justice*, Massachusetts: The Belknap Press.

Schmidt, E. (1992). *Peasants, traders and wives: Shona women in the history of Zimbabwe, 1870 – 1939*, London: Heinemann.

Sreenivasan, G. (2002) Errors about errors: Virtue Theory and Trait Attribution, *Mind*, Volume 111, pp.47 – 67.

Tshuma, A. (2015) Reframing post-Mugabe justice: A critical need for a truth and reconciliation commission, *African Journal of Political Science and International Relations,* 9(7): 308 – 320.

Van Niekerk, J. (2013) 'Ubuntu and moral value,' *PhD Thesis*, University of the Witwatersrand: Johannesburg.

Velasquez, M, Andre, C. Shanks, T. and Meyer, M. J. (1992) 'The common good,' in: *Issues in Ethics*, Volume 5, Number 1. https://legacy.scu.edu/ethics/publications/iie/v5n1/common.html

Wallenstein, P. (2015) *Understanding conflict resolution*, Sage: London.

Chapter 15

Indigenous and Christian Forms of National Healing: A Case for the Global Political Agreement in Zimbabwe

Tobias Marevesa

Introduction

Violence has become cancerous in Africa and the world over. This violence has manifested itself in different ways such as ethnic strife, armed struggles, religious extremism, and terrorism among others. In recent history, Zimbabwe was besieged by politically-motivated violence which rocked the country between 2000 and 2008. The violence was orchestrated by the major political parties which are the Zimbabwe African National Union Patriotic Front (ZANU-PF), the Movement for Democratic Change-Tsvangirai (MDC-T) and the Movement for Democratic Change-Mutambara (MDC-M), in preparation for the presidential and parliamentary elections between 2000 and 2008. The subsequent talks that were held in an effort to end this violence led to the birth of the Global Political Agreement (GPA) which was signed between the aforementioned major political parties in Zimbabwe, namely, ZANU-PF led by Robert Mugabe, MDC-T of Morgan Tsvangirai, and MDC-M of Arthur Mutambara with the mandate of forming a transitional government in preparation for a free, fair and credible election (Raftopoulos, 2013).

The purpose of this chapter is to interrogate the relevance of the inclusion of traditional and religious mechanisms for national healing in the GPA in Zimbabwe. Based on the data gathered, the research observed that the GPA did not achieve the anticipated objectives in the context of national healing in Zimbabwe. The chapter argues that the GPA could have done better in bringing about reconciliation if the Organ on National Healing, Reconciliation, and Integration could have incorporated people and institutions with the capacity for conflict resolution drawn from the traditional and religious domains.

The chapter concludes that the inclusion of traditional leaders, traditional healers (*n'angas*), church leaders, spirit mediums, local communities and other relevant stakeholders would have brought the much needed reconciliation and peace in Zimbabwe during the GNU era.

The Global Political Agreement (GPA) and the formation of the Government of National Unity (GNU) in Zimbabwe

The GPA was an arrangement which culminated in a power-sharing government known as the Government of National Unity. The GPA was signed on 5 September 2008 by Mugabe, Tsvangirai and Mutambara (Chipaike, 2013; Hofisi, Manyeruke and Mhandara, 2013). As part of the agreement, Mugabe was to be the President, but was to relinquish some executive power to Tsvangirai who was to serve as Prime Minister, while Mutambara was to serve as the Deputy Prime Minister (Raftopoulos, 2007; Muzondidya, 2009; Muzondidya, 2013; Masaka, 2010; Tatira and Marevesa, 2011; Mapuva, 2010). This came as a result of the Southern African Development Community (SADC)-led negotiations brokered by the then President of South Africa, Thabo Mbeki (Raftopoulos, 2013; Hofisi, Manyeruke and Mhandara, 2013).

The GNU became operational in February 2009 (Chipaike, 2013). This brought a lot of hope and relief to Zimbabweans after years of economic and political difficulties. This was because the GNU was an inclusive government that was put in place as a conflict-resolution measure with the mandate to crafting a new constitution and prepare free, fair and credible elections.

Chiwara, Shoko, and Chitando (2013) argue that the GNU has received different interpretations. Those who supported the GNU argue that it reduced inflation which had ravaged the economy for almost a decade. It is true that the introduction of the multi-currency system in 2009 brought significant progress in addressing the economic challenges which bedevilled the country. In addition, the dollarization of the economy helped to stabilize prices of goods. As well, due to the stability, some basic commodities and foodstuffs, which had hitherto disappeared from the shop shelves, became readily available. This was coupled with an improvement in the provision of some social services. As well, according to Alexander and McGregor (2013), there was also a notable number of workers who were back at work because the economy had improved.

The GNU instituted a number of key constitutional commissions which were established in consultation with all the GPA signatories. These commissions include the Media Commission, Anti-Corruption Commission, and the Human Rights Commission. In addition, there were some reforms in some sectors of the government such as the media and politics which brought a new page of democracy, progress and development. The constitutional reform process, while slow because of political bickering among the political parties, however, succeeded in completing its major mandate of doing public outreach programmes that led to the drafting of a new constitution. Manyeruke and Hamauswa (2013) posit that the constitution from the Constitutional Parliamentary Select Committee (COPAC) came as a people-driven document, which means that it was a product of prolonged negotiations among the major political parties in Zimbabwe.

Politically, the formation of the GNU helped in reducing polarization and tension in Zimbabwe. The Zimbabwe Institute (2011) asserts that during the GNU, there was a notable decrease in politically motivated arrests, violence, abductions and murders as compared to the period before it. However, there were isolated pockets of violence; intimidation and political tension nationally. There were traits of arbitrary arrests and harassment of the civic groups, victimization and intimidation of human rights and political activists, and disregarding of court orders (Mashiri, 2013). This was a major setback of the GNU because it failed to bring the warring parties together by utilizing the Organ on National Healing, Reconciliation and Integration (ONHRI) and the Joint Monitoring and Implementation Committee (JOMIC) which were mandated to bring transitional justice, healing and reconciliation. It is against this background that even during the inclusive government there was politically-motivated violence. In fact, some critics argue that the GNU failed "to address issues relating to transitional justice, healing and reconciliation" (Chiwara, Shoko, and Chitando, 2013:36).

On the whole, the inclusive government was a fragile political agreement which did not solve all the challenges which the country was facing. Among others, there was extreme contestation for the control of the government and state power within the GNU. This resulted in the slowdown of the political and economic growth and development of the country (Mashiri, 2013).

Given the persistence of incidence of political violence and intolerance during the period 2009-2013, it is quite apparent that the GNU did not succeed in bringing about lasting peace in Zimbabwe. It is, therefore, important to assess what could have been done by the GNU to bring about national healing and lasting peace in the country. This chapter will analyse the role played by religious stakeholders, both indigenous and Christian, in national healing during the tenure of the GNU in Zimbabwe. It will also challenge political players, both within the GNU and after, for failing to seriously consider the role of religious institutions in conflict-resolution.

The GNU and its peace-building and national healing mandate

There are different forms in the indigenous religion and the church in Zimbabwe that are capable of bringing peace and reconciliation. This section will interrogate the Shona indigenous forms of justice, national healing and reconciliation during the Government of National Unity (GNU). These traditional and religious forms that could have been utilized by the GNU are the belief and respect of spirits, *n'anga,* traditional leaders, cultural values, among others. This will be discussed after a brief survey of the sections in the GPA that gives the GNU power and mandate to promote national healing and unity in the country. As outlined earlier in this chapter, Zimbabwe was rocked by politically-motivated violence from 2000 to 2008. This was worsened by the 2008 presidential elections which were disputed by the major political parties namely, ZANU-PF, MDC-T, and MDC-M. Again as clearly enunciated earlier, the political impasse resulted in the SADC being tasked to broker the conflict in Zimbabwe. The intervention of

SADC led to the signing of the GPA which paved the way to the formation of the GNU.

The GNU was a transitional government tasked with preparing for fresh elections and ensuring lasting peace in Zimbabwe. Article VII of the GPA laid provisions to promote equality, unity and national healing. In Section 7.1, the GNU was directed among other things to:

c)....give consideration to the setting up of a mechanism to properly advise on what measures might be necessary and practicable to achieve national healing, cohesion and unity in respect of victims of pre- and post-independence political conflict;

d)... strive to create an environment of tolerance and respect among Zimbabweans and that all citizens are treated with dignity and decency irrespective of age, gender, race, and ethnicity, place of origin or political affiliation.

It was on the basis of Section 7 (c) of the GPA document that the Organ for National Healing Reconciliation and Integration (ONHRI) was put in place to lead the national healing process. As an organ of the GNU, the ONHRI had the mandate of advising the government on measures to be taken to promote national healing, cohesion and unity.

Lamentably, the ONHRI demonstrated minimum expertise in advising the GNU and coordinating communities in creating conditions that promoted peace (Chipaike, 2013). In actual fact, the GNU and the political parties that constituted it blundered by assuming that politicians would be able to lead a programme of national healing and reconciliation. It is therefore being argued that conflict resolution, peace-building and national healing in Zimbabwe could have been more effective if the 'traditional' political and religious institutions as well as Christian churches had been considered. The chapter will now turn to these options.

The chief (*ishe*)

The first element that could have been very important in bringing about conflict transformation, national healing and peace was the involvement of the traditional leadership as represented by the chiefs (*ishe*, among the Shona people of Zimbabwe). In the Shona religion and customs, the chief is an embodiment of tradition and culture (Chiwara, Shoko and Chitando, 2013). He is the leader of all the people in his community and is the custodian of the land where people get life. During the pre-colonial period, according to Nkomo (1998), chiefs had executive, ritual and judicial powers and always enjoyed the support of their subordinates and the people under their jurisdiction.

The major role of chiefs was to resolve conflicts and disputes through the traditional court (*dare*). Chiwara, Shoko and Chitando (2013) note that the chief was the last court of appeal for the village headmen referred cases which they had failed to settle to him. As the chief presided over the traditional court, he was helped by advisors (*machinda*) who made it a point that there was peace, harmony and unity within the community. The chief's court dealt with a variety of cases which included divorce, quarrels, compensation, breaking taboos, theft of cattle among others, hence the chief was both a "religious and political ruler" (Bourdillon, 1976:137).

In Shona cosmology, as in many other parts of Africa, chiefs mediate between their subjects and the spirit guardians (Shoko, 2007). Since the pre-colonial period, they have played the important role of spearheading and overseeing the organisation of rituals such as *mukwerere* (rain-inducing ceremony) to make sure that there is enough rain and fertility on the land. There is no doubt that chiefs still command a great deal of respect from their subjects in independent Zimbabwe. Given the importance of the traditional leaders to indigenous societies, the GNU could have utilised the involvement them in national healing, conflict resolution and reconciliation.

Avenging spirits

Shona religious beliefs and practices are rich in principles of conflict resolution and reconciliation. This section focuses on the institution of avenging spirits (*ngozi*) among the Shona. Avenging spirits are the spirits of the dead people who died in anger, such as victims of murder, who may want to seek revenge (Sibanda, 2016; Chiwara, Shoko and Chitando, 2013; Bourdillon, 1976). The family of the person who murdered a person would consult a traditional healer (*n'anga*) who would help to settle the dispute and bring harmony between the angry spirit and the family.

The Shona believe that "*Mushonga wengozi kuiripa*" (The solution to *ngozi* is restitution or compensation) (Sibanda, 2016: 353). When not appeased, the *ngozi* can cause mayhem in a family to an extent of wiping the whole family. The avenging spirits can only be compensated by the payment of blood money, a herd of cattle or a girl child (*Ibid*). The belief in avenging spirits could have been handy if it was utilised by the GNU which could have publicized it in order to discourage many sections of the population from engaging in violence. The traditional chiefs could have been used to spearhead the process and ensure that perpetrators of political violence were tried at the *dare* after which they paid compensation to the families of their victims.

Chiwara, Shoko and Chitando (2013) rightly pointed out that the inclusive government could have seen the need to conduct traditional ceremonies to appease the spirits of the victims of politically-motivated violence. If such cleansing ceremonies had been undertaken during the GNU period, spearheaded by the ONHRI with the assistance of chiefs, they could have gone a long way in reconciling conflicting parties that had been involved in political violence from 2000 to 2008. The concept of *ngozi* is a deterrent measure in society because if other people witness a person or family being tormented by the avenging spirits, few people would commit the same offence of killing. Therefore, the fear of *ngozi* may instil discipline in the entire society but, this can only be realised when the traditional leaders emphasise the importance of not engaging in violence.

The traditional medical practitioners (*n'anga*)

The *n'anga* (traditional medical practitioners) might also have played a significant role in bringing national healing if they had been incorporated in the GNU. According to Chiwara, Shoko and Chitando (2013:41), *n'angas* may be referred to as diviner-healers. Their major task is to give advice to difficult issues and questions which affect people. In addition, their role is to heal people with different ailments. As herbalists, they mainly deal with medicine and give prescriptions to patients. *N'angas* can also do other duties such as *kupinga musha* (protecting a home using magic) and *rukwa* (boosting agriculture using magic) (Chiwara, Shoko and Chitando, 2013). According to Shoko (2007), herbalists are also believed to use spiritual powers to provide medicine for love, luck and employment, and heal both individuals and society. It can be argued that herbalists/*n'angas* could have played a pivotal role in bringing national healing and reconciliation in the Government of National Unity in Zimbabwe. This is evidenced by the various roles they play, particularly in cleansing and exorcising avenging spirits and in bringing sanity, to individuals and communities.

Cultural values

Zimbabwean societies have many cultural values which could have been instrumental in bringing national healing. According to Chiwara, Shoko and Chitando (2013), Shona cultural values which include ethics and morals through the concept of *unhu* (personhood), for example, nurture good behaviour and peaceful co-existence. The Shona word *unhu* (personhood) is etymologically derived from *vanhu* (people) who collectively determine what is to be *munhu* (a person) (Ibid). This concept believes in working together rather than operating as individuals. Another pertinent issue of *unhu* is identity in relation to human rights. According to Chidester (1992: 82), *unhu* is premised on the belief that, "A human being is a human because of other human beings". The Shona concept of *Munhu munhu navanhu* (a person is a person through other persons), is vital. From this cultural point of view, personhood is articulated in the course of giving through inclusive acts of hospitality (*Ibid*). Based on this, a person has the right to life, security, and freedom in relation to a communal set of social and political ethics, all enshrined by belonging to the community of the living and the living-dead.

Human rights

In Shona indigenous culture, there are some aspects which show human rights. According to Chiwara, Shoko and Chitando (2013), these aspects promote human rights in that, they protect, sustain, and bring about human life, self-respect, and uprightness among others. The aspect of human rights in Shona indigenous culture is evident in marriage, chieftainship and ritual practice. In this regard, there are particular issues under the mentioned areas of human rights which include *mombe youmai* (mothers' cow), *chiredzwa* (appreciation of child caring) *zunde ramambo* (chief's food storage in times of drought), *kugarwa nhaka* (inheriting the deceased's estate), *sara pavana* (inheritance of the deceased's family) and *ubuntu* (personhood). In addition, there are rituals which promote human rights such as *kupayira* (child naming), *kutsikisa mapoto* (stepping over protective porridge), *mhinza mumba* (home-bringing ceremony) (Chiwara, Shoko and Chitando, 2013; Mushishi, 2009). Based on the research of the above scholars, it can be argued that in Shona indigenous culture there are elements of promoting human rights. Nevertheless, it could have been a noble and prudent way to involve the Shona indigenous culture in bringing national healing, peace, cohesion and conflict-resolution in the GNU.

The Church and national healing in Zimbabwe

After high levels of violence and political polarisation which were experienced in Zimbabwe, the church could have been very useful in bringing national healing and peace. This is because churches are generally associated with tolerance, reconciliation and peace. As an organisation, the Christian church's teachings are based on the premises that Jesus Christ came to redeem humanity and so the Cross becomes an apex of liberation. Chiwara, Shoko and Chitando (2013) assert that in the Bible, justice, love and peace have to do with slaves being set free from bondage, with care of widows and orphans, with kindness to strangers and sojourners, with compassion for the sick and disabled, but also with fair wages to workers, economic security, the inclusion of the marginalized, liberation from oppression, ecological justice and the end of the war. It is against this background that the church could have been an instrumental platform to bring about national healing and conflict resolution had it been included to participate. There are church organisations like the Evangelical Fellowship of Zimbabwe (EFZ), the Zimbabwe Catholic Bishops' Conference (ZCBC) and the Catholic Commission of Justice and Peace (CCJP). Some of these church organisations were the voice of the voiceless in Zimbabwe since the colonial period.

According to Chiwara, Shoko and Chitando (2013), the ZCBC acted as the voice of the voiceless in 1983 when they wrote a communique entitled *Reconciliation is Still Possible* showing that they (ZCBC) vehemently denounced and condemned the atrocities of the Gukurahundi and encouraged the government to respect and maintain law and order in the provinces of Matabeleland and Midlands. In addition, the CCJP members played a crucial role in the negotiations between ZANU PF and ZAPU which culminated in the signing of the Unity Accord on 22 December 1987 (Chiwara, Shoko and Chitando, 2013). Muzondidya (2011) rightly noted that the agreement's major achievement was the eradication of the political violence that had rocked Matebeleland and Midlands provinces.

Surprisingly, churches remained marginalised by the ONHRI in the peace-building process (Chitando, 2011). As Chiwara, Shoko and Chitando (2013) correctly note, national healing and reconciliation are embedded in moral obligations and the church-based organisations can claim moral authority and legitimacy to lead the National Healing and Reconciliation Process since politicians may not be neutral in conflict situations. It can be observed that politicians are not experts of conflict transformation and healing. Chitando (2011) also lays some blame on the churches themselves for not positioning themselves to be visible as potential players in resolving conflict during the GNU era.

Conclusion

Both 'traditional' and 'modern' non-state institutions are valuable resources of peace-building, national healing, conflict resolution and reconciliation. These institutions were severely underutilized in Zimbabwe during the GNU era. Cultural values could have been appropriated to create and establish peace and tolerance. Other facets of indigenous spiritual beliefs could also have been utilised. The indigenous role of traditional chiefs as guarantors of peace could also have been seriously considered. The concept of *ubuntu* and human rights that sustain communal co-existence could also have been a valuable resource in promoting national healing. All the said aspects are of great importance and value that could have brought positive input in the avoidance of violence in the era of the inclusive government in Zimbabwe. Despite the fact that the Shona indigenous beliefs are despised by some people, they are of paramount importance to the policy makers in Zimbabwe if they are to attain national healing and reconciliation. In a similar way, churches can also be utilized to preach peace to politicians and communities.

References

Alexander, J. and McGregor, J. (2014) 'Introduction: Politics, patronage and violence in Zimbabwe, In: Journal of Southern African Studies, 39:4, pp. 749-763.

Bourdillon, M. F. (1976). *The Shona People: Ethnography of the Contemporary Shona with Special Reference to their Religion.* Gweru: Mambo Press.

Chidester, D. (1992) *Religions of South Africa*, London: Routledge

Chipaike, R. (2013) The Zimbabwe Government of National Unity as a conflict transformation mechanism: A critical review, *Southern Peace Review Journal*, 2(1): 17-34.

Chitando, E. (2011) 'Prayers, politics and peace: The church's role in Zimbabwe's crisis, in: *Open Space*, Issue 1, pp.43-48.

Chitando, E. and Manyonganise, M., (2011) 'Voices from faith-based communities,' in: Murithi, T. and Mawadza, A. (eds.), *Zimbabwe in transition: A view from within,* Johannesburg: Fanele.

Chiwara, A. Shoko, T. and Chitando, E., (2013) 'African Traditional Religion and the Church: Catalysts for national healing in Zimbabwe in the context of the Global Political Agreement,' in: *Southern Peace Review Journal,* Volume 2. Number 1, pp.35-55.

Chung, F. (2007) Re-*living the Second Chimurenga: Memories from the liberation struggle in Zimbabwe,* Harare: Weaver Press. Government of Zimbabwe, 2008. *Global Political Agreement,* Harare: The Ministry of Constitutional and Parliamentary Affairs.

Hofisi, S. Manyeruke, C. and Mhandara, L. (2013) The church and political transition in Zimbabwe: The Inclusive Government Context, *Journal of Political Administration and Governance,* 3, (1):103-114.

Hudleston, S. (2005) *Face of courage: A biography of Morgan Tsvangirai,* Cape Town: Double Storey.

Kanyeze, G. (2004) 'The Zimbabwe economy, 1980-2003: a ZCTU perspective', in: D Harold –Barry (Ed.), *Zimbabwe: The past is the future,* Harare: Weaver Press.

Kriger, J. N. (2003) *Guerrilla veterans in post-war Zimbabwe: Symbolic and violent politics 1980-1987,* Cambridge University Press: Cambridge.

Mapuva, J. (2010) Government of National Unity (GNU) as a conflict prevention strategy: Case for Zimbabwe, *Journal of Sustainable Development in Africa,* 12(6): 11-26.

Masaka, D. (2010) *Zimbabwe's Government of National Unity (GNU): A panacea to an economy in a state of crisis,* Lap Lambert Academic Publishing: Saarbrucken.

Moyo, A. (1987) 'Religion and politics in Zimbabwe,' In: Peterson, K. H. (ed.) *Religion, development and African identity,* Uppsala: Nordiska Afrikainstitutet

Mushishi, C. (2009) 'Aspects of Budga traditional religion which promote human rights,' unpublished *DPhil Thesis,* University of Cape Town: South Africa.

Muguti, T. Tavuyanago, B. and Hlongwana, J. (2012) untenable marriages: Situating governments of national unity in Africa's political landscape, *International Journal of Developing Societies,* 1(4): 149 – 158.

Muzondidya, J. (2013). 'The opposition dilemma in Zimbabwe: A critical review of the politics of the Movement for Democratic Change (MDC) parties under the GPA transitional framework, 2009-2012,' in: B. Raftopoulos (Ed.). *The hard road to reform: The politics of Zimbabwe's Global Political Agreement,* Harare: Weaver Press.

Muzondidya, J. (2011) 'Zimbabwe's failed transition: An analysis of the challenges and Complexities in Zimbabwe's transition to democracy in the post-2000 period,' in: T. Murithi, and A. Mawadza, (Eds.), *Zimbabwe in transition: A view from within,* Johannesburg: Fanele.

Muzondidya, J. (2009) 'From buoyancy to crisis, 1980-1997,' In: B Raftopoulos and A, Mlambo (Eds.) *Becoming Zimbabwe: A history from the pre-colonial period to 2008,* Harare: Weaver Press.

Nkomo, J. (1998) 'Compiling specialised dictionaries in African languages: Isichazamazwi SezoMculo as a special reference,' in: Chiwome, E. M. and Gambahaya, Z. (eds.) *Culture and development: Perspectives from the South,* Harare: Mond Books Publishers.

Raftopoulos, B. (2009). 'The crisis in Zimbabwe, 1998– 2009,' in: B. Raftopoulos and A. Mlambo (Eds.) *Becoming Zimbabwe: A history from the pre-colonial period to 2008,* Harare: Weaver Press.

Raftopoulos, B. (2004) 'Current Politics,' In: D. Harold-Barry (ed.), *Zimbabwe: The past is the future: Rethinking land, state and nation in the context of crisis,* Harare: Weaver Press.

Raftopoulos, B. (2013) 'An Overview of the GPA: National conflict, regional agony and international dilemma,' in: B. Raftopoulos (Ed.), *The hard road to reform: The politics of Zimbabwe's Global Political Agreement,* Harare: Weaver Press.

Sadomba, Z. W. (2011) *War veterans in Zimbabwe's revolution: Challenging neo-colonialism, settler and international capital,* Harare: Weaver Press: Harare.

Sachikonye, L. (2011) *When a state turns on its citizens: Institutionalized violence and political Culture,* Auckland Park: Jacana Media.

Sachikonye, L. M. (2000) 'The promised land: From expropriation to reconciliation and *Jambanja*', in: B. Raftopoulos and Savage

(Eds.), *Zimbabwe injustice and political reconciliation,* Harare: Weaver Press.

Shoko, T. (2007) *Karanga indigenous religion in Zimbabwe: Health and well-being,* Aldershot: Ashgate Publishers.

Tatira, L. and Marevesa, T. (2011) 'The Global Political Agreement (GPA) and the persistent political conflict arising there from: Is this another manifestation of Council of Jerusalem', in: *Journal of African Studies and Development,* 3 (10): 187-191.

Vestraelen, F. J. (1998). *Zimbabwean realities and Christian responses,* Mambo Press: Gweru.

Zimbabwe Catholic Bishops Conference, 2 June 2005,'Pastoral letter,' Harare.

Chapter 16

Conflict, Justice and Peace from an African Indigenous Cultural Perspective: The Case of the Vatsonga People of Mozambique, South Africa, Swaziland and Zimbabwe

Steyn Khesani Madlome & Osborne Risimati Chauke

Introduction

Conflict is an inevitable phenomenon among human beings and any other living organisms. For peace and tranquillity to prevail among human beings, there should be a way of resolving these conflicts. Conflicts are witnessed at different levels in the society and they have varying causes and effects. There are different lenses through which cultures can view conflicts. As well, ways of restoring peace also differ from culture to culture.

The aim of this chapter is to highlight some common conflicts which disturb peace among the Vatsonga communities across borders and how they are resolved using African indigenous cultural mechanisms, notably the Vatsonga speaking people found in Zimbabwe, South Africa, Mozambique and Swaziland. Using the Vatsonga case, the chapter argues that some of the major disputes within communities can be settled amicably from an Afrocentric vantage point to the satisfaction of the people involved in the same way or even far much better than other points of view elsewhere. African indigenous cultural aspects of the Vatsonga, which are based on the values of Ubuntu/*Vumunhu*,[1] are used as a tool to bring justice, peace and healing in the community. The chapter also shows that both parties involved in a conflict will benefit from the methods employed in resolving it for the good of the community as well. The

---

[1] *Vumunhu* is the Vatsonga term for Ubuntu. Generally Ubuntu is taken to mean African communal life which expresses principles of humanness, caring and the spirit of mutual support.

327

chapter, therefore, recommends incorporating African indigenous cultural ways of achieving justice and peace in the process of resolving conflicts.

Historical background of the Vatsonga people

The Vatsonga are a cross-border ethnic group found in Zimbabwe, South Africa, Mozambique and Swaziland (Mathebula, 2014). They may also be found in small pockets in countries like Lesotho and Zambia. This group of people has a common language and culture even though there might be small differences here and there due to contact with other groups in their respective countries. In supporting this claim, Mathebula, Nkuna, Mabasa and Maluleke (2007:1) aver that "in the 1720s, Portuguese and Dutch identified the Tsonga as linguistically and culturally belonging to one group despite the fact that they belonged to different chiefdoms". Most of the cultural practices that are performed by the Vatsonga across the colonially-inspired borders of southern Africa are basically the same. These include; how Vatsonga view death, burial rituals, male and female initiation ceremonies, ancestral worship, traditional marriages, and many other traditions (Khosa, 2009). Xitsonga, their language, is spoken by nearly 2 million people in South Africa, some 1.5 million in Mozambique, over 100 000 in Zimbabwe and a few thousand people in Swaziland and Zambia (National African Language Resource Centre, 2017).

The Vatsonga, like any other African ethnic groups, have socio-cultural beliefs when it comes to fundamental community issues. They believe in administering justice from a Xitsonga perspective which is largely linked to the Ubuntu/*Vumunhu* concept (Rwelamila, Talukhaba and Ngowi, 2014). There could be some uniqueness in how they solve other issues due to cultural differences with other groups. The African indigenous justice system is victim-centred and also aims at reconciling victims and offenders, as well as restoring order in the community (Elechi *et al*, 2010). Another thing to take note of is that African justice systems have been heavily influenced by Western systems and the Vatsonga are no exception (*Ibid*).

Even though there might be influence from other cultures, there are some aspects which are still notable among the generality of the people in the scattered Vatsonga communities. Among others, chiefs (*Tihosi*) still command respect from their subjects and the subjects in turn recognise and respect these traditional leaders (Khosa, 2009). All Vatsonga chiefs on the Zimbabwean side belong to the Vahlengwe clan of the Cawuke (fire) totem. In Mozambique and South Africa, however, chiefs belong to various other clans. What is common is that their chieftainship is lineal, directly from father to the eldest son and it is not based on rotation as other ethnic groups do. This succession plan is very clear and simple (Nhlapo, 2017). In addition, the Vatsonga across the numerous borders also value and practice traditional rites of passage for both boys and girls. This is known as *ngoma* and *khomba* for boys and girls respectively. There is no operation undertaken on girls. They are both taught to behave in a way which is acceptable to the society. Furthermore, the Vatsonga elderly women in all the different countries of southern Africa dress themselves in traditional skirts (*xibelani*), a cloth over their shoulders (*miceka*) and some bracelets in their arms (*vusenga*) and legs (*madeha*).

Conceptualising conflict resolution, peace and justice: A global overview

This section gives an overview of the concepts and practices related to conflict resolution, peace and justice among human beings across the world. Different scholars have discussed these issues basing on conflicts that occur in various communities across the globe. This overview helps to give a comparison with what really happens among the Vatsonga in as far as issues of conflict, conflict resolution, peace and justice are concerned

Symonides and Singh (1996) highlight the importance of peace in the world by taking note of the fact that there are many violent conflicts across the globe. They also aver that the main goals of the United Nations are to achieve permanent peace and security. They argue that peace has to be founded upon the intellectual and moral solidarity of mankind. They also underline the United Nations Educational and Scientific Organisation's (UNESCO) objective, as

329

highlighted in its constitution, which stresses the construction of the defence of peace in the minds of men and women. This means that peace is an important component in life which all people have to abide with. Symonides and Singh (*Ibid*) further point out some causes of conflict and violence which make peace an issue of critical importance. Among them are xenophobia, ethno-nationalism, racism and discrimination against minority groups, hatred, suspicion, intolerance, poverty, religious extremism and violation of human rights.

Furthermore, Symonides and Singh (1996) recommend that the culture of violence found in many contemporary societies should be replaced by a culture of peace which is based on non-violence, tolerance, mutual understanding and solidarity, as well as the ability to solve conflicts peacefully. They also point out that democracy is an important prerequisite for the construction of a culture of peace. They argue that democracy creates an environment which is conducive for building lasting peace (*Ibid*).

It is interesting to note that while Symonides and Singh (1996) argue that peace and justice are guided by written laws and precepts, the Vatsonga generally believe that they are written in people's hearts. The end result remains the same though. There could, however, be slight differences when it comes to the issue of administering justice and bringing peace through democratic means. Under the Vatsonga traditions, every man is allowed to air his views but strong social orders on customary law come from the chief's advisers (SAHO, 2011). Thus, in the Vatsonga culture the kind of democracy referred to may not be the same as in Western cultures. In addition, what Westerners may regard as written laws guiding peace and justice may achieve the same desired results as the guidance provided by elders in various African cultures including the Vatsonga.

Carneiro, Novais and Neves (2014) have shown that conflict is an inevitable and a natural phenomenon in human life. They argue that since conflicts cannot be avoided, the only way forward is to find means of solving them. Carneiro, Novais and Neves (2014) discuss two main approaches of resolving conflict, namely: litigation in the courtroom and alternative methods. In their view, alternative methods such as indigenous cultural jurisprudence have advantages over the prosecutorial ones, including contextual richness.

Kariuki (2015) discusses successes and challenges of conflict resolution strategies involving elders in Africa. He shows how colonialism and Western legal traditions have impacted negatively on African ways of conflict resolution. Kariuki (Ibid) argues that despite imposing Western methods of administering justice, African justice systems still have a central place in resolving conflicts in Africa. He goes on to examine some successes and challenges faced by elders in resolving disputes in different African states. He examines countries such as Kenya, Uganda, Rwanda, Ethiopia, Botswana and South Africa. In the countries listed above, he focuses on specific ethnic groups except South Africa where he just generalizes. On South Africa, he mentions that there is respect of customary law but there are limitations when it comes to handling of certain issues. South Africa is a multicultural society which does not have homogeneous ways of resolving disputes as implied by what Kariuki writes. He also shows that religion, through its spiritual appeal, has a great influence on traditional ways of resolving disputes (*Ibid*).

Francois du Bois (2007: 15) defines justice as a practice concerned "with giving people their due." He further argues that there is a very close connection between justice and law since various aspects of law are related to dimensions of justice. He says law has an ability to do justice. Du Bois (*Ibid*) also examines different forms of justice, namely distributive and commutative or corrective justice. Distributive justice is concerned about distributing goods and treating people equally. Corrective justice pertains to rectifying disturbances through the process of distributing goods. This concept of justice has some similarities with the Vatsonga justice system in the sense that their traditional tribunals, while aimed at the good of the community, aim at treating individuals equally and democratically as much as possible (SAHO, 2011).

Elechi, Morris and Schauer (2010) discuss the restoration of justice from an African perspective and point out that the main goal of administering justice is to appease victims and at the same time reintegrate offenders back into the community. They also state that the primacy of the African concept of justice lies in its efforts towards the restoration of relationships and peace which had been affected by conflicts. In their view, the African indigenous justice system is effective since all stakeholders participate in the process of conflict resolution and decisions made there are reached through a consensus. They also aver that this jurisprudential process fosters the spirit of oneness and communitarian principles whose main characteristics include caring for one another. The welfare of an individual is given much value since it is the base on which the survival of the community depends. Elechi, Morris and Schauer (Ibid) also point out clearly that even though African cultures are diverse, and culture itself is not static, there are some of its tenets which survived external influences and colonialism.

Drawing insights from the contribution of Elechi, Morris and Schauer (2010), this chapter seeks to identify some 'traditional' Tsonga methods of resolving conflicts which will help strengthen African justice systems which are helpful to the society at large. This should be done to the satisfaction of all members of the community since everyone has right to air their views in certain issues affecting individual members.

In his examination of the efficiency of courts, Fix-Fierro (2003) finds that people have varying opinions about this system in European countries. He says some people describe courts as slow, expensive, unfair, and inefficient. He argues that if opinion polls were anything to go by in countries like, Germany, France and Mexico, then the administration of justice in the world is in a state of crisis. He goes on to highlight that this sense of crisis is widespread to the extent that there are evils such as widespread corruption, lack of independence, politicisation, inadequate legal training of judges, court employees and attorneys and limited or no access to the majority of the people. This scenario is also common in 'modern' judicial systems in many African countries, most of who inherited Western forms of administering justice.

Nhlapo (2017) examines customary law in post-Apartheid South Africa where the country's Constitution recognizes it as an equal component of the legal order together with the common law. In his study, Nhlapo (*Ibid*) seeks to ascertain whether customary law has been integrated into the mainstream legal system and, if so, in what form. In order to achieve this, he analyses key judicial decisions and law reform initiatives. His study uses the notion of 'living law' as the point of departure and concludes that the cause of integration has not been well served by either the judiciary or the legislature. He argues that both the judiciary and the legislature have shied away from protecting the deep values embedded in customary law in favour of Western notions. Nhlapo (*Ibid*), thus, calls for a different approach that is more accommodative to the values underpinning customary law.

Nhlapo (*Ibid*) also gives some examples of cases where there were some clashes between women's rights and the cultural rights which are protected by the South African constitution, but impacting negatively on women. He cites cases of customary marriage and chieftainship as examples. He also noted that the South African constitution does not adequately capture many aspects of Xitsonga customary law. He draws some differences between a 'living law' and the general customary law. However, Nhlapo mainly focuses on the debates of rights and cultural aspects which are enshrined in the South African constitution which, to some extent, are influenced by Western laws. Some of the rights are contrary to the Vatsonga world view and bring confusion into their culture (*Ibid*). This chapter, therefore, examines Vatsonga culture, paying particular attention at how best it can be used to improve conflict-resolution processes in the contemporary world.

Common conflicts and the administration of justice among Vatsonga

This section deals with common conflicts among the Vatsonga and how they are administered as part of efforts to bring peace and harmony in the community. Most conflicts among the Vatsonga emanate from domestic matters, social, political, cultural and economic issues. The conflicts are varied in nature, for example, intrapersonal, interpersonal, intergroup and intragroup as discussed below.

Intrapersonal conflict

Intrapersonal conflict is when an individual has no peace or is having conflicts within his/her mind. Carneiro *et al* (2014:12) aver that: "These conflicts happen within ourselves, when we face situations in which contradictory values or convictions must be weighted and a decision or action, based on them, taken."

This type of conflict mainly affects one person but, basing on the Ubuntu philosophy, it may end up affecting the whole community. Such conflicts happen among the Vatsonga and are mainly caused by issues such as marital problems, poverty, health ailments and economic challenges. If such problems are left to persist, they lead to depressions and more complex health problems. Among the Vatsonga, it is the duty of the elders, starting from the family level up to community, to identify people with such conflicts in order to help them. At family level, aunts, uncles or grandparents are the ones who engage a person who suffers from an intrapersonal conflict. If one fails, he or she may seek help from another relative who is well known to the individual whose conflicts are to be resolved. These people will try to have counselling sessions with the affected individual (Interview with Hobyani, 2018).

For instance, if there is a case where a young man impregnates two ladies and becomes undecided on what to do, either to marry two wives or to deny responsibility of the other one. In such a case, elders from the family call him to discuss the matter. Since they live in a community where the issue of polygamy is not a problem, Vatsonga counsellors can just advise him to marry two wives. Another reason that will make them take such a decision is the fact that it would have happened before in their locality and that it would be a taboo to let a neighbour's child to suffer the shame of having a child out of wedlock. As such, the young man would be invited to 'wear the shoes' of the parents of the daughters and to imagine the shame it brings to that family (*Ibid*).

Other methods used are preventative in nature. The individual is taught that in life he or she can meet such situations. This is also the work of Vatsonga traditional initiation schools which apply to both men and women. These institutions are known as *khomba* and *ngoma* for girls/women and boys/men respectively (Mapindani, 2018). This practice is prevalent among the Vatsonga in Zimbabwe, Mozambique and South Africa. At the initiation schools, both groups are taught to be responsible people and are prepared to meet difficult situations (*Ibid*). In addition, they are encouraged to find their way out of any kind of conflicts they are likely to face in life. As Mapindani (2018: 6) notes: "Boys are introduced to the hardness of times in life so as to become men of great bravery and responsibility in their future socio-cultural and political orientations." Vatsonga initiation schools are, therefore, very useful in preparing boys and girls to overcome intrapersonal conflicts and enable them to fit well in their communities.

The Vatsonga also encourage the sharing of information as a way of helping to overcome intrapersonal challenges. At the family level, for example, children are taught to open up through discussion platforms known as *ehubyeni / eb'andleni* or traditional courts (Personal observations, 2018). In many instances, Vatsonga young boys and men were, and still are, discouraged from mixing with their sisters and mothers during the time they will be waiting for evening meals. They would make their own fire at some distant place from the kitchen where their food would be brought. During this time they would be told entertaining stories that keep them occupied to the extent of not agonizing over their intrapersonal challenges. In addition, they would draw a lot of lessons from what is taught to them during that time (Interview with N'waRisimati, 2018).

Interpersonal conflicts

The Vatsonga, as any other people who have different opinions and varying interests, have some interpersonal conflicts which, if not managed properly, may leave them without peace among themselves. Interpersonal conflicts can happen within a family where brothers, sisters, parents and children or any other family member have different views about a particular issue. This type of conflict involves two or more individuals and can be seen as a struggle between interdependent parties (Bergmann and Volkema, 1994).

At the family level, when children have such conflicts it is the duty of aunts and uncles to chip in and resolve the disputes (Kariuki,

2015). Parents have trust in these people and they do not interfere with the process of conflict resolution. What they only want is to see peace being restored between their children. When parents are the ones conflicting about any issues, close relatives are the ones who try to mediate and restore peace. When the issue is more complex, they may seek advice from aunts and uncles as well. If these fail, the matter may be taken to the in-laws through the wife's aunt if it is a marital issue. The aunt may seek help from other relatives so that they can counsel and advise accordingly (*Ibid*).

If it is in the case that the husband has married a second wife, the matter is brought to the attention of elders in the family (Kariuki, 2015). Polygamy among the Vatsonga is not a taboo, but what is only wanted is that the husband should notify the first wife about his intentions to marry a second or third wife. This is done by giving a beast to the wife. Not informing the wife is taken as undermining the authority of the wife and it leads to the husband being sanctioned. When the husband marries secretly, the wife has a right to claim for compensation (*Ibid*). The other family members who are tasked to settle the matter have to see to it that he has paid what is due to the wife. Once this is done, there are no more quarrels expected pertaining to the marriage of another wife or wives. The family is supposed to continue living in peace as before. If a wife continues quarrelling or shows that she is not contented, the husband has a right to send her to her parents for counselling (*Ibid*). Ordinarily, she should come back after a reasonable time when it is assumed that she had received enough advice (*Ibid*).

In the case of a general misunderstanding between a boy and a parent, an uncle is called to resolve the issue and if the child is a girl, the aunt is involved. A parent has to respect the views of the person who would have been tasked to handle the matter. Parents know very well some strengths and weaknesses of their relatives, so they choose someone whom they know can handle the matter. They would not choose someone who is known to be incompetent in resolving family disputes (*Ibid*).

Intragroup conflict

Intragroup conflict is one that takes place between members of a group. As Carneiro, Novais and Neves (2014: 12) state: "Intragroup conflicts take place between individuals that belong to a same group, that is, those individuals often share interests, cultural aspects, objectives and other identifying characteristics." The Vatsonga share some cultural values, norms and other characteristics which have to be maintained for peace to prevail among them (Mathebula *et al*, 2010). Common disputes that arise are marital disagreements, cultural clashes and land conflicts. Pertaining to land, conflicts often arise when neighbours fight over of boundaries of the land allocated to them by traditional leaders. Others may encroach into somebody's territory unknowingly or knowingly. In most cases, such conflicts are not solved at the family level. Such matters are usually handled by village heads. If they fail to settle the matter, they take it to the headman who in turn passes it on to the chief if he cannot solve it (Aiyedun and Ordor, 2016). Among Vatsonga, there are some elderly people who are considered to be more knowledgeable than others when it comes to historical information and events. These people are sometimes invited to identify the boundaries since they have lived in the area for quite a long time. In most cases, it is rare to find people who dispute what would have been said by these elders because they would be independent people and not related to the conflicting parties (Interview with Hanyani, 2018).

On the issue of marriage, it is usually the non-payment of bride price which makes some people within the same group to conflict. Such issues are usually handled by the chief. There are stipulations set by Vatsonga chiefs to regulate the amount of money or number of beasts to be paid as bride price in their respective areas of jurisdiction. In Zimbabwe, for example, Tsonga chiefs stipulate that beasts charged as bride price should not exceed eight. Again if a person feels he can pay in the form of money, there is a stipulated amount to be paid as an equivalent. This has to be followed throughout the area of his jurisdiction. In Chief Tshovani's area of jurisdiction around the year 2000, for instance, the amount was pegged at US$200. No people were allowed to dispute these figures

(Interview with Chauke, 2018). Given these stipulations, the settlement of bride price was usually conducted amicably. Lobola should be treated as a token of gratitude rather than a payment (Baloyi, 2016).

Even though the majority of Vatsonga people believe in practicing their culture, there are certain elements of the society who feel offended if forced to partake in some rituals such as *ngoma* which is a male circumcision ceremony. This usually happens when those affiliated to some religious sects such as Christianity reject such indigenous cultural practices. Chiefs usually preside over these issues even though sometimes those who feel offended many a time rush to 'modern' courts of law (Interview with Hanyani, 2018).

Intergroup conflict

Intergroup conflict takes place when two groups with different cultures, values and goals clash due some differences (Carneiro *et al*, 2014:12). Members of the conflicting groups will be in solidarity with each other and in most cases the conflicts involve large groups around the world (Bar-Tal, 2011). In cases where the Vatsonga are in the majority, they tend to be united against any perceived moves that seem to undermine their culture. In cases where they may try to team up against being invaded, traditional leaders take leading roles in resolving some conflicts. However, they seem to fight some losing battles and end up compromising since the government' s court system is the one which usually presides over such matters. This shows that some Tsonga indigenous jurisprudential practices have been severely curtailed in the contemporary world when it comes to resolving intergroup conflicts. These sentiments were aptly noted by Chauke, an elderly Tsonga informant, during an interview: *"Sweswi loko mi onhelana ku rihelana ka kona i mali na ku pfalelana makhotsweni. Loko ku ri huvo yi kona kambe yi hava matimba ya ku tirhisa tindlela ta ndhavuko,"* meaning: "If there is a matter between people, the penalty is to pay using money or being locked up in a jail. The traditional tribunal is there, but it has no power to use cultural ways" (Interview with Chauke, 2018).

On the cultural aspect, there have been intergroup conflicts on the issue of male initiation when some people who are non-Tsonga find themselves in a territory where the Vatsonga will be involved in such practices. In such cases, the chiefs will stand to defend their people and in most cases they win. There were some reports that those who accidentally encroached into the boundaries of the initiation camps will automatically be obliged join the team (Interview with N'waMarilele, 2018).

The Tsonga indigenous court system

The Tsonga indigenous courts are convened in open spaces designated for that purpose. Selected elders (*madoda*) preside over issues together with the traditional leader. However, other members of the community present are allowed to air their views. This makes the Vatsonga traditional justice system to be more inclusive and effective since various views are allowed to be heard and decisions taken there are reached unanimously (Elechi, Morris and Schauer, 2010). This creates an opportunity for greater transparency in passing judgments and reduces chances of contested verdicts, bribery and corruption since many people will be in attendance.

The Vatsonga traditional leaders' courts preside over civil issues starting from family level up to community level. The cases are first attended to by the village head, then by the headman and finally by the chief's tribunal depending on the gravity of the issue. When found guilty, the offenders are made to pay court fees and to compensate the offended. However, the charges are minimal (Aiyedun and Ordor, 2016). The compensation paid is not given as a punishment but a way or reintegrating the offender into the community and also to appease the family which was affected by the offence (Kariuki, 2015).

In support of the above issue, Elechi, Morris and Schauer (2010: 74) avers that: "Justice making in the African indigenous judicial system is also an opportunity for the re-socialisation of community members and the relearning of important African values and principles of restraint, respect, and responsibility". This means the members who are caught on the other side of the community expectations are given a chance for re-socialising with other community members. They do not have to be banished from the community or to be put behind bars so that when they come back they will be good people acceptable in society. They should just reform whilst living among other community members. Other people can still learn from this situation unlike when they do not see the person who is meant to be on rehabilitation. People can still come from jail and commit similar crimes on the very instant they are released which means the prison system is not as effective as letting the offender reform whilst within the community.

Another reason for compensating the offended is a way of warning would-be offenders from committing similar offences and to restitute the aggrieved. There are some advantages of paying directly to the offended as compared to the government-run courts which usually take money from the offender. Sometimes they put the offender in jail whilst the offended is still suffering some loss due to the acts of the offender. Members of the community are also taught not to bear grudges against each other and that they must learn to forgive one another. It is quite apparent that African indigenous justice systems, such as that of the Vatsonga, seem to strive more at reconciling conflicting parties than 'modern' judicial systems which are rather punitive in nature (Kariuki, 2015).

Past and present ways of administering justice within Tsonga royal families

In a Tsonga royal family, issues have always been kept private. As well, disputes within the royal family were always kept private. They were settled internally and never publicly at the courts (Interview with N'wa-Hobyani, 2018). Such measures were put in place to protect the integrity of the royal family in the eyes of the commoners (*Ibid*). During the pre-colonial period, for example, it was common Vatsonga practice for boys from the royal family who caused problems to be taken to a solitary place for discipline. While in secluded areas such as forests, the delinquent boys would be punished in various ways such as being made to dig pits, in addition to being beaten up. As one elderly Tsonga informant stated during an interview: *"Khale a ku biwa munhu a tshwomoka switshamu leswi,"* meaning: "A long time ago, a person was beaten thoroughly until the buttocks had some sores" (Interview with Chauke, 2018). Such punishments on deviant members of the royal family were always kept secret from the public (*Ibid*). Secrecy was therefore critical in handling disputes within the royal family. This was done to protect the integrity of the ruling dynasty and maintain social cohesion.

During the pre-colonial period, it was taboo for a commoner to offend a member of the royal family. If, for example, a commoner impregnated a girl from the royal family, he was captured and killed, sometimes together with the girl (Interview with N'wa-Hobyani, 2018). The situation has, however, changed with time and death is no longer one of the penalties for offending the royal family, such as impregnating the chief's daughter. Xahumba, a Tsonga informant from Zimbabwe's Chiredzi South District, for example, had this to say: *"Loko kuri n'wana wa xisati a nga nyimbisiwa leti se i ta muti wa hosi ntsena. Kumbe na vohahani,"* meaning *"*If it is the chief's daughter, such a matter is left for the chief's family only, or for the aunties" (Xahumba, Interview: 2018).

Conclusion

Basing on the experiences from the Vatsonga people from across southern Africa, this chapter has shown that while conflict is an inevitable phenomenon of human life, different ethnic groups in Africa have specific historical and cultural methods of resolving it. It has discussed types of conflict and the varying methods to resolve them at various levels namely: intrapersonal, interpersonal, intragroup and intergroup among the Vatsonga. The role of initiation schools and elders in resolving intrapersonal and interpersonal conflicts at the family level have been examined. Their role largely involves conflict resolution through counselling and guiding people involved in disputes. Traditional leaders such as village heads, the headmen and chiefs are also important stakeholders depending on the magnitude of the matter being handled. The chapter has noted some of the advantages of the Tsonga indigenous court system, for example, its efforts to reconcile parties, sometimes through compensating the aggrieved in dispute in a bid to attain lasting peace.

References

Aiyedun, A. & Ordor, A. (2016) Integrating the traditional with the contemporary in dispute resolution in Africa, *Law, Democracy and Development*, Vol. 20, pp.155-173.

Baloyi, M. E. (2016) The "vat-en-sit" Union as a threat to the stability of African Marriage in South Africa: African Theological pastoral perspective. *Phronimon,* 17 (2): 1-16.

Bar-Tal, D. (2011) *Inter-group conflicts and their resolution: A social psychological perspective*, Psychology Press: New York.

Bergmann, T. J. and R. J. Volkema (1994) 'Issues, behavioral responses and consequences in interpersonal conflicts,' in: *Journal of Organizational Behavior*, Volume 15, pp.467-471.

Carneiro D., Novais P., Neves J. (2014) 'Traditional and alternative ways to solve conflicts,' in: *Conflict Resolution and its Context: Law, Governance and Technology Series*, Volume 18, pp.11-37.

Du Bois, F. (Ed.) (2007) *Law in Wille's principles of South African Law*, Cape Town: Juta and Company.

Elechi O. O. Morris S. V. C. and Schauer, E. J. (2010) 'Restoring justice (Ubuntu): An African perspective,' in: *Indigenous Criminal Justice Review*, Volume 20, Number 1, pp.73-85.

Fix-Fierro, H. (2003) *Courts, justice and Efficiency: A socio-legal study of economic rationality in adjudication*, Hart Publishing: Oxford.

Kariuki, F. (2015) Conflict Resolution by Elders in Africa: Success Challenges and Opportunities, Kariuki Muigua & Co. Advocates Publisher: Nairobi

Khosa, M. A. (2009) Symbolism in Xitsonga Cultural ritual ceremonies, *M.A Dissertation*, University of Limpopo, R.SA.

Mapindani, A. (2018) The *Ngoma* Initiation Rite: A Distinctive Vatsonga Cultural Mainstay in Zimbabwe. *Africology: The Journal of Pan African Studies*, 11 (2): 83-91.

Mathebula, M. (2014) 800 Years of Tsonga History. Sasavona Publishers and Booksellers: Burgersfort.

Mathebula, M, Mabasa, H, Nkuna, R and Maluleke, M (2007) Tsonga History Discourse Tsonga History Blog; Blog Archive September 12 2007.

Nhlapo, T. (2017) 'Customary law in post-apartheid South Africa: Constitutional confrontations in culture, gender and 'living law,' in: *South African Journal on Human Rights*, 33 (1): 1-24.

Rwelamila, D. D., Talukhaba, A.A., and Ngowi, A.B. (2014) Practising Ubuntu and Leadership for good governance. African Journal of Public Affairs, 17 (4): 30-41.

SAHO (2011) Tsonga. www.sahistory.org.za/article/tsonga. Accessed 27/06/18.

Symonides, J. and Singh, K. (1996) 'From a culture of violence to a culture of peace,' in: *Peace and Conflict Issues Series*, UNESCO Publishing: Paris.

Chapter 17

The Prospects of Reconciliation, Healing, Justice and Peace in 21st Century Africa: Concluding Remarks

Fidelis Peter Thomas Duri, Ngonidzashe Marongwe & Munyaradzi Mawere

The prospects of peace, healing and justice in Africa in particular and the world in general lie in concerted efforts by all stakeholders to address the causes and dynamics of conflict in given geographical, socio-economic and political settings. The collection of chapters in this text aptly demonstrate that the pursuit of peace, healing and justice cannot be achieved without the complementary efforts of various individuals and institutions. The first stage towards this end has to be diagnostic, that is, identifying the source and cause of particular conflicts and incidences of violence. An understanding of the socio-historical context is an important prerequisite for addressing particular conflicts (Khadlagala, 1997) in any given context. It should be acknowledged, however, that it was not possible for this book to cover all forms of violence bedevilling 21st century Africa given the breadth and depth of the subject. The subsequent stages involve dialoguing and settlement of the conflicts in a manner that seeks to achieve lasting peace, healing and justice.

The diagnostic phase, as Chapters 1-7 illustrate, involves identifying various forms of violence in many societies before seeking the most appropriate measures to address them. The political elite, as Chapters 1, 2 and 7 show, for example, contribute considerably towards the eruption of violence and the disruption of peace in many countries during the 21st century. As David Tobias and Joseph Tagarirofa argue in Chapter 1, the shrinkage of democratic space and the heavy-handedness of governments in dealing with the grievances of the ordinary people have a realistic potential of provoking both popular protests and sporadic nationwide acts of defiance. In Chapter 2, Nancy Mazuru articulated how the state's development agendas, such as resettlement programmes, have often been implemented violently and without making arrangements for alternative accommodation and other provisions thereby abusing a plethora of rights for many citizens. In Chapter 7, James Hlongwana has illuminated how power struggles between political parties makes life unbearable for many ordinary people. Focusing on Mozambican Civil War in which the ruling FRELIMO Party is battling against RENAMO rebels, Hlongwana demonstrates how the ordinary Ndau speaking people have been caught up in the crossfire, clearly illustrating that where giants clash, it is the grass that suffers. Chapters 1, 2 and 7, therefore, are critical to this text by demonstrating how the political elite sometimes contribute in causing disharmony among the very populations whose security they claim to be safeguarding.

This text has also shown how some incidents of violence and social discord in contemporary Africa are rooted in longstanding socio-cultural beliefs. In Chapter 3, for example, Ngonidzashe Marongwe, David Tobias and Tinashe Mawere proffer an occult explanation, rooted in age-old indigenous beliefs in witchcraft and sorcery, coupled with prevailing socio-economic insecurities, for the prevalence of sperm-harvesting escapades by female rapists on male victims in 21st century Zimbabwe. Similarly, in Chapter 5, Nancy Mazuru discusses how many ritual murders in Zimbabwe are motivated by superstitious discourses that seek to attain instant riches and address pressing insecurities during times of severe socio-economic hardships. The irony of these discourses is that, in their attempts to resolve prevailing dissonances within communities, they actually generate more conflicts and incidents of violence.

Religious extremism constitutes one of the major sources of violence in many parts of Africa and the world over. In Chapter 4, for example, Jacob Tagarirofa explore the gender dimensions of violent religious conflicts most of which involve Islamic extremists in contemporary Africa. He challenges the commonly-held gender stereotype of men as perpetrators and women as victims of violence in religious conflicts. He argues that both men and women can be agents and victims during incidents of religious violence. Thus, attempts to resolve religious conflicts can be rendered futile if either men or women are regarded as homogeneous groups in terms of their involvement and experiences.

This text has also unravelled the nexus between advancements in information technology, infidelity and the upsurge in cases of domestic violence. In Chapter 7, for instance, Nancy Mazuru acknowledges that communication technology such as mobile phones, the internet and social media platforms have enhanced networking across the world but laments how they have in many cases spurred incidents of infidelity and domestic violence between married couples.

Given the various forms of violence prevalent in contemporary Africa, a pragmatic approach of attaining lasting peace, healing and justice has to be adopted by various stakeholders. Many chapters in this text argue that state-centred or elitist conflict-resolution strategies alone cannot solve the problem. Instead, several chapters advocate for a more complementary and/or holistic and contextualised approach that involves state and non-state actors. State actors include the political elite, law-enforcement agents and 'modern' or Western justice systems while interventions by non-governmental organisations, churches and African indigenous jurisprudence constitute part of the non-state mechanisms. As many chapters suggest, the nature and context of a particular conflict or incident of violence determine the resolution strategy or strategies to be implemented. There is, therefore, no prescription or rigid formula of achieving lasting peace, healing and justice.

Although most chapters in the second section of this text underline the importance of 'everyday' or 'bottom-up' approaches of conflict-resolution, they are fully cognisant of the critical role that the state and its structures can contribute towards this end. Among other things, the state has law-enforcement agents and judicial organs to maintain peace and execute justice. Furthermore, the state can institute judicial commissions of inquiry and can use the press and other media platforms in efforts to resolve conflicts and ensure lasting peace and justice. Problems arise, however, when some sections of the political elite are interested parties in some conflict situations. Again, as Fidelis Duri notes in Chapter 9, the state, as in the case of new millennium Zimbabwean case, can be also be an unreliable guarantor of peace and justice if it exercises an overriding influence over the judiciary, law-enforcement agencies and other organs of national healing. In addition, some conflicts are deeply rooted in indigenous socio-cultural beliefs and practices which 'modern' judicial systems cannot either fully appreciate or adequately handle. Thus, as Tobias Marevesa noted in Chapter 14, the Organ for National Healing Reconciliation and Integration (ONHRI), an arm of national healing and national reconciliation instituted in Zimbabwe during the period 2009-2013, failed to make a meaningful impact largely because of the conflicting interests among the political elite within its ranks and its failure to draw some of its members from church and indigenous institutions.

Given these circumstances, many chapters in this volume acknowledge non-state actors as important stakeholders in the conflict resolution process. Many chapters in this text have underscored the vital role played by African indigenous institutions in this regard. In Chapter 8, for example, Ngonidzashe Marongwe has highlighted the popularity and effectiveness of *kuripa ngozi* (appeasing avenging spirits) as a transitional justice mechanism among many rural Shona people in contemporary Zimbabwe. In Chapter 9, Fidelis Duri also acknowledges the value of *kuripa ngozi* as a viable conflict-resolution practice that heals social fissures and guarantees lasting peace in Zimbabwean post-conflict societies. The institution of *kuripa ngozi* should, however, be practised in a manner that does not violate the freedoms and rights of some people. As Duri argued in Chapter 11, the practice of marrying off young girls in order to appease the avenging spirit of a murdered person sacrifices the rights and liberties of girl children, and at times boy children, under the guise of seeking peace and justice. Such practices result in societal discord by appeasing the dead and their bereaved families at the expense of innocent young people whose childhood and adulthood are both compromised.

Court gatherings (*Dare* among the Shona people of Zimbabwe) convened by chiefs and village heads have been one of the most effective conflict-resolution mechanisms since the pre-colonial period. As Erasmus Masitera notes in Chapter 13, the *Dare* system is very relevant institution in the resolution of disputes in 21st century

Zimbabwe because of the inclusive nature of its deliberations, what Ayittey (1998: 91) calls "participatory democracy," which goes a long way in ensuring lasting peace, healing and justice. It is necessary to quote George Ayittey (1998: 87-88) at length in order to capture useful insights on the operations of the *Dare* institution in many African societies since recorded historical times:

Under normal governance, the Chief would inform the Council of Elders on the subject to be dealt with, and those wishing to do so would then debate it. Routine matters were resolved by acclamation. Complex matters would be debated until the council reached unanimity. Decisions so reached were sure of acceptance by the rest of the tribe since the councillors were influential members of the community.

Generally, the chief would remain silent and watch the councillors' debate. His role was to weigh all viewpoints, not to impose his decision on the council; doing so would defeat the purpose of the council's debates. The chief did not rule; he only led and assessed the council's opinions. If the council did not reach unanimity on a contested issue, the chief would call a village assembly to put the issue before the people for debate. Thus, the people served as the ultimate judge or final authority on disputed issues.

Village meetings began with the chief explaining the purpose of the meeting. He would not announce any decision reached in council meetings; he would merely state the facts involved and order discussions to begin. His advisers would open the debate and would be followed by headmen or elders. Then anyone else wishing to speak or ask questions might do so. These deliberations continued until a consensus was reached. In such a process of consensus building, minority positions are not only heard but also taken into account. In a majority-rule process, on the other hand, a minority position can be ignored. Consensus is far more difficult to reach on many issues, and that was one reason why African political tradition is noted for the length of time, sometimes days and even weeks, it took to reach a consensus. But once reached, there was unity of purpose since all participated in the decision-making process. Note that consensus, by its very nature is the antithesis of autocracy. One cannot impose one's will in a system that is traditionally structured to reach decisions by consensus.

Freedom of expression was an important element of village assemblies. Anyone- even those who were not members of the tribe- could express his views freely. Sensible proposals or ideas often were applauded, and inappropriate ones were vocally opposed. Dissent was open and free, with due respect to the chief. Thus, the *Dare* system can be a very useful conflict-resolution mechanism in 21st century Africa given that it was "open and inclusive" since "no one was locked out of the decision-making process. One did not have to belong to one political party or family to participate in the process; even foreigners were allowed to participate" (*Ibid*: 91). In the Horn of Africa during the 1990s, Prendergast (1997) also noted the importance of local initiatives in which traditional leaders such as chiefs, headmen and community elders were actively involved in peace-building at a time when District Councils had failed to make meaningful progress.

Furthermore, the *Dare* is a sustainable conflict-resolution strategy that is more reconciliatory than punitive. As Fred-Mensah (2005: 1) observed, many African indigenous conflict-resolution initiatives constitute social capital because of their capability "to hold members of a group together by effectively setting and facilitating the terms of their relationship…Sustainability facilitates collective action for achieving mutually beneficial ends." Tafese (2016: 22-23) reiterates that most African indigenous conflict-resolution mechanisms "are part of a well-structured, time-proven social system geared towards reconciliation, maintenance and improvement of social relationships…In this way, African societies emphasise social harmony as the overriding ideology of social control." This is aptly exemplified by the concept of the *Ubuntu* philosophy among the indigenous communities of Southern Africa such as the Xhosa (Masina, 2000).

This text has also demonstrated that linguistic cultural measures can also be employed to deliver messages of restraint and prevent violent confrontations during times of conflict. In Chapter 12, Prosper Hellen Tlou has articulated how the Vhaveṇda people in the Beitbridge peri-urban area of Zimbabwe near the border with South

Africa improvised names for purposes of identification of conflict and also as a way of conveying different coded messages that advocated for peace, restraint and tolerance in conflict-riddled situations. There is no doubt, that "linguistic innovation is one of the critical resources ordinary people utilise as they seek to negotiate crisis situations" (Duri, 2014: 42-43). In particular, nomenclature is an important form of media, one of the reflections of a society's lived experiences and a critical strategy of coping with dispensations characterised by conflict and socio-economic hardships (Chiumbu and Musemwa, 2012; Kadenge, 2012).

The role of churches in conflict-resolution, peace-building and healing should not be underestimated. As Conrad Chibango has argued in Chapter 10, church institutions are important watchdogs of peace and justice in Zimbabwe as elsewhere. As other scholars of conflict have noted, religious organisations can be vital agents in resolving the scourge of violence in Africa through their theology of conflict resolution which emphasises the mobilisation of local communities to embrace the principles of partnership, hospitality, forgiveness and reconciliation (Cunningham, 1996; Gatwa, 2001). In addition, church leaders can play a meaningful role as principles and non-partisan mediators in conflict situations (Gatwa, 2001).

Furthermore, as Tobias Marevesa argues in Chapter 14, there is also need for complementarity between the efforts of church organisations and African indigenous institutions in the pursuit of harmony in 21st century Africa. This strategy has worked in many war-torn areas across the globe. The final report of the Truth and Reconciliation Commission of Liberia (2012), for example, cited the successful efforts of religious leaders, particularly from the Roman Catholic Church, and traditional authorities such as chiefs in the peace process that led to the 2003 Comprehensive Peace Agreement in Accra, Ghana.

Broadly, this book laments the scourge of violence and human insecurity in 21st century Africa, yet it is optimistic about the future of the continent. Future hopes lie in innovative and coordinated approaches by various stakeholders that create a sustainable environment for conflict-prevention, conflict-resolution and peace-building in Africa and beyond.

References

Ayittey, G. B. N. (1998) *Africa in chaos*, St. Martin's Press: New York.

Chiumbu, S and Musemwa, M. (2012) 'Introduction: Perspectives of the Zimbabwean crisis,' in: S. Chiumbu and M. Musemwa (eds.) *Crisis! What crisis? The multiple dimensions of the Zimbabwean crisis*, Cape Town: Human Sciences Research Council Press.

Cunningham, T. F. (1996) 'Conflict resolution strategies and the church,' Doctorate of Theology Thesis, Pretoria: University of South Africa, Available at: https://core.ac.uk/download/pdf/43175838.pdf, Accessed 6 April 2018.

Duri, F. P. T. (2014) 'Linguistic innovations for survival: The case of illegal panning and smuggling of diamonds in Chiadzwa, Zimbabwe (2006-2012)' in: *Africana*, Volume 7, Number 1, pp.41-60.

Fred-Mensah, B. (2005) '*Nugormesse*: An indigenous basis of social capital in a West African community,' IK Notes, Available at: www.worldbank.org.afr/ik/default.htm, Accessed 6 April 2018.

Gatwa, T. (2001) 'Churches and conflict resolution in Rwanda: A model,' Available at: https://tharcissegatwa.wordpress.com, Accessed 6 April 2018.

Kadenge, M. (2012) 'Linguistic negotiation of the Zimbabwean crisis,' in: S. Chiumbu and M. Musemwa (Eds.) *Crisis! What crisis? The multiple dimensions of the Zimbabwean crisis*, Cape Town: Human Sciences Research Council Press, pp.143-160.

Khadlagala, G. (1997) 'African mediation,' in: D.R. Smock (ed.) *Creative approaches to managing conflict in Africa: Findings from the United States Institute for Peace-funded project*, Washington: The United States Institute for Peace, pp.3-5.

Masina, M. (2000) 'Xhosa practices of *Ubuntu* for South Africa,' in: I.W. Zartman (ed.) *Traditional cures for more conflicts: Africa's conflict 'medicine'*, Boulder: Lynne Reinner Publishers, pp.169-182.

Prendergast, J. (1997) 'Building on locally-based and traditional peace processes,' in: D.R. Smock (ed.) *Creative approaches to managing conflict in Africa: Findings from the United States Institute for Peace-funded project*, Washington: The United States Institute for Peace, pp.16-21.

Tafese, T. (2016) 'Conflict management through African indigenous institutions: A study of the Anyuaa community,' in: *World Journal of Social Science*, Volume 3, Number 1, pp.22-32.

Truth and Reconciliation Commission of Liberia, (2012) 'The role of religious and traditional institutions during conflict and in peace-building,' in: *Journal of Religion, Conflict and Peace*, Volume 5, Issue 1 and 2, Available at: www.religionconflictpeace.org, Accessed 6 April 2018.

www.ingramcontent.com/pod-product-compliance
Lightning Source LLC
Chambersburg PA
CBHW060023030426
42334CB00019B/2156